Corporate Governance and China's H-Share Market

CORPORATIONS, GLOBALISATION AND THE LAW

Series Editor: Janet Dine, *Director, Centre for Commercial Law Studies, Queen Mary College, University of London, UK*

This new and uniquely positioned monograph series aims to draw together high quality research work from established and younger scholars on what is an intriguing and under-researched area of the law. The books will offer insights into a variety of legal issues that concern corporations operating on the global stage, including interaction with WTO, international financial institutions and nation states, in both developing and developed countries. Whilst the underlying foundation of the series will be that of company law, broadly-defined, authors are encouraged to take an approach that draws on the work of other social sciences, such as politics, economics and development studies and to offer an international or comparative perspective where appropriate. Specific topics to be considered will include corporate governance, corporate responsibility, taxation and criminal liability, amongst others. The series will undoubtedly offer an important contribution to legal thinking and to the wider globalisation debate.

Titles in the series include:

Human Rights and Capitalism
A Multidisciplinary Perspective on Globalisation
Edited by Janet Dine and Andrew Fagan

Company Law in the New Europe
The EU *Acquis*, Comparative Methodology and Model Law
Janet Dine, Marios Koutsias and Michael Blecher

EU Corporate Law and EU Company Tax Law
Luca Cerioni

Corporate Governance and China's H-Share Market
Alice de Jonge

Corporate Governance and China's H-Share Market

Alice de Jonge

Department of Business Law and Taxation, Faculty of Business and Economics, Monash University, Australia

CORPORATIONS, GLOBALISATION AND THE LAW

Edward Elgar

Cheltenham, UK • Northampton, MA, USA

Published by
Edward Elgar Publishing Limited
The Lypiatts
15 Lansdown Road
Cheltenham
Glos GL50 2JA
UK

Edward Elgar Publishing, Inc.
William Pratt House
9 Dewey Court
Northampton
Massachusetts 01060
USA

A catalogue record for this book
is available from the British Library

Library of Congress Control Number: 2007942976

ISBN 978 1 84720 907 8

Printed and bound in Great Britain by MPG Books Ltd, Bodmin, Cornwall

Contents

Preface

This book examines the post-listing evolution of the first nine Chinese companies to be listed on the Hong Kong stock exchange in 1993–94. It also provides a comprehensive summary of the various law reforms which have formed the background to that evolution over the past 12 years. What emerges is not, as one might predict, a story of the tensions between Hong Kong-based western-derived common-law notions of the corporation versus Chinese socialist, collectivist state-controlled ideas of the corporation. Nor is the classical evolutionary model from law and economics demonstrated by, for example, selection and survival of only the more 'efficient' reforms in corporate governance within H-share firms and the H-share market generally. Rather, corporate structures within the H-share market have been built upon those in existence in earlier times. Two sources of path dependence are identified and analysed. First, the corporate structure of individual H-share firms has emerged from the state-ownership structures of the Mao era, and their evolution has been determined by the tensions between the interests of different parties involved in the ownership/management of the firm. Only some of these interests have had both incentive and power to (usually) impede or (less frequently) advance change. Second, as well as influencing the structure and business strategies of individual firms over which they have direct or indirect control, different state agencies have also influenced the identity and timing of corporate governance reforms generally within the PRC. This story of path dependence sheds light on the reason why, despite pressures to converge, mainland China and Hong Kong vary so significantly in their corporate ownership structures. It also provides a basis for explaining why some important differences are likely to persist.

This book reflects the law as at December 2006. It has not been possible to more fully take into account reforms occurring after that date.

Acknowledgments

This book is dedicated to the memory of Professor Malcolm Smith, friend, guide and mentor to myself and many others at the University of Melbourne.

I would also like to acknowledge the tremendous help and support of Professor Tim Lindsey, whose guidance and assistance made many things possible. Thanks also to my husband Ian for his love and support, for believing in me, and for picking up the pieces when necessary. Thanks to Kathryn Taylor for her patient and generous assistance in the final presentation of layout, and thanks also to Joseph Nunez for help in producing the graphs provided in Appendix 2.

A. de Jonge

1. Introduction: legal transplants, convergence and regionalism in Chinese corporate law reform

I INTRODUCTION AND OVERVIEW

A number of different approaches have been taken by those who have analysed corporate law reform in China. One group of writers, who can be called 'transplant theorists', have focused on the way in which western concepts of the company have been applied in the drafting of Chinese company and securities legislation. Some have complained of the legal confusion arising from thoughtless transplantation of western company-law concepts into a Chinese political and social context,[1] while others have seen an auspicious melding of the 'organizational structure of Western capitalist business into a socialist regime'.[2] Issues of corporate governance preoccupy many of these writers, with several questioning whether mechanisms aimed at overcoming 'agency problems' arising within the western model of the corporation are appropriate for solving possibly different problems, in the different environment of China.[3]

Some analysts of law and corporate governance in China have tried to identify the sometimes confusing variety of foreign influences upon the system, pointing out that, while many aspects appear to have been adapted from civil-law systems such as those of Germany and Japan, still other aspects appear to be based on the example of Hong Kong's success as a common-law based centre of market-oriented business enterprise. Often preoccupied with questions of 'convergence', these writers occasionally hope that future reforms will make the Chinese system more like Anglo-American systems, and less like those of continental Europe or Japan.[4]

Another group of writers has focused upon the many tensions and fluctuations of power occurring between the centre and the regions in a large country such as China, with some writers even going so far as to predict the eventual breaking up of the 'empire'.[5] Other observers have not gone so far, but have simply observed the obvious tensions, and examined the emergence of multiple economic, cultural and legal regions within China,[6] with important consequences for regional approaches to corporate law and policy.[7] Others have emphasized the need to remain aware of differences in the *level* (central vs regional) and *degree* (eg. majority owned or controlling minority interest) of state control when analysing management behaviour and firm performance of listed SOEs in China.[8]

This book is influenced by all of these approaches to analysing company law and securities markets in China. It begins, however, with the observation that all equity systems involve a balance of power and obligations shared between government and participants in the securities markets under its jurisdiction. Finding this balance is inevitable, if only because government must determine how, and to what extent, it wishes to regulate the behaviour of the various actors operating in the equities market. It is the state, moreover, which must ultimately enforce the rights and obligations attached to securities traded within its jurisdiction. The way in which powers and obligations are shared between government and the market community is determined by laws and institutions, and these will differ according to the cultural, social and economic conditions in which they emerge.

In mainland China, the defining feature of the equity market must surely be the pervasive presence of the state on both sides of the fence. That is, the state not only provides the rules and institutions within which the securities community must operate, but the state is itself is a major equity stakeholder and participant in the market.[9] Many writers have pointed out this feature of the Chinese securities markets, and some have also noted that such a feature is not unique to China, but may be typical of developing markets in socialist political systems.[10] The case studies provided in this book provide an opportunity to explore the implications of this feature of the Chinese system for those Chinese companies which have listed their shares on the Hong Kong Stock Exchange.

H-share enterprises – China-based firms incorporated under mainland laws but with shares listed on the Hong Kong stock exchange – must operate within, and according to, the rules of two very different systems. The Chinese mainland is widely perceived as having an underdeveloped legal system. Likewise, corporate governance standards within China-incorporated firms are often seen as either lacking or deficient in their operation.[11] In sharp contrast to this, Hong Kong is commonly seen as having a well-developed market economy, with a set of regulatory controls and legal safeguards in place derived from Britain that meets western standards. The important point here is that H-share firms inevitably reflect the political, economic and social preoccupations of mainland Chinese governments, yet must at the same time recognize and comply with the demands made by the Hong Kong legal system and securities market.

Applying the classical evolutionary model from law and economics, two predictions might have been made about the future of the H-share market in China. First, it might have been predicted that corporate governance within H-share firms would reflect the tensions between two different legal systems, and two different ideas of what the corporation is, how it should be managed, and the purposes it should serve.[12] Successful firms would be those which most efficiently adapted to the sometimes conflicting demands of the Hong Kong securities market, on the one hand, and of the mainland legal, political and economic systems, on the other. In particular, firms which both quickly and selectively adapted their corporate governance structure and practices, taking the most efficient features of each system, would tend to survive.

A second prediction about legal reforms within the H-share market might also have applied the classical evolutionary model from law and economics. According to this model, corporate governance legal reform within the H-share market (and possibly also within publicly-listed Chinese firms in general) would tend to identify and select the most efficient features of the mainland and Hong Kong corporate governance systems. In a globalizing and increasingly connected world, Chinese law makers have also had other corporate governance systems in economically advanced economies to turn to for inspiration. These are typically divided into two basic models: the Anglo-American model centred on the primacy of the market, and the European model centred on the financial intermediary as owner and controller of the firm. In theory, Chinese law makers should have had the luxury of selecting and adapting the most efficient features of both models when developing an indigenous share-market.

What this book demonstrates, however, is that neither of these predictions has been, or is being, fulfilled. Rather, corporate governance practices and corporate governance law reform in China are more accurately viewed as an adaptation to the Chinese political/economic environment. Within individual firms, management decision making has tended to reflect the tensions between often diverging political policy aims of various state agencies involved in ownership and/or oversight of the firm. Likewise, attempts by the Chinese leadership to reform corporate governance standards and practices can be seen as a series of responses to problems that have emerged during the processes of globalization and economic reform. That these responses have not always proved to be the 'best' or most 'efficient' answer to the perceived problem is precisely because of the path-dependent nature of reform.[13] Saddled with the burden of strong State and Party involvement in every aspect of corporate life, and with the equally heavy burden of local protectionism and the politics of national–provincial rivalries, corporate governance reform in

China has followed a unique path all of its own, unlike that followed by any other jurisdiction.

The first chapter of this book provides a theoretical background for the legal analysis and case studies which follow. It provides a summary of the way in which 'transplant' theorists such as Watson and others[14] have analysed and, often prematurely, judged the 'success' or otherwise of attempts to incorporate western ideas of the corporation into Chinese legislation. Some scholars have argued that law reform can serve to initiate or at least facilitate change, such that the future could see management practices and company behaviour in China converging towards those found in western markets.

Another important body of China scholarship emphasizes the importance of regional differences, and the need to avoid nation-wide generalizations in the Chinese context. This scholarship also point to the constantly shifting and widely divergent nature of central–regional relations in China, another feature of the country that pervades nearly all aspects of law and policy. In the case of corporatized and listed SOEs, for example, there may be important differences between those privatized SOEs controlled by central government ministries and those controlled by provincial government authorities.[15] Protectionist tendencies within provincial government authorities may hinder the implementation of western-style corporate governance law reforms at the company level in some areas, but not in others. Central–regional relations can also determine the extent to which corporatized SOEs in 'strategic' industry sectors are treated differently and managed differently from other enterprises. And as power relations between the centre and the region alter over the years, those shifts and changes may be reflected in changes of company control and management.

Chapter 2 of this book provides an historical overview of the birth and development of the H-share market, beginning with the listing of the first H-share firm, Tsingtao Brewery, in July 1993. In essence, the story told is of a mainland government used to maintaining rigid control over all Chinese enterprises learning how to 'let go', and allow companies to operate according to free® market forces. On the Hong Kong side of the border as well, authorities have experienced a steep learning curve in determining precisely what level of regulatory control is most appropriate for locally-listed mainland firms. What Chapter 2 demonstrates is that the actual selection of the nine mainland firms to be allowed to list 'overseas', and the order of their listing, is a story of tensions between local (regional) power bases and interests on the one hand, and the central government's desire to control the entire process on the other. It is also a story reflecting tensions between the various national-level ministries involved in oversight of the strategic industry sectors (such as petroleum) from which the nine vanguard H-share firms were selected. It is this tension between the interests of different state agencies, and the constant negotiations which mediate this tension, that remains a constant feature in the story of Hong Kong-listed Chinese firms, especially those listed during the early years of the H-share market.

Chapters 3 and 4 provide a legal and regulatory background for the case studies that follow. In doing so, these chapters reveal two major weaknesses which have characterized and continue to characterize the Chinese regulatory system for listed corporations. First, there is the dispersed and disparate nature of the system, with regulatory control divided between a number of different agencies at different levels of government. As Chapter 3 demonstrates, there is no 'single' regulator of listed companies, either on the mainland or in Hong Kong. In mainland China, the China Securities Regulatory Commission (CSRC) is simply the 'lead' regulator amongst a number of different state agencies at different levels of government (central and regional) each of which is responsible for different aspects of company operations and management. All firms and business enterprises in China, regardless of ownership, are affected to some degree by government policies, both national and local, which are administered through various state supervisory agencies. State policies provide incentives or disincentives (carrots and sticks) that can have a significant effect upon business decision making. Moreover, all firms in China fall under the supervision of at least one (usually more), state ministry to which all proposals for expansion, diversification, re-organization etc. must be submitted for approval. Government policy and funding support for mergers and takeovers, tax-relief and/or funding support for such things as research and development initiatives and new projects, as well as direct government involvement in corporate restructuring initiatives, are just some of the ways in which government policies drive business in China.

The weaknesses inherent in dividing regulatory control amongst different state entities, not all of which have common interests or aims, have only partially been overcome by moves towards centralization of control over listed assets in China.[16] In the case of H-share enterprises, however, control has always had to be shared with the Hong Kong authorities, primarily the Hong Kong Stock Exchange authority (Hong Kong Exchanges and Clearing Limited, hereafter HKEx) and the Securities and Futures Commission (SFC). For a number of reasons these Hong Kong regulatory agencies are limited in the effectiveness with which they can enforce corporate governance standards, act to protect minority shareholder interests, or otherwise act to impose western-derived norms on Chinese firms. These reasons are explained in Chapter 3, and include a number of cultural and legal obstacles hindering the efficiency of cross-border cooperation between Hong Kong and mainland securities authorities.

The second major weakness inherent in the Chinese regulatory system for listed companies lies in the numerous and overlapping *personal* relationships between government and management which pervade that system. These are highlighted in Chapter 4, which looks at regulatory reforms in China and Hong Kong specifically aimed at improving corporate governance standards in listed firms. Corporate governance reforms have been aimed both at making listed firms more independent of government,[17] and at altering the way in which *internal* aspects of corporate management operate. The noticeable thing about these reforms is the extent to which they appear to have been modelled upon recent reform initiatives in the US, the UK and Australia following a series of corporate collapses that revealed weaknesses in the corporate governance systems of those jurisdictions. The problem is, however, that these jurisdictions are characterized by securities markets with dispersed shareholdings, where shareholders and companies interact on an arm's-length basis. The US, the UK and Australia are all said to have an 'outsider' system of corporate ownership and control typical of Anglo-American legal systems. The same cannot, however, be said of China. Rather, mainland China has obvious features in common with the 'insider' systems of countries such as Japan and Germany. In these systems, shareholdings are more concentrated, and shareholders and creditors are more actively in the control of companies. Reforms aimed at overcoming 'agency' problems and strengthening shareholder rights may well be appropriate in 'outsider' systems, where market efficiency is an importance mechanism for quality control of corporate governance standards. Similar reforms may not, however, be appropriate, or may not achieve the desired objectives, in a different system where different ownership patterns prevail. This raises the possibility that, rather than solving the corporate governance problems of the Chinese listed market (including the H-share market), the current reform process could instead simply serve to disguise the current extent of state control, and allow current problems to be perpetuated.

Chapter 4 of this book also reveals the way in which the interests of the state have been and still are represented within listed Chinese firms. The conclusion is reached that, while protection for minority shareholder interests has improved under recent reforms, it is the State, through a variety of personal allegiances and connections, which remains a dominant presence on the board of most publicly listed Chinese corporations, including those listed in Hong Kong. Personal linkages are possibly the most significant and important aspect of the State's presence in business life in China. This is partly a consequence of state equity ownership, partly due to the paternalism of many state policies (especially in strategic industry sectors), and partly a consequence of the current paucity of management experience, training and expertise in mainland China. Even when the non-executive and independent directors (who must now comprise at least one-third of all directors on the board of Hong Kong-listed Chinese companies) are being appointed, firms in China typically turn to government circles to find the necessary level of education and experience. Non-executive directors might come from the local branch of a government-owned bank, for example, or from a local university. The result is a significant overlap between both state and company personnel, although different individuals may be more or less closely involved with different institutions and different state policy concerns. Not surprisingly, changes in the composition of a firm's management personnel often reflect the fluctuating influence of different state organs (eg. central ministry or provincial government authority) over the firm. This creates an environment where the loyalties of company management can be torn in different directions, to the detriment of the company and/or its minority shareholders.

Chapter 5 provides individual case studies of the nine firms chosen to be in the first batch of companies approved for H-share listing. Selected in 1993 to become the first-ever Chinese firms listed outside the mainland, the nine firms were, in order of appearance on the market, Tsingtao Brewery Co. Ltd (Tsingtao) (15.07.93), Shanghai Petrochemical Co. Ltd[18] (26.07.93), Beiren Printing Machinery Holdings Ltd (06.08.93), Guangzhou Shipyard International Co. Ltd (06.08.93), Maanshan Iron and Steel Co. Ltd (03.11.93), Kunming Machine Tool Co. Ltd[19] (07.12.93), Yizheng Chemical Fibre Co. Ltd[20] (29.03.94), Tianjin Bohai Chemical Industry (Group) Co. Ltd[21] (17.05.94) and Dongfang Electrical Machinery Co. Ltd (06.06.94). What these case studies most obviously reveal is the pervasive influence of the State in almost every aspect of business decision making over the 12 years since the nine firms were listed. This is for several reasons. First, the fact that the State has retained a majority percentage of company equity even after listing has meant that the State, as shareholder, has been able to nominate, and ensure the election of, its own representatives in company management. Second, state policies in the form of both incentives and disincentives (carrots and sticks) have had significant influence, both directly and indirectly, on firm strategy. Direct government involvement in corporate restructuring initiatives has also been used to ensure that firm business strategy accords with state-driven aims and policies.

Strong state involvement in business has a number of consequences, some of which are positive and others negative, when viewed from a traditional business development viewpoint. More importantly for the present context, state involvement in business decision making is neither singular nor homogenous. Rather, diverse and disparate versions of the State exist, potentially representing power elites at the local, regional and central government levels, respectively. While tensions exist within each level between diverse departmental aims and interests, the more obvious and influential tensions so far as the nine firms examined are concerned are those between regional (provincial) governments on the one hand, and the national central government on the other.

The case study method as an approach to legal analysis can be justified most when it provides a basis for building a new theory that can then be tested qualitatively at the broader level.[22] That is precisely what is being attempted here. While many analysts have discussed the (imported western) notion of the corporation when applied to a Chinese context, and others have examined the tensions that exist between the region and the centre in China, no-one has yet applied the idea of tensions between different forms of the state (in particular between regional and national state agencies) to the actual operation of the modern Chinese firm.

The choice of the nine companies examined as the case study sample is justified primarily on the basis that these firms were the very first Chinese-incorporated firms to be listed outside China. Selecting these nine firms therefore ensures the longest period of time over which the life of the listed firm can be examined, providing the best opportunity for properly supported conclusions to be reached about their development. What is also true is that the first batch of nine firms was chosen by the Central Government to represent a range of different Chinese industry sectors and regions. This selection was, itself, a political process, as further revealed in Chapter 2. Thus, it is no surprise to find that the nine firms selected to be in the first batch of H-shares were heavily weighted towards heavy industry and manufacturing, reflecting the political influence and economic importance of these sectors in China at the time.[23]

Chapter 6 discusses the role of the market in corporate governance and firm strategy. In particular, this chapter asks whether or not the H-share market can be said to be 'efficient' in the sense that H-share prices respond to information published by, and about, individual firms. What are the implications of the relative lack of liquidity in the H-share market in this context? Reference is made to recent findings by Cheung et al. of 'a positive and significant relationship between CGI [corporate governance index score] and MTBV [market-to-book-value] . . . for China-related companies listed in Hong Kong'. Chapter 6 also examines recent reforms to takeover and merger laws in China that are creating a more competitive environment for corporate control. The extent to which the 'disciplinary' effect of the market on firm behaviour is actually strengthened as a result, however, remains to be seen.

The concluding chapter of this book sums up the complex interrelationships between the various forces operating within and upon China's H-share firms. An examination of these forces reveals that the questions which most preoccupy those who must regulate, advise and make decisions about and on behalf of the H-share firm are questions which arise as a result of the (often conflicting) interests, aims and demands of the regional power élite (local or municipal government) versus those of the central national power élite. A subsidiary thesis is that corporate ownership systems characterized by concentrated shareholdings, in the case of China by concentrated state share-holdings, are not always, or inevitably, inferior to those systems characterized by dispersed shareholdings and greater levels of reliance on the market for finance. Nor are 'insider' systems of corporate control and ownership necessarily less 'efficient' in allowing firms to adapt to market forces.

II THEORETICAL BACKGROUND

A The Story of the Company with Chinese Characteristics

Many commentators have noted the influence that the principal–agent model of the corporation has had on company law in Anglo-American legal systems.[24] This model is one which assumes that corporations are run well when directors (agents) make decisions in the 'best interests of' shareholders (principals). When directors fail to do this, inefficient 'agency costs' result.[25] In order to overcome these agency costs, Anglo-American legal systems give primacy to the interests of shareholders, and impose obligations on company management to exercise their decision-making powers in a manner which furthers the interests of the company and its shareholders.[26] In contrast to this model of the corporation found in Hong Kong and other Anglo-American jurisdictions, the Japanese and German systems expressly require that stakeholder interests are recognized in corporate decision making. This is achieved essentially through two mechanisms: structural transparency of the corporate form, and participation by stakeholder interests in corporate decision making. The aim is to ensure that the benefits of the corporate form can be fully realized for customers, employees and the community as well as for the shareholder.

In Germany, structural transparency and cooperation in corporate decision making are facilitated by two main features: a two-tiered board structure and a system of co-determination. The two-tiered board system consists of the management or executive board and the supervisory board.[27] The members of the executive board manage the company and the supervisory board members control and monitor the management board.[28] Independence of the supervisory board is maintained by legislation which provides the two boards with totally separate functions. The system of co-determination operates through the structure and mechanisms of the supervisory board. By requiring that a certain proportion of supervisory board members must be employees, the system ensures that the supervisory board provides a mechanism through which employee representatives can safeguard employee interests.[29]

What light does the 'shareholder vs stakeholder' debate in western corporate theory cast on the history and development of Chinese corporate law? An understanding of variations between models of the corporation, and principles underlying those variations in different western jurisdictions, helps to identify the sources from which different aspects of China's company and securities regime have been borrowed. For example, the two-tiered board structure mandated for all listed Chinese firms has clearly been borrowed from the European/ Japanese model of the corporation, while the more recently developed rules aimed, *inter alia*, at introducing a minimum number of 'independent directors' onto the board of all listed Chinese companies, and empowering those directors in their oversight role, are clearly derived from the United States reforms introduced by Sarbanes-Oxley Act of 2002. In other words, the student of China's legal system needs first of all to understand the extent to which modern Chinese company and securities laws consist of transplanted Western corporation law. The more difficult, but more important task, is then to understand the way in which, in a new cultural context, even the most basic provisions of transplanted law are liable to be interpreted in new and unexpected ways. This involves understanding not just how this process has occurred, but also why the same rule, when 'transplanted' to a different environment, has apparently been interpreted in so many different ways.

B China's Legal System and the Transplant Effect

Two main themes are discernible in Western legal transplantation discourse. Convergence theorists contend that nation-states are enmeshed in an inevitable and accelerating shift towards internationalization. As telecommunications, urbanization, international investment and international trade increase, regional differences, which in the past inhibited successful legal transplantation, disappear. Convergence theorists have also tended to assume that Western corporate laws, especially those of the United States, both can and should form the model for a global legal template.[30] The opposing point of view originates from Montesquieu's scepticism that laws cannot traverse cultural boundaries.[31] He proposed that laws express the spirit of nations and are consequently deeply embedded in, and inseparable from, their geographic, customary and political context. Other scholars have also reached the conclusion that laws are culturally specific and do not transplant with much success, or at least that, to have any hope of being effective, legal transplants must first comprehend and accommodate the ideological, institutional and cultural differences between donor and recipient country.[32]

Other writers have sought theoretical alternatives to the unproductive convergence and cultural–essentialist dichotomy. Otto Kahn-Freund, for example, has found 'degrees of transferability' amongst laws; with some so deeply embedded in their social and institutional matrices as to render transplantation to different cultural contexts virtually impossible, whilst others may be more readily absorbed into different ideological, institutional, social and cultural national legal recipes.[33] Drawing on this insight, John Gillespie has postulated that

1. The success of legal transplantation is strongly influenced by the congruence between the ideological content of transplanted laws and host country political–legal ideologies.[34]
2. Transplanted law is profoundly influenced by the way institutional structures distribute state power, and the legal cultures (epistemologies) informing official thinking.[35]
3. Certain laws require specific configurations of state and non-state interest groups such as market support organizations (eg. banks, accountants, markets and the media) to function effectively.[36]

The research undertaken for this book provides valuable support for each of these three working postulates. The case studies provided in Chapter 5 also demonstrate the way in which both ideological and institutional aspects of mainland politics have continued to shape firm management decision making, despite exposure to market forces and Western standards of corporate governance via the offshore listing process, and despite recent law reforms on the mainland which appear to incorporate Western ideas of the corporation and corporate governance standards. As Professor Ruskola has also argued, the story of company law reform in modern China is largely a story of the difficulties which state enterprises have had in gaining independence from the politics of state policy determination and administration.[37]

Why should it be so difficult for modern Chinese companies, even those most exposed to foreign markets and influences, to achieve independence from the constraints imposed by mainland ideological and institutional forces? And why should twentieth-century attempts to transplant Western corporations law, and Western ideas of corporate governance, into the

Chinese context have achieved such limited success? According to Ruskola the reason for this limited success is, at least partly, 'a function of [an] ideology that believes in the fundamental unity of a social and political whole'.[38] To justify this conclusion, Ruskola points to the differences between the 'traditional Chinese view of the corporation as a kinship group'[39] on the one hand, and the individualistic contract-based view of recent Western (American) jurisprudence on the other. According to Ruskola, even when Chinese state enterprises succeed in gaining a degree of independence from the bureaucratic system, their relationship to the bureaucracy is still coloured by familial conceptualizations reminiscent of the rhetoric that defined clan corporations' role within the imperial state. Today, every state entity is supervised by an 'administrative agency in charge' (*xingzheng zhuguan bumen*), colloquially known as the 'mother company' (*mu gongsi*).[40] In addition, each state entity typically owes a subsidiary duty of loyalty to a number of other administrative units as well. When these other units interfere with enterprise management, the problem is described as having 'too many mothers-in-law (*popo duo*)'.[41]

Ruskola thus finds that, despite their surface similarities, Chinese and Western corporations' laws are based on diametrically-opposed justifications for a similar entity, the Chinese view being based on a belief in the moral primacy of the collective, while American corporate scholarship has been preoccupied by the need to justify the existence of the corporation in a way that accords with liberal individualism.[42] He concludes that the two views are unlikely to converge in a meaningful way 'so long as their legal, political, and discursive interpretations remain informed by distinct local understandings of the nature and purpose of corporations'.[43]

While the 'family' analogy is to some extent justified, Ruskola arguably takes it much too far in discussing the modern Chinese corporation. Certainly, the analogy becomes somewhat strained when discussing large, overseas-listed Chinese corporations. What it does help to highlight, however, is the tensions and 'discontents' that are part of the modern Chinese regulatory system, including the parts of that system aimed at regulating corporate and securities trading behaviour. The reality of different levels of regulatory oversight each representing different political interests is not a matter of kinship-style overlapping relationships. It is quite straightforwardly a matter of political power, and of the way in which political tensions can affect business decisions and corporate behaviour. In particular, a number of writers have pointed to the importance of regional identity and regional protectionism in Chinese political and economic life. How does the 'regionalized' nature of China's regulatory systems, and hence its economy, affect the behaviour of Hong Kong-listed Chinese firms? One hypothesis of this book is that political tensions between the region and the centre within mainland China have had a much more significant impact on the behaviour of Hong Kong-listed Chinese firms than have the differences and tensions between Hong Kong and mainland securities law.

C Over the Mountain and Far Away: the Centre and the Region in the Chinese Regulatory Experience

A number of scholars have examined regionalism and the process of decentralization in the Chinese context. Segal, Goodman and others have noted that decentralization, both before and during recent decades of reform since 1978, has caused fault lines to appear in the structure of authority as power has flowed from the central government to the provinces. Historically, China has experienced a number of periods of regional disintegration, most notably during the Warring States period (c. 450–221 BC) and during the Warlord Era of 1916–1928.[44]

So far as the period since 1978 is concerned, David Goodman has argued that 'there is a new pattern of economic regionalism unlike earlier regionalisms experienced in China'.[45] He points to three key initiatives of the era of economic reform that started with the Third Plenum of the Eleventh Central Committee of the Chinese Communist Party (CCP) in December 1978 which are typically held to have encouraged local political autonomy, and to contain the seeds for potential political disintegration.[46] One is the decentralization of economic management, which has taken a number of forms. Within the state sector there has been the decentralization of economic management and decision making, with lower levels taking over functions and responsibilities previously the preserve of superior levels. More recently, some of these functions have been reclaimed by central government authorities, reflecting the constant ebb and flow of centre–region tensions which has long characterized China's internal political and economic systems. In addition, governments and the state sector at all levels have divested themselves of large areas of business activity which have now been taken over by private enterprise and by the 'privatized' (formerly state and collectively-owned) sector.

Allied to decentralization is the development of a more market-oriented and market-determined economy. By the early 1990s, few prices were still fixed by the State, and resource allocation decisions were increasingly left to the market. One consequence has been the development of highly localized markets for both supply and distribution. Fiscal decentralization has significantly strengthened the tie between local officials' financial and career rewards and the growth of local government revenue. Efforts to expand the revenue base have led local officials to mobilize resources and bend existing rules for local enterprises' market-oriented activities that compete with those promoted by governments in other localities.[47] Greater provincial autonomy has also allowed provincial leaders to succumb to protectionist instincts in protecting local revenue-generating activities from competition from other provinces. This has been made much easier to achieve against a background of rapid economic growth since the beginning of the reform era. Over the two and a half decades since 1978, China's economy has grown at an annual rate of almost 10 per cent, although, beginning from a small base, its GDP is still only a quarter that of Japan.[48]

Rapid economic growth has also been a result of China's policy of the 'open door' – a policy which has had, possibly unintended, decentralizing consequences as well. Opening up to foreign capital, foreign technology and foreign management expertise has been an integral part of the leadership's drive to modernize the economy and to join (or rejoin) the international economy and the World Trade Organization. As Goodman points out, 'The CCP's determination since the late 1970s to utilize its economic and geographic comparative advantages in the international economic system may also have assisted in the development of a new economic regionalism'.[49] Although South China, with Guangdong Province being the most obvious example, is in the vanguard, other economic regions are also developing relationships with the international economy outside of China, especially in East Asia. Regions that have been able to develop such relationships no longer depend on central government support or approval for their economic activities. Economic integration between Guangdong and Hong Kong is now such that the movement of goods and people across the border has become virtually unrestricted. Fujian's industrial dependence on Taiwan has been noted by a number of writers. In addition, Japanese, Taiwanese and, since 1992, Hong Kong investment and activities in Jiangsu and Zhejiang have been steadily increasing; Shandong and Northeast China have ties with South Korea and the Russian Far East; Xinjiang is becoming economically integrated with the Turkic republics of the former USSR; and Yunnan's economic relationships with Burma (Myanmar) and Thailand are considerable.[50]

Not surprisingly, therefore, a significant number of observers have concluded that there is 'no threat to the ruling capacity of the central leaders . . . more dangerous than the threat of regionalism, which derives from the changes that have occurred in central–regional relations as a result of the economic reforms'. According to these observers, the decentralization of economic functions, which has been essential for carrying out the reforms, has also led to a devolution of political power to such an extent that the capacity of the central government has been brought into doubt.[51] Some writers have even gone so far as to compare the centrifugal tendencies of

Chinese Regionalism to those which led to the Soviet Union's recent experience of imploding communism. As Goodman convincingly points out, however, there are a number of reasons why this interpretation is suspect, the analogy strained, and a more subtle understanding of autonomy and regionalism in China is needed.[52]

The cultural determination of regionalism in the PRC is clearly an important factor in relations between the centre and the provinces, most noticeably in the non-Han areas known as 'Autonomous Regions' and concentrated in the border areas of North, Northwest and Southwest China. But even within these areas, separate cultural identity does not necessarily mean political disintegration or provincial separatism. The capacity of the central government to control the regions has always been qualified in China, not least because of China's size, local diversity and the staggering growth of its population in the last century. Even at the heights of its power, central rule has necessarily been limited by decentralization, local autonomy, and some circumvention of central directives. This did not indicate trends towards regionalism in the sense of open and long defiance of the central government by local leaders, who had the capacity to act autonomously on major issues. Instead, departures from central directives have generally been limited. Often, a degree of license in interpreting central directives has even been necessary for the effective operation of China's sprawling political system.[53]

While there may be tensions between the centre and the regions/provinces, their relationship is by no means necessarily always antagonistic. In the first place, whatever else has happened in the PRC since the start of the reform era in 1978, it remains a Communist Party state. The role of the Chinese Communist Party (CCP) has changed with reform, but it still controls the appointment of senior local leaders, and still exercises that control assiduously, especially at provincial level.[54] With the possible exception of the major non-Han areas, there are no organizations outside the party-state system that might claim to articulate the wishes of a province or region. Economic development might bring entrepreneurs in a region into conflict with the centre, but that conflict is then mediated by local leaders whose careers depend on their superiors within the CCP, even though they will need to compromise with local demand if they are to ensure compliance with central direction and policy.

In summary, therefore, the position of regional political leadership, as well as the traditions of the CCP which have always encouraged a degree of local flexibility in national policy implementation, have combined to ensure that regionalism has been a constant feature of the PRC's political process and not necessarily a symptom of political disintegration. It is usual to find policies under experimentation regionally before national adoption, and central and local leaders frequently combine to lobby on behalf of specific policy initiatives. The relationship between centre and region is then perhaps more usefully interpreted in terms of negotiation rather than conflict.[55]

What happens when negotiations between the centre and the region become the background against which a new type of business enterprise – the corporation limited by shares – is created and then expected to strive for economic (business) success? Here I draw on Lin's insight that, 'In the reform era, effective manipulation of state action – ie., making gains from ad hoc favourable treatment by the state – constitutes a necessary condition for the success of firms' in China. When placed against the background of a deliberate policy of fiscal decentralization, what this means is that success for the modern Chinese company depends very largely on management's ability to understand and manipulate the negotiating process between different levels of the State in the effort to attract the most effective form of favourable treatment. The working hypothesis of this book is that this is just as true for the overseas-listed Chinese firm (H-share company) as it is for any other Chinese enterprise.

NOTES

1. See eg. Teema Ruskola 'Conceptualizing corporations and kinship: comparative law and development theory in a Chinese perspective' [1999–2000] 52 *Stanford Law Review* 1599–1729, 1705, and Fang Liufang, 'China's corporatization experiment', [1995] 5 *Duke Journal of Comparative & International Law* 149–269, 260.
2. Gao Xiqing, 'The perceived unreasonable man – a response to Fang Liufang' [1995] 5 *Duke Journal of Comparative & International Law* 271–288; Robert C. Art & Minkang Gu, 'China incorporated: the first corporation law of the People's Republic of China', (1995) 20 *Yale Journal of International Law* 273–308.
3. See eg. On Kit Tam, *The Development of Corporate Governance in China* (Edward Elgar, 1999). Edward S. Steinfeld, *Forging Reform in China: The Fact of State-Owned Industry* (Cambridge University Press, 1998).
4. See eg. Merton H. Miller, 'Alternative strategies for corporate governance' and Haiying Zhao, 'Restructuring Chinese state-owned enterprises: a contractual approach', in G.J. Wen and D. Xu (eds), *The Reformability of China's State Sector* (World Scientific, 1996) at 3–16 and 119–130 respectively.
5. See eg. W.J.F. Jenner, *The Tyranny of History: The Roots of China's Crisis* (Allen Lane Penguin Books, 1992), and see John Fitzerald, 'Reports of my death have been greatly exaggerated: The history of the death of China', in David S.G. Goodman & Gerald Segal (eds), *China Deconstructs: Politics, Trade and Regionalism* (Routledge, 1994) 21–58.
6. Jin Huang & Andrew Xuefeng Qian, '"One country, two systems", three law families and four legal regions: the emerging inter-regional conflicts of law in China' [1995] 5 *Duke Journal of Comparative & International Law* 289. See also Raymond Wacks, 'One country, Two Grundnormen? The Basic Law and the Basic Norm', in *Hong Kong, China and 1997: Essays in Legal Theory* (Raymond Wacks, ed., 1993) at 151.
7. For discussion see Dali Yang, 'Reform and the restructuring of central–local relations'; Brantly Womack and Guangzhi Zhao, 'The many worlds of China's provinces: foreign

trade and diversification' and David S.G. Goodman and Feng Chingyi, 'Guangdong: Greater Hong Kong and the new regionalist future', in David S.G. Goodman & Gerald Segal (eds), *China Deconstructs: Politics, Trade and Regionalism* (Routledge, 1994) at 59–98, 131–176 and 177–201, respectively. See also Chi Zhang, Thomas C. Heller & Michael M. May, 'Carbon intensity of electricity generation and CDM baseline: case studies of three Chinese provinces' [2005] 33 *Energy Policy* 451–465.

8. See eg. Kin Cheung Liu, 'State control and performance evaluation: The case of a state-owned enterprise in China' (1995) 8:6 *International Journal of Public Sector Management* 39–50; and Andrew Delios, Zhi Jian Wu and Nan Zhou, 'A new perspective on ownership identities in China's listed companies' (2006) 2(3) *Management and Organization Review* 319–343.
9. At the end of 1995, State shares made up 54 per cent of the total shares of listed Chinese companies. A number of policies have since ensured a decline in this figure, but as at the end of 2001, the State still owned 47.7 per cent of total shares: Madam Jiang Qianggui (Vice Minister of the State Economic and Trade Commission), 'Speech at the Meeting on Summarizing the Experience of Establishing Modern Enterprise Systems in Listed Companies' (abstract), 27 December 2002. Downloaded from the State Economic and Trade Commission website (http://www.setc.gov.cn.)
10. According to Mark Roe, for example, socialist political systems inevitably produce an 'insider' system of corporate ownership and control. An insider system is said to be one where shareholding is said to be concentrated in the hands of block-holders, and where shareholders and creditors are more actively involved in the control of companies: Mark Roe, 'Political preconditions to separating ownership from corporate control' (2000) 53 *Stanford Law Review* 539.
11. See eg. Fang Liufang, above n.1, and G.J. Wen and D. Xu (eds), *The Reformability of China's State Sector* (World Scientific, 1996).
12. For an overview of different views on the nature and purposes of the business corporation, see Lynn A. Stout, 'On the nature of corporations. *Symposium: Unincorporation: A New Age?*' (2005) 1 *University of Illinois Law Review* 253 and Lynn Stout, 'On the nature of corporations' (2004) 9(2) *Deakin Law Review* 775.
13. For a discussion of path dependency, see Mark J. Roe, 'Chaos and evolution in law and economics' [1996] 109 *Harv. L. Rev.* 641 and see Lucien Arye Bebchuk and Mark J. Roe, 'A theory of path dependence in corporate ownership and governance' (1999) 52 *Stanford Law Review* 127. See also Randall Peerenboom, 'Globalization, path dependency and the limits of law: administrative law reform and the rule of law in the People's Republic of China' [2001] 19:161 *Berkeley Journal of International Law* 161.
14. Alan Watson, 'Aspects of reception of law' (1996) 44 *American Journal of Comparative Law* 335. For overview and discussion of the views put forward by Watson and others, see Richard G. Small, 'Towards a theory of contextual transplants' (2005) 19 *Emery International Law Review* 1431.
15. For a demonstration of the importance of distinguishing between various sorts of government ownership, see Andrew Delios, Zhi Jian Wu and Nan Zhou, 'A new perspective on ownership identities in China's listed companies' (2006) 2:3 *Management and Organization Review* 319–343.
16. Since 1998, regulatory control over listed company behaviour has been centralized in the China Securities Regulatory Commission (CSRC) and control over listed state assets has been centralized in the State-owned Assets Supervision and Administrative Commission (SASAC): Leila Fernandez-Stembridge and Jean-François Huchet, 'What's next for China's SOEs?' (2006) 169(5) *Far Eastern Economic Review* 32, 32–33.
17. Notably, the 'Three Segregations' policy (separation of parent organization and listed company personnel, assets and finance) as implemented in the *Public Share Offerings by Listed Companies Tentative Procedures* [3710/00.04.30]. Promulgated by the China Securities Regulatory Commission on, and effective as of, 30 April 2000. Translated (July–August 2000) 14(6) *China Law & Practice* 45–49. See especially article 4(1).
18. Since re-named Sinopec Shanghai Petrochemical Co. Ltd.
19. Later re-named Jiaoda Kunji High Tech Co. Ltd.

20. Since re-named Sinopec Yizheng Chemical Fibre Co. Ltd.
21. Since re-named Tianjin Capital Environmental Protection Co. Ltd.
22. See further Robert K. Yin, *Applications of Case Study Research* (2nd edn, 2003); Robert K. Yin (ed.), *Case Study Anthology* (2004); Roger Gomm, Martyn Hammersley & Peter Foster, *Case Study Method: Key Issues, KeyTexts* (2004); Robert K. Yin, *Case Study Research: Design and Method* (3rd edn, 2003).
23. What was noticeable about the H-share market even as recently as 2000 was the absence of firms from the services sector. The first Chinese bank, for example, was not listed in Hong Kong until June 2005. By the end of 2006, banking firms make up the largest percentage of the capitalization of the H-share market. Before 2000, however, it was the petrochemical sector which took up most of the market capitalization in the H-share market. For a statistical overview of listed H-share companies, including date of listing and capitalization, see Hong Kong Stock Exchange Website, Data and Statistics, China Dimension, List of H Share Companies, available at http://www.hkex.com.hk/data/chinadimen/CD_HMB.htm, last updated 30 June 2007, accessed on 5 July 2007.
24. For discussion see Lynne Stout, 'On the nature of corporations' (2004) 9(2) *Deakin Law Review* 775; Bryan Horrigan, 'Fault lines in the intersection between corporate governance and social responsibility (2002) 25:2 *UNSW Law Journal* 515; Lucian Arye Bebchuk and Mark J. Roe, 'A theory of path dependence in corporate ownership and governance' (1999) 52 *Stanford Law Review* 127, and Wayne Gumley, 'Can corporations law reform save the planet? Seeking a missing link between environmental and economic policies', in Gerald Acquaah-Gaisie & Val Clulow (eds), *Enhancing Corporate Accountability: Prospects and Challenges Conference Proceedings*, Melbourne, 8–9 February 2006, 239, 243–244.
25. For further discussion, see Michael Spisto, 'Stakeholder interests in corporate governance: Is a new model of governance a change for the better for South Africa? – Part 1', (2005) 18 *Australian Journal of Corporate Law* 129; D. Bailes, 'Watch your corporation' (1995) 3(1) *Journal of Business Law* 24; P. Jiang and L.F. Fang (eds), *New Corporate Law Textbook*, 9th edn (Legal Publishing House, 1998) pp. 48–50, as cited in Y Wei, *Comparative Corporate Governance: A Chinese Perspective*, Global Trade and Finance Series, Vol. 3 (Kluwer Law International, 2003) 2.
26. Section 181(1) of the Australian *Corporations Act*, for example, provides that A director or other officer of a corporation must exercise their powers and discharge their duties (a) in good faith in the best interests of the corporation; and (b) for a proper purpose.

    The generally-accepted common law test defines 'best interests of the company' to mean the interests of the company's shareholders, or, where a company is insolvent, its creditors: Therese Wilson, 'The pursuit of profit at all costs: corporate law as a barrier to corporate social responsibility' (2005) 30:6 *Alternative Law Journal* 278, citing *Greenhalgh v. Ardene Cinemas* [1945] 2 All ER 719 and *Kinsela v. Russell Kinsela Pty Ltd (In Liq)* (1986) 4 NSWLR 722. See further, Peter Henley, 'Were corporate Tsunami donations made legally?' (2005) 30(4) *Alternative Law Journal* at 154. See also Parliamentary Joint Committee on Corporations and Financial Services, Australian Parliament, *Corporate responsibility: managing risk and creating value* (June 2006), available at: http://www.aph.gov.au/Senate/committee/corporations_ctte/corporate_responsibility/report/report.pdf.
27. In German, the Vorstand and the Aufsichtsrat: Spisto, Michael, 'Stakeholder interests in corporate governance: is a new model of governance a change for the better for South Africa? – Part 1', (2005) 18 *Australian Journal of Corporate Law* 129 at 140.
28. For example, the supervisory board may, *inter alia*, examine the business decisions made by the management and may examine all financial statements and accounts: ibid.
29. Ibid. 141.
30. See further, John Gillespie, 'Transplanted company law: an ideological and cultural analysis of market-entry in Vietnam' (2002) 51 *International & Comparative Law Quarterly* 641; B. Black and R. Kraakman, 'A self-enforcing model of corporate law' (1996) 109(8) *Harvard Law Review* 1911–82; Sarah Biddulph, 'Through a glass darkly: China, transparency and the WTO' (2001) 3(1) *Australian Journal of Asian Law* 59, 91–2.

31. John Gillespie, 'Transplanted company law: an ideological and cultural analysis of market-entry in Vietnam' (2002) 51 *International & Comparative Law Quarterly* 641, 644; citing Montesquieu, 1749, *De L'Esprit des Lois* (The Spirit of Laws), Livre I Gallimard, Paris, reprint J.P. Mayer and A.P. Kerr (eds), (1970). See also Pierre Legrand, 'Comparative legal studies and commitment to theory' (1995) 58 *Modern Law Review* 263–83; Tahirih V. Lee, 'Risky business: courts, culture and the market place' (1993) 47 *University of Miami Law Review* 1335, 1338.
32. See eg. Pierre Legrand, 'The impossibility of "legal transplants"' (1997) 4 *Maastricht Journal of European and Comparative Law* 111, 119.
33. Otto Kahn-Freund, 'On uses and misuses of comparative law' (1974) 37 *Modern Law Review* 1, 6, 7–11, 27; Otto Kahn-Freund, 'Common law and civil law – imaginary and real obstacles to assimilation', in Mauro Cappelletti (ed.), *New Perspectives for a Common Law Europe* (1978) 160.
34. John Gillespie, 'Transplanted company law: an ideological and cultural analysis of market-entry in Vietnam' (2002) 51 *International & Comparative Law Quarterly* 641, 645–646, citing Robert Gordon, 'Critical legal histories' (1984) 36 *Stanford Law Review* 65, 108. See also Alan Hunt, 'Dichotomy and contradiction in the sociology of law', in P. Beirne and R. Sharlet (eds), *Marxism and Law* (1982) 87–89; Maureen Cain, 'Gramsci, the state and the place of law', in David Suggerman (ed.), *Legality, Ideology and the State* (1983) 111–15; Alan Hunt, 'The ideology of law: advances and problems in recent applications of the concept of ideology to the analysis of law' (1985) 19 *Law Society Review* 11, 13–19.
35. John Gillespie, 'Transplanted company law: an ideological and cultural analysis of market-entry in Vietnam' (2002) 51 *International & Comparative Law Quarterly* 641, citing Pierre Legrand, 'The impossibility of legal transplants (1997) 4 *Maastricht Journal of European & Comparative Law* 119. See also Susan Silbey, 'Making a place for a cultural analysis of law' (1992) 17 *Law and Social Inquiry* 41.
36. John Gillespie, 'Transplanted company law: an ideological and cultural analysis of market-entry in Vietnam' (2002) 51 *International & Comparative Law Quarterly* 641, citing Kahn-Freund, 'On the uses and misuses of comparative law' (1974) 37 *Modern Law Review* 12–14; and Gunther Teubner, 'Legal irritants: good faith in British law or how unifying law ends up in new divergences' (1998) 61 *Modern Law Review* 30–2.
37. Teema Ruskola, 'Corporations and kinship' (2000) 52 *Stanford Law Review* 1599, 1693.
38. Ibid. 1693.
39. Ibid. 1600–1605.
40. Ibid. 1693, citing Fang Liufang, 'China's corporatization experiment' (1995) 5 *Duke Journal of Comparative & International Law* 149, 155, n.13.
41. Ibid. 1693–94, citing Donald C. Clarke, 'Regulation and its discontents: understanding economic law in China' (1992) 28 *Stanford Journal of International Law* 283, 293.
42. Ibid. 1606.
43. Ibid. 1600.
44. David S.G. Goodman, 'The politics of regionalism' in David S.G. Goodman & Gerald Segal (eds), *China Deconstructs: Politics, Trade and Regionalism* (Routledge, 1994) 3; further noting that it is far from clear that the conditions which have on occasion encouraged a high degree of regionalism in the past are those that apply in the late 20th and early 21st century.
45. David S.G. Goodman & Gerald Segal, 'Preface' in David S.G. Goodman & Gerald Segal (eds), *China Deconstructs: Politics, Trade and Regionalism* (Routledge, 1994) at viii.
46. David S.G. Goodman, 'The politics of regionalism' in David S.G. Goodman & Gerald Segal (eds), *China Deconstructs: Politics, Trade and Regionalism* (Routledge, 1994) 1–20 at 4–5.
47. Yi-min Lin, *Between Politics and Markets: Firms, Competition, and Institutional Change in Post-Mao China* (Cambridge University Press, 2001) at 5.
48. C.H. Kwan, article written for *The Straits Times*, accessed 23 November 2004 at http://www.rieti.go.jp/en/. See also Bernard Wasow, 'Should We Trust China', *The Globalist*, 30 March 2004, available at http://www.theglobalist.com/ and Phil Ruthven,

'Continued economic growth will make this the Chinese Century', *On Line Opinion* 17 November 2003, available at http://www.onlineopinion.com.au/.

49. David S.G. Goodman, 'The politics of regionalism' in David S.G. Goodman & Gerald Segal (eds), *China Deconstructs: Politics, Trade and Regionalism* (Routledge, 1994) 5.
50. Ibid., 5–6.
51. Ellis Joffe, 'Ruling China after Deng', in Orville Schell and David Shambaugh (eds), *The China Reader: The Reform Era* (Vintage Books 1999) at 148.
52. David S.G. Goodman, above, n. 49, 5–6.
53. Joffe, above, n. 51, 148.
54. Goodman, above, n. 49, 4.
55. Ibid.

2. Birth pangs of a market: creation and development of China's cross-border share markets

I INTRODUCTION

The listing on domestic stock exchanges of Chinese State Owned Enterprises (SOEs) emerged in the 1980s as part of the central government's combined aims of getting the state out of enterprise operations and promoting the marketization of the economy. The water was first tested by the central treasury, which began issuing treasury bonds in 1981. It was not long before many central and locally-controlled state-owned enterprises (SOEs) began issuing financial and construction bonds to provide badly needed funds for the country's economic reconstruction. Both the China International Investment Corporation and the Bank of China floated public bonds in the early 1980s,[1] and local bonds were floated in major municipalities like Fujian, Guangdong and Xiamen.

Legal and economic reform initiatives in China are often tried out first at the regional/local level before being adapted for nationwide implementation. The growth of securities markets provides a good example of this. Markets for the sale of enterprise equities and bonds originally developed in pockets throughout the country, and were regulated through a series of rules promulgated by provincial and municipal governments. Thus, the first Chinese companies to issue domestic shares ('A-shares') did so under regional government encouragement and control. The Joint Investment Co in the Baoan County of Shenzhen issued the first public share certificates in 1983 under provincial Shenzhen regulations. In November 1984, the Shanghai Feiyue Hi-fi Corp floated 10 000 shares at Rmb 50 a share, and two months later the Tan Yanzhong Realty Co issued 100 000 shares of the same par value. Both issues were handled by the Trust and Investment Company of the Shanghai Branch of the PBOC.[2] Both in Shenzhen and in Shanghai the regulatory authorities followed the pattern adopted in other regions of vesting regulatory power over issues of securities by local enterprises in the local branch of the People's Bank of China (PBoC).[3]

By the late 1980s, a secondary market had begun to develop with the emergence of 'trading centres' scattered across the country in major cities like Guangzhou, Changzhou, Wuhan, Tianjin Harbin and Dalian under local government supervision.[4] By the end of 1992, there were about 5000 such 'trading centres'.[5] The first permanent domestic capital markets for public trading of shares were largely experimental and confined to the two regional centres of Shanghai and Shenzhen where China's two main national exchanges were formally established in 1990 and 1991, respectively.[6] At first, the two exchanges enjoyed high levels of autonomy in regulating the development of exchange listing requirements and approval processes, but the rapid and successful expansion of the securities markets to include a nationwide coverage of listed firms led the central government to tighten its control.

The *Standard Opinion for Joint Stock Limited Companies* (the Standard Opinion)[7] was issued in early 1992 to provide the first national-level set of regulations for the formation of joint stock shareholding companies able to issue publicly traded shares. National level rules for the issue and trading of domestic A-shares were promulgated in April 1993, when the *Administration of the Issuing and Trading of Shares Tentative Regulations* were promulgated by the State Council.[8] The Standard Opinion was supplanted when the China's first-ever national *Company Law* came into effect on 1 January 1994.[9] By the year 2000, over 1000 companies had listed on the two exchanges, and equity market capitalization had risen to RMB 5 trillion.[10] By 2004, the combined capitalization of the Shanghai and Shenzhen Stock Exchanges was US$447.7 billion, ranking it as the thirteenth-largest stock market in the world.[11]

As noted in Chapter 1, one of the most important aspects of China's economic reform since 1978 has been the 'open door' policy, which has aimed to bring about China's integration into the global economy. And an important part of this aim has been the closer integration of the mainland and Hong Kong economies. Just six years after the central government under Deng Xiaoping announced the 'open door' policy, Margaret Thatcher signed the bilateral treaty by which Britain agreed to return the territory of Hong Kong to Chinese control. Ever since then, Hong Kong, one of the most open economies in the world, has developed an ever-closer partnership with mainland China, previously one of the most closed economies ever known. The handover ceremony on 1 July 1997 formalized the legal status of Hong Kong's return to the mainland, but by then the linkages between the two economies had already become indissoluble.

The *Basic Law*, a mini-constitution for the Special Adminstrative Region of Hong Kong, now confers in-principle legal and economic autonomy, such that Hong Kong's financial and economic affairs are to be determined exclusively by Hong Kong laws. At the same time, economic partnership and integration between Hong Kong and the mainland is closer than ever before. China has been Hong Kong's largest trading partner since 1985. The mainland share of Hong Kong's total trade has risen over the years from 9.3 per cent in 1978 to 45 per cent in 2005. The Chinese mainland was also Hong Kong's largest import source, accounting for 45 per cent of Hong Kong's total imports in 2005. In the other direction, Hong Kong was the mainland's third-largest trading partner (after Japan and the US) in 2005. According to China's Customs Statistics, bilateral trade between the Mainland and Hong Kong amounted to US$136.7 billion (9.6 per cent of the mainland's total external trade) in 2005.[12]

The Chinese mainland and Hong Kong signed the Closer Economic Partnership Arrangement (CEPA) on 29 June 2003 and the implementation details on 29 September 2003. This was followed by Phase II of CEPA announced on 27 August 2004 and CEPA III announced on 18 October 2005. The Closer Economic Partnership Agreements now ensure zero tariff entry to China for all products of Hong Kong origin,[13] and significantly enlarged market access to China for most of Hong Kong's major service sector enterprises.[14] So far as direct investment is concerned, Hong Kong is the largest source of overseas direct investment in the Chinese Mainland. By the end of 2005, of all the overseas-funded projects registered in the Chinese mainland, 45.9 per cent were tied to Hong Kong interests. Utilized capital inflow from Hong Kong amounted to US$259.5 billion, accounting for 41.7 per cent of the national total.

The Chinese mainland is also one of the leading sources of inward investment in Hong Kong. Based on Hong Kong statistics, the Mainland's cumulative direct investment in Hong Kong was HK$1020.1 billion at the end of 2004, accounting for 29 per cent of the stock of inward direct investment. As of December 2005, 335 companies listed on the Hong Kong stock exchange were controlled by mainland interests, comprising H-share, red-chip and private companies with total market capitalization of HK$3.2 trillion (US$409 billion).[15]

So far as Chinese listings on the Hong Kong stock exchange are concerned, cross-border negotiations had begun early in the 1990s, and were formalized by the Chinese–Hong Kong *Memorandum of Regulatory Co-operation on Regulation of Mainland Enterprises Listed in Hong Kong* signed on 19 June 1993.[16] Similar Memorandums of Understanding (MoUs) have also been entered into with regulatory authorities in London, Singapore and the United States to facilitate the listing of Chinese enterprise securities in those jurisdictions. An important outcome of the MoU negotiations was the introduction of Mandatory Provisions to be included in the Articles of Association of all Hong Kong-listed mainland companies.

These Mandatory Provisions resulted from joint efforts by the Hong Kong Securities Commission and the State Restructuring Commission of the PRC to bring corporate governance standards within Hong Kong-listed mainland firms more into line with those prevailing in other Hong Kong listed firms. In Hong Kong, the Mandatory Provisions are required under, and supplemented by, the HKEx Listing Rules. In the PRC, they are enforced through, and supplemented by, the *Special Regulations of the State Council concerning Floating and Listing of Shares Overseas by Companies Limited by Shares*[17] and the *Notice on the Implementation of Essential Clauses in Articles of Association of Companies Listed Overseas*.[18] Since 1993, the Mandatory Provisions have ensured that all H-share firms have certain binding clauses in their Articles of Association which serve to subject directors, supervisors and senior management to a number of important fiduciary duties owed to the company and its shareholders.

II CHINESE EXPLOITATION OF THE HONG KONG STOCK EXCHANGE PRIOR TO 1990

The international aspects of Hong Kong's return to the mainland have obliged the central Chinese government to take the lead in formally negotiating key elements of economic and legal integration, including the 1997 return of Hong Kong to Chinese sovereignty, the CEPA, and the formal agreements (MoUs) under which mainland companies were to be allowed to list on the Hong Kong stock exchange. In terms of actually forging practical economic and business linkages with Hong Kong, however, it has often been the provincial and municipal governments which have been the main players. Thus, well before mainland companies were officially allowed to list directly on the Hong Kong stock exchange (HKEx), there was already significant Chinese interest in the HKEx, primarily through 'back-door listings' or significant stake building. Back-door listings involve a Hong Kong company being taken over by a mainland holding company controlled by a central government ministry, or by a provincial or municipal government. The takeover target is typically a Hong Kong shelf company or company in financial distress.[19] After the acquisition, the mainland company injects its capital into this Hong Kong 'shell' company, and the Hong Kong 'shell' is then used as a listing vehicle by the mainland parent.[20]

The first generation of mainland-controlled listed vehicles in Hong Kong arrived in the 1980s in the form of vehicles established by mainland central-government ministries and provincial/municipal governments eager to establish a financial base in the territory.[21] These mainland-controlled,

Hong Kong-incorporated companies are known as 'red chips' and became popular investment vehicles for Western investors seeking a part of the mainland economic boom without the hazards of exposure to the legal, political and economic risks of direct exposure to the mainland market. Examples include:

- Guangdong Enterprises (Holdings) Limited established in Hong Kong on 3 June 1980 (under the name of Guangdong Enterprises Ltd until 1986), originally established as a window for investment into Guangdong under the direction of the Guangdong provincial government;[22]
- Guangdong Investment, a controlled subsidiary of Guandong's leading holding company Guangdong Enterprises (Holdings) Ltd;[23]
- GITIC Enterprises, controlled by Guangdong International Trust and Investment Corporation (GITIC). First created in 1950 under the direct control of the Guandong provincial government, in 1980 GITIC was established as the Guangdong provincial government's principal funding vehicle in international markets; [24]
- China Everbright group set up in Hong Kong in 1983 by the State Council;[25]
- China Resources, originally set up in Hong Kong in 1948 as China Resources Company and reorganized under the control of the Ministry of Foreign Trade and Economic Cooperation (MOFTEC) in 1983 under the new name of China Resources (Holdings). China Resources (Holdings) acquired a back-door listing in 1992, which was renamed China Resources Enterprise Ltd;[26]
- China Travel was originally founded in 1927 and now operates under the State Council. Its Hong Kong subsidiary, China Travel Service (Holdings) HK Ltd was founded in 1985, and listed its own subsidiary in 1992 under the name China Travel International Investment Hong Kong Ltd.[27]

The Tiananmen Square crackdown in June 1989 was a major setback to the international appetite for red chips, as enthusiasm for China turned to invective against a politically repressive pariah.[28] But interest in China-related stocks soon revived, and was greatly stimulated by President Deng Xiaoping's 1992 reform-promotion tour of southern China. There was a wave of mainland investment in shell companies on the HKEx in 1992–1993, with more than 15 back-door listings between spring 1992 and July 1993.[29] Central government ministries began to dominate in this period, establishing red-chip investment vehicles in centrally-controlled industry sectors such as aerospace,[30] non-ferrous metals[31] foodstuffs[32] and shipping.[33] Local tycoons in Hong Kong like Li Ka-Shing occasionally came to the aid of these ministries to act as a conduit and aid the smooth takeover of a shelf company.[34] Another notable feature of red chips established during 1992–1994 was the way in which they quickly diversified into the speculative areas of real estate and property development.[35]

The Shanghai and Beijing municipal governments would not succeed in floating Hong Kong based investment vehicles until 1996 and 1997, respectively.[36] This was a period during which centralized control over local initiatives was weakened by factional preoccupations within central government circles during the months immediately prior to and following the illness and death of Deng Xiaoping.[37] In 1992, however, the central government's exertion of power and influence under Deng Xiaoping was at a high point. Not surprisingly, therefore, 1992 was also the year that the mainland authorities took measures to assert control over red-chip listings by establishing a centralized approval mechanism for all Hong Kong listings by Chinese subsidiaries. It was also the year when official communications were formally established between the Hong Kong stock exchange and the mainland regulatory authorities to discuss the possibility of listing China-based enterprises on the Hong Kong stock exchange directly, instead of via Hong Kong-incorporated listing vehicles.[38]

A Central Government Reaction to the Flight of Capital to Hong Kong

The takeover of shelf companies to achieve a 'backdoor listing' in Hong Kong or other international markets has typically been followed by the transfer of mainland-based assets to these vehicles to improve share asset-backing levels, and hence share price. Needless to say, the central government very quickly became concerned about this flow of assets out of the country, and eventually became alarmed at the very success of the red-chip market, which very quickly began to outperform even the blue chip Hang Seng index. The State Council issued a *Notice on Suspension of the Purchase of Overseas Enterprises and Further Strengthening the Administration of Overseas Investment* in 1993,[39] in an attempt to control the acquisition of red-chip 'shell companies' outside China. Until 1997, however, it was relatively easy for red-chip companies, which did not, strictly speaking, fall within the supervision of mainland Chinese authorities, to conduct restructuring and raise funds from overseas for new investments easily.[40]

In June 1997, however, the CSRC in conjunction with the State Council introduced the *Notice on Further Strengthening the Administration of the Listing and Issuing of Shares Overseas* (also called the 'Red Chip Notice').[41] The purpose of the Red Chip Notice, as with measures directed towards the H-share firms, was to protect domestic assets from being transferred to overseas ownership. This was accomplished by putting into place more stringent requirements for reporting to, and obtaining approval from, Chinese authorities. The Red Chip Notice targets both listed and unlisted companies registered outside mainland China, and ensures that any China-based Red-Chip parent company cannot inject Chinese assets into the foreign firm through acquisition, share swap or any other type of deal without the approval of the CSRC and other relevant government agencies.[42] In addition to controlling the transfer of assets abroad, article 4 of the Notice 'reaffirms' the *Notice of the State Council on Suspension of the Purchase of Overseas Enterprises and Further Strengthening the Administration of Overseas Investment* issued in 1993, to prohibit domestic firms from purchasing shares overseas for the purpose of listing their own 'shell' company.

The 1997 Notice was followed on 9 June 2000 by the CSRC's *Issues Relevant to the Overseas Issue and Listing of Shares by Overseas Companies with Interests in Mainland China Circular* to further control the process of 'backdoor' listings on overseas exchanges by Chinese enterprises.[43] The 2000 Circular makes it clear that the CSRC considers asset injections as an unauthorized sale of state assets, and approval will only be issued in special cases.

The government also sought to stem the flow of assets out of China via the red chips by providing an alternative venue for raising foreign capital – allowing direct listings on overseas exchanges for mainland-incorporated SOEs for the very first time. The first foreign exchange accessed would be Hong Kong.[44] And, right from the beginning, Beijing has maintained a watchful eye on H-share listings with regard to the valuation and transfer of company assets, which are monitored by the central government agency now known as the State-Owned Assets Supervision and Administration Commission (SASAC), previously known as the State Assets Management Bureau. Through the discipline established by this practice, the government has prevented massive transfers of China's assets offshore.[45]

III DEVELOPMENT OF THE CHINESE H-SHARE MARKET

A The Selection and Flotation of the First Batch of H-share Companies 1992–1995

It was in September 1992 that the State Council of China published its list of the first nine SOEs selected to be the first ever to issue H-share equities. Thus, the process of preparing these firms for listing in Hong Kong was actually taking place at the same time as the negotiations over the Chinese–Hong Kong memorandum of understanding, and the preparation of the Mandatory Provisions.

Intergovernmental tensions between central and provincial authorities became evident early on, and affected both the size and timing of approved H-share issues. One source of friction was the central Finance Ministry's policy directive that localities which failed to fully subscribe to the assigned quota of state treasury bonds would not receive preferential treatment in issuing securities. In an attempt to overcome the shortfall in sales of central government bonds, the State Council also made it clear that localities that subscribed to the assigned quota of state treasury paper would receive preferential treatment in issuing stocks.[46]

The State Council thus began restricting new issues of A-shares (Chinese domestic shares) in order to encourage bond purchases by Chinese individuals and organizations (legal persons). In a move that incensed the Shanghai and Shenzhen authorities, Beijing ordered Tsingtao Brewery, one of the SOEs selected for listing in Hong Kong, to shrink the size of its planned A-share issue from 40 per cent of total share capital down to 11.11 per cent, and to increase its number of shares offered in Hong Kong from an originally planned 25 per cent of total shares to 38.54 per cent. Local authorities in Shenzhen and Shanghai saw this move as stealing business away from their own markets, noting that the enforcement of bond purchases was hurting the whole A-share market in other ways as well.[47]

The first H-shares, issued by Tsingtao Brewery Corporation (Tsingtao), were opened for offer in Hong Kong on Tuesday 29 June 1993,[48] and began trading on the Hong Kong Stock Exchange on 15 July 1993. It had originally been thought that the much larger Shanghai Petrochemical Company Limited (Shanghai Petrochemical) IPO would take place first, but when the difficult and controversial nature of that offering became clear, it seems that Beijing was persuaded that the Tsingtao listing would be a more suitable one with which to test the waters. The cautious approach being adopted in Beijing was further evidenced by the authorities' initial refusal to allow primary listings to proceed in New York, London or any other place outside of China apart from Hong Kong. They believed that the Hong Kong market for China-based issues should be developed before proceeding further.[49] Thus, the original Shanghai Petrochemical plan for a dual primary listing in Hong Kong and New York was finally abandoned on the instructions of Beijing. Instead, there was a single offering, which took place in three parts: a share sale in Hong Kong, a public sale of ADRs in the United States and a sale of GDRs (global depository receipts) outside the United States.[50]

The use of experimental legislation in regional areas as precedents for drafting new laws at the national level has long been a characteristic of Chinese legal reform. What is interesting about the development of the H-share market is the way in which the region (Hong Kong) was forced to confront and find solutions to new legal problems raised throughout the creation of a new H-share market. For example, the Hong Kong offer of Shanghai Petrochemical H-shares, which took place between 6 July and 16 July 1993, was characterized by a number of controversial issues that, never having arisen before, had to be resolved 'on the run'. Two issues in particular were the subject of vigorous debate: the first involving the rules around the use of 'book building' as the procedure for IPO price determination,[51] and the second involving the use of price 'stabilization' as a form of benign market rigging to ensure orderly distribution of shares immediately following a new share issue.[52] The debate, while probably detrimental to the overall success of the Shanghai Petrochemical offering itself (because it helped make that offering so very controversial), can be viewed as a positive development in the evolution of Hong Kong as an international financial centre. A capital market with international credibility cannot develop in an environment where brokers and the media cannot offer a whole range of opinions on a whole series of issues, and that is not just limited to financial matters.[53] The fact that some brokers felt unable to comment publicly on the more sensitive aspects of the Shanghai Petrochemical offering, however, also raised concerns in some circles about the fate of press freedom under future Chinese rule.[54]

Prior to 1993, a fixed price system of IPO price determination had traditionally been used for Hong Kong IPOs. In mainland China, the CSRC also followed a fixed-price system and, at least until 1999, placed severe restrictions on listing candidates' ability to determine their own issuing prices. So, when the underwriters of the Shanghai Petrochemical H-share offer announced that a process of 'book building'[55] would be used to determine the final share price,[56] it became instantly controversial. Book building typically involves a series of consultations between the lead underwriter and institutional investors to determine the most appropriate price range for an IPO which then helps, closer to the actual transaction date, to fix the best price at which the investment bank can clear the book. It can also dictate who takes the shares (institutional bidders), which can sometimes preclude retail investors. The Hong Kong fixed-price system, on the other hand, allows for a strong element of retail participation which has always been a feature of local listings in the territory. The fixed-price period of sale can, however, be cumbersome, particularly in the case of very large listings like the Shanghai Petrochemical offer, where institutional and international investors are needed. Book building has only recently become a feature of mainland Chinese IPOs, and would not have been allowed for a mainland listing in 1993. The price-setting mechanism for the Shanghai-Petro H-share offering, however, was subject only to Hong Kong law, which contained no actual prohibition on book-building exercises, and so it was allowed to proceed.

The Shanghai Petrochemical issue became even more controversial when the underwriters included a statement in the published prospectus that they reserved the right to stabilize the price of the company's shares, contrary to the accepted orthodoxy that stabilization is illegal in Hong Kong. To be fair, the prospectus also made it clear that 'If stabilization transactions in the H shares [were] effected in Hong Kong they [would] be executed and reported to the market for public dissemination in accordance with the Rules of the Hong Kong Stock Exchange and [would] be in strict compliance with the securities laws of Hong Kong and the requirements of the regulatory authorities'.[57]

International practice varies as to whether, and in what circumstances, stabilization is allowed. While stabilization is ubiquitous in the Euromarkets and specifically allowed in the US and UK[58] (although only in specified limited circumstances), the legality of stabilization under Hong Kong law was not formally resolved when the Shanghai Petrochemical prospectus was issued, or during the offer period.[59] Indeed, Hong Kong law under the *Securities Ordinance* (now repealed) regarding stabilization was famously unclear. Section 135, which purported to ban stabilization under the law relating to false markets, was unhelpful. To get a conviction, a prosecutor had to show that the market price of securities had been stabilized by sales and purchases transacted by persons acting in collaboration, and aiming to secure a market price not justified by the assets or profits of the issuer of the securities. But the question of a how a 'justifiable price' should be determined was not dealt with, instead being left for expert witnesses to argue over.[60] Nor was it ever made clear whether section 135 applied to transactions carried out overseas, or to pre-listing transactions.[61]

When a share price stabilization scheme was proposed in the Shanghai Petrochemical prospectus, the Securities and Futures Commission in Hong Kong (SFC) was quick to take a firm line in clarifying the question of its legality. The SFC made it quite clear that it would view any attempt by the sponsoring banks to move into the market to support the price by offering to buy at a set level as a clear contravention of section 135.[62] What the sponsors (Merrill Lynch and Peregrine Capital) were permitted to do, however, was to 'cover' the issue by buying shares in Hong Kong to meet demand from outside the territory. The stabilization question was not resolved until nearly 10 years later when, in 2002, new rules aimed at attracting more companies to list in Hong Kong were introduced, and the SFC finally agreed to allow price-stabilizing actions during share offerings for a limited 30-day period. The rules now permit companies staging share offerings worth more than HK$100 million to support the share price in the first 30 days after listing.[63]

The Beiren issue and listing came after Tsingtao and Shanghai Petrochemical H-shares had already begun trading, and at the same time as Guangzhou Shipyard International issued its first batch of H shares. The public offer of 100 million Beiren H-shares took place in Hong Kong in late July 1993, with subscriptions closing on 28 July 1993. The timing of the offer was not optimal, coming as it did at a time when investors were becoming cautious about H-shares, partly owing to the poor market reaction to the first two H-shares. In addition, both the Beiren issue prospectus and commentators warned prospective investors that Beiren's reliance on the domestic market would leave it more exposed to China's currency risk than in the case of the other H-share firms. On the other hand, some commentators viewed Beiren as a positive long-term investment opportunity, pointing out that, if the renminbi remained steady, then the company's prospects in a market of rising demand for printing machines were very bright indeed.[64] '[W]ith an order book that is full for 18 months, Beiren's earnings can hardly be considered at risk', said one commentator.[65] Also in favour of a successful Beiren H-share issue was the low subscription price, giving a price–earnings ratio of around 11.5 times.[66] This was the lowest price amongst the first nine H-shares, and considerably lower than the P/E ratio of 17.89 times (fully diluted) for the most expensive H-share amongst the first batch of nine (Tsingtao Brewery). Of course, with 16 leading Hong Kong brokerages acting as underwriters for the Beiren issue, the success of the float was in any event probably guaranteed from the start.[67] In the result – and despite being compared favourably in the press with the more expensive Guangzhou Shipyard share offer, and keen interest from institutional investors – the Beiren H-share issue was a mere 24–25 times oversubscribed, well below the 76–77 times attracted by Guangzhou Shipyard.[68]

Both Beiren and Guangzhou Shipyard H-shares began trading in Hong Kong on 6 August 1993. Then, in late October 1993, the central government announced that, encouraged by the successful listing of the first four H-share companies, it would soon allow more state-owned enterprises to issue shares on overseas markets. Twenty-two enterprises were included in the second batch of companies approved for listing overseas, and the relative speed with which they were selected and listed demonstrates the Chinese government's eagerness to further develop the H-share market.

The Maanshan Iron & Steel and Kunming Machine Tool H-share listings took place in November and December 1993, respectively, and were relatively uncontroversial. Yizheng Chemical Fibre was next, with a public offer of one billion Yizheng H-shares in March 1994. Yizheng shares were listed on the HKEx and began trading on 29 March 1994. Then, in April 1995, in what was described as a 'crash placing', an extra 400 million Yizheng H-shares worth $980 million were put up for sale by British investment bank SG Warburg. Shareholder approval for the issue of 400 million new H-shares 'within six months' had been obtained only the week before the placing. Approval from the CSRC and the HKEx was also required. The fact that everything was put into place ready for the placing to proceed only hours after approval from the authorities was obtained demonstrates the company's confidence that such approval would not be withheld.[69]

Whether or not such confidence was well founded, the fact that approval was given with such apparent readiness demonstrates a growing level of sophistication and flexibility among Chinese authorities in their approach to fund raising by state-controlled companies. On the mainland side, there was also the fact that authorities were well aware that Yizheng's original plan for reducing company debt by issuing domestic A shares had been stymied by the CSRC's own crackdown on new A-share issues. To make the crackdown more palatable, the CSRC recognized the need to ease up on access to alternative avenues (including the Hong Kong market) for 'standard-bearing' enterprises in need of finance.[70]

The authorities thus had a motive for experimenting with new methods of share placing and equity-based fund raising. In Yizheng's case, the placing method adopted by SG Warburg was the first of its kind involving an H-share, and resembled the more common 'bought deal', in which an investment house takes a large line of existing stock onto its own books, effectively absorbing all the market risk, and then rapidly pushing the shares out to clients.[71] In the result, the strategy appears to have been successful, and the new H-shares began trading on the Hong Kong Stock Exchange on 26 April 1995.[72]

The Tianjin Bohai H-share offer which followed appears to have been badly timed, with the market tainted by speculative investment during the earlier H-share offerings and sour economic news about the Chinese economy in general – inflation, rising debt levels in state-run enterprises and mounting unemployment. The new shares were sold at 12.6 times Tianjin Bohai prospective earnings (on a fully diluted basis), with a subscription rate that was 0.25 oversubscribed – by far the lowest subscription rate of the eight stocks which had been issued to that date.[73] Trading began on Tuesday 17 May 1994.

The Tianjin Bohai issue also raised concerns about the lack of disclosure amongst Chinese listed enterprises. Press reports revealed rumours, supported by circumstantial evidence, that mainland-Chinese authorities had sought the help of underwriters to ensure the issue was fully subscribed. It was not long before the rumours were confirmed as being true. The Tianjin Bohai public offering closed at noon on 6 May 1994, but the number of applications seemed to fall short of the amount offered early in the morning. At least two of the sub-underwriters, Peregrine Capital and SG Warburg, received calls from the mainland authorities requesting them to file more applications.[74] Under the underwriting system, the lead underwriters, Jardine Fleming and China Development Finance (an offshoot of the Bank of China) were obliged to take up the shortfall if the issue was undersubscribed. But they appear to have been bypassed, with the co-underwriters being asked to pick up the extra shares. (The underwriting syndicate comprised eight co-underwriters and six principal sub-underwriters.)

Under the Rules Governing the Listing of Securities on the Stock Exchange of Hong Kong Limited (the Listing Rules), underwriters can direct their associate operations, such as fund management arms, to acquire shares during the initial offer period, and the information does not have to be disclosed. It is considered a whitewash or face-saving approach to subscribe for the shares at the last minute and take positions and sell the shares when they think the time is appropriate. Very often, the majority shareholder or some financial advisers would be the market makers and the downside risk is therefore lessened.[75]

But many analysts and commentators compared the Tianjin Bohai case unfavourably with what had occurred in the case of Shanghai Petrochemical, where underwriters revealed the fact that they had subscribed for the shares right from the beginning. As well as breaching stock exchange information disclosure protocols, these commentators felt that 'the mainland authorities' attempt to whitewash the subscription indicate[d] its unrealistic attitude to H-share issues and [the overly-] high expectation of the merchant banks'. The government was criticized for not facing up to the problems, determined to believe that everything about H-share listings had to be successful.[76]

New rules governing overseas listing by state-owned enterprises were issued by the mainland authorities in August 1994. The new 30-point Code helped to clear up many of the uncertainties that had emerged during the first few Chinese enterprises' listings in Hong Kong. By specifically recognizing some of the previously unofficial practices adopted during these listings, it also demonstrated the Chinese authorities' willingness to adjust to different market environments, and to fit in with common practices of stock markets overseas. For instance, the new Code expressly allowed overseas-listed companies to issue Depository Receipts or derivatives. Also expressly permitted were over-allotments of shares in the case of oversubscription for new share offerings, a method which had already been used by Shanghai Petrochemical the year before,[77] despite the fact that the practice of inserting green-shoe provisions into underwriting agreements allowing an underwriting syndicate to buy more shares from the issuer in the case of oversubscription during an IPO was in fact not ratified by the Hong Kong authorities until November 1994.[78] In mainland China, the *Tentative Opinion for Over-placement Option* promulgated by the CSRC on 3 September 2001 served to formalize the legality of green-shoe options and outline rules applicable to such options.[79]

The last of the first batch of nine companies selected for listing to reach the market in Hong Kong was Dongfang Electrical. The Dongfang Electrical experience illustrates the way in which firms involved in the issue and trading of H-shares have occasionally had problems keeping up with new legal rules as reforms have been introduced. The lead international underwriter for Dongfang Electrical H-shares, Nomura International (Hong Kong), was found by the Hong Kong Stock Exchange (HKEx) listing committee to have been in breach of rule 10.08(1) governing the listing of securities. The rule was introduced on 16 March 1994, only shortly prior to the Dongfang H-share offer. It requires all IPO sponsors to ensure that multiple, or suspected multiple, applications for securities offered to the public for subscription are identified and rejected. Nomura was found to have submitted multiple applications on behalf of a client for the 112.5 million-share public offer. Nomura admitted that it had failed to identify and reject the multiple applications, and also admitted to 'certain control weaknesses'. The listing committee noted that, following an internal review carried out by Nomura, the firm had tightened up its internal procedures to avoid occurrence of a similar incident in future, and also said that the announcement of the breach was not a public censure.[80]

B The Evolving Mainland Securities Markets

The H-share listing plans of the first nine Hong Kong-listed Chinese companies were each developed as part of a package of proposals for corporate financing which included a domestic listing. Unlike most later Hong Kong-listed Chinese firms,[81] every one of the first nine H-share firms undertook a domestic share issue and listing within months of their H-share issue. And, just as the procedures for H-share IPOs in Hong Kong were not free of problems, so also were early share issues on China's domestic securities markets sometimes fraught with difficulties.

First, there have been the different rules governing IPOs in each of the different markets. Thus, for example, there are different requirements for preparing and releasing prospectuses, as well as for price-setting, subscription and allotment of shares, depending on whether the company is under-

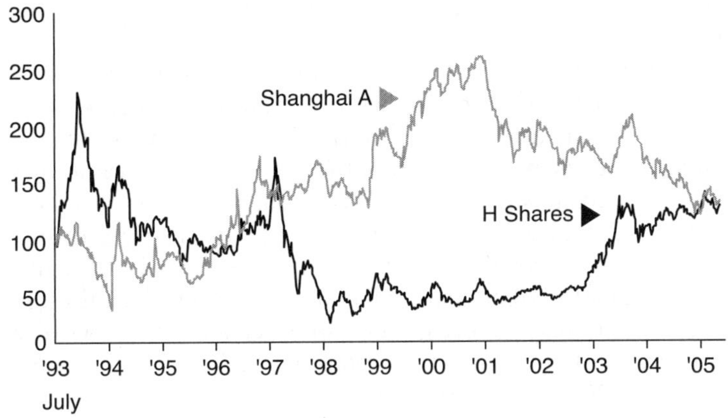

Source: Published in (2005) 168(11) *Far Eastern Economic Review* 9; FACTIVA.

Figure 2.1 Two roads converged: price performance of Shanghai-traded A-shares and Hong Kong-traded H shares

taking an IPO of H-shares on the Hong Kong Exchange, or issuing A-shares onto a domestic Chinese exchange.

There are also differences in the way the different markets respond when an IPO takes place. Beginning in mid-1997, H-share prices and A-share values of dually-listed firms began to diverge sharply. Demand for tradable A-shares issued on the mainland was high,[82] while foreign investor caution began to play a dampening role on demand for new H-share issues in Hong Kong. As a result, companies dually listed on a PRC stock exchange and in Hong Kong found that their common A-share stock typically traded at a significant premium (on an equivalent currency basis) on the mainland over their Hong Kong-listed H-shares. To be sure, the price gap between domestic and foreign share values of dually-listed Chinese companies has narrowed in recent years, from about 380 per cent in 2001, to only about 30 per cent at the end of 2005 (see Figure 2.1).[83] But, according to some views, the A-share market still remains overvalued compared with overseas markets, despite a significant decline in recent years.[84]

Not surprisingly, this price divergence has created difficulties in the simultaneous listing of companies in both the PRC and Hong Kong, since, under the PRC *Company Law*, shares offered at the same time must be sold at the same price.[85] The solution has been to ensure, in the case of most Hong Kong-listed Chinese firms, that IPOs for A-shares do not take place simultaneously with IPOs for H-shares of the same company. Instead, IPOs for the same firm in the two markets have been staggered, sometimes occurring up to 12 months apart.

Early problems unique to the A-share market arose from the use of the 'lottery ticket method' used for share allocation. Under this method, prospective investors not only had to travel to the city where the offer was taking place (Shenzhen or Shanghai), they also had to successfully buy an IPO application form, and then hope they would be one of only 10 per cent of application form holders who would be granted the right to subscribe, depending on the results of a lottery draw to determine the final allocation of shares. What subscribers paid for under this system was thus, not just the money for the shares allotted, but also the cost of travel to the relevant venue, the time cost of queuing to purchase subscription lottery tickets, and the cost of the IPO application form-cum-lottery ticket itself. Moreover, in many cases the distribution of the winning applications was largely over before it began, as most of the successful applications had already been allocated to the friends and family of those involved in the listing process – those able to 'go through the back door'.[86] In the case of the Shanghai Petrochemical A-share offering, the IPO was made even more controversial by the decision to split the first offering of Shanghai Petrochemical A-shares between Shenzhen and Shanghai, under two separate systems for the allocation of shares. The presence of different allocation systems in the two cities resulted in widely divergent prices for investors buying in Shenzhen and Shanghai, respectively, with Shanghai investors paying twice that paid by their counterparts in Shenzhen.

Both Beiren and Guangzhou Shipyard companies issued A-shares in early 1994, several months after their respective H-share issues. Beiren launched its public A-share offering in Beijing, while the Guangzhou Shipyard A-share offer occurred in the southern cities of Shanghai and Guangzhou. The offer of Beiren A-shares was initially restricted to Beijing residents, and was conducted by means of a lottery selection in which winning certificates allowed holders to subscribe for and purchase up to 500 shares in four Beijing-based companies: Beiren itself, Beijing Light Bus Co., Beijing Town and Country Trade Centre and Beijing Department Store. The Beijing share lottery sale revealed yet another problem with the lottery process in China, the swift growth of a vigorous black market where lottery coupons were selling at almost ten times the face value. Limited supply of coupons in a market of very high demand appears to have aggravated the effects of investor inexperience and lack of sophistication to create an environment where local investors approached the whole process as a gambling exercise, rather than as a chance for long-term investment.[87] This was despite government propaganda that emphasized both the illegal nature of black market trade in stock purchase certificates, and the risks of buying stocks compared to the 'absolutely safe' option of buying treasury bonds. Government two-and-three year treasury bonds in fact went on sale on 1 April 1994, within days of the Beiren A-share offer.[88] In the event, the Beiren Printing A-share offer was ten times oversubscribed, making it the least popular of the four Beijing stocks included in the lottery coupon sale.[89]

In the case of the Guangzhou Shipyard A-share issue, about 53.1 million share-subscription forms were sold, entitling each applicant to 500 A shares *if* they were successful in a lottery held on 9 October 1993. Each lottery winner then had ten days to subscribe for no more than the maximum number of A-shares until the subscription period ended on Tuesday 19 October 1993.[90] The chances of being successful in the original lottery was about 3.69 in 1000, making the average cost of acquiring each share 1.08 yuan more than the issue price of 5.23 yuan.[91] Even though the first day of trading in Guangzhou Shipyard A-shares delivered a paper profit to shareholders of 28 per cent, this gain is not so impressive when the cost of buying subscription forms is taken into account.[92] The only potential share applicants exempt from the uncertainties and disappointments of the lottery process were the company's employees, who, between them, were entitled to subscribe for a total of 28 396 400 shares, with each applicant guaranteed at least a minimum number of shares. The employee share offering was very quickly fully allocated. Guangzhou Shipyard employee-held shares became publicly listed (subject to certain restrictions on their transfer), in Shanghai on 31 May 1994 at an initial price of 5.23 yuan.[93]

Yizheng's A-share issue of a mere 200 million shares did not take place until January 1995. In fact, approval had been given in 1993 for the company to issue 600 million A-shares as part of a plan for reducing company debt, but the CSRC was becoming concerned about a flood of new A-share issues resulting in a long-term decline in the market value of the domestic securities markets, and was only initially prepared to give approval for the public issue of 200 million A-shares to proceed in 1995. Yizheng A-shares were listed and began trading on the Shanghai Securities Exchange on 11 April 1995.

The lottery method of offering shares was not altered until 1995 when a new method was introduced for the Tianjin Bohai and Dongfang Electrical A-share IPOs. Under the new share allocation method, Tianjin Bohai and Dongfang Electrical guaranteed an equal minimum number of 100 shares for each successful subscriber, with applications processed on a 'first-come-first-served' basis. Whether or not subscribers would be able to buy more shares than the minimum number would depend on the total number of applications received. In addition, all investors interested in the shares had to do was to buy them through underwriters in their local city, instead of travelling all the way to the site of the issue. Application buy orders were sent through computer stations linked to the Shanghai or Shenzhen exchange, and successful applicants only ever had to pay for the shares subscribed for at the relevant fixed issue price – unlike under the lottery ticket method.[94]

The new method of allocating A-shares through a minimum guaranteed number of shares for each successful subscriber was a great improvement on the system but not without its own problems. During the Tianjin Bohai A-share issue (which came more than a year after the firm's launch onto the Hong Kong stock exchange), the problem encountered was a practical one. On the very day that the first Tianjin Bohai A-shares were launched onto the open market (Friday 16 June 1995), an avalanche of orders for the shares jammed the Shanghai stock exchange's national electronic trading network and triggered a suspension of A- and B-share trading during the morning session. By the time subscriptions closed on Saturday, the marine chemicals manufacturer had received orders for about 199 million shares from 187 264 ordinary Chinese investors for the issue of 68.98 million shares.[95]

As well as the more efficient share allocation method, further reasons for the shares' popularity were the relatively cheap price of 2.50 yuan a share (HK$2.32) and the relatively small size of the issue.

The same share allocation method was used in the Dongfang Electrical A-share issue, and here the authorities found themselves confronted by a legal quandary as well as a practical one. A total of 60 million A-shares were issued, priced at 4.10 yuan each. In the result, the offer was nearly 59 times oversubscribed, with applications for 3.53 billion shares received from a total of 799 658 potential investors. Share orders were keyed into computer systems across the country linked to the Shanghai stock exchange's main trading system. Given the limited number of shares available, only 600 000 subscribers, chosen on a first-come-first-served basis, got any shares at all, with each successful applicant receiving only 100 shares each. This was a record in Shanghai's recent stock history, as never before had so many shareholders owned so few shares in a new issue.[96]

The problem was that, under Chinese securities regulations, a company cannot list unless it has at least 1000 investors who own more than 1000 shares each.[97] In other words, the 100 share per investor status quo meant that Dongfang lacked a legal basis for listing. Eight weeks after the issue, Dongfang still could not be listed.[98] Although Shanghai exchange officials finally gave permission for the Dongfang A-shares to begin trading on 10 October 1995,[99] the company was required to bring itself into line with listing requirements as soon as possible.[100]

The CSRC has only recently begun to relax its strict control over the price-setting process for new A-share issues, and its ability to withhold approval for IPOs whose price falls outside permissible limits.[101] It was not until 1999 that the CSRC issued a new *Circular on Further Improving Methods of Issuing Shares*,[102] under which a listing candidate and its lead underwriter are free to set the issue price, within a scope confirmed by the CSRC, through the book-building method.[103] But this did not solve the problems of price instabilities and fluctuations which typically followed a new share listing. Nor did it prevent criticisms, especially in the early years, about the lack of transparency in the way IPOs were priced, basically a matter of negotiation between the listing applicant and the securities regulatory authorities. There were many complaints that IPOs were overpriced and not transparent.[104]

Lack of transparency and fairness for IPO pricing was just one of a number of factors that by late 2004 had brought about a dramatic decline in the value of China's domestic stock exchanges. Many domestic investors had been 'burned' after purchasing overpriced shares in newly listed firms that later failed. Demand for shares was also depressed by the growth in alternative avenues for investment. The third depressing influence was the government's declared determination to persist with plans to release a large number of non-tradable state-owned shares onto the market, leading to fears of further dilution and depression of A-share values generally. There was a need to curb the continued growth of the market, as companies appeared as keen as ever to ask the investing public for funds, despite the overall market decline. In order to stabilize the market, all new IPOs were suspended in September 2004, and no new A-share issues took place for over 12 months, until May 2006.

New *Measures for the Administration of Initial Public Offerings of Shares and the Listing Thereof* (the IPO Measures) became effective on 18 May 2006, and signalled the reopening of the PRC stock market after more than one-year's suspension of new share sales. The Measures are aimed both at achieving the resumption of the market's key role of fund-raising, and at reshaping the shareholder structure of listed companies. New Listing Rules were also issued by the Shanghai and Shenzhen stock exchanges following the implementation of, and in order to complement, both the new Measures and the central government's new *Company Law* and *Securities Law* which came into effect on 1 January 2006. Under the new IPO rules, the minimum registered capital requirement for listed firms remains at Rmb 50 million (US$6.25 million) which must be paid-up before the listing. As for a minimum public float, the New Listing Rules maintain the old standard of 25 per cent of the issuer's total issued share capital for most firms, but reduce the standard for issuers that have a total share capital of more than 400 Rmb million, from 15 per cent, down to 10 per cent of total share capital.

In line with the government's 'five separations' policy for government-controlled listed firms, the IPO Measures require that the issuer must be fully independent of its controlling shareholder and other companies controlled by that shareholder, in respect of its ownership of operating assets, its business system, business organization, financial system and personnel. In particular:

- The issuer's senior officers must not take positions other than a directorship or a supervisory role with the issuer's controlling shareholder or companies controlled by such a shareholder;
- The issuer's financial personnel must not keep any concurrent post with the issuer's controlling shareholder or companies controlled by such a shareholder;
- The issuer must not share the same bank account with its controlling shareholder or companies controlled by such a shareholder;
- The issuer's articles of association must clearly specify the approval authority and procedure for external security so as to prevent any irregular provision of security to the issuer's controlling shareholder or companies controlled by such a shareholder;
- The controlling shareholder or companies controlled by such a shareholder must not own or operate any business competing with the issuer.

A number of 'trial' Measures and Circulars dating from as early as 1996 were consolidated and repealed by new *Measures for the Administration of the Offering and Underwriting of Securities* (the Offering and Underwriting Measures) which came into effect on 19 September 2006.[105] The Offering and Underwriting Measures both complement and add to the provisions of the new 2006 *Securities Law* concerning the offering and underwriting of shares. The Offering and Underwriting Measures represent the culmination of a series of efforts by the CSRC to enforce transparency and fairness in IPO pricing. Mechanisms such as fixed pricing and pricing according to price–earnings ratios were criticized for lacking flexibility and depriving underwriters of pricing freedom. The Offering and Underwriting Measures address these problems by leaving IPO pricing to be determined through a two-stage pricing inquiry process involving qualified institutions (Inquiry Recipients) such as securities investment fund management companies, securities companies, trust and investment corporations, finance companies, insurance institutional investors and qualified foreign institutional investors.[106]

The first stage of the pricing inquiry process is the preliminary inquiry, on the basis of which the offer price range is determined, and the second stage is book-building, on the basis of which the specific offering price is determined. For IPOs involving fewer than 400 million publicly offered shares, at least 20 Inquiry Recipients must participate and provide valid quotations, while for IPOs involving more than 400 million publicly offered shares, at least 50 Inquiry Recipients must participate and provide valid quotations. An Inquiry Recipient cannot participate in the book-building inquiry or off-line placement if it has not participated in the initial price inquiry, or if it participated in the initial price inquiry but did not make a valid quotation.[107] This provision closes a loophole in the old pricing procedure, which allowed institutions to submit arbitrary quotations without intending to subscribe.[108]

Securities offering can be conducted through online issuances (via the electronic system of securities exchanges) or offline placements organized and completed by underwriters. Where both procedures are used, offline placements and online issuances must be conducted simultaneously.[109] This is to help ensure equal access to issuances by public (individual) investors.[110] For IPOs involving at least 400 million shares, a private placement of shares may also be made with a strategic investor. This provision is aimed at attracting long-term capital for newly listed companies, so that strategic investors must commit themselves to a lock-up period of at least 12 months before a private placement is permitted.[111]

When domestic A-shares are issued in China they are usually distributed by one or more securities companies under an underwriting agreement. Under articles 28–33 of the new *Securities Law*, an underwriting agreement must be for a period of no longer than 90 days,[112] and can be either a 'best efforts underwriting' agreement or a 'firm commitment underwriting' agreement.[113] In most cases, the issuing price will be determined through consultations between the issuer and the underwriter.[114] Securities to be offered to the public with a total face value exceeding Rmb 50 million must be distributed by a distribution syndicate comprising a securities company acting as chief underwriter and participating security companies. Securities underwritten on a best efforts or firm commitment basis must be first sold to subscribers, and not set aside or retained by underwriters. The 2006 *Securities Law* contains new provisions on underwriting to extend the range of financial misdemeanours liable to incur penalties, including inaccurate or misleading information or material omissions from official reports or from any other information disclosure. It also outlaws 'improper competitive methods'[115] adopted by some underwriters when touting for business, and penalizes issuers using the funds they raise for purposes other than those stated in their offering documents.[116]

In order to prevent the kind of price instability so commonly associated with IPOs in China over recent years, the new stock exchange Listing Rules impose an extended lock-up period for general shareholders of 36 months whenever an IPO takes place. So far as the controlling shareholder is concerned, the lock-up period begins on the listing date, while for general shareholders who acquire shares within 12 months prior to the IPO, the lock-up period commences from the date on which the shareholder was registered as a shareholder of the issuer. Approval for the IPO will only be given after such shareholders have signed an undertaking in relation to the lock-up requirement.[117]

So far as follow-on issues are concerned, the market was reopened for new equity offerings by already-listed companies when new *Measures for the Administration of Securities Offerings by Listed Companies* (the Follow-on Offerings Measures) became effective on 8 May 2006.[118] The Follow-on Offerings Measures clarify the rules governing follow-on offerings of shares by already listed companies, and give publicly listed companies more funding options to expand through private placements and secondary sales to the public. A follow-on public offering increases the listed company's total number of shares of outstanding stock, and is generally easier than for an initial offering. The Measures only set restrictions on the maximum amount of shares to be issued in a follow-on public offering when the subscribers are existing shareholders of the issuer. In such a case, the value of the issued shares should not exceed 30 per cent of the issuer's share capital.

So far as the price of follow-on shares is concerned, the new Measures provide that the price of shares issued in a follow-on public offering must not be lower than the average of the issuer's shares in the 20 trading days prior to the publication of the prospectus. Issuers and underwriters will need to convince investors that this price-range is justified, a task which has been made even more challenging by higher probity standards relating to the content of prospectuses and other investment documents. On the same day the Follow-on Offerings Measures were issued, the CSRC also promulgated revised versions of two guidelines on the format and content of application documents and prospectuses for public offerings of shares.[119] All directors, supervisors and senior managers of the issuer must sign the prospectus and guarantee the accuracy of the information disclosed in the prospectus, and bear joint and several liability.

As well as clarifying the rules for follow-on public share offerings by listed companies, the Measures provide guidance on the requirements to be met by registered issuers performing private placements of securities. In a private placement, a listed company issues shares to a limited number of designated investors.[120] The terms of the placement are usually described in a 'private placement memorandum' and no formal offer document is required. Other requirements are also less stringent than those applying to public follow-on offerings. The Measures do not place any qualification requirements on designated investors to a private placement. However, if the designated subscriber is a 'foreign strategic investor' under the *Measures for the Administration of Strategic Investments in Listed Companies by Foreign Investors*[121] (Strategic Investment Measures) the investor will have to:

a. comply with quantitative requirements (owning at least US$100 million of offshore assets or managing at least $500 million of offshore assets);
b. obtain an 'in principle' approval from the Ministry of Commerce prior to subscribing to new shares issued by private placement, and
c. satisfy a range of prudential conditions.

Under the Follow-on Offerings Measures, new shares issued by private placement are subject to a one-year lock-up period. New shares subscribed by a controlling shareholder or the de facto controller (and any enterprise controlled by the controlling shareholder or de facto controller) are subject to a lock-up period of three years. The price of the newly issued shares must not be less that 90 per cent of the average price of the issued shares within the last 20 transaction days before the date of pricing.

Many other aspects of the regulatory regime governing listed companies in China have also undergone significant change since the first H-share listings. And many of the legislative changes since 1993 have ostensibly been aimed at making listed companies more independent of government involvement in firm management, and more answerable to market forces and independent shareholders. Before discussing these reforms, however, it is necessary to understand the regulatory framework within which they have occurred.

NOTES

1. Tan Lay Hong, 'The legal and regulatory framework of securities markets in the PRC', [1998] 7:1 *Asia Pacific Law Review*, p. 69 at 69; citing Magasaki Igarashi, 'Chinese bonds in the introduction of foreign capital', 82 *China Newsletter* 9–15, and Pitman B. Potter, 'The legal framework for securities markets in China: the challenge of maintaining state control and inducing investing confidence' (1992) 7 *China Law Reporter* 61.
2. Tan Lay Hong, 'The legal and regulatory framework of securities markets in the PRC', [1998] 7:1 *Asia Pacific Law Review*, p. 69, at 71 citing 'State Commission Outlines Shareholding System', special report by the State Commission for Restructuring the Economic System, *JPRS–CAR-92-059*, 3 August 1992 pp. 34–39; 'Article on Joint Stock Companies, Stock Markets', *JPRS–CAR-92-079*, 21 October 1992 pp. 20–27; and 'Shanghai Re-establishes Securities Market', *JPRS–CAR-90-011*, 12 February 1990 pp. 31–34. Also noting that the B-share issue was pioneered by the Shanghai Vacuum Electronic Devices Co Ltd on 30 November 1990, citing 'On China's Stock Market Development', *JPRS-CAR-93-018*, 19 March 1993 pp. 16–19.

3. On the issue of the overlap in jurisdictional oversight between the PBoC and the CSRC and the need to eliminate this overlap, see Chapter 7, Conclusions and Recommendations in World Bank (Anjali Kumar, Kwang Jun, Anthony Saunders, Susan Selwyn, Yan Sun, Dimitri Vittas, David Wilton), *China's Emerging Capital Markets* (FT Financial Publishing Asia Pacific, 1997) esp. at 256–257.
4. Tan Lay Hong, 'The legal and regulatory framework of securities markets in the PRC', [1998] 7:1 *Asia Pacific Law Review*, p. 69 at 71, citing P. Schroeder, 'Rebuilding China's securities markets' (May–June 1991) *The China Business Review*, 20–21.
5. Tan Lay Hong, 'The legal and regulatory framework of securities markets in the PRC', [1998] 7:1 *Asia Pacific Law Review*, p. 69 at 71, citing R. Nottle, 'The development of securities markets in China in the 1990s' (1993) 11 *Company and Securities Law Journal* 503; Mei Xia, P.D. Grub and Jian Hai Lin, *Re-emerging Securities Market in China* (Quorum Books, 1992) pp. 103–116.
6. Tan Lay Hong, 'The legal and regulatory framework of securities markets in the PRC', [1998] 7:1 *Asia Pacific Law Review*, p. 69 at 71, noting further that the forerunner of the Shanghai Stock Exchange was the Shanghai Jing'an Trading Centre, which started in 1986 with the stocks of just two companies, the Yangzhong Industrial Co and Feili Hi-Fi Corp worth RMB 5 million. See also China Securities Regulatory Commission, *China Securities and Futures Markets*, April 2004, at 3, which gives December 1990 as the date on which both the Shanghai and Shenzhen exchanges were established – a date which is not consistent with other reliable sources.
7. *Standard Opinion for Joint Stock Limited Companies*, issued on 15 May 1992 by the State Restructuring Commission.
8. *Administration of the Issuing and Trading of Shares Tentative Regulations* promulgated on, and effective from, 22 April 1993 by Order Number 112 of the State Council. Published as *Provisional Regulations on the Administration of the Issuing and Trading of Stocks* in *China Laws for Foreign Business – Business Regulation* at para. 13-574.
9. Translated as *The Company Law of the People's Republic of China* (adopted at the Fifth Session of the Eighth National People's Congress; promulgated by Order No. 16 of the President of the PRC on 29 December 1993, in L.A. Tokley & Tina Ravn, *Company and Securities Law in China* (Sweet & Maxwell Asia, 1998).
10. Erica Leung, Lily Liu, Lu Shen, Kevin Taback and Leo Wang, 'Financial reform and corporate governance in China', MIT Sloan School of Management, 50th Anniversary Proceedings, June 2002, Cambridge, Massachusetts (http://www.mitsloan.mit.edu/50th/corgovchina.pdf), citing CSRC 2000).
11. Chi Kuen Simon Wu, 'Single securities market in China' (2006) 14(1) *Asia Pacific Law Review* 19, at 21, citing World Federation of Exchanges, 'Equity 1.1: Domestic Market Capitalization' (6 May 2005) http://www.fibv.com/publications/EQUITY104.pdf accessed 18 March 2006.
12. Figures taken from the Hong Kong Trade Development Council's 'Market profile on Chinese mainland' (updated to 6 October 2006) available via the Trade Development Council's website at http://www.tdc.com.hk/.
13. Under CEPA, the mainland began to apply zero tariff to 374 import items. Phase II of CEPA (announced on 27 August 2004), provided zero tariff level entry into the mainland for a further 713 Hong Kong origin products, while under CEPA III (announced on 18 October 2005) the mainland agreed to give all products of Hong Kong origin tariff-free treatment: from the Hong Kong Trade Development Council's 'Market profile on Chinese mainland' (updated to 6 October 2006) available via the Trade Development Council's website at http://www.tdc.com.hk/.
14. For details, see the Hong Kong Trade Development Council's 'Market profile on Chinese mainland' (updated to 6 October 2006) available via the Trade Development Council's website at http://www.tdc.com.hk/.
15. Ibid.
16. I.A. Tokley & Tina Ravn, *Company and Securities Law in China* (Sweet & Maxwell Asia, 1998) paras 5.19–5.20.

17. Adopted 4 July 1994 by the Twenty-second Session of the Standing Committee of the State Council, Promulgated 4 August 1994 by the State Council, translated in CCH Asia *China Laws for Foreign Business – Business Regulation* para. 13-552.
18. *Zhengweifa* (1994) Document No. 21. Promulgated 27 August 1994 by the Securities Committee of the State Council and the State Commission for Restructuring the Economic System. Translated in CCH Asia *China Laws for Foreign Business – Business Regulation* para. 13-410.
19. For example, the ailing Hong Kong-listed TV manufacturer Conic Investment was 'bleeding red ink' when it became the takeover target for China Aerospace Corp. in 1992: Charles de Trenck, 'The growth of China's key conglomerates' in Charles de Trenck et al., *Red Chips and the Globalisation of China's Enterprises* (revised second edn, Asia 2000 Ltd, 1998) 43–80, 59.
20. Dongwei Su, *Chinese Stock Markets: A Research Handbook* (World Scientific Publishing Ltd, 2003) 345.
21. 'Fortune found at the back door', *South China Morning Post* (Hong Kong) 14 September 1993.
22. Charles de Trenck, 'Guangdong Enterprises and Guandong Investment' in Charles de Trenck et al, *Red Chips and the Globalisation of China's Enterprises* (Revised 2nd ed, Asia 2000 Ltd, 1998) 153–181, 153.
23. Charles de Trenck, 'The growth of China's key conglomerates' in Charles de Trenck et al., *Red Chips and the Globalisation of China's Enterprises* (revised 2nd edn, Asia 2000 Ltd, 1998) 43–80, 70–73. The Hong Kong stock code for Guangdong Investment Ltd is 270. Guangzhou Investment Co Ltd has also been listed by the Guanzhou municipal government as stock code 123.
24. Ibid. 70–73. GITIC as been de-listed since the bankruptcy of its mainland parent in 1998.
25. Ibid. 60–61. Hong Kong-listed red chips forming part of the China Everbright group include China Everbright International Ltd (stock code 257) and China Everbright (stock code 165).
26. Ibid. 67–68. China Resources Enterprise Ltd stock code in Hong Kong is 291.
27. Ibid. 67–68. China Travel International Investment Hong Kong Ltd's stock code in Hong Kong is 308.
28. Gareth Hewett, 'Patience needed for huge gains', *South China Morning Post* (Hong Kong) 19 January 1995.
29. Ibid.
30. Beijing-based China Aerospace Corp oversees functions in aerospace and defence on behalf of the central government. By 1998 it controlled more than 300 research centres and three universities. China Aerospace arrived in Hong Kong in 1992 via a takeover of the Hong Kong-listed ailing TV manufacturer Conic Investment. The listed vehicle was re-named China Aerospace International Holdings Ltd: Charles de Trenck, 'The growth of China's key conglomerates', in Charles de Trenck et al., *Red Chips and the Globalisation of China's Enterprises* (revised 2nd edn, Asia 2000 Ltd, 1998) 43–80, 59.
31. In 1993, ONFEM Holdings Ltd became the Hong Kong-listed flagship of China National Non-Ferrous Metals (CNNC), which in turn controlled some 80 per cent of China's market for non-ferrous metals throughout the 1990s. Its other Hong Kong-listed investment vehicles include Silver Grant International Industries Ltd, also acquired in 1993, and Oriental Metals, and Simsen Metals, both listed in 1994: Charles de Trenck, 'The growth of China's key conglomerates', in Charles de Trenck et al., *Red Chips and the Globalisation of China's Enterprises* (revised 2nd edn, Asia 2000 Ltd, 1998) 43–80, 65. See also 'Fortune found at the back door', *South China Morning Post* (Hong Kong) 14 September 1993.
32. China National Cereals, Oils and Foodstuffs Import & Export Corp (China Ceroil Food), formed in the early 1950s under MOFTEC, by the late 1990s was China's principal importer of grain, edible oils and other food products. Its Hong Kong-listed vehicle, China Food Holdings, was established and listed in 1992. In the early 1990s, China Ceroil Food also invested in real estate in Hong Kong and Beijing through its

listed flagship Top Glory International: Charles de Trenck, 'The growth of China's key conglomerates', in Charles de Trenck et al., *Red Chips and the Globalisation of China's enterprises* (revised 2nd edn, Asia 2000 Ltd, 1998) 43–80, 60. Both China Food Holdings and Top Glory International have since been de-listed.

33. China Ocean Shipping Co (COSCO) reports to the Ministry of Communications. In August 1994 the group reorganized and incorporated and listed its flagship Hong Kong subsidiary COSCO (HK) Group Ltd.
34. 'Fortune found at the back door', *South China Morning Post* (Hong Kong) 14 September 1993. Examples include Shougang Corporation, supported by Hong Kong tycoon Li Ka-shing: Gareth Hewett, 'Patience needed for huge gains', *South China Morning Post* (Hong Kong) 19 January 1995.
35. Charles de Trenck, 'The growth of China's key conglomerates', in Charles de Trenck et al., *Red Chips and the Globalisation of China's enterprises* (revised 2nd edn, Asia 2000 Ltd, 1998) 43–80, especially at 58–79. Su Dongwei also notes the way in which red-chip investment in real estate has played a major part in boosting real estate prices in both Hong Kong and the mainland: Su Dongwei, *Chinese Stock Markets: A Research Handbook* (World Scientific Publishing Ltd, 2003) 346.
36. Shanghai Industrial Holdings Ltd, controlled by the Shanghai Municipal Government's investment arm Shanghai Industrial Investment (Holdings) was listed in 1996. Beijing Enterprises Holdings Ltd, controlled by the Beijing government's unlisted company Beijing Holdings Ltd (formerly Scriven Trading Ltd) was listed in May 1997: Charles de Trenck, 'The growth of China's key conglomerates', in Charles de Trenck et al., *Red Chips and the Globalisation of China's Enterprises* (revised 2nd edn, Asia 2000 Ltd, 1998) 43–80, 75 and 58–59.
37. Deng Xiaoping's death was announced in February 1997. The subsequent rise to power of Zhu Rongji and Jiang Zemin, and its implications for SOE reform, is described in Charles de Trenck, 'Chinese capitalism and Chinese companies', in Charles de Trenck et al., *Red Chips and the Globalisation of China's Enterprises* (revised 2nd edn, Asia 2000 Ltd, 1998) 19–42, 38–39.
38. Gareth Hewett, 'Patience needed for huge gains', *South China Morning Post* (Hong Kong) 19 January 1995.
39. Referred to in Article 4 of the 1997 *Red Chip Notice*, which 'reiterates the spirit provided in the "Notice of the State Council regarding suspension in purchasing foreign enterprises and further reinforcement of administation of foreign investments"' (Guo Fa, 1993, No. 69) in prohibiting domestic organizations and enterprises to conduct purchasing shell companies for listing by way of purchasing controlling share rights of foreign listed companies': I.A. Tokley & Tina Ravn, *Company and Securities Law in China* (Sweet & Maxwell Asia, 1998) 257.
40. Su Dongwei, *Chinese Stock Markets: A Research Handbook* (World Scientific Publishing Ltd, 2003) 55, 345–347.
41. Translated under the title 'Notice regarding the further reinforcement of administration on the issue of foreign shares and listing overseas' in I.A. Tokley & Tina Ravn, *Company and Securities Law in China* (Sweet & Maxwell Asia, 1998) 256–257.
42. Su Dongwei, above, n. 95.
43. *Issues Relevant to the Overseas Issue and Listing of Shares by Overseas Companies with Interests in Mainland China Circular*, Promulgated by the CSRC on 9 June 2000, translated in (July–August 2000) 14(6) *China Law & Practice* 26–27.
44. Kent Chen, 'Further overseas listings planned for US or Europe', *South China Morning Post* (Hong Kong) 29 October 1993.
45. For discussion see Charles de Trenck, 'The growth of China's key conglomerates', in Charles de Trenck et al., *Red Chips and the Globalisation of China's Enterprises* (revised 2nd edn, Asia 2000 Ltd, 1998) 43–57, 55–57.
46. Kent Chan, 'Poor bond sales will not affect float plan', *South China Morning Post* (Hong Kong) 18 June 1993.
47. Staff Reporters, 'State Council orders bigger Tsingtao float', *South China Morning Post* (Hong Kong) 27 June 1993.

48. This was just in time to avoid the need for preparing new sets of accounts under the 6-month current accounting rule in Hong Kong under which accounts contained in listing documents expire for the purposes of making an offering on 31 June and 31 December each year.
49. Ivan Tong, 'Local market viewed as test for China listings', *South China Morning Post* (Hong Kong) 27 July 1993. See also Ivan Tong and Carrie Lee, 'Petrochemical may hold back giant flotation', *South China Morning Post* (Hong Kong) 24 June 1993.
50. The Shanghai Petrochemical issue of 1.68 billion H-shares (half of which were set aside for Hong Kong), was badly received in the territory, with a final subscription rate of a mere 1.77 times, in contrast to the Tsingtao Brewery IPO which was more than 100 times oversubscribed. One problem was that the Hong Kong offering was closed first, before the international offering. Hong Kong subscribers thus had to bear the risk of a failed international offering, paying an up-front amount of $1.74 per share, and having to wait about two weeks to learn the final price set for the US market (HK$1.58 per share): Kerry Wong, 'Call to improve underwriting practices of HK', *South China Morning Post* (Hong Kong) 8 August 1993. See also Ray Heath, 'SFC rejects any stabilization scheme for Shanghai Petro', *South China Morning Post* (Hong Kong) 22 July 1993.
51. See eg. Kerry Wong, 'Call to improve underwriting practices of HK', *South China Morning Post* (Hong Kong) 8 August 1993.
52. Ray Heath, 'SFC rejects any stabilisation scheme for Shanghai Petro', *South China Morning Post* (Hong Kong) 22 July 1993.
53. Gareth Hewett, 'Speaking out will help bring more Tsingtao's', *South China Morning Post* (Hong Kong) 16 July 1993.
54. Ibid.
55. 'Book building' is a process used mostly in America under which the lead investment bank in an IPO or share placement talks to the clients, issues a prospectus then goes on a road-show with the transaction. Indications of price are taken from institutions, or institutions may be asked to make a non-binding bid for stock within a given price range. On building the book and completion of the marketing, new talks begin with the clients, the institutional investors and other brokers as to what price can be agreed upon as an offer price. At this stage firm undertakings are taken and the final price is set just ahead of the transaction going forward. In some cases, the final price may be taken at below expectations to ensure a good after market, and to make investors feel they received some benefit: 'A closer look at US book building', *South China Morning Post* (Hong Kong) 22 July 1993.
56. Subscribers were advised that the final share price, to be determined only after a process of book building had taken place in the United States and globally, would range between HK$1.55 to $1.74 a share. Subscribers paid an initial $1.74 per share, and successful applicants would be entitled to a refund of the difference between the amount paid and the final issue price reached at the end of the US book-building period: 'A closer look at US book building', *South China Morning Post* (Hong Kong) 22 July 1993. See also Gareth Hewett, 'Merrill chief warns mainland listings could be lost', *South China Morning Post* (Hong Kong) 28 July 1993.
57. See Shanghai Petrochemical Company Limited, *Prospectus for Initial Public Offering of H-shares*, 5 July 1993, 14–15.
58. 'Stabilisation should be written into law', *South China Morning Post* (Hong Kong) 2 August 1993. This article notes that stabilization as a form of benign market rigging to ensure orderly distribution of shares immediately after their issue is a common practice in internationally syndicated offerings, where distribution of the securities continues after the offer has closed. It may take place before or after the issue, and consists of buying in the market at or below the initial issue price on the grey or official markets. In the US, stabilization is only permitted to prevent or slow a fall in the share's open market price during share distribution. It usually occurs during offers of common stock. In the UK, one stabilizing manager may, under certain publicity and pricing conditions, stabilize during a (normally) 30-day period.

59. Ibid.
60. Ibid.
61. Ibid. See now sections 274–275 of the *Securities and Futures Ordinance* (Chapter 571) 2003 (Hong Kong) which define 'false trading' and 'price rigging', and sections 295–296 which make both false trading and price rigging offences in Hong Kong.
62. Ray Heath, 'SFC rejects any stabilisation scheme for Shanghai Petro', *South China Morning Post* (Hong Kong) 22 July 1993.
63. The rules provide that stabilizing bids for shares should only be made to reduce short-term price fluctuations and cannot be higher than the public offer price for shares. They are permitted for 30 days from the start of trading, after which disclosure of certain information on stabilizing transactions undertaken must be made. The new rules, which were modelled closely on the British equivalent, came into effect on the same day the new *Securities and Futures Ordinance* went into operation in 2003. See Enoch Yiu, 'SFC agrees to allow price-stabilising actions for 30 days on $100m offers', *South China Morning Post* (Hong Kong) 10 July 2002. See also Enoch Yiu, 'SFC proposes price support for IPOs', *South China Morning Post* (Hong Kong) 9 February 2002, and Simon Pritchard, 'A case for rules and disclosure', *South China Morning Post* (Hong Kong) 10 November 2000.
64. Kerry Wong, 'Brokers back new offerings', *South China Morning Post* (Hong Kong) 30 July 1993.
65. Simon Davies, 'Beiren pricing sets it apart from the crowd', *South China Morning Post* (Hong Kong) 30 July 1993.
66. See Beiren Printing Machinery Holdings Limited, *Prospectus for Share Issue of 100 000 H Shares*, 23 July 1993, p. iv for further details, noting that the issue price of RMB2.30 (HK$2.08) represented a 1993 price–earnings ratio of around 8.6 times on a weighted average basis, or 11.5 times on a fully diluted basis. See also Kerry Wong, 'Lower prices on offer for next mainland listings', *South China Morning Post* (Hong Kong) 18 July 1993, and Simon Davies, 'Beiren pricing sets it apart from the crowd', *South China Morning Post* (Hong Kong) 30 July 1993.
67. Kerry Wong, above, n. 119.
68. See Mark Evans, 'Utilities lead index surge to top off winning week', *South China Morning Post* (Hong Kong) 31 July 1993. See also Hu Cui-Ping, 'Steel giant plans $3.9 stock offer', *South China Morning Post* (Hong Kong) 20 October 1993. Note also that the Beiren subscription rate was basically in line with earlier merchant broker forecasts of 20–30 times.
69. Ray Heath, 'Warburg sells $1b shares in Yizheng', *South China Morning Post* (Hong Kong) 26 April 1995.
70. Ibid.
71. Ibid.
72. Yizheng Chemical Fibre Company Limited, *Annual Report 1995*, 1.
73. 340 million H-shares were offered, and applications for about 340.86 million were received.
74. Kerry Wong and Ivan Tong, 'China in plea to bail out Bohai', *South China Morning Post* (Hong Kong) 15 May 1994.
75. Ibid.
76. Ibid.
77. Renee Lai, 'Listing code clears up uncertainties', *South China Morning Post* (Hong Kong) 20 August 1994.
78. Renee Lai, 'Warburg exercises option to buy Harbin Power shares on market', *South China Morning Post* (Hong Kong) 21 December 1994; noting that it was in December 1994 that China's Harbin Power Equipment Co, a major competitor to Dongfang Electrical, became the first initial public offering in Hong Kong to make use of the green-shoe option. The company's underwriter, SG Warburg exercised the option when it purchased HPEC shares for the purpose of short-covering on the first day of trading of the H-share counter. In the Shanghai Petrochemical H-share issue, options were granted allowing the Underwriters to require the Company to issue an aggregate of up

to 252 million additional H-shares (or a corresponding number of ADSs in the case of the US and International Offerings) solely to cover over-allotments in the combined offering. The options were, in the event, never exercised.

79. The green-shoe option is granted by an issuer to lead underwriters who can oversell the issuer's shares for as much as 15 per cent of the total amount. Within 30 days of the listing of shares (and depending on market conditions), lead underwriters can purchase an issuer's shares from the market. At that time they can also request the issuer to issue more shares to investors who have applied for subscription to the oversold portion of shares: Yang TieCheng, Zhang Nan and Alan Xu, 'A rule pushed by the market: china's new measures for offering and underwriting securities' (December 2006–January 2007) 20(10) *China Law & Practice* 25–27, 26–27.
80. Nicholas Ionides, 'Nomura escapes censure', *South China Morning Post* (Hong Kong) 21 July 1995.
81. Of a total of 140 Chinese companies currently listed on the Hong Kong stock exchange, only 40 also have A-shares listed on a domestic exchange (List of H-Share Companies, available at http://www.hkex.com.hk/data/chinadimen/CD_HMB.htm, last updated 30 June 2007, accessed on 5 July 2007).
82. This was because both the number of potential shareholders and the amount of unused savings (capital) held by ordinary Chinese was so high.
83. Weijian Shan, 'The mystery of China's sinking stocks' (December 2005) 168(11) *Far Eastern Economic Review* 5, 6.
84. Ibid.
85. Michael G. DeSombre and Weiheng Chen, 'Unloading state-owned shares: another trial under new rules (June 2005)' 19(5) *China Law and Practice* 17.
86. Leung et al., 'Financial Reform and Corporate Governance in China', MIT Sloan School of Management, 50th Anniversary Proceedings, June 2002, Cambridge, Massachusetts (http://mitsloan.mit.edu/50th/corgovchina.pdf), citing Yang, Dal, 2001.
87. 'Stock price forced up by traders', *South China Morning Post* (Hong Kong) 13 April 1994, citing reports in the official mainland newspaper *China Daily* on 12 April 1994.
88. Geoffrey Crothall, 'Government bonds draw good support', *South China Morning Post* (Hong Kong) 4 April 1994.
89. Ibid.
90. Wong Joon San, 'Shipyard set to list in Shanghai', *South China Morning Post* (Hong Kong) 25 October 1993.
91. 'Guangzhou Shipyard in demand', *South China Morning Post* (Hong Kong) 1 October 1993.
92. GSI A-shares closed trade on 28 October 1993 at 6.69 yuan, a premium of 1.46 yuan on the issue price of 5.23 yuan. For comment, see Christine Chan, 'Paper profit of 28pc in shipyard float', *South China Morning Post* (Hong Kong) 29 October 1993.
93. According to the first PRC *Company Law* (which came into effect on 1 July 1994) the directors, supervisors and managers of the company who used their entitlements to subscribe for A-shares were not permitted to transfer their shares in Guangzhou Shipyard while they remained in any senior capacity with the company: Guangzhou Shipyard International Company Limited *Annual Report 1995*, 109.
94. Foo Choy Peng, 'China revamps listings', *South China Morning Post* (Hong Kong) 25 July 1995.
95. An additional 43.51 million shares were reserved for employee subscribers, making an issue total of about 112.495 million A-shares: Foo Choy Peng, 'Investors bring down network in rush for shares', *South China Morning Post* (Hong Kong) 17 June 1995. See also Foo Choy Peng, 'Tianjin Bohai Chemical Industry (Group) public issue is about 28 times over-subscribed', *South China Morning Post* (Hong Kong) 19 June 1995.
96. Foo Choy Peng, 'Dongfang gets record response', *South China Morning Post* (Hong Kong) 6 July 1995.
97. This rule remains in force: see 'listing requirements' at the Shanghai stock exchange website: (http://www.sse.com.cn: accessed December 2005).

98. 'Share hand-out prevents listing', *South China Morning Post* (Hong Kong) 30 August 1995.
99. Foo Choy Peng, 'Dongfang's A-share in star display', *South China Morning Post* (Hong Kong) 11 October 1995; noting that the A-shares opened at 12.98 yuan (about HK$12) against the issue price of 4.10 yuan, exceeding even the most optimistic expectations of 10 yuan, and closed the day at 16.91 yuan with more than 70 per cent of the 60 million Dongfang A-shares changing hands. Speculative activity by small shareholders ('stir frying') appears to have been an important reason for the stock's roaring debut.
100. Certainly compliance with the relevant listing rule appears to have been achieved by 1999, by which time there were only 44 187 holders of domestic listed A-shares, making an average shareholding of around 1358 shares for every shareholder: Dongfang Electrical Machinery Company Limited, *1999 Annual Report* 10.
101. *Circular on Further Improving Methods of Issuing Shares* issued by the China Securities Regulatory Commission on 28 July 1999. Discussed in E. Anthony Zaloom and Hongchuan Liu, 'New rules for A-share issues' (September 1999) 13(8) *China Law & Practice* 42.
102. Ibid.
103. Prior to 1999, the CSRC had generally prohibited private placements that were in conjunction with a public offering. But this changed with the 1999 Circular which specifically permitted qualifying companies to conduct A-share issues through a combination of public offerings to ordinary investors and private placement to Chinese legal persons, something which is now specifically permitted by the 2006 Amended *Securities Law*.
104. 'China decides to resume issuance of IPOs', *People's Daily Online* 14 January 2005 (accessed at http://english.people.com.cn/ on 10 January 2006).
105. Promulgated by the CSRC on 17 September 2006, translated (December 2006–January 2007) in 20(10) *China Law & Practice* 48–61, and discussed in Yang TieCheng, Zhang Nan & Alan Xu, 'A rule pushed by the market: China's new measures for offering and underwriting securities' (December 2006–January 2007) 20(10) *China Law & Practice* 25–27. Article 68 of the new Measures repeals a number of earlier measures and circulars, including the *Circular Concerning Several Issues on Trial Implementation of IPO Pricing Inquiry System*, released by the CSRC on 30 August 2004. The August 2004 Circular was the first to propose requiring all firms planning IPOs to first conduct a full pricing inquiry, involving consultations with institutional investors, and with the results of that inquiry to then form the basis for deciding the final IPO price: CSRC, *Circular Concerning Several Issues on Trial Implementation of IPO Pricing Inquiry System (Exposure Draft)*, 30 August 2004; (available at the CSRC website http://www.csrc.gov.cn/).
106. Article 5, *Measures for the Administration of the Offering and Underwriting of Securities* [3700/ 06.09.17]. Promulgated by the China Securities Regulatory Commission on 17 September 2006 and effective as of 19 September 2006. Translated (December 2006–January 2007) in 20(10) *China Law & Practice* 48–61, 48–49.
107. Ibid., Article 30.
108. Yang TieChang, Zhang Nan and Alan Xu, 'A rule pushed by the market: China's new measures for offering and underwriting securities' (December 2006–January 2007) 20(10) *China Law & Practice* 25–27, 25.
109. Article 31, *Measures for the Administration of the Offering and Underwriting of Securities* [3700/ 06.09.17]. Promulgated by the China Securities Regulatory Commission on 17 September 2006 and effective as of 19 September 2006. Translated (December 2006–January 2007) in 20(10) *China Law & Practice* 48–61.
110. Yang TieChang, Zhang Nan and Alan Xu, 'A rule pushed by the market: China's new measures for offering and underwriting securities' (December 2006–January 2007) in 20(10) *China Law & Practice* 25–27, 26; noting that 'Under the previous regulation, online subscriptions were conducted after the completion of offline pricing and placements. This two-stage process was frequently used by institutional investors who used

the same fund to subscribe to stocks online and offline. . . . According to a CSRC statement regarding the two-stage process, the previous IPO rate allotted to public investors was below 1%.'

111. Article 24, *Measures for the Administration of the Offering and Underwriting of Securities* [3700/ 06.09.17]. Promulgated by the China Securities Regulatory Commission on 17 September 2006 and effective as of 19 September 2006. Translated (December 2006–January 2007) in 20(10) *China Law & Practice* 48–61.
112. Article 33, *Amended PRC Securities Law* (2006) [3700/05.10.27]. Promulgated on 27 October 2005 and effective as of 1 January 2006. Translated (February 2006) in 20(2) *China Law and Practice* 31–84. See also articles 38–50, *Measures for the Administration of the Offering and Underwriting of Securities* [3700/ 06.09.17]. Promulgated by the China Securities Regulatory Commission on 17 September 2006 and effective as of 19 September 2006. Translated (December 2006–January 2007) in 20(10) *China Law & Practice* 48–61.
113. These terms are defined in article 28 of the *Amended PRC Securities Law* (2006). [3700/05.10.27]. Promulgated on 27 October 2005 and effective as of 1 January 2006. Translated (February 2006) in 20(2) *China Law and Practice* 31–88. See also article 39 of the *Measures for the Administration of the Offering and Underwriting of Securities* (3700/ 06.09.17) promulgated by the CSRC on 17 September 2006 and effective on 19 September 2006. Translated (December 2006–January 2007) in 20(10) *China Law & Practice* 48–61.
114. Article 34 of the Amended PRC *Securities Law* provides that, 'If shares are issued at a premium, the issuing price shall be determined through consultations between the issuer and the securities company handling the underwriting': *Amended PRC Securities Law* [3700/05.10.27]. Promulgated on 27 October 2005 and effective as of 1 January 2006. Translated (February 2006) in 20(2) *China Law and Practice* 31–88. See also Article 22 of the *Measures for the Administration of the Offering and Underwriting of Securities* (3700/ 06.09.17) promulgated by the CSRC on 17 September 2006 and effective on 19 September 2006. Translated (December 2006–January 2007) 20(10) *China Law & Practice* 48–61.
115. See articles 29, 190–191 and 193 of the *Measures for the Administration of the Offering and Underwriting of Securities* (3700/ 06.09.17) promulgated by the CSRC on 17 September 2006 and effective on 19 September 2006. Translated (December 2006–January 2007) in 20(10) *China Law & Practice* 48–61. See also Chi Kuen Simon Wu, 'Single securities market in China' (2006) 14:1 *Asia Pacific Law Review* 19, at 37.
116. The IPO Measures provide clear guidelines to control the use of proceeds from new share sales, in line with the principle set out in article 15 of the Amended *Securities Law* (2006) that such proceeds must be used only in accordance with the approved purpose of the fund as described in the share prospectus.
117. Jinrong Liu and Chengwei Liu, 'China re-opens its doors to the IPO market' (July/August 2006) 20(6) *China Law & Practice* 22–24, 23; also noting that, following the amendment of the 1994 *Company Law* and the 1998 *Securities Law*, the IPO Measures abolish the requirement for a one-year tutorial by a sponsor and the ban on private placements within 12 months prior to the IPO.
118. *Measures for the Administration of Securities Offerings by Listed Companies* [3700/06.05.06] promulgated by the CSRC on 6 May 2006 and effective as of 8 May 2006. Translated (July–August 2006) in 20(6) *China Law & Practice* 47–63.
119. Jean-Marc Deschandol and Charles Desmeules, 'New rules on equity offerings: lifting the ban on China's share sales' (July/August 2006) 20:6 *China Law & Practice* 17; citing *Listed Companies Public Offerings Information Disclosure Contents and Formats Guidelines No. 10 and 11*; *Guidelines for the Contents and Formats for Information Disclosures by Companies That Offer Securities to the Public (No. 10)*; *Application Documents for Public Offers of Securities by Listed Companies*, issued by the CSRC on 8 May 2006 and *Guidelines for the Contents and Formats for Information Disclosures by Companies That Offer Securities to the Public (No. 11)*; *Prospectuses for Public Offers of Securities by Listed Companies*, issued by the CSRC on 8 May 2006.

120. See Part Three, articles 36–39, *Measures for the Administration of Securities Offerings by Listed Companies* [3700/06.05.06] promulgated by the CSRC on 6 May 2006 and effective as of 8 May 2006. Translated (July–August 2006) in 20(6) *China Law & Practice* 47–63; and see article 10 of the *Amended Securities Law* (2006) [3700/05.10.27]. Promulgated on 27 October 2005 and effective as of 1 January 2006. Translated (February 2006) in 20(2) *China Law and Practice* 31–88.
121. Jean-Marc Deschandol and Charles Desmeules, 'New rules on equity offerings: lifting the ban on China's share sales' (July/August 2006) 20(6) *China Law & Practice* 17, 18. The Strategic Measures were Jointly issued by the Ministry of Commerce, the CSRC, the State Administration of Taxation, the State Administration of Industry and Commerce and the State Administration of Foreign Exchange on 31 December 2005 and effective on 30 January 2006.

3. Securities, regulatory authorities and H-share enterprises

I INTRODUCTION

H-share firms are subject to regulatory control from both sides of the mainland–Hong Kong border. The aim of this chapter is first to describe the broader role and powers of the regulatory institutions which oversee the securities markets in mainland China and in Hong Kong, and second to outline the framework within which H-share listing applications are assessed and approved by the different regulatory authorities. This will then provide the institutional context for discussing the corporate governance reforms outlined in Chapter 4, and the case studies presented in Chapter 5.

II THE CHINESE SHARE MARKET: AN OVERVIEW

The Chinese legal system contains no express classification of shares into different types. Since its very earliest days, however, the China equity market has been notable for its rapid diversification into a bewildering variety of shares.

A A-Shares

A shares are domestically listed shares of Chinese companies which, until very recently, have been available to Chinese investors only. A-shares can be further divided into three different classes: state-owned shares, legal person shares and 'social' (publicly owned) shares. According to Chao Xi, the legal strategy of dividing company shares into three classes based on the attributes of the shareholders was adopted in order to 'secure the dominant position of state-ownership in larger companies transformed from SOEs'.[1] State-owned shares are typically held by the central and local governments (represented by local financial bureaus, state asset management companies or investment companies) and by the parent of the joint-stock company (typically an SOE or a wholly state-owned company). The establishment of the State Assets Supervision and Administration Commission, or SASAC, in March 2003 served to consolidate a large number of previously diversified avenues for state ownership of shares under a single umbrella. It also served as a mechanism for bringing a number of previously locally-controlled SOEs under central government control.[2]

Legal person A-shares are shares held by such domestic institutions as industrial enterprises, non-bank financial institutions and technology and research institutes. State-owned shares and legal person shares are not tradable on the stock exchange. Social shares, which are generally tradable on the stock exchanges, are shares held mostly by individuals (including enterprises employees) and by private institutions in some cases. Offical statistics show that each of the three classes account for about one-third of all outstanding shares of Chinese listed companies.[3] These figures reveal the State's direct shareholding in listed companies, but do not take into account the State's indirect shareholding through the mechanism of the 'state-owned legal-person share'. This sub-category of legal person shares was introduced by the Tentative Measures Concerning Administration of State-Owned Equities of Joint Stock Companies. Legal person shares held by SOEs and state-owned institutions fall into this sub-category. When the State's indirect shareholding through such entities is taken into account, ultimate effective control of up to 84 per cent Chinese listed companies may, in fact, lie in the hands of the State.[4]

As at April 2003, a total of 1219 Chinese firms had issued tradable A-shares listed on one of the two domestic exchanges in Shanghai and Shenzhen. A total of 580.8 billion A-shares had been issued by December 2003 and raised a total of RMB 761.7 billion yuan. The market capitalization of A-share companies amounted to RMB 4152.1 billion, of which the market capitalization of tradable shares was RMB 1230.6 billion.[5] In other words, most of the securities market capital in China has been locked up in the form of non-tradable shares. Despite reforms introduced since 1999 aimed at gradually bringing an end to this split share structure, by the end of 2004 there were still 454.3 billion or 64 per cent of total listed shares in China that were not freely tradable. Most of these non-tradable shares (74 per cent) were state-owned shares.[6] Reform efforts have been aimed both at converting non-tradable shares into tradable shares, and at opening up China's domestic A-share market to approved overseas institutional investors.

B B-Shares

B-shares, also known as 'domestically listed foreign investment shares' or 'special renminbi-denominated shares', are ordinary shares of Chinese shareholding companies that are listed and traded on the domestic securities exchanges. B-shares are denominated in RMB, but are subscribed for and traded in either US currency or Hong Kong dollars. B-shares have exactly the same ownership and dividend rights as do A-shares, but they can only be subscribed for and traded by foreign legal and natural persons and other entities, legal and natural persons from Hong Kong, Macau and Taiwan, and Chinese citizens who are resident abroad.

The regulatory framework for domestically-listed B-shares is primarily found in the *Provisions on Listing of Foreign Investment Shares Inside China by a Shareholding Company* issued by the State Council on 25 December 1995 and the *Provisions on Listing of Foreign Investment Shares Inside China by a Shareholding Company: Implementing Rules* introduced on 3 May 1996.[7] Both sets of rules supplement the *Company Law* of 1993–1994 which also sets out national-level regulatory standards for share-listing requirements, listing approval processes and procedures for the issuing and assignment of securities. Numerous other laws, regulations and rules also govern different aspects of China's securities and futures markets – markets which now encompass seven different types of financial instruments.[8]

The original goal of the B-share market was to attract foreign investors, but the market has always remained so illiquid, and so small, as well as being encumbered by all the perceived 'country risks' associated with investment in China, that it has never attracted any more than minimal interest. B-shares accounted for a mere 5 per cent of the tradable capitalization of the A-share market, until 20 February 2001, when Chinese investors with foreign exchange were finally permitted to invest in B-shares.[9] This move propelled the Shanghai B-share index from 78 to a high of 239 in May 2001. The index dropped back to a trading range of about 160 in late 2002, still more than double its previous level. By 1993, about 70 per cent of B-share investors were in fact overseas or domestic Chinese. Chinese domestic demand for B-shares is largely due to the fact that Chinese citizens hold about $75 billion in savings, while Chinese institutions have savings of about $48 billion – and both groups are now investing in B-shares.[10] The government has also acted to stimulate the sluggish B-share market by allowing private companies to issue B-shares. In August 2000, Hebei Dixian Knitwear became the first private company to list on the B-share market in Shenzhen.[11] China's small B-share market expanded from 85 companies with listed B-shares in 1996 (43 in Shenzhen and 42 in Shanghai) to a total of 111 such companies as of December 2003.[12] But because China's currency is still not convertible on the capital account, the A-and B-share markets have remained separate. Although A- and B-shares represent equal company ownership rights, this is certainly not reflected in the relative prices of the two classes of shares, which instead reflect the very different demand and supply forces operating in what can be seen as two different markets.

C H-Shares

H-shares are issued by Chinese-incorporated firms and denominated in RMB, but subscribed for and traded in the foreign currency of the overseas market of listing. As noted above, H-share issues were initially approved in 'batches', and separate lists of the successful applicants for listing approval were released periodically. By the end of the 1990s, however, individual companies had much more control over the timing of their own H-share IPOs, and applications were being considered and decided upon separately rather than in batches. Recent examples of significant H-share listings include the HK $2.23 billion IPO and subsequent Hong Kong listing by China Oilfield Services (a subsidiary of China Offshore Oil) in November 2002, and China Telecom's US$1.43 billion IPO and dual listings in New York and Hong Kong.

Prior to 1999, Chinese companies listed overseas were mainly the foreign-listed arm of a large State-Owned-Enterprise. Overseas-listed SOEs were mainly those that were considered of vital importance to the national economy. More recently, the H-share market has seen the entry of small and medium enterprises and more privately-owned companies have ventured abroad. Many of these are now listed as high-tech companies on Hong Kong's recently established (1999) Growth Enterprise Market (GEM). Examples include Chengdu Top Sci-Tech Co Limited and Jiangsu Nandasoft Company Limited.

By December 2003, a total of 93 Chinese companies had issued shares outside of China, raising 27.1 billion US dollars in total. Of these companies, 30 also had domestically listed A-shares, while 12 of them had dually listed in Hong Kong and New York.[13] Also by the end of 2003, three Chinese companies had chosen to list shares in Hong Kong and London, while one company had listed in three markets: Hong Kong, New York and London. One Chinese company was listed both in Hong Kong and in Singapore, while one company was listed singly overseas in Singapore (ie. without first being listed in Hong Kong). By mid-2007, the number of Hong Kong-listed Chinese firms had risen to 143: 100 firms with H-shares listed on the Main Board of the Exchange, and 43 with shares listed on the Hong Kong Growth Enterprises Market (GEM). Of these, 35 companies also had domestic A-shares listed on one of the mainland exchanges.[14]

III THE CSRC: ITS ROLE AND ITS POWERS

The CSRC officially took over regulatory control of the mainland securities market from the Securities Commission of the State Council in 1998, when the *Securities Law* empowered it as an independent governing body answerable only to the central State Council.[15] The 1998 *Securities Law* vested in the CSRC the dual power of overseeing and managing the securities market and of standardizing existing law and regulations within a unified legal framework. After 1998, regulatory control over the national securities markets and China's two established securities exchanges thus became more centralized, and local and municipal governments were removed altogether from the formal decision-making process in relation to new IPOs.[16] The change was one which represented a 'drastic departure from previous practices'.[17] Local and municipal governments were no longer to play the active role they had previously in formulating securities-related regulations and policies, or in the approval and selection of individual enterprises for listing.

Despite moves towards centralization, regulatory control over listed companies and other securities market players remains divided amongst several government institutions. Chinese listed companies report to multiple government regulatory authorities, with each governing body exerting different levels of influence over the company's management and business direction. Likewise, supervision and control of market intermediaries such as securities companies, fund management companies,[18] financial asset management companies and trust investment companies has now been divided between the CSRC, the China Banking Regulatory Authority[19] (CBRA) and the China Insurance Regulatory Commission. What will be critical for the future of financial system regulation and development in China is to establish an effective coordination mechanism among the three watchdogs. This will especially be the case as different businesses in the finance sector are gradually integrated.[20] In late 2003, the central government issued the *Memorandum of Understanding on Division of Responsibilities and Cooperation in Financial Supervision and Regulation among the CBRC, the CSRC and the CIRC*[21] to formally establish separate regulatory organs for the banking, securities and insurance industries, respectively. More recently, this separation of regulatory control according to industry was given formal legislative recognition in the 2006 *Amended Securities Law* which specifically vests the CSRC with responsibility for supervising the activities of a range of market intermediaries including securities companies, securities depository and clearing institutions, and securities service institutions.[22]

One thing which may continue to blur the distinction between banking and securities services is the fact that, under the new *Securities Law*, securities companies are now allowed to lend money and stock to clients.[23] Stock or cash lending by securities companies was prohibited under the 1998 *Securities Law*. Pursuant to Article 142 of the revised Securities Law, however, securities companies can now provide stock/cash lending services to their clients with CSRC approval. Commercial banks are still prohibited from lending for stock trading purposes. The new Securities Law does not require securities companies intending to provide financing to their clients to obtain approval from the CBRC, which generally regulates lending businesses. It will be important to coordinate the regulation of stock and cash lending services and, in particular, the way in which the CBRC and the CSRC ensure that bank funds do not flow into stock trading via various forms of direct and indirect relationships between banking and non-banking financial organizations.[24] Coordination between the three financial-service regulatory agencies may be assisted by the fact that they all fall under the unified supervision of the national audit office.[25]

Supervising the activities of over 100 securities brokerages[26] that have emerged to take advantage of the rapidly growing Chinese securities markets has now became a major challenge for the Chinese authorities. Instances of corruption and inefficiency in the brokerage industry have been extensively described in the mainland and Hong Kong press, and the details are not important here.[27] Part of the problem is political. For example, government officials have occasionally urged, or even directed, brokerages to buy up shares at times of market decline, particularly when significant political events, such as the 1997 and 2002 Communist Party Congresses, were being staged. Officials have wanted to ensure that resentment amongst investors, many of whom have seen their assets evaporate over the past few years, remains subdued on politically sensitive occasions.[28] The danger, of course, is that such an environment can give rise to opportunities for otherwise illegal activities such as 'churn trading' to take place with impunity, further distorting share prices.

By 2004 the CSRC was finally forced to take action. Starting with China Southern Securities in January 2004, the CSRC has orchestrated the takeover of at least eight major brokerage firms. Several have been placed in the hands of the asset management companies set up in 1999 to work out non-performing loans accumulated by the state banks. In addition, the CSRC created a 'blacklist' of 63 high-risk brokerages – nearly half the total – many of which have since been closed or reorganized.[29] Enforcement efforts have been hindered, however, by limited resources. In 1997, the World Bank noted the need for the government to strengthen the CSRC, which at the time had a single Beijing-based office of some 120 staff.[30] By 2003, the CSRC reportedly still only had about 40 of its staff dedicated to legal enforcement and supervision of over 1200 listed companies, and its financial resources remain equally inadequate.[31]

Another problem, limited CSRC powers of enforcement, has been partly overcome by recent reforms. The new 2006 *Securities Law* has expanded the scope and nature of the securities under the CSRC's regulation, and contains significant new powers for the CSRC. In particular, the CSRC is given more powers to conduct investigations, including the power to freeze the accounts of people or units under investigation without an order from a judicial organ,[32] and power to make on-the-spot inspections (*xianchang jiancha*).[33] This does a lot but does not go all the way in solving the lack of independent enforcement powers that has so far handicapped the CSRC in carrying out its functions. For example, the CSRC must still coordinate any effort to penalize rule breakers with the Ministry of Public Security,[34] and, in the case of Hong Kong-listed Chinese firms, with the HKSE, the SFC and other regulatory authorities in Hong Kong. Much of the CSRC's daily activity is, in fact, channelled into overcoming the limitations imposed by inadequate resources and coordinating with the complex array of different institutions which exist at various levels of government throughout China. For example, the CSRC typically shares regulatory authority over any individual listed firm with both the Ministry responsible for the industry in which the firm operates and local authorities where the firm is located. The CSRC alone thus lacked the capacity to investigate or understand all levels of the company's activities and finances, or the actions of its management. Moreover, the local authorities commonly have an interest in protecting the company, rather than in cooperating with the CSRC to expose possible malpractice.

The CSRC also has no power to suspend or de-list H-shares listed on the Hong Kong Exchange. However, nearly one-third of H-share firms also have a significant portion of their equity listed domestically, and the CSRC does have control over this part of the firms' issued capital. Even where action is taken to suspend or terminate the A-share listing status of a particular enterprise, however, trading in H-shares issued by the same firm may remain apparently unaffected. So, for example, when the A-shares of Jilin Chemical were suspended in late April 2003 after the company posted its third consecutive annual net loss in 2002, trading in Jilin's H-shares was seemingly unaffected. In fact, Jilin's H-shares rose 5.08 per cent on the very day its A-shares were suspended by mainland authorities, probably because of the profit reported by the firm for the first quarter of 2003.[35] This demonstrates yet again the separate nature of the two markets in which H-share companies operate.

Part Eleven of the Chinese *Securities Law* spells out a number of offences and the relevant penalties which must or may be imposed by the CSRC acting in conjunction with the exchanges and local authorities. The most commonly used sanction is the published criticism issued by the Exchange on which the relevant company is listed. The criticism can apply to the company itself, and/or to any company or public official found guilty of acts or omissions affecting the company's shares. Public criticism can also be used in conjunction with the imposition of an additional penalty, such as a fine or other administrative penalty. If necessary, the CSRC can place companies and/or persons under judicial investigation. Severe breaches of the law can result in a company being delisted altogether and/or, in the case of any professional involved in such a breach, revocation of a licence to operate in securities-related areas. In 2001, for example, the CSRC revoked the securities licences of at least five local accounting firms found to have been involved in the improper preparation of listed-company financial reports,[36] and more than 15 mainland listed companies were criticized or punished by the CSRC for fraudulent disclosure, distorting financial statements, misuse of listing proceeds, occupation of listing profits by its controlling shareholders or other violations of securities-related rules.[37] None of these cases involved H-share companies or the rights of H-share shareholders. Questions thus remain over the extent to which the CSRC would be willing or able to exercise jurisdiction over mainland citizens responsible for breaches of Hong Kong regulatory requirements.

Criminal actions have also recently become a feature of the CSRC's arsenal for combating securities market malfeasance. China's first criminal case in the securities sector occurred when the CSRC brought criminal charges against seven individuals, alleging they had manipulated the stock of the Shenzhen-listed China Venture Capital Group Ltd from December 1998 to January 2001. The case involved more than 100 businesses and individuals and over 120 securities trading firm offices in more than 20 provinces. Behind the 120 trading firm offices were 66 securities brokerage and investment trust companies.[38]

The CSRC's more rigorous approach to enforcement of the rules over recent years appears to have been at least partly stimulated by the appointment of independent outside experts mostly from Hong Kong – people like chief adviser to the CSRC Anthony Neoh (practising lawyer and former chair of the Hong Kong Securities and Futures Commission) in 1998, and CSRC vice-chair Laura Cha (US-trained lawyer and former HKSFC vice chair and president of operations).[39] Whether or not this impetus continues remains, however, to be seen.

A Standards and Procedures for Approving IPOs in Mainland China

Public listing as a means of obtaining easy access to funds has always been a limited and much sought-after commodity in China. Moreover, particularly in the early years, the listing of public companies was largely politically driven. A system of quotas was established by the central regulators and administered in the provinces. Each province was given a number of SOEs that could be listed, and it was up to local leadership to determine which firms would list. Certain performance requirements had to be met, but the process was full of political pitfalls, and bore little resemblance to market forces.[40]

In theory, consideration of SOEs for listing should be based primarily on their financial health and, preferably, the best SOEs should be listed first. The reality during the early years was, however, that provincial governments used scarce quotas for companies which needed money the most. Because the listing law specified that a company had to show three years of continued profits to qualify for listing – a provision borrowed from Hong Kong – provincial governments often bundled operations which had profits with enterprises that needed money when establishing joint stock companies able to apply for listing. Even entities with no apparent synergies were bundled together and in some cases the management personnel of organizations that got bundled together did not know each other until just before going public.[41] Understandably, it became much more difficult to obtain listing approval after provincial government involvement in listing applications was abolished with the coming into effect of China's first *Securities Law* in 1998. The record number of listing application rejections in the two years following the coming into effect of the *Securities Law* (approximately 40 per cent of applications rejected in the period to end 2000) demonstrates the presence of a much more demanding hurdle for listing applicants to qualify.[42]

Even today, the selection of companies to be publicly listed is still to some extent made by the state, rather than the market. This is particularly the case for companies applying to list on one of the two domestic exchanges, where the State Planning Commission and the CSRC are still concerned to maintain control over the total amount of capital that can be raised from the market, as well as over the proportion of listed enterprises from different industrial sectors and provincial regions. The quota system, although no longer officially in force, still operates in a looser de facto manner to indicate to various ministries and local governments whether or not business enterprises under their management would be looked upon favourably if market listing was sought.

Within the CSRC there are several departments, each responsible for different aspects of the regulatory process.[43] Guarding the gate of entry to the market are the Public Offering Supervision Department (PO Department) and the CSRC's Public Offering Review Committee (POR Committee) first established by Chapter 14 of the 1998 *Securities Law* and the *Interim Measures on the Public Offering Review Committee of the CSRC*.[44] Application documents are first submitted to the PO Department for initial review, and then forwarded to the POR Committee for its consideration. The POR Committee is empowered to review and evaluate listing applications against a legislated set of listing criteria. In practice, recommendations made by the POR Committee have, by and large, been adopted by the CSRC, making the Committee the de facto decision-making body for public offering applications.[45]

The POR Committee comprises 25 members, including five CSRC staff members and 20 external experts (some of whom are full-time members).[46] The POR Committee is responsible for making a recommendation regarding listing applications to the CSRC. Recommendation decisions are usually decided upon by majority vote of seven Committee members who sit on each individual listing-application hearing panel.

In regard to membership of the Committee when individual listing applications are heard, Article 23 of the *Securities Law* 2006[47] provides that persons involved in the approval of applications to issue shares may not have a material connection with, or accept gifts from, the applicant or hold shares of the applicant or have any private contact with the applicant. As yet, however, there are no procedures for applicants to be informed of the identities of the seven members in any listing hearing, and the level of secrecy still surrounding the approval process effectively denies applicants any way of challenging the membership of a particular listing committee panel. This has been the case even despite the wording of Article 23 which expressly provides that 'verification and approval procedures shall be made public, and shall be subject to supervision according to law'. The reality, however, has been that, until recently at least, committee members have been able to vote anonymously, rendering both listing applicants and the public effectively unable to challenge committee members on conflict of interest issues, even where a listing decision seems to be manifestly inconsistent with previous decision-making practices or with decisions regarding other similar applications.

Article 24 of the new *Securities Law* 2006[48] provides applicants and the public with some protection by requiring that the CSRC must reach a decision on listing applications within three months from receiving the listing application documents; and, further, that reasons must be given if an application is rejected. Despite this theoretical right to obtain reasons for refusal to approve an application, the lack of any regular avenue for placing CSRC listing decisions on the public record has, until recently, made it impossible for applicants to challenge a decision to reject. The situation still compares favourably, however, with the situation in Hong Kong, where the HKEx Listing Committee is not obliged to, and rarely does, provide any reasons for its decisions on listing-related matters.[49]

It was in mid-2003 that CSRC vice-chair Laura Cha Shih May-lung announced that the CSRC would begin to announce publicly the identities of the members involved in a listing application hearing, that Committee members would no longer be able to vote anonymously and the listing committee's decisions would be made public by the CSRC. These reforms have now been implemented, putting China ahead of several more mature markets elsewhere, including Hong Kong, where lack of transparency still serves to deny many applicants an effective avenue for challenging listing decisions on administrative law grounds.[50]

New Administrative Law reforms have also served to make the CSRC more accountable for its decision-making processes. Corporate plaintiffs have now become both able and willing to institute actions against the CSRC and other government regulatory authorities on administrative law grounds for wrongful decision making. In 2000, for example, the CSRC lost a lawsuit to Hainan Kaili Central Development & Construction. The company, which had been seeking an A-share listing since 1998, said the CSRC had breached its rules in rejecting the firm's application. Beijing No 1 Intermediate Court ordered the commission to reconsider Hainan Kaili's application within two months.[51]

More recently, the CSRC has issued new *Measures on the Public Offering Review Committee* (POR Measures) that became effective on 9 May 2006.[52] The POR Measures establish a three-stage approval process for new issue applications. The first step follows the filing of application documents by the Sponsor, and involves preliminary examination and verification by the CSRC Issuance Department. Stage two involves an ad hoc meeting by an issuance verification commission consisting of seven members (selected amongst a group of five CSRC officials and 20 external professionals or specialists). The ad hoc issuance verification commission is in charge of examining the application documents prepared by the issuer, its accountants, financial advisers, legal counsel and valuation institution. Following the examination, the commission makes a recommendation to the CSRC, which will then approve or disprove the application, mainly based upon the commission's report. Private share placements are subjected to a simplified version of these approval procedures under the POR Measures.

While the CSRC has the main regulatory role when it comes to the issuing of shares by a company, it is the two national stock exchanges (in *Shanghai* and *Shenzhen*, respectively) which have primary control over the daily trading of domestic shares, and which also receive and scrutinize listing applications.[53] While the new *Securities Law* lists certain minimum conditions that a company must meet before its shares can be listed (article 50), a stock exchange may specify listing conditions that are more stringent than those specified in the legislation, so long as those conditions are first approved by the CSRC. Likewise, the new *Securities Law* outlines the circumstances under which a stock exchange must suspend (article 55) or terminate (article 56) the listing and trading of a listed company's shares, but the stock exchange may also specify in its listing rules the circumstances under which suspension or delisting will occur.[54] This appears to represent a return to decentralization compared to the previous *Securities Law*, under which the CSRC rather than the exchanges controlled the suspension and delisting process. As early as 2001, however, the CSRC's *Suspending and Terminating the Listings of Loss-making Listed Companies Implementing Procedures* delegated legal authority to the two national stock exchanges in regard to decisions on suspending the listings of companies that turn into consecutive losses.[55]

So far as H-share listing and trading are concerned, however, the mainland Chinese exchanges have no role to play. Rather, once approval for the issue of new H-shares is received from the CSRC, the applicant enterprise must amend its articles of association in compliance with Hong Kong requirements, and the listing application is then submitted to the Hong Kong Stock Exchange. The main requirements which have to be met for CSRC approval prior to submitting application documents to Hong Kong are contained, inter alia, in the 1994 *Special Regulations of the State Council Concerning Floating and Listing of Shares Overseas by Companies Limited by Shares*[56] and in Special Assessment Guidelines, the most recent of which were issued by the State Council on 14 July 1999 and 21 September 1999, to regulate listing of PRC enterprises on Hong Kong's Main Board and the GEM, respectively. Approval by the CSRC will generally be granted provided that the requirements of the 1999 Notices are complied with.[57]

Until 2000, H-share firms were all controlled by *unlisted* state-controlled China-based parent organizations, and, in most cases, the H-share parent enterprise, with no remaining profit-making assets under its direct control, had little or no potential to seek listing status on its own. It was not until July 2000, that Beida Jade Bird Universal was separated from its Shanghai-listed A-share parent company Beijing Tianqiao Beida Jade Bird, and made its listing on the GEM Board of the HKEx. Tong Ren Tang Technologies followed suit, separating from Shanghai-listed Beijing Tongrentang Ltd and making its IPO in Hong Kong in 2004. Other Hong Kong-listed firms controlled by mainland-listed parent companies include Chengdu Top Tech, Shanghai Fudan Microelectronics and Lianhua Supermarket. Lianhua's was the first spin-off from an A-share listed company to be listed on the HKEx Main Board rather than the GEM Board.[58]

In August 2004 the CSRC released a new circular designed to enhance its control over the number of mainland-listed firms seeking a subsequent listing in Hong Kong. The *Certain Issues Regarding the Regulation of Offshore Listing of Subsidiaries of Domestic Listed Companies Circular*[59] (the Spin-off Circular) provides a legal framework within which already listed Chinese firms can now apply to list a newly-formed subsidiary overseas. From the perspective of the listed parent company, a spin-off means additional funding. When the parent to begin with holds more than one set of viable business assets, the subdivision through spin-off can help to rationalize the P/E ratios of separate listed assets. Problems arise, however, when a listed parent spins off its core or most important business assets for an offshore listing, leaving it without the necessary 'critical mass' of profit-making operations and assets to support its separate existence as a listed entity. The risk that such a spin-off could seriously erode the interests of its shareholders explains why, when listed companies announce a proposed spin-off, the share price usually declines.

Prior to the release of the Spin-Off Circular, the CSRC treated applications for Offshore Spin-off Listings filed by A-share listed companies on a case-by-case basis. The Spin-Off Circular now clarifies the criteria for domestically listed companies to carry out spin-off listings. The Circular seeks to ensure that a parent firm will not become so depleted in value after the spin-off listing occurs that it needs to rely on its entitlements from, and interests in, the offshore-listed subsidiary to maintain its mainland share value and independent viability. This is done by requiring the clear separation of assets, financial accounts and management between the listed parent company and its subsidiary, and requiring that a minimum level of value (in terms of assets and operations) must remain with, and be independently controlled by, the mainland-listed parent firm applying for a spin-off listing. Section 2 of the Circular sets out eight qualifications that a Listed Parent Company must meet before its controlled subsidiary can issue shares for listing offshore. These include the following requirements:

- The entitlement of the Listed Parent Company to the distribution of the net profit of the Controlled Subsidiary . . . shall not account for 50 per cent or more of the total net profit of the Listed Parent Company reflected in its consolidated financial statements.
- The entitlement of the Listed Parent Company to the net assets of the Controlled Subsidiary . . . shall not account for 30 per cent or more of the [total] net assets of the Listed Parent Company reflected in its consolidated financial statements.
- The Listed Parent Company must not compete with the Controlled Subsidiary in the same line of business, and each must have separate assets and financial accounts, with no management personnel in one entity allowed to serve concurrently in the other.
- Management of the Listed Parent Company and the Controlled Subsidiary should have no direct personal interest in pursuing the spin-off project (item (vi) of Section 2).

Once CSRC approval for the Hong Kong listing has been obtained, it remains for the H-share listing applicant to satisfy the Hong Kong authorities that Hong Kong listing requirements have been met.

IV THE SECURITIES AND FUTURES COMMISSION & THE HONG KONG STOCK EXCHANGE: ROLE, STRUCTURE AND POWERS

Volatility of the financial markets in the wake of the Asian financial crisis of 1997–1998 and a large number of corporate collapses in the Hong Kong market revealed inadequacies in the regulatory system. In Hong Kong prior to the merger and demutualization of the exchanges in 1999–2000, securities regulation was fragmented and overly-reliant on self-regulation by the private sector in the form of two member-owned, or mutualized, exchanges and three clearing houses.

Hong Kong's Financial Secretary announced comprehensive reform of the stock and futures exchanges in his 1999 Budget Speech. The members of both the Stock Exchange of Hong Kong Ltd and the Hong Kong Futures Exchange Ltd facilitated the proposed reform by voting overwhelmingly in favour of demutualizing and merging the exchanges and clearing houses in September 1999. Together with Hong Kong Securities Clearing Company Limited, the demutualized Stock Exchange of Hong Kong Ltd and Hong Kong Futures Exchange Ltd became wholly-owned subsidiaries under a new entity, Hong Kong Exchanges and Clearing Ltd (HKEx). With the demutualization, the holding of shares in HKEx was no longer a prerequisite for trading on either exchange, as trading rights were separated from ownership. HKEx subsequently became only the third exchange in the world to be publicly listed when its shares commenced trading, by introduction, on the Hong Kong stock exchange on 27 June 2000.[60]

The listing of HKEx was designed to ensure that it would have no controlling shareholder when it became a public listed company. To begin with, however, the government, without holding any shares in HKEx, had power to appoint eight of the 15 directors, thereby ensuring it had effective control of the HKEx board. The structure of the board of directors of HKEx was, however, modified at the annual general meeting of 2003 to ensure that the number of directors appointed by the government can now be 'no more than' the number of directors elected by its shareholders.

The introduction of a new 'ministerial' system of government which came into effect in Hong Kong on 1 July 2002 also served to alter the regulatory structure for Hong Kong's financial markets. In summary, the present Hong Kong regulatory structure for financial markets now comprises three separate tiers, the functions of which can be summed up as 'macro policy', 'watchdog' and 'operational'. Responsibility for regulation of the banking and securities industries, oversight of the governance of companies' provident funds and oversight of the insurance sector all fall within the purview of the Secretary for Financial Services and the Treasury. Sitting at the apex of the regulatory regime, he is entrusted with the responsibility of formulating and implementing government policy in relevant areas.[61]

At the next level is the Securities and Futures Commission (SFC).[62] Established as an independent statutory body under the recently enacted *Securities and Futures Ordinance* (2003),[63] the SFC has a broad range of powers and functions relating to maintaining and promoting the fairness, efficiency, competitiveness, transparency and orderliness of the securities industry in Hong Kong.[64] It exercises supervisory and regulatory authority over the activities of recognized exchange companies and other institutions and persons conducting securities trading activities.

The SFC has responsibility for detecting market malpractices with statutory implications. Its powers include the power to carry out on its own initiative, or in cooperation with the HKEx, investigations into 'market misconduct', and it can take action to penalize firms and individuals responsible for such misconduct. Under s. 183 of the 2003 SFO, the SFC is vested with broad powers of investigation into suspected market misconduct including, inter alia, the following:

a. require the production of documents and 'an explanation or further particulars' of the documents produced.
b. require a person to appear before the SFC for an interview and require answers to 'any question relating to the matters under investigation' that the investigator might ask during the interview. A person is not entitled to refuse to answer such questions simply because his answer might tend to implicate him in wrongdoing.
c. demand answers to written questions raised by the investigator (a new power).
d. demand a person verify answers given by way of a statutory declaration.

It is a criminal offence for a person to fail to cooperate with the SFC or supply misleading information during an investigation by the SFC.[65]

The SFO has been drafted in broad terms to ensure that virtually all *types* and *degrees* of market misconduct are caught under the new disciplinary regime, ranging from relatively minor infractions of industry rules (eg. failing to advise of a change of business address), through to the more serious forms of market misconduct such as insider trading, various forms of market manipulation ('price rigging', 'false trading' and 'stock market manipulation') or the dissemination of false information. This broad coverage is achieved by establishing two parallel penalty regimes, one criminal and one civil, each prohibiting 'market misconduct'.[66] In cases where sufficient evidence is available to satisfy the criminal standard of proof, breaches of the criminal law will continue to be handled by the courts rather than the SFC.[67] Where insufficient evidence exists to support criminal action, the matter is dealt with as a civil matter by the Market Misconduct Tribunal (a panel comprising a High Court judge and two lay members), which replaced the Insider Trading Tribunal in 2003.[68] The SFC itself deals with cases where the matter is relatively minor or outside the jurisdiction of the Market Misconduct Tribunal. Appeals from a decision by the SFC can be taken to the newly-constituted Securities and Futures Appeal Tribunal (also a panel comprising a High Court judge and two lay members). There is also a review process to monitor the procedural practices of the SFC conducted by the Chief Executive-appointed Process Review Panel. Finally, the SFO also gives a statutory right of civil action enabling any person who suffers financial loss as a result of market misconduct to recover damages. Holders of H-shares, for example, can theoretically initiate legal proceedings against any director or other company insider, to recover losses arising from insider trading or other market misconduct.

The SFO also has a broad *geographical* reach, and applies to conduct in Hong Kong that manipulates prices in markets outside Hong Kong, as well as to conduct outside Hong Kong that manipulates Hong Kong markets.[69] For example, s. 291 of the SFO is drafted broadly enough to give the SFC jurisdiction over mainland directors or other company 'insiders' involved, or allegedly involved, in insider trading, which is broadly defined.[70]

While theoretically the SFC's powers of investigation stretch across the border into mainland China, in practice the SFC requires the cooperation and assistance of mainland officialdom to carry them out effectively. Low Chee Keong suggests that effective cross-border cooperation might be promoted if the SFC were to start exercising its powers through a process of 'moral persuasion'. Low notes the example of the CSRC in mainland China which is known to call up directors of companies to 'express its views', particularly where it suspects breaches of fiduciary duties. The gradual introduction of such practices into SFC culture might assist cooperative enforcement efforts between the SFC and the CSRC as well as between the SFC and other regulatory authorities in mainland China.[71]

The SFC exercises no *direct* day-to-day supervisory or regulatory control over listed companies or their officers. Just as the requirements which must be met by listed companies and their officers are set out in the Listing Rules rather than the SFO, so also it is the HKEx and not the SFC which is responsible for monitoring and regulating compliance with those requirements.[72] It is the HKEx alone which is party to the HK Listing Rules, and which is accordingly empowered to enforce compliance by market participants with those Rules. The SFC is not privy to the contract contained in the Listing Rules, and cannot enforce the terms of the same. However, as a for-profit company, a major aim of HKEx is also to maximize profits for its shareholders. Its revenues are principally derived from initial and annual listing fees, and from the trading levy imposed on securities and futures transactions. The potential thus exists for the HKEx to be confronted by situations where its regulatory enforcement role and its desire to maximize income may conflict. To prevent and handle such conflicts of interest and to enhance regulatory efficiency, the HKEx has signed two memoranda of understanding with the SFC to define their respective roles and functions. Under these MoU it is the SFC which is responsible for any matters associated with the continued listing of HKEx on the Hong Kong Stock Exchange. This arrangement allows the SFC to assume a more active and broader role as the principal regulator, especially since it is perceived to be more impartial than the HKEx in relation to matters that may conflict with the business interests of the latter.[73]

The problem still remains, however, that, while the SFC has the right to accept or reject any amendment to the Listing Rules proposed by HKEx, it does not have the power to compel HKEx to act where the latter chooses not to. The potential thus exists for the HKEx to be confronted by conflict of interest situations over which the SFC may have little control. Part of the problem has been the 'old boys club' dynamics that operate within the HKEx board, which has traditionally been dominated by the nominees of large, institutional shareholders. One accusation is that it has often been less than rigorous in its enforcement style, particularly when it comes to protecting the interests of minority shareholders.[74]

Recent proposals for reform have recommended that the SFC should take over the Exchange's regulatory role completely, and that the HKEx should no longer be the body responsible for enforcing the Listing Rules. Such proposals, unsurprisingly, have been opposed by the HKEx which 'has made it clear it would like to maintain the dual filing system and share vetting with the SFC',[75] as well as retaining its current enforcement responsibilities. With regard to regulation of listing sponsors, however, the HKEx appears to have adopted a somewhat different attitude. The exchange has recognized that, since the SFC is the one which issues licences to sponsors (who may be securities firms, issuing houses or investment banks), 'it would be natural for the commission to handle the regulation of sponsors'.[76]

In regard to its role as supervisor and regulator of day-to-day activities on the HKEx, the aims of the Exchange are spelt out in the Listing Rules. The Exchange aims to ensure that:

1. the issue and marketing of securities is conducted in a fair and orderly manner and potential investors are given sufficient information for a properly informed assessment of an issuer;
2. investors and the public are kept fully informed and immediate disclosure is made of any information, to be evenly disseminated, which might reasonably be expected to have a material effect on market activity in, and the prices of, listed securities;
3. all holders of listed securities (of the same class) are treated equally and fairly; and
4. directors of a listed issuer act in the best interests of its shareholders as a whole, particularly where the public represents only a minority of the shareholders.

In the event of a breach of the Listing Rules, the HKEx has a range of options, including power to issue a private reprimand; power to make a public criticism of a listed company or any of its officers;[77] power to suspend trading in an issuer's securities; and the ultimate penalty of delisting a company's securities altogether under Chapter 6 of the Listing Rules. The HKEx may also cooperate with the SFC, which has stronger investigative, prosecutorial and enforcement powers, to correct and/or penalize abusive transactions or market misconduct.

A Screening of H-share Listing Applications by the Hong Kong Stock Exchange

At the operational front-line of the market in Hong Kong is the HKEx, which is responsible for administering the *Rules Governing the Listing of Securities on the Stock Exchange of Hong Kong* (the Listing Rules). The Listing Rules set out the contractual obligations that are imposed upon the stock exchange, issuers and their advisers for the seeking and maintenance of listings on the Hong Kong Stock Exchange Main Board. Chapter 8 of the Listing Rules sets out the basic conditions which have to be met as a prerequisite to the listing of equity securities. In particular, both the issuer and its business must be considered suitable, so that an issuer or group (other than an investment company) whose assets consist wholly of cash or short-dated securities is not normally considered suitable for listing. The issuer, or its group, must also normally have a trading record of not less than three financial years under substantially the same management. The expected total market capitalization at the time of listing of a new applicant must be at least HK$200 million, and total capitalization of securities held by the public must be at least HK$50 million. The listing applicant must also satisfy the profit test in rule 8.05(1)[78] or the market capitalization/revenue/cash flow test in rule 8.05(2)[79] or the market capitalization/revenue test in rule 8.05(3).[80] In addition, the Exchange must be satisfied that there will be sufficient public interest in the business of the issuer and its securities, and an open market in the securities for which listing is sought. This normally requires that at least 25 per cent of an issuer's listed securities are held by the public, though in the case of issuers with a high expected market value (over HK$4000 million) this percentage may be as low as 10 per cent. Where an issuer has more than one class of securities, the total securities held by the public on all regulated markets at the time of listing must be at least 25 per cent of the issuer's total share capital. However, the class of securities for which listing is sought must be not less than 15 per cent of the issuer's total share capital.

In addition to the normal listing requirements, issuers incorporated in the PRC (H-share issuers) must also comply with the requirements spelt out in Chapter 19A of the Listing Rules. Chapter 19A begins by noting that, although under PRC law domestic shares (A-shares) and foreign shares (H-shares) are all shares of a PRC issuer, the two kinds of shares in effect operate in separate markets, one of which is not based on a common law system, and each subject to different investor demands. It is for this reason that compliance with additional requirements, modifications and exceptions to the Hong Kong Listing Rules are necessary in order for a PRC issuer to list on the HKEx. In addition, the issuing agreement that must be entered into with the HKEx by all issuers of equities listed on the Exchange will, in the case of an issuer incorporated in the PRC, be based on the Listing Agreement text set out in Part 1 of Appendix 7 of the Listing Rules, together with such modifications or additions as the Exchange considers appropriate.[81]

A PRC issuer who is a new applicant must also retain the services of a sponsor (or other financial adviser/professional firm acceptable to the exchange) who is closely involved in the preparation of listing documents and must sign the listing application before lodging it. In sponsoring a PRC company for listing, the sponsor has a particular responsibility to satisfy himself that the PRC applicant is suitable to be listed and that its directors and supervisors appreciate the nature of their responsibilities and can be expected to honour their obligations under their directors' or supervisors' undertakings, the Listing Rules and the Listing Agreement and applicable laws and regulations in both mainland China and Hong Kong.[82] If securities of the PRC issuer are, or are to be, listed on any other stock exchange(s), the sponsor must make a written submission to the Exchange stating whether in the sponsors opinion the PRC issuer's directors appreciate both the differences and similarities between H shares and the shares listed on such other stock exchange(s) and between the rights and obligations of holders of such shares, and the basis for such an opinion. The sponsor must also explain how the PRC issuer's directors propose to coordinate and comply in a timely manner with their obligations under the requirements of the Hong Kong Exchange and such other stock exchange(s).

Whereas under Rule 3.02 the legal requirement for a sponsor normally ends once the applicant has been listed, Rule 19A.05 modifies this rule so as to require PRC issuers to retain the services of a sponsor for at least one year. In its role after listing, the sponsor must inform the PRC issuer on a timely basis of any amendment or supplement to the Exchange Listing Rules and any new or amended law, regulations or code in Hong Kong applicable to such issuer, and must also provide advice on all continuing requirements under the Exchange Listing Rules, the Listing Agreement and applicable laws and regulations. The sponsor also acts as the PRC issuer's principal channel of communication with the Exchange in Hong Kong, except where the authorized representatives of the PRC issuer are frequently/commonly present in Hong Kong.[83] Where this is not the case (as is typically true for issuers incorporated in the PRC) the issuer's authorized representatives, or their stand-ins must be readily contactable by the Exchange by phone (and fax where available).

While the Exchange is not responsible for the licensing of sponsors, or for selecting the listing applicant's sponsor in individual cases, its does exercise considerable power through its ability to indicate that the sponsor chosen by an applicant is not acceptable. The message in such cases would be clear: choose a different sponsor or place the listing application in peril. Despite this, a number of corporate scandals and fraud allegations in companies during 2002 raised concern that some listing sponsors had not been discharging their responsibilities.[84] It also became obvious that there was a need for the SFC and HKEx to cooperate more effectively in the regulation of sponsors. In a bid to improve the quality of regulation and oversight of such sponsors, in May 2003, the SEHK and the SFC put forward for consultation a number of proposals for the better regulation of listing sponsors, and a number of new rules emerging from the process were put into place in December 2003. The new rules now feature much tougher entry requirements for companies wanting to be listing sponsors, as well as making their duties much clearer.[85] In addition, although not party to the Listing Rules, sponsors must now agree to observe the guidelines set out in the recently issued model code for sponsors now found in Appendix 9 of the Listing Rules.

Under the Appendix 9 code of conduct, sponsors and their employees must sign a declaration in the listing prospectus of any company whose listing they have sponsored, vouching for the accuracy of the information contained therein. Sponsors must also undertake to cross-check the reports of auditors and surveyors and carry out site visits.[86] To ensure independence, sponsors must not hold more than 5 per cent of the equity in the listing candidate.[87] The HKEx has also recently begun to focus regulatory attention on other professionals responsible for helping companies to list. Individuals who breach the code of conduct contained in Appendix 9 of the Listing Rules can be placed on a blacklist and their names published on the HKEx web site. Individuals targeted under the new 'naming and shaming' scheme can also be banned from being involved in any new listings or merger deals.[88]

V THE NEED FOR CROSS-BORDER COOPERATION AND ISSUES OF CROSS-BORDER DISPUTE RESOLUTION

As Chapter 19A of the Hong Kong listing rules notes, 'although under PRC law [mainland listed] shares and foreign shares [issued by a Chinese company] are all shares of a PRC issuer, the two kinds of shares in effect operate in separate markets subject to different investor demands'. Thus, the Hong Kong authorities have always shared their role as supervisor of listed H-share firms with the CSRC and other mainland authorities. It is the Hong Kong authorities who exercise primary authority over the H-share market and all aspects of that market *qua* market. Thus, for example, it is the Hong Kong SFC which possesses the power to inquire whether or not trading in a particular firm's H-shares indicates market malpractice and whether or not such market malpractice has in fact taken place. It is also the HKEx that retains the final say over whether or not Chinese firms will be permitted to list, or remain listed, on the Hong Kong Main Board or the GEM.

It is the HKEx that retains final powers for determining the requirements that all Chinese companies listed in Hong Kong must meet to be listed in Hong Kong, and these can include such things as requirements relating to the composition of the listed company's board of directors, or a listed firm's debt–equity composition. But it is the mainland authorities that exert practical control over most of the firm's management personnel, as well as over its assets and business operations. Likewise, decisions regarding whether or not a particular Hong Kong-listed firm and/or any of its senior management have failed to comply with Hong Kong requirements are made by the HKEx under Hong Kong laws. But carrying out investigations into, for example, the business operations and/or on-site accounts of an H-share firm to check compliance with Hong Kong requirements requires assistance from, and action by, the mainland authorities.

The two legal systems do overlap in a number of different ways. For example, the HKEx Listing Rules require Chinese listing applicants to declare formally that all requirements imposed by relevant PRC laws have been met. The listing applicant's prospectus must also contain a summary of relevant PRC laws affecting the applicant company. The summary should cover matters such as relevant securities and company laws, foreign exchange controls or restrictions, any relevant laws affecting the listing applicant's business operations, and any relevant taxation issues. In addition, Rule 19A.37 provides that:

> Information to be supplied by PRC issuers in a listing of documents or accounts notwithstanding any obligation in the Exchange Listing Rules, the Statutory Rules or any obligation imposed by the laws of Hong Kong *shall not be less than that required to be supplied by the PRC issuer under applicable PRC law*. (Emphasis added)

Mainland law likewise requires that all overseas-listed Chinese firms must comply with all laws, regulations and guidelines in the relevant overseas jurisdiction. In both China and Hong Kong a number of other rules and regulations provide further evidence of the authorities' concern to ensure that Hong Kong-listed Chinese firms remain in compliance with laws and regulations on both sides of the border. Achieving this aim requires effective channels of communication and cooperation between authorities on both sides of the border.

The effectiveness with which the HKEx and the SFC are able to supervise and regulate the H-share market on a day-to-day basis also depends to a large extent on the quality of communication and cooperation between the authorities on both sides of the Hong Kong–Mainland border. Good communication is needed to ensure that the HKEx is kept informed of changing mainland requirements for listed firms, and of any relevant developments affecting the mainland securities markets. Likewise, in order to enter or inspect the premises or operations of, or the on-site account books kept by, a firm located on mainland territory, Hong Kong government officers must first obtain the assistance of mainland officialdom – in particular the CSRC and its employees, servants and agents. It is the CSRC which exercises powers under the *Amended Securities Law* to perform random checks on mainland-based listed companies in order to ensure proper disclosure of financial information and proper use of proceeds from new share issues. The CSRC is also empowered to check the working papers of mainland-registered accountants on which audit opinions are based. In carrying out such inspections, the CSRC is primarily concerned to ensure compliance with mainland regulations and accounting standards. For the HKEx to be aware that such investigations are taking place, and/or to receive information regarding the results of such investigations, the mainland authorities must be both willing and able to cooperate.

Dispute resolution in the context of an H-share firm also requires cross-border involvement and cooperation. Disputes can arise either under the Listing Agreement between the listed H-share firm and the Stock Exchange and/or under the H-share firm's Articles of Association which is the contract between the firm, its management and its owners (shareholders). In the case of H-share firms, the standard Listing Agreement that must be signed requires the H-share issuer to enter into a contract with every director and officer of the company under which the directors and officers undertake to comply with all requirements of the Hong Kong Listing Rules and all requirements of the company's Articles of Association. Any dispute between the listed firm and a member of senior management arising under the contract between them must be resolved by arbitration either by the China International Economic and Trade Arbitration Commission or by the Hong Kong International Arbitration Centre, at the election of the party seeking arbitration. In addition, both mainland and Hong Kong regulations require that the Articles of Association of listed H-share firms must provide that disputes arising under the company's Articles be resolved by arbitration either by the China International Economic and Trade Arbitration Commission or by the Hong Kong International Arbitration Centre, at the election of the party seeking arbitration.[89] The award made by the arbitral body 'shall be final and have binding force'. As some commentators have been quick to note, one of the implications of this provision is effectively to preclude access to the courts of law in Hong Kong for foreign shareholders in the event of a dispute with a listed mainland company, its management or domestic shareholders. Moreover, the effect iveness with which the relevant arbitration tribunal can conduct arbitrations arising under a listing agreement or a company's articles of association clearly depends on the tribunal's ability to gain access to relevant evidence and witnesses situated on the opposite side of the border.

The point here is that, within the cross-border context in which H-shares operate, the extent to which legal requirements are maintained and enforced depends on how effectively obstacles to cross-border communication and cooperation between regulatory organs and government officials are overcome. These obstacles are many: legal, physical, economic, political and cultural. Legally, Chapter 6 of the HKEx Listing Rules empowers the HKEx to order the suspension, cancellation and/or withdrawal of listing of any equity listed on the Exchange, including the shares of any H-share firm. Trading in the shares of an H-share firm may be suspended if the firm fails to maintain a prescribed minimum of assets, fails to submit proper accounts at regular intervals, or otherwise fails to meet the requirements of Hong Kong Law. Trading in a particular H-share may also be suspended if unusual price movements or turnover levels are detected. But, so far as the mainland assets and any mainland-listed equities of the firm are concerned, it is the mainland authorities that remain in control.

Physical obstacles to cross-border cooperation include difficulties in obtaining access to evidence and witnesses located on the opposite side of the China–Hong Kong border. The economic constraints are mainly those imposed by scarcity of resources, while the political and cultural obstacles concern different approaches to investigation and law enforcement on both sides of the border. Law enforcement officers trained in the political and cultural reality of China's one-party market socialism may have a very different understanding of the way in which investigations and prosecutions should be conducted from their Anglo-trained Hong Kong counterparts, particularly when state officials and state assets are concerned.

NOTES

1. Chao Xi, 'Transforming Chinese enterprises: ideology, efficiency and instrumentalism in the process of reform', in John Gillespie & Pip Nicholson (eds) *Asian Socialism and Legal Change: the Dynamics of Vietnamese and Chinese Reform* (Asia Pacific Press at the Australian National University, 2005) 91–114, 101.
2. Leila Fernandez-Stembridge and Jean-François Huchet, 'What's Next for China's SOEs' (2006) 169(5) *Far Eastern Economic Review* 32–36, 32–33.
3. Chao Xi, above n.177, citing 1998 figures available on the CSRC website (http://www.csrc.gov.cn/CSRCSite/eng/esmintr.htm,) as follows: 'by the end of 1998, state-owned shares totalled 86.6 billion shares, 34.25 per cent of the total equity of Chinese listed companies; legal person shares totalled 71.6 billion shares, 28.35 per cent of the total equity; tradable shares totalled 86.2 billion shares, 34.11 per cent of the total equity (among which A-shares 24.06 per cent, B-shares 5.30 per cent, H-shares 4.75 per cent)'.
4. Ibid., citing Liu Xhaojia, et al., 'The theory of ultimate ownership, ownership structure and firm's performance [*Zhongji Chanquan Lun, Guquan Jieguo yu Gongsi Jixiao*]' (2003) 4 *Economic Research Journal* [*Jingji Yanjiu*] 51–62; also citing He Jun, 'An empirical analysis of corporate governance of the listed companies [*Shangshi Gongsi Zhili de Shizheng Fenxi*]' (1998) 5 *Economic Research Journal* [*Jingji Yanjiu*] 50–57, who found that the State was in absolute control (control over 50 per cent of votes) of 24.3 per cent of Chinese listed companies.
5. CSRC, *China's Securities and Futures Markets* (April 2004), p. 4. Available from the CSRC website at (http://www.csrc.gov.cn).
6. Xiao Yu, 'Ending the split share structure: government interferes to correct a long-standing plague', (28 May 2005) *Beijing Review* accessed at (http://www.bjreview.com.cn/En-2005/05-28-e/bus-2.htm) in January 2006. The total number of corporate shares listed on China's two bourses as at the end of 2004 was 714.9 billion.

7. Formulated in accordance with Article 85 of the *Company Law* 1994. Discussed by Jackie Lo, 'New PRC Securities Law fails to fully unify regulation of securities issues in China' (February 1999) 13(1) *China Law and Practice* 21. Lo notes that both the *Listing of Foreign Investment Shares Inside China by a Company Limited by Shares Provisions* and the *Implementing Rules* formulated thereunder were promulgated on, and effective from, the same date, ie. on 25 December 1995.
8. In addition to A-shares, B-shares, treasury bonds, corporate bonds, treasury bond repurchases, convertible bonds and securities investment funds are also available.
9. The *Notice Regarding B-share Investment by Chinese Citizens* which allowed domestic individual investors to open B-share accounts and trade B-shares in foreign currency was promulgated by the CSRC on 19 February 2001: CSRC, *China's Securities and Futures Markets* (April 2004) 14. Available from the CSRC website at (http://www.csrc.gov.cn).
10. Ji Chen and Stephen C. Thomas, 'The ups and downs of the PRC securities market', (2003) 30(1) *The China Business Review* 36, at 40.
11. Ibid.
12. These 111 B-share companies had issued a total of 19 billion B shares, raising RMB 35.6 billion yuan by December 2003: CSRC, *China's Securities and Futures Markets* (April 2004) 14. Available from the CSRC website at (http://www.csrc.gov.cn).
13. In New York, H-shares are traded in the form of American or Global Depositary Receipts (ADRs or GDRs), which are receipts for shares in non-domestic companies entitling the domestic holder to all dividends and capital gains in the underlying shares. For discussion of the 'N-share' market as it is known, see World Bank (Anjali Kumar, Kwang Jun, Anthony Saunders, Susan Selwyn, Yan Sun, Dimitri Vittas, David Wilton), *China's Emerging Capital Markets* (FT Financial Publishing Asia Pacific, 1997) 190–191.
14. List of all H-share companies available at the Hong Kong Exchanges and Clearing Ltd (website at http://www.hkex.com.hk/), Data and Statistics – China Dimension.
15. *PRC Securities Law* [3700/98.12.29]. Promulgated on 29 December 1998 and effective as of 1 July 1999. Translated (February 1999) in 13(1) *China Law & Practice* 25–66.
16. See now Article 7 of the 2006 *Amended PRC Securities Law* which provides that the CSRC 'shall implement centralized and unified regulation of the nationwide securities market according to law'. See also Part Ten (Articles 178–187): *Amended PRC Securities Law* [3700/05.10.27]. Promulgated on 27 October 2005 and effective as of 1 January 2006. Translated (February 2006) in 20(2) *China Law and Practice* 31–88.
17. Leung et al., above n. 65, 9.
18. At the end of 2003, there were 34 fund management companies running 54 closed-end funds and 56 open-end funds with net assets of RMB 169.9 billion yuan under management: China Securities Regulatory Commission, *China's Securities and Futures Markets* (April 2004) 4. (Available from the CSRC website at http://www.csrc.gov.cn.)
19. A new law to establish and empower the China Banking Regulatory Commission came into effect on 1 February 2004. Under the new law, the CBRC takes over regulatory powers and functions formerly vested in and exercised by the People's Bank of China, China's central bank: *Performing the Regulation Function Originally Performed by the People's Bank of China by the China Banking Regulatory Commission* (L3600/03.04.26). Effective as of 1 February 2004. Summarized in New Law Digest (May 2003) 17(4) *China Law and Practice*.
20. See Xinhuanet, 'New law justifies banking watchdog', available through the website of the China Economic Information Network at http://www.ce.cei.gov.cn/; and Bloomberg, 'China moves closer to a unified regulatory regime', *South China Morning Post* (Hong Kong) 29 December 2003.
21. Available at http://www.csrc.gov.cn/.
22. *Amended PRC Securities Law* (2006) [3700/05.10.27]. Promulgated on 27 October 2005 and effective as of 1 January 2006. Translated (February 2006) in 20(2) *China Law and Practice* 31–88. See especially articles 122, 155, 169 and 179. Securities service institutions include investment and financial consultancies, asset appraisal institutions, credit rating agencies and accounting firms that offer securities-related services (article 169).

23. Yang Tiecheng, Alan Xu and Allen Zhong, 'Steady as she goes – China's new Securities Law' (December 2005/January 2006) 19(10) *China Law & Practice* 16, 17.
24. Ibid.
25. See eg. article 9 of the *Amended PRC Securities Law* (2006) above, n. 198.
26. As of December 2003, there were 133 securities companies licensed to operate in China: China Securities Regulatory Commission, *China's Securities and Futures Markets*, April 2004; available at the CSRC website, http://www.csrc.gov.cn/.
27. See, for example, 'Hazy forecast for capital reform', *South China Morning Post* (Hong Kong) 22 November 2004 (from China Economic Quarterly) and Elaine Chan, 'CSRC urges fund managers to toe line' *South China Morning Post* (Hong Kong) 10 December 2004.
28. Reuters, 'Beijing urges brokerages to bolster markets', *South China Morning Post* (Hong Kong) 29 October 2002.
29. 'Hazy forecast for capital reform', *South China Morning Post* (Hong Kong) 22 November 2004 (from China Economic Quarterly).
30. World Bank (1997) above, nn. 189, 257.
31. Ji Chen and Stephen C. Thomas, 'The ups and downs of the PRC securities market', (2003) 30(1) *The China Business Review* 36, 38.
32. Compare article 168(4) of the 1998 PRC *Securities Law* (above, n. 191) and article 180(6) of the *Amended PRC Securities Law* (2006). [3700/05.10.27]. Promulgated on 27 October 2005 and effective as of 1 January 2006. Translated (February 2006) in 20(2) *China Law and Practice* 31–88.
33. Article 180(1) of the *Amended PRC Securities Law* (2006), above, n. 198.
34. Steven Shi, 'Corporate governance with Chinese characteristics', 13(2) *Company Secretary* 10, 12.
35. Eric Ng, 'Jilin Chemical stock frozen', *South China Morning Post* (Hong Kong) 26 April 2003, noting that Jilin was delisted by the CSRC after reporting a loss of 1.02 billion yuan (about HK$956 million) in 2002, despite the fact that the firm had just reported a net profit of 193.29 million RMB for the first quarter of 2003. The company was left to apply for resumption of trading in its shares under the relevant exchange listing rules.
36. Leung et al., above, n. 65, 10.
37. Cai Shu Mo and Deng Ying Xia, 'Corporate governance: obstacles and new developments', *South China Morning Post* (Hong Kong) 12 April 2002.
38. Ji Chen and Stephen C. Thomas, 'The ups and downs of the PRC securities market', (2003) 30:1 *The China Business Review* 36, 38.
39. Ibid.
40. Leung, et al., above, n. 65.
41. Ibid.
42. Ibid.
43. See *Circular of the General Office of the State Council on the Functions, Internal Organization and Staffing of the China Securities Regulatory Commission.*
44. See now article 22 of the *Amended Securities Law* (2006) [3700.05.10.27]. Promulgated on 27 October 2005 and effective as of 1 January 2006. Translated (February 2006) in 20(1) *China Law and Practice* 31–83.
45. CSRC, *China's Securities and Futures Markets* (April 2004) 9.
46. On 11 December 2003 the CSRC announced reforms designed to streamline its four-year-old listing committee and to introduce more transparency into the listing-approval process. In place of an 80-member committee half-filled by government officials, the new slimmer body now comprises 25 people, drawn from a wide range of interest groups including government agencies, financial intermediaries, institutional investors, stock exchanges, academic institutions and overseas professionals. There are 13 full-time members, including three seconded by the CSRC and 10 outside members. See further: Bei Hu, 'Mainland reforms listing panel', *South China Morning Post* (Hong Kong) 12 December 2003.
47. Compare article 15 of the 1998 *Securities Law*: above, n. 191.
48. Compare article 16 of the 1998 *Securities Law*: above, n. 191.

49. Low Chee Keong, 'Regulating the regulators' (2002) 12(12) *Company Secretary* 42–45, 44.
50. Bei Hu, 'Mainland reforms listing panel', *South China Morning Post* (Hong Kong) 12 December 2003.
51. Mathew Miller, 'Hainan construction company wins landmark case against CSRC', *South China Morning Post* (Hong Kong) 20 December 2000; Bei Hu, 'Regulator fights ruling', *South China Morning Post* (Hong Kong) 6 January 2001; Bei Hu, 'Narcissus shareholders sue CSRC, Shanghai exchange over delisting', *South China Morning Post* (Hong Kong) 27 April 2001; Staff Reporter in Shanghai, 'Court raps watchdog for breaking regulations', *South China Morning Post* (Hong Kong) 7 July 2001 and 'CSRC loses Kaili appeal', *South China Morning Post* (Hong Kong) 8 July 2001.
52. New Law Digest (23 July 2006) http://www.chinalawandpractice.com/, accessed January 2007.
53. Articles 48, 52–54, *Amended Securities Law* (2006), above, n. 220.
54. Ibid., articles 55(5) and 56(5).
55. Article 3 of the *Suspending and Terminating the Listings of Loss-making Listed Companies Implementing Procedures* [3710/2001.02.22]. Promulgated by the CSRC on 22 February 2001. Translated (April 2001) in 15(3) *China Law & Practice*. For discussion see Lawrence S. Yee and Jason Yu, 'Time to go: new CSRC de-listing regulations' (April 2001) 15(3) *China Law & Practice*.
56. August 1994, the *Special Regulations of the State Council Concerning Floating and Listing of Shares Overseas by Companies Limited by Shares*. Adopted 4 July 1994 by the Twenty-second Session of the Standing Committee of the State Council. Promulgated 4 August 1994 by the State Council. Translated in *China Laws for Foreign Business – Business Regulation* Para. 13–552 (pp. 17,169–17,179).
57. Pursuant to the 1999 Notices, the documents which must be submitted to the CSRC along with the application for overseas listing include a report which outlines the applicant's business operations and shareholding structure, then details the intended use of the proceeds from the initial public offering; the business objectives for the future of the company to be listed; the risk factors involved and the costs or expenses incurred in the fund-raising exercise. A sponsor's report is also required, which must contain an analysis of the feasibility of the listing and state the sponsor's intention to underwrite the securities of the PRC enterprise.
58. 'Regulations for the Overseas Listing of the Subsidiary of A Domestic Listed Company' (November 2004) *CNPUpdate: Greater China Supplement*, available at http://www.cnplaw.com/en/cnpupdate/2004/_gcpg_11.htm; accessed January 2007.
59. Issued by the CSRC on 21 July 2004, released on 10 August 2004. Zheng Jian Fa [2004] No. 67. Extracted (September 2004) in 18(7) *China Law and Practice* 37.
60. Chi Kuen Simon Wu, 'single securities market in China' (2006) 14:1 *Asia Pacific Law Review* 19, 23; Betty M. Ho, 'Demutualization of organized securities exchanges in Hong Kong: The great leap forward' (2002) 33 *Law & Policy in International Business* 283, 286–287; and Andreas M. Fleckner, 'stock exchanges at the crossroads' (2006) 74 *Fordham Law Review* 2541.
61. Low Chee Keong, 'Regulating the regulators' (December 2002) 12(12) *Company Secretary* 42–45, 43.
62. Ibid.
63. Originally established pursuant to the *Securities and Futures Commission Ordinance*. The *Securities and Futures Commission Ordinance* and nine other pieces of legislation were consolidated in the *Securities and Futures Ordinance* passed by LegCo on 13 March 2002 and which came into effect in 2003.
64. See especially articles 4 and 5 of the *Securities and Futures Ordinance* (Hong Kong) 2003. For discussion, see L. C. Keong, above, n. 237, 43.
65. Alan Linning, 'Disciplinary focus of the SFC' (July–August 2003) 4(4) *Hong Kong Securities* 26–27.
66. Parts XIII and XIV of the *Securities and Futures Ordinance* (Hong Kong) 2003, respectively.

67. Offences under Part XIII of the SFO are punishable by up to 10 years' imprisonment and a fine of up to $10 million: A. Linning, above, n. 241, 26.
68. A. Linning, above, n. 241.
69. Stephen Fletcher and Brian van Langenberg, 'An overhaul of the SAR's financial markets' (April 2003) 4(13) *Company Secretary* 8.
70. Division 2, Part XIV, *Securities and Futures Ordinance* (Hong Kong) 2003.
71. L. C. Keong, above, n. 237, 45.
72. Ibid., 43.
73. Ibid.
74. See further Christine Loh, 'Mandate under challenge: Christine Loh's Newsletter', received by email on 4 May 2003 from cloh@civic-exchange.org. Loh notes that the cosy atmosphere of the Exchange was somewhat shaken by the election to the board, on 16 April 2003, of two new directors, David Webb and Oscar Wong, whose avowed mission was to look after the rights of minority shareholders.
75. Enoch Yiu, 'Exchange wants SFC to be sole regulator of listing sponsors', *South China Morning Post* (Hong Kong) 24 December 2003.
76. Ibid.
77. Rule 2A.09, *Hong Kong Stock Exchange Listing Rules* (as at July 2007). Available at the HKEx website at http://www.hkex.com.hk.
78. Under this test, the new applicant must have a trading record of not less than three financial years during which the profit attributable to shareholders for the two years preceding the listing should be, in aggregate, not less than HK$30 million and, for the most recent year, should be not less than HK$20 million.
79. Under this test, the new applicant must have a market capitalization of at least HK$2 billion at the time of listing, revenue of at least HK$500 million for the most recent audited financial year and positive cash flow from operating activities carried out by the new applicant, or its group, that are to be listed of at least HK$100 million in aggregate for the three preceding financial years.
80. Under this test, the applicant must have a market capitalization of at least HK$4 billion at the time of listing, revenue of at least HK$500 million for the most recent audited financial year and at least 1000 shareholders at the time of listing.
81. The additional requirements usually required by the Exchange in respect of PRC-based issuers are set out in part D of Appendix 13 of the Listing Rules.
82. See Listing Rule 3 and Appendix 9.
83. Rule 3.05.
84. Enoch Yiu, 'HKEx to shame shoddy sponsors', *South China Morning Post* (Hong Kong) 31 May 2003.
85. Ibid.
86. Ibid.
87. Ibid.
88. Ibid.
89. Chapter XX, Article 163, *Notice on the Implementation of Essential Clauses in Articles of Association of Companies Listed Overseas*, Promulgated 27 August 1994 by the Securities Committee of the State Council and the State Commission for Restructuring the Economic System: Articles of Association of Companies Listed Overseas. Translated in *China Laws for Foreign Business – Business Regulation* para. 13–410.

4. Internal governance structures within the H-share firm: solving agency problems in a cross-border environment

I INTRODUCTION: THE H-SHARE COMPANY AND INSIDER CONTROL

A recent study by the World Bank defines Corporate Governance as 'the set of mechanisms available to shareholders for influencing managers to maximize the value of shareholder's stock and to fixed claimants such as banks and employees for controlling the agency costs of equity'.[1]

The OECD's revised Principles of Corporate Governance defines it as follows:

> a set of relationships between a company's management, its board, its shareholders and other stakeholders. Corporate governance also provides the structure through which the objectives of the company are set, and the means of attaining those objectives and monitoring performance are determined.[2]

Both of these definitions imply and accept the 'principal–agent' model of the corporation which has dominated much of western corporate scholarship over the past century or more.[3] This model, however, is one which has increasingly come under pressure in recent years. The first arena of questioning has been by scholars who have examined the experience of 'transplanting' western corporate law concepts into an alien environment – Vietnam under *Doi Moi*,[4] for example, or China under Deng Xiaoping.[5]

In the case of China-focused scholars, many have concluded that, despite the undoubtedly western origin of much of modern Chinese corporations law, the modern Chinese listed firm remains a far cry from the western idea of the corporation as a 'nexus' of contracts between independent parties at arm's length. In the case of H-share companies, the difference arises because the process of corporatization has been distinctly different from the concept of privatization as understood in other countries. Whereas privatization generally involves a complete or partial transfer of control over publicly-owned assets to the private sector, the Chinese government has typically retained control over Hong Kong-listed SOEs, even after corporatization.[6]

Many observers have described China's insider control model of corporate organization, with its high levels of State ownership, connectedness and control, and have highlighted the problems that arise as a result of these characteristics.[7] The fundamental difficulties facing the implementation of corporate governance standards in China's major listed companies are thus well known and include the following:

1. dominance of the state as major shareholder;
2. non-transferability of most state shares;
3. dominance of key man/chairman, nominees of controlling shareholder etc;
4. extensive use of related party transactions;
5. weak position of minority shareholders;
6. independent directors have very few real powers;
7. lack of transparency partly due to accounting standards that fall short of international standards; and
8. a legal system that provides few real remedies for disgruntled shareholders.

These problems have often been attributed to differences between mainland and Hong Kong company and securities laws, particularly in the area of shareholders' protection and directors' duties. Until recently, PRC law contained few effective safeguards against directors' abuse of their powers, and no specific provision to guard against oppression of minority shareholders by major shareholders. So far as Hong Kong-listed Chinese firms are concerned, the most important initiative for overcoming this perceived lack of shareholder protection under PRC law has been the introduction of Mandatory Provisions in the articles of association of all Chinese companies listed on the HKEx.

Two long-standing problems in regard to H-share enterprises have been the difficulty of separating Government and enterprise, and ensuring management accountability to minority shareholders. The first really serious efforts to tackle these problems through legislative means came in March 1999, when the State Economic and Trade Commission and the CSRC issued the *Further Standardizing Operations and Reform of Companies Listed Outside China Opinion*.[8] The 1999 Opinion specifically encourages the 'separation of government and enterprise',[9] and requires overseas-listed firms to bear risks and liabilities independently, keep separate accounts, have separate management personnel, maintain separate operations and separate assets and reduce related transactions between controlling entity and listed firm.[10] The joint Opinion also stresses the importance of 'strengthening directors' responsibilities', and takes the first step towards ensuring the presence of independent directors on the boards of all foreign-listed Chinese firms.[11]

The remainder of this chapter focuses upon those reforms in mainland China and in Hong Kong which have had the most recent and significant impact upon corporate governance practices in H-share firms. These reforms include measures aimed at enhanced minority shareholder protections, enhanced standards of professionalism and independence for the board of directors and the supervisory committee, and improved accounting and reporting standards. The most recent of these reforms on the mainland are contained in a new *Company Law*[12] and new *Securities Law*, both of which came into effect on 1 January 2006. In Hong Kong, a new *Securities and Futures Ordinance* came into effect in 2003, replacing and consolidating 10 earlier pieces of legislation that previously had regulated various aspects of the securities markets. The HKEx Listing Rules have also undergone significant amendment and reform over the years since 1993. The conclusion is reached that, despite significant legislative reform on the books, remarkably little has really changed in the political influences that still determine the making of major decisions within H-share enterprises.

II THE H-SHARE COMPANY: ITS SHAREHOLDERS, DIRECTORS, SUPERVISORS AND MANAGERS

Under the framework established by the combination of Chinese and Hong Kong laws to which H-share firms are subject, there are three tiers for the exercise of internal decision-making powers within every H-share enterprise. The highest level is the shareholders' general meeting which, under the Chinese *Company Law*, exercises ultimate power to supervise and control the company's business activities, as well as the power to appoint and dismiss directors and supervisors. The second level consists of the board of directors, responsible for managing the company according to shareholders' direction, and the supervisory committee, responsible for supervising the decision making of directors and management. The third level is the general manager and other senior executive personnel who are responsible for the day-to-day operation of the firm. While this structure is meant to ensure that shareholder rights are protected, including minority shareholder rights, this aim has not always been achieved in practice. Part of the problem stems from the fact that government and quasi-government institutions own the bulk of shares of listed mainland companies. Where the state is the majority shareholder, it often becomes impossible or difficult to make managers responsible to government regulators, let alone to small individual investors.[13]

Recent reforms have thus been two-pronged in their aims. First, the aim has been to get the State out of corporate ownership and management, and second, the aim has been to modify the power balance between the different 'tiers' of the Chinese company to strengthen the powers of shareholders, and make company directors and managers more accountable.

A The Shareholders' Meeting

Under the 1994 *Company Law*, the shareholders' general meeting was vested with what one commentator has described as 'an extraordinarily wide range of decision making powers . . . including managerial powers normally exerted by the board of directors in other jurisdictions'.[14] Article 38 of the 1994 *Company Law* which lists the 'functions and powers' of the shareholders' general meeting, has been retained in the 2006 *Company Law*. By reserving vital decision-making powers to the shareholders' general meeting, article 38 serves to limit the managerial power of the board of directors, thus potentially helping to reduce the adverse effects of any abuse of powers or wrongdoing by directors. In theory, article 38 also establishes the shareholders' meeting as an avenue through which minority shareholders can have their voice heard and can influence corporate decision making. In practice, however, minority shareholders in Chinese firms have had little incentive or inclination even to attend shareholders' meetings, let alone join together in the numbers required to convene such a meeting. And this remains the case today, despite recent reforms expressly aimed at protecting minority shareholder rights in listed Chinese firms.

In early 2002, the CSRC issued a new Regulatory Opinion on Standardising Shareholders' General Meetings of Listed Companies[15] and a new set of Guidelines for Corporate Governance of Listed Companies (the Corporate Governance Guidelines).[16] Both of these instruments emphasize the importance of shareholder rights. Chapter One of the Corporate Governance Guidelines deals specifically with shareholder rights, while Chapter Two deals with the particular position and behaviour of the controlling shareholder. Article 2 states that minority shareholders should have equal status with other shareholders, while Article 4 gives all shareholders the right to protect their interests through civil litigation and other legal action. Article 8 requires that companies make 'a genuine effort' to use modern technologies in shareholders' annual general meetings to improve shareholder participation. Also, article 11 gives institutional investors more weight in the decision-making processes, including the nomination of directors.

In 2004, the CSRC moved to further 'curb the abuse of control of listed companies' by controlling shareholders. The *Strengthening the Protection of the Rights and Interests of Public Shareholders Several Provisions* (the Protection of Public Shareholders Provisions) established, on a 'trial basis', a system wherein public shareholders would have greater voting rights on material matters of the company. The Protection of Public Shareholders Provisions require that major decisions (concerning the issue of new shares or the listing of a new subsidiary by the company, or any other decision having a material impact on the interests of public shareholders of the company), must be adopted by an affirmative vote at the shareholders' meeting and passed by a simple majority of the voting rights held by public shareholders who participated in the vote. The results of the vote must be published by the company together with details of the number of public shareholders who participated in the vote, the total number of shares held by them, the percentage of the company's public shares they account for and the result of their votes. The Protection of Public Shareholders Provisions also expressly impose fiduciary duties upon the controlling shareholder and party in actual control of a listed company toward both the company and its public shareholders.[17]

Part Four of the new *Company Law*[18] deals with the establishment and organizational structure of public companies (companies limited by shares), and contains several new provisions aimed at protecting minority shareholder rights. The functions and powers of the shareholders' general meeting are dealt with in Section Two (articles 99–108). The shareholders' meeting is the company's most powerful authority, and exercises its decision-making powers inter alia to elect and replace directors and supervisors of the company, and determine their remuneration.[19] A shareholders' general meeting must be held at least once a year. An extraordinary shareholders' meeting must occur within two months if requested by a single shareholder or two or more shareholders holding shares accounting for 10 per cent or more of the company's shares (article 101).[20] The new *Company Law* also enables shareholders holding 3 per cent or more of a company's shares to put forward a motion to the board of directors 10 days prior to a shareholders' meeting.[21] The motion must then be circulated to all shareholders before being submitted to the meeting for consideration and vote. This power is supported by provisions which improve minority shareholder access to company information and records. Shareholders now have the right to access and make copies of not only the shareholders' meetings and company financial statements, but also the resolutions of the board of directors and the board of supervisors.[22] Directors, supervisors and senior officers must attend shareholder meetings upon request by shareholders, and answer inquiries from the shareholders.[23]

If the company wishes to expand, reduce or otherwise alter its share capital and/or share composition, or amend its articles of association, the approval of at least two-thirds of the voting rights of shareholders who are present at an annual or interim meeting must first be obtained (article 104).[24] The board of directors also cannot decide to purchase or sell major fixed assets of the company without such two-thirds approval at a shareholders' meeting. A company's decision to provide security for a shareholder or for its de facto controlling person must be approved at a shareholder's meeting by a majority of the voting rights held by disinterested shareholders;[25] while a decision to provide security exceeding 30 per cent of the company's total assets to any third party requires the approval of a two-thirds vote in favour by those present at a shareholders' meeting (article 122).[26] A shareholder who opposes a resolution on the merger or division of the company adopted at a shareholders' general meeting may request the company to purchase his or her shares.[27]

So far as Hong Kong-listed Chinese firms are concerned, Chapter 14 of the HKEx Listing Rules vests the shareholders' meeting with powers of oversight over an even broader number of company decisions. Chapter 14 provides that any 'major transaction', 'very substantial transaction' or 'connected transaction' entered into by a listed company must be approved by shareholders in general meeting. A listed company is normally required to send a circular to shareholders giving detailed information about these transactions. In addition, an opinion is required by an independent expert acceptable to the Exchange as to whether the transaction is fair and reasonable, which must set out the reasons for reaching that opinion.[28] For a 'very substantial transaction' or 'connected transaction', any person interested in the transaction must abstain from voting at the general meeting during which the transaction is to be approved.

New amendments to the HKEx Listing Rules were introduced in early 2004, and became effective on 1 April 2004. The 2004 amendments introduced a revised Chapter 14 on notifiable transactions and a new Chapter 14A on connected transactions. The new Chapter 14A contained, inter alia, a newly codified definition of 'continuing connected transactions' and association requirements to formalize the HKEx's current practice with respect to exemptions and ongoing review requirements for such transactions. One result has been that virtually every listed H-share firm has been obliged to send, for the first time, a circular to shareholders seeking approval at an extraordinary shareholders' meeting of newly agreed annual caps (over a three-year period) for continuing connected transactions between the listed company and its parent organization. This is probably a key improvement in terms of alerting ordinary shareholders of the nature and extent of such transactions. From the point of view of the ordinary shareholder, the circular not only comprises a separate notification and information source about the company's connected transactions, but also contains much more detail about the nature and extent of those transactions than is contained in the company's Annual or Interim Reports. The 2006 revisions to the mainland *Company Law* discussed above simply serve to complement this reform.[29]

The new PRC *Company Law* also introduces more flexibility in the voting system used during shareholder meetings. It allows the articles of association of a limited liability company to allocate voting rights between shareholders in proportions different from their respective contributions. Shareholders may also receive dividends and/or enjoy priority subscription for new equity in proportions different from their capital contribution ratios.[30] In addition, the new *Company Law* enables a company limited by shares to adopt a cumulative voting system at shareholders' meetings for the election of directors and supervisors. Under the cumulative voting system, the number of votes available to a shareholder is equal to the number of shares held by the shareholder multiplied by the number of positions up for election. All votes may be cast for the same director.[31]

By the end of 2006, two of the nine companies examined in this book had altered their articles of association to introduce a system of cumulative voting for election of directors.[32] The two firms are Shanghai Petrochemical and Guangzhou Shipyard. Both companies are, however, effectively controlled by the SASAC, with 55.56 per cent of company equity in the case of Shanghai Petrochemical, and 42.61 per cent of company equity in the case of Guangzhou Shipyard. The point here is that, when cumulative voting is introduced into a context of extensive state control, it appears to have little or no effect on the process of nominating directors or on the final composition of the board. In the case of Shanghai Petrochemical, the introduction of cumulative voting was not even enough to ensure compliance with the requirement under Appendix 14 of the Hong Kong Listing Rules for listed firms to ensure that the roles of board chairman and company chief executive officer (CEO) should be separate and vested in different individuals.[33]

Despite these reforms aimed at strengthening shareholder rights and encouraging minority shareholder participation in the management of listed Chinese firms, it is still the case that, for a variety of reasons, individual mainland shareholders rarely attend company meetings. At the 2004 Annual General Meeting of Guangzhou Shipyard, for example, only seven out of a total of 52 426 shareholders bothered to attend.[34] The seven shareholders who attended represented approximately 44.73 per cent of the total shares of the Company, of which 42.61 per cent was controlled by the State. In effect, the shareholders' meeting seems to have operated as a mechanism for facilitating State involvement in the appointment of management and firm decision making, and not at all as a venue for facilitating minority shareholder voices. After so many years during which the State has effectively controlled company decisions, there has simply been no opportunity for a practice of shareholder activism to emerge, and public awareness of shareholder rights remains in its infancy.

B Individual and Minority Shareholder Rights

1 Background: the first twelve years

Hong Kong law permits minority shareholders to start a derivative action in the name of shareholders in cases where directors have breached their fiduciary duties. The PRC *Civil Procedure Law* does not provide for any such procedure. Prior to 2006, the closest thing to a derivative action under PRC law was article 111 of the *Company Law* 1994, which gave shareholders the right to initiate proceedings in the People's Court to restrain any resolution adopted by the shareholders' general meeting or board of directors of the firm if the resolution is in breach of any law, or infringes the lawful rights and interests of shareholders. The 1994 *Company Law* also contained clauses in connection with fiduciary duties of managers and directors, but these clauses had little practical force as they were drafted in very general terms. Moreover, there was no attempt in the *Company Law* to guard against or deal with oppression of minority shareholders by the majority shareholders of a listed firm. It was therefore left for the Hong Kong authorities, under the HKSX Listing Rules, to ensure that all listed H-share enterprises contain in their Articles of Association mandatory provisions that allow minority shareholders to commence action against defaulting directors, and that also accord minority protection similar to that available under Hong Kong law.

Until recently, however, political hang-ups and the absence of a case-law system have presented major obstacles to such actions in mainland China. While the 1994 *Company Law* conferred certain rights on shareholders, those rights were provided without any mention of civil remedies. Many fundamental issues, such as which court had jurisdiction, and who was the proper plaintiff in cases of securites fraud, remained unresolved. As a result, most of the early shareholder suits were dismissed by the courts, even before a hearing. Even for those investors who did get to argue their case before a court, difficulties in proving the existence of a causal relation between a claimed misrepresentation and alleged losses, and problems in calculating such losses, proved to be insurmountable.[35]

Article 63 of China's first *Securities Law*, which came into effect in 1998, allowed investors who incurred losses as a result of a misrepresentation, a misleading statement or material omission in a prospectus, financial and accounting report or annual report, to claim compensation from the issuer and/or underwriter responsible for the misrepresentation. The responsible director(s), supervisor(s) and manager(s) in the issuer or underwriter's company were also made jointly liable for such compensation.

A surge in shareholder suits following the passage of the 1998 *Securities Law* was clearly something the PRC Supreme Court was unprepared for. Its initial response was to issue a notice (on 21 September 2001) stating that, owing to 'the weakness of the current securities civil liability system and limits on the quality of judges', the court 'would not accept and hear such cases for the time being'.[36] In the face of mounting criticism from market participants, however, the Court was forced to alter its stance. And so, in January 2002, the Court issued a Circular effectively lifting the four-month freeze on shareholder actions.[37]

Encouraged by the 2002 Circular, an explosion of shareholders suits arose, with more than 900 suits filed in 2002, beginning in January when the Haerbin Intermediate People's Court formally accepted a civil misrepresentation case brought by three shareholders against Daqing Lianyi Petrochemical Shareholding Co. This case was reportedly the first shareholder civil remedies action accepted by a people's court.[38] Then, in early November 2002, a 60-year-old Shanghai housewife became the first mainland stock investor to win a settlement from a mainland-listed company for false disclosure.[39]

The enthusiasm for suits quickly cooled, however. Despite the issuance of the Circular, shareholders remained ill-equipped to pursue an effective remedy. While the Circular did solve such procedural issues as acceptance of cases and which courts were competent to hear them, many other key issues remained unresolved. Containing only seven clauses, the Circular remained too sketchy on details to be of much practical use. Issues not dealt with include such questions as the burden of proof between plaintiff and defendant, and permitted methods of loss calculation.[40]

Against this background, the PRC Supreme People's Court promulgated the *Trial of Civil Damages Cases Arising from Misrepresentation in the Securities Market Several Provisions* (the Provisions), which replaced the 2002 Circular on 1 February 2003. The definition of misrepresentation was expanded in the Provisions to include not only fraudulent records (also covered in the 2002 Circular), but also three other categories of fraud: misleading statements, material omissions and improper disclosure, not covered by the Circular. In addition, the Provisions substantially increase the scope of potential defendants who can be held liable for misrepresentation. Apart from the issuer and its directors, managers and underwriters as provided in article 63 of the 1998 *Securities Law*, the Provisions make it clear that sponsors, promoters and controlling shareholders of the issuer, the intermediary agencies (such as accounting firms, law firms and asset appraisal firms) involved, and persons directly responsible for misrepresentation in the intermediary agencies can all be held jointly liable for misrepresentation. In some cases, even journalists and market commentators can be found liable.[41]

One limitation of the Provisions, however, is that, before the court can agree to hear a misrepresentation case, a government authority must first have imposed administrative or criminal punishments on the persons responsible for making the misrepresentation. The Provisions make such a precondition easier to satisfy by expanding the number of government agencies that have the power to discipline public companies. Despite this, the precondition does appear to limit unnecessarily the right of a person to bring a lawsuit. Moreover, given the limited resources of the CSRC and other government authorities, and the many practical difficulties, only a small percentage of companies and individuals responsible for misrepresentation are eventually caught and punished by any government agency.[42]

Under the Provisions, investors can file a suit jointly with other investors as an alternative to individual suits. So long as the number of plaintiffs is decided before the hearing, joint actions are therefore possible. Plaintiffs may also select two to five litigation representatives and each litigation representative can authorize one or two attorneys. China's stock market is characterized by large numbers of small individual investors and, for most, the tremendous costs of bringing an individual legal action against a public company are simply too high vis-à-vis the relatively small amount claimed. The possibility of coordinated joint action provides an attractive alternative. The problem is that, if an investor does intend to bring a joint action with other investors, the coordination, travel and transaction costs can be very high. With a couple of exceptions, all lawsuits on misrepresentation must be filed with the intermediate court in the locality of the public company's place of business.[43] Shareholders not residing in that locality may be deterred by the costs of travel, while shareholders who do live in the same locality are more likely to be affected by local political influences weighing against proceeding with the action against the company.

The Provisions do make it significantly easier for plaintiffs to seek compensation for losses due to fraud, by making it clear that the burden of proof lies on the defendant. Securities fraud plaintiffs no longer have to satisfy the requirement imposed by the PRC *Civil Law General Principles*, under which a direct causal relation between the alleged tortious act and the loss must be established. Establishing causation can be extremely difficult, if not impossible, for plaintiffs in misrepresentation cases, not least because of the many factors that can often operate together to influence the movement of stock prices. Article 21 of the Provisions provides that promoters, issuers or listing companies shall bear strict liability for misrepresentation. Other persons are also assumed to be liable for misrepresentation, unless they can establish absence of fault. According to article 18, the plaintiff only needs to prove that (1) the misrepresentation made directly concerned the securities invested in; (2) the plaintiff purchased such securities on or after the date of the misrepresentation and before the misrepresentation was disclosed or corrected; and (3) the plaintiff suffered losses when reselling the securities or, while holding such securities after the date, the misrepresentation was disclosed or corrected. An important contribution to the determination of loss causation in securities misrepresentation cases was also made in the Daqing Lianyi Petrochemical case when the court, in its December 2004 final judgement, elaborated for the first time on the concept of the systemic risk of the securities market.[44]

Finally, when it comes to calculating losses suffered by successful securities fraud plaintiffs, the Provisions provide, for the first time, a clear legal basis and guidelines on how to calculate such losses. Slowly, then, Chinese courts have begun to render decisions in shareholder lawsuits against listed companies, and this in turn has helped to make shareholder lawsuits more viable as an enforcement tool – a process which has gained further momentum with the coming into effect of the new *Company Law* and a revised *Securities Law* in 2006.

2 Civil Remedies for shareholders under the new company & securities legislation

Articles 20, 21 and 149 of the new *Company Law* introduce new rules governing the relationship between shareholders and company management; accompanied by civil liabilities. Article 21, for example, provides that directors, supervisors, officers and anyone else who exercises control over the company (including a controlling shareholder) must pay 'compensation' for any damage they cause to the company's interests by taking advantage of their affiliations.[45] The company is entitled to any gains made by a director or senior officer who commits any of the actions proscribed by article 149 in violation of his or her duty of loyalty to the company.[46]

Prior to 2006, civil liability in the course of securities issuance or trading only existed on the basis of proven misrepresentation, leaving investors facing any other kind of market malpractice, such as share price manipulation or insider trading, without an effective remedy. The amended PRC *Securities Law* specifies civil remedies for a number of additional violations, including matters involving corporate governance. For example, article 76 of the *Securities Law* now provides civil remedies for insider trading.

Private enforcement of the new *Company Law* is bolstered by several provisions providing shareholders with the right to seek court intervention to compel compliance with certain corporate governance matters. For example, shareholders can now petition the people's court to revoke any shareholder or board resolution that violates the company's articles of association or that was passed at an improperly convened meeting or using an improper voting method (*Company Law* 2006, article 22).

For the first time, the new *Company Law* now provides basic procedures for shareholder derivative lawsuits. This is an important new development in Chinese law, and serves to close a number of procedural gaps that previously existed. Derivative lawsuits protect company shareholders (especially minority shareholders) by allowing one or more shareholders to initiate a claim in the name of the company, in order to prevent or remedy injury to the company. Such lawsuits thus represent a temporary usurpation by shareholders of the decision-making power of the board of directors, as opposed to direct lawsuits, which are brought by shareholders on their own behalf.[47]

Shareholder derivative lawsuits are now made possible under article 152 of the new *Company Law*. Article 152 first allows shareholders who alone or jointly have held at least 1 per cent of the company's shares for at least 180 days in succession to request the supervisory board to initiate legal proceedings against a director who has violated any laws, administrative regulations or the company's articles of association causing losses to the company. In the case of such a violation by a supervisor, the request can be made to the board of directors. If the supervisory board or board of directors fails to act on the request, or if there are urgent circumstances requiring prompt action to protect the company's interests, the shareholder(s) who made the request may directly institute proceedings in a people's court in their own name.[48] Similar procedures can be used by shareholders to institute legal proceedings against a third party who has infringed upon the lawful rights and interests of the company, causing the company to incur a loss.[49]

Article 153 provides a procedural counterpart to article 152 for shareholder direct lawsuits. It allows shareholders to bring direct lawsuits against a company's director or senior officer who violates any provision of laws, administrative regulations or the company's articles of association and causes losses to the shareholders themselves (as opposed to the company). As Anderson and Guo point out, however, determining whether the harm is suffered by the shareholders or by the company is not always an easy matter.[50]

Moreover, in contrast to the United States and other jurisdictions with well developed rules relating to shareholder lawsuits, the new *Company Law* provides very limited guidance with respect to the causes of action that should proceed as derivative actions rather that direct actions. Article 149 of the Company Law does provide that gains made by directors or senior officers who commits any of the breaches of fiduciary duty listed in that article 'shall belong to the company', suggesting that such breaches are likely to be treated as derivative actions. Similarly, article 47 of the new *Securities Law* provides that, if a director, supervisor, senior official or major shareholder (over 5 per cent equity) of a listed company sells shares of that company within six months of acquiring those shares, or re-purchases shares within six months of selling the same, the gains obtained therefrom belong to the company, and the board of directors must act to recover such gains.

At least until Chinese case law and court rules develop to the stage where things become clearer, it may well be that shareholders will prefer to initiate direct actions under article 153 rather than derivative actions under article 152, regardless of the appropriateness of doing so. The two compelling reasons for such a preference are, first, the desire to avoid the more complex and onerous procedural restrictions of article 152, and secondly because any monies recovered in a derivative lawsuit are generally paid to the company, while recovery in a direct action allows the monies to be paid to the plaintiff shareholder(s).

On 28 April 2006, the Supreme Peoples' Court issued the *Provisions on Several Issues concerning the Application of the PRC Company Law (1)* (Company Law Interpretations),[51] which address certain procedural issues regarding the application of the new *Company Law* to civil lawsuits and clarify certain issues related to the standing requirements for shareholders who seek to initiate derivative lawsuits. Future interpretations may also serve to clarify some of the uncertainties that remain.

While the new legislation represents a significant step forward, more is needed to bring protection provided to Chinese investors in line with that provided to their counterparts in other markets internationally. To begin with, many have been disappointed by the express exclusion of class actions as a permitted channel for investors to bring a lawsuit. Partly this is because of the 'no claim, no acceptance' principle which has long been part of Chinese law, and means that courts will not accept or hear cases of those who have not filed a claim. In other words, historically there has so far never been a basis for class actions under Chinese law, and this, in turn, explains the lack of experience or resources of Chinese courts in dealing with such actions.[52]

What Chinese law does provide, however, is basic joint action procedures for two classes of cases: first, where one of the parties is numerous but certain, and second, where the persons comprising one of the parties are numerous but uncertain at the commencement of the action. Article 55 of the *Civil Procedure Law* regulates joint action where 'the subject matter of the action is of the same category and one party is numerous and of an uncertain number upon commencement of the lawsuit'. Theoretically, this type of joint litigation is allowed as a procedural device for shareholder lawsuits, other than securities-related misrepresentation cases which are still regulated by the 2003 Provisions on securities market misrepresentation lawsuits discussed above. There are no direct legal impediments to using the article 55 joint action for shareholder claims triggered by most violations of the new *Company Law*. The People's Courts have, however, preferred individual actions or the more restrictive joint actions with a fixed number of plaintiffs, and have remained resistant to joint actions where the plaintiff class membership remains uncertain.[53]

Under article 183 of the new *Company Law*, shareholders holding 10 per cent or more of a company's shares have the right to petition the People's Court to liquidate the company when the company's managerial problems threaten to damage shareholder's interests. This introduces a significant addition to China's bankruptcy regime, and provides an avenue to the liquidation of a company which can be compared to the 'contributory' petition for winding up available under article 179 Hong Kong's *Companies Ordinance*. Under Part V of the *Companies Ordinance*, any shareholder ('contributory') who has held his shares for at least six months may apply to the High Court for the winding up of the company (article 179), and the court may grant the petition and wind up the company if, inter alia, 'the court is of the opinion that it is just and equitable that the company be wound up' (article 177). Under Part X of the *Companies Ordinance*, the provisions of Part V in regard to contributory petitions apply equally to foreign-incorporated companies that are listed on the Hong Kong stock exchange.[54]

C The Role of Independent Directors and Qualified Personnel in the Management of Listed Chinese Companies

Perhaps the most important implication of the dominant role of state ownership in China's listed companies is the control the state can exercise over directorship and managerial nominations and appointments. According to the *Company Law*, a board of directors should consist of from five to 19 directors.[55] The Mandatory Provisions then establish the typical corporate structure whereby the board of directors is made directly accountable to the shareholders' meeting, and under which directors, supervisors and managers owe specific fiduciary duties to the company and its owners. A certain degree of independence is required of all directors and supervisors in that they must avoid conflict of interest situations in the performance of their duties. Directors must make full disclosure and must not vote in respect of any board resolution in which they have a direct or indirect interest. The Mandatory Provisions also specifically prohibit the company from giving any loan, or providing any guarantee to secure a loan made, to any director, supervisor or officer of the company. Share ownership and remuneration levels of directors, supervisors and senior management must be disclosed in every Annual Report.

In 2002, the business journal *Asiamoney* conducted a corporate governance poll of companies throughout the Asian region. Some 121 firms of a total 197 companies polled responded to the survey, 12 of the respondents coming from China. Responses provided by the 12 Chinese firms that returned completed questionnaires indicate that in the average Chinese firm:

- The board of directors has about 15 directors, of whom perhaps three or four are independent non-executives;
- the full board formally meets for two or four meetings per year; and
- most Chinese companies take votes at shareholder meetings through a poll (proportionate to the number of shares held) rather than through a show of hands.[56]

By far the greatest majority of directors of H-share companies are nominated by the controlling shareholder (usually representing the State), but this situation is beginning to change. Change is most noticeably occurring in those companies such as Tsingtao Brewery that have introduced a significant foreign partner, and where nomination committees have been established.

In 2002, the CSRC and the State Economic and Trade Commission issued a regulatory Notice requiring all listed companies to carry out an internal inspection of corporate governance standards and to prepare a formal report on the results of the inspection.[57] New *Guidelines Regarding Independent Directors in Listed Companies* issued in August 2001 also required every listed firm to introduce, by 30 June 2003, a system for ensuring that at least one-third of directors on its board are 'independent' within the legal meaning of that term (article 3).[58] The tables provided in Appendix 1 of this book show the increase in the number of independent directors over the period 1994–2005 for the nine H-share firms examined in Chapter 5.

Article 1(3) of the *Independent Director Guidelines* seeks to ensure that at least one of the independent directors is a qualified accounting professional. This rule complements Listing Rule 3.10 of the Hong Kong listing rules which provides that at least one of the independent non-executive directors on the board of all Hong Kong-listed issuers must have 'appropriate professional qualifications or accounting or related financial management expertise'. Rule 3.24 of the Hong Kong-Listing Rules further provides that every listed issuer must ensure that at all times it employs on a full-time basis a qualified accountant who is a fellow or associate member of the Hong Kong Society of Accountants (or similar body) who must be a member of the senior management of the listed issuer (preferably an executive director) and whose job includes oversight of the issuer and its subsidiaries in connection with its financial procedures and internal controls.[59] This provision is particularly important as a necessary complement to the stricter accounting and disclosure requirements that H-share firms are now subject to, as further discussed below.

In principle, an independent director may only hold concurrently the position of independent director in a maximum of five listed companies. If an independent director fails to attend a board meeting in person for three consecutive times, he or she may be removed from his or her position at the next shareholders' meeting. The only other reason for which an independent director may be removed from office is where the independent director concerned fails to meet the 'independence' requirements imposed by the Guidelines, or becomes no longer qualified to hold the position of a director as stipulated in the *Company Law*.[60] The Guidelines thus provide Independent Directors with the protection of guaranteed security of tenure for the entire period of the term for which they have been appointed. If an independent director resigns or is removed from office, the CSRC in China, and the Exchange in Hong Kong, must be notified of the reason.[61]

The role of the Independent Director is to safeguard the overall interests of the company, with particular attention paid to protecting the rights and interests of minority shareholders.[62] Independent Directors are specifically vested by the Guidelines with special powers additional to those stipulated in the *Company Law* and other relevant laws and regulations. In particular, the independent directors of a listed company must provide an independent opinion on any important matters coming before the board of directors or the shareholders' meeting, including such things as the nomination appointment or replacement of any director or member of senior management, remuneration of directors or senior management and major related-party transactions and major financial transactions.

In addition, with the approval of at least one-half of all the independent directors, any independent director may independently engage the services of an external auditing or consulting organization, propose the appointment or removal of an accounting firm engaged by the company, propose the holding of an interim shareholders meeting and/or solicit proxies before the holding of a shareholders' meeting. Finally, and importantly, listed companies must provide all necessary assistance and support, including financial assistance, for independent directors to perform all their functions and duties properly and effectively.[63]

One major shortcoming of the independent director system in China is the lack of qualified manpower available to fill board and management positions. In more developed markets, directors are more likely to be brought in on the basis of their professional qualifications and experience. In China, however:

> Most corporate managers still aspire to a civil service rank and are concerned about how their superiors in the political and administrative hierarchy assess their performance. This assessment may be quite arbitrary or subjective and be based on such indicators as profits, political correctness and the discharge of social obligations. Furthermore, local governments may have incentives that are not aligned with the plans of companies that operate on a national or international scale.[64]

Recent corporate scandals in America and elsewhere show that even highly-qualified and experienced directors do not always fulfil their duties or act honestly, but the lack of managerial expertise in China creates equally serious problems. A number of Chinese enterprises are solving the lack of local qualified personnel by turning elsewhere, and paying high salaries for top talent from other markets,[65] but it will take many years before China can provide the kind of home-grown talent it now needs.[66] A recent report of the IFF Equity Advisory Group also notes that, owing to the non-merit-based promotion system, state-controlled companies fail to attract quality managers at the senior-most level, while lack of worthwhile incentives ensures that the best business school graduates nearly always prefer joining a multinational corporation or setting up their own business to joining an SOE. The report recommends that the government needs to put more emphasis on corporate governance 'capacity building' by introducing training programmes for managers, senior executives and directors.[67]

In line with this recommendation, Article 5 of the Independent Director Guidelines ensures that independent directors and nominees for independent directors must take part in training organized by CSRC and its authorized institutions. And Article II provides that, as well as having all of the ordinary qualifications required for all persons acting as directors of listed companies, persons acting in the position of independent director must also have a basic knowledge of the operation of listed companies and be familiar with the relevant laws and regulations. In addition, all independent directors must have no fewer than five years' work experience in law, economics or other professional area required by his or her performance of the duties of an independent director.

In Hong Kong, the Listing Rules were amended in 2003 to require at least three independent non-executive directors on the board of all Hong Kong-listed companies.[68] In the case of PRC-incorporated listed firms, an additional requirement was imposed that at least two of the independent directors must come from Hong Kong. The Hong Kong Listing Rules also place particular importance on the position of company secretary, which must be held by a qualified person having knowledge of Hong Kong laws and accounting rules. Thus Lianhua Supermarket, China's largest supermarket, was forced to delay its Hong Kong listing plans when its application for waiver on appointing a mainlander as company secretary was rejected, and it was required to appoint a suitably qualified independent Hong Kong secretary instead. Lianhua was also required to ensure at least two independent Hong Kong directors on its board.[69]

At present, 'board secretaries' in mainland China are expected to concern themselves primarily with providing secretarial support to, and 'serving' the board of, directors and its members. In contrast, company secretaries in more developed markets have a much broader role in the capacity of secretary for the entire company, not just its board. The title 'board secretary', rather than 'company secretary' as in Hong Kong, or 'corporate secretary' as in North America, also serves to imply a lesser status, and to downgrade the overall importance of the role they perform.[70] The Hong Kong Institute of Company Secretaries (HKICS) has argued that there is a need to enhance the role and status of board secretaries in mainland firms, and has begun providing assistance to their mainland counterparts, including the introduction of professional training courses for H-share board secretaries and senior management. Most recently, a new Association of Board Secretaries of Listed Companies was established in Shanghai, but, as the Hong Kong Institute of Company Secretaries has pointed out, the new Shanghai association was established under the direction and supervision of, and remains dependent upon, the securities authorities in Shanghai. In sharp contrast, the Institute of Company Secretaries in Hong Kong operates as an independent non-profit professional organization, and is neither controlled by, nor financially dependent on, the Hong Kong government authorities.[71]

Most H-share companies, including all of the nine case-study firms examined in Chapter 5, have now amended their articles of association to comply with the minimum compulsory requirements of China's Corporate Governance Guidelines and the Independent Director Guidelines. Recent amendments to individual company articles have also ensured a high degree of ostensible compliance with the amended HKEx Listing Rules, including the Code of Best Practice in Appendix 14 of the Listing Rules.[72]

One reason for such a high level of compliance is that, not only is the Code relatively easy to comply with, but non-compliant companies are expressly required by paragraph 34 of Appendix 16 to explain their non-compliance in the relevant Annual Report.

Mainland-listed firms, however, have been more reluctant to comply. In early 2004, the CSRC revealed that around 36 per cent of mainland-listed firms missed the June 2003 deadline to fill at least a third of their board positions with independent directors. Moreover, some firms with independent directors had withheld negative information from them – in some cases even refusing to invite them to board meetings.[73] Other committee-related reforms, such as the introduction of Audit Committees and other independent board Committees also remain rare amongst mainland listed Chinese companies, but are much more common amongst their foreign-listed counterparts.

D Introducing a Committee System on the Boards of Listed Chinese Companies

All listed companies are required by the *Independent Director Guidelines* to ensure that any subordinate committee established on the board of directors in accordance with the 2002 *Corporate Governance Guidelines* must have independent directors making up at least one-half of its membership. The *Corporate Governance Guidelines* establish recommended, but not mandatory, guidelines for the establishment of a number of subordinate committees on the boards of all listed enterprises, such as a nomination committee, a remuneration committee and/or an auditing committee.

Article 14 of the *Code of Best Practice* contained in Appendix 14 of the Hong Kong Listing Rules provides that listed company boards should establish audit committees to supervise the company's financial reporting processes and internal financial controls. The committee should be appointed from amongst the non-executive directors and a majority of the non-executive directors should be independent. Article 14 then refers its readers to the 'Guide for the Formation of An Audit Committee', published by the Hong Kong Society of Accountants in December 1997, for further guidance on the establishment of audit committees. More recently, the establishment of an audit committee has been turned from a 'best practice' recommendation into a requirement, now contained in Rule 3.21 of the Hong Kong *Listing Rules*.

Most Hong Kong listed companies, including most H-share companies, have now established audit committees. Other committees, such as nomination and remuneration committees, have been introduced more slowly, but they are appearing. The Tsingtao Brewery board of directors, for example, established three special committees in 2001: a nomination committee, an audit committee and a remuneration committee.[74] By the end of 2002, these committees had been restructured to form a strategy and investment committee, an audit and finance committee and a Human Resource and Corporate Governance Committee. As at the end of 2002, all but the strategy and investment committee were chaired by an independent director, and had a membership consisting of a majority of independent directors.[75] As shown in the tables provided in Appendix 1, all of the nine companies examined as case studies in this book had established audit committees by the end of 2005, though not all had established nomination or remuneration committees.

In regard to remuneration committees, these may prove to be an important part of a wider process of introducing incentive mechanisms (currently noticeably lacking in most listed Chinese firms) that tie a management team's performance to its compensation.[76] For example, the aim of Tsingtao's Remuneration Committee, according to the company, is to 'give top management staff an incentive payment, or impose a penalty, according to an evaluation of that staff-member's "annual achievement" for the year'.[77] The range of incentive mechanisms available to remuneration committees has recently expanded under the 2006 *Securities Law* which, for the first time, now permits the issuance of stock options to directors of listed Chinese firms. The *Administrative Measures on Stock Incentives in Listed Companies*, published in 2006, provide more detailed implementation rules for listed companies when adopting stock options and other stock incentive plans. The *Measures* require that a stock option plan be drafted by the remuneration/appraisal committee of the firm, which may retain an independent financial consultant to provide opinions on the draft plan. Independent directors' opinions and a legal opinion are also required. The draft plan can then be approved by the board of directors and then filed with the CSRC, which has 20 working days to raise any objection to the plan. If there is no objection by the CSRC, the draft plan can then be referred to the shareholders' general meeting for its approval.

While stock options, which hold out the promise of substantial wealth if the stock price rises above the exercise price of the options, are often seen as an important tool for aligning manager and shareholder interests, they can also act perversely. This is because share options give managers an incentive to maintain an appearance of corporate success, at least in the short term. They have an incentive to undertake corporate initiatives whenever they think the market will respond to them, even if they themselves are doubtful of the longer-term value of these initiatives. Managers holding incentive options also have an unusual incentive to substitute share repurchases for a portion of the dividend payout, since the direct effect of such a substitution is to increase the value of the managers' options.[78]

The future will no doubt provide opportunities for examining the longer-term effect of permitting the use of stock options as management incentives in the context of the Chinese listed firm. Here it suffices to note the potential for using such incentives to attract better-quality talent into SOE management, while at the same time recognizing that their use may not always operate in an entirely predictable or desirable manner.[79]

E Improving the Role and Status of Supervisory Committees in Listed Chinese Firms

As mentioned above, China's board governance structure is designed loosely on Germany's two-tier board structure. Article 118 of the new *Company Law* ensures that every listed company must have a supervisory board of not fewer that three members. Newly-enhanced powers outlined in articles 54 and 55 of the *Company Law* now complement the provisions in the Mandatory Articles which bestow on the supervisory board powers, inter alia, to

- examine the company's financial records and affairs;
- investigate at the company's expense and with the assistance as deemed necessary of professional advisers an investigation into any irregularities discovered in the company's operations
- attend meetings of the board of directors as non-voting attendees and raise questions and make suggestions about matters arising from board resolutions and otherwise supervise the directors and senior officers in the performance of their company duties;
- propose the dismissal of directors or senior officers who violate laws or administrative regulations or breach the company's articles of association or shareholders' resolutions and/or require a director or senior officer who commits an act detrimental to the interests of the company to rectify that act and/or institute a derivative action against a director or senior officer who commits such violations; and
- propose the holding of an extraordinary shareholders' meeting and, if the board of directors fails to convene such a shareholders' meeting, to convene and preside over such a meeting and submit motions to any shareholders' meeting.[80]

Article 118 also ensures another important role for the supervisory board: acting as a conduit of communication between senior management and the workers of a company. At least one-third of the supervisory board must comprise workers' representatives who must be democratically elected by the staff and workers of the company. Workers' representatives can also be included on the board of directors of a company, although none of the nine companies examined as case studies here appear to have made any express provision in their articles of association for such representation to occur.

According to a 2006 report by the the IFF Equity Advisory Group, while recent reforms have served to clarify and enhance the role and powers of supervisors and the supervisory committee, a number of significant shortcomings still remain. Important differences between the German and the Chinese model render the Chinese supervisory board ineffective, in that it is unable to perform a supervisory role equivalent to its German counterpart. The supervisory board in China is much smaller than the supervisory board in Germany, and much weaker in its functions and powers. In particular, the supervisory board in most listed companies typically has almost no decisive power to stop or correct any actions of directors or senior officers. Nearly always, the supervisory board can only 'investigate' a suspected irregularity which can then be reported to the shareholders' general meeting, which may itself, however, be controlled by one or two majority shareholders.[81]

There is also the problem of the lack of independence of individual supervisors and thus of the Supervisory Board as a whole. Although the Independent Director Guidelines ensure that independent directors now exist on the boards of all listed Chinese companies, no similar requirement exists in relation to the Supervisory Board. The only guarantee of a supervisor's independence lies in the rule that a supervisor cannot concurrently hold a position as director, manager or chief financial officer of the company in which he is a supervisor.[82] But directors or senior personnel of one company can, it would appear, hold a position as supervisor on the supervisory committee of any other enterprise, including any related enterprise.

The result of these differences between the Chinese system and the German means that, in many respects, the supervisory board in a typical Chinese company is only symbolic, and mostly does little more than rubber-stamp decisions taken by the board of directors as the main decision making authority. As the EAG Task Force Report notes,

> This duplication and overlap of functions creates redundancy in the corporate governance structure. Further, it dilutes the authority of the board of directors and increases administrative costs for companies. . . . Chinese current board structure, while giving the illusion of a two-tier board structure, in practice is more like a muddled one-tier (Anglo-Saxon) board.[83]

The Task Force therefore recommended that future reform should be aimed at 'Rationalising the board governance structure by eliminating redundancies caused by the quasi two-tier structure.'[84] The Report leaves open whether this should be done by eliminating the supervisory board in Chinese companies altogether, or by reforming the size, powers and functions of the supervisory board to make it more akin to the German model.

What the Task Force fails to recognize is the importance and potential of the supervisory committee as an avenue for introducing worker representation into the management structure of listed Chinese firms. Much has been written about the poor state of employment conditions and workers' rights in the modern Chinese context. The forces of globalization and marketization in particular have forced those former SOEs which have survived to cut staff numbers significantly in the name of efficiency and profitability. Appendix 1 indicates the dramatic nature of staff cuts over the period since 1993. All of the nine case study companies have reduced staff numbers significantly in the past 10 years, in the case of Guangzhou Shipyard by as much as one-third.[85] All nine firms also carry a significant burden of pension support for former employees. If these nine firms are typical of listed former SOEs, and there is no reason to believe they are not, it may well be that the supervisory committee has performed and/or could perform a valuable function in protecting workers' rights and the rights of laid-off workers (including pension entitlements), despite the obvious fact that worker representation has failed to prevent significant staff cuts.

F The Role of the Party Committee in Chinese Corporate Governance

The 'five separations' policy has served to close off many avenues, such as through the control of corporate assets, which previously enabled the State to influence corporate decision making. Ostensibly at least, the only avenue through which the State can still exercise direct internal influence, over corporate strategy is through its role as majority shareholder, where that still exists. Majority shareholder status not only enables the State to determine, or at least influence, the agenda and outcomes of shareholder meetings, but also to control to a significant degree the nomination and election of senior company management. The Government's recently announced determination to release State-held shares onto the share market for purchase by non-state shareholders (see below, at Part C, p. 122) would seem to suggest that the State's ability to make use of its majority shareholder status to influence corporate strategy is going to decline significantly in the very near future. There is, however, one important feature of the Chinese corporation that is likely to preserve the State's presence and influence even in those firms where the State has disappeared, or almost disappeared, as shareholder/owner: the Party Committee of the Company.

Article 19 of the 2006 *Company Law* provides:

> For the establishment of an organization of the Communist Party of China and the carrying out of Party activities in a company in accordance with the charter of the Communist Party of China, a company shall provide the necessary conditions for the activities of the party organization.

What is even more significant than the mere presence of an obligatory 'party organization' (which always takes the form of the Party Committee) within the individual corporation is the presence of senior Party Committee office-holders in the senior management of the firm. For example, in 2005, each of the nine companies examined in Chapter 4 has at least two, and in one case seven, Party Committee office-holders on the board of directors of the firm. Party Committee office-holders are also present on the Supervisory Committee and in senior company management.

As Chao Xi has pointed out, article 19 not only provides solid justification for the Party Committee to exist and operate in the Chinese company, it also expressly refers to 'the Charter of the Communist Party of China' and mandates that the Party Committee of the company must operate according to its terms. According to Chao Xi, this may in effect give the Party's Constitution implicit statutory authority to supplement, or even supplant, the *Company Law* in its application to the Party Committee of the company. This interpretation seems more plausible if one examines the Party's Constitution; article 32 of which provides that 'The Party's grass-roots organisation' (ie. the Party Committee):

> acts as the political nucleus and works for the operation of the enterprise. [It] guarantees and supervises the implementation of the principles and policies of the Party and the state in its own enterprise and backs the shareholders' general meeting, the board of directors, the supervisory board and the manager (factory director) in the exercise of their functions and powers according to law. [It] relies wholeheartedly on the workers, supports the work of the workers' congress and *participates in the decision making of major matters in the enterprise*. (Emphasis added)

A CPC Central Committee Circular issued in 1997, dealing with companies transformed from SOEs, appears to confirm that the Party Committee may lawfully participate in corporate governance in accordance with Party directives. The circular provides a broad definition of the 'major matters in the enterprise' referred to in article 32 of the Party Constitution to include 'all matters discussed and decided by the shareholders' general meeting and the board of directors'. The Circular also appears to impose an obligation on the board of directors to take the views of the Party Committee into account in all decision making, as well as bestowing power on the Party Committee to require the board of directors to 'rectify' any decisions found to contradict party policies, guidelines and laws.

Equally significant is the way in which the 1997 Communist Party Circular 'encourages' Party cadres to become directly involved in the day-to-day management of the company, and expressly permits the Party Secretary to serve concurrently as the chairman of the board of directors. Other members of the Party Committee are also expressly encouraged to become members of the board of directors, the supervisory committee and senior management of newly corporatized SOEs 'in accordance with law'. Thus, for example, in June 2005, both the Chairman of the Board and Chairman of the Supervisory Committee of Shanghai Petro held senior positions in the firm's Communist Party Committee.[86] Likewise, in 2003 both the Chairman of the Board and Chairman of the Supervisory Committee of Dongfang Electrical also held senior positions in the parent firm's Party Committee.[87]

As Chao Xi has noted, the 1997 Circular demonstrates the Party's desire to take a leading role in the management of corporatized SOEs by maintaining the Party's ability to participate, directly or indirectly, in corporate governance and decision making.[88] On the one hand, these provisions are useful in describing and confining the imprecise, but in practice extensive, decision-making power of the Party Committee and its role in the functioning of new governance organs. On the other hand, however, they serve to blur the boundaries of decision making of the various governance organs prescribed by the Company Law in a way that becomes especially problematic if and when broader Party aims and policies come into conflict with the best interests of the individual company and its shareholders. Also problematic is the fact that the Party Committee of the company is subject to none of the various legal duties and liabilities that the board or its individual directors are subject to, making the Party Committee a potentially very powerful governance organ with little or no accountability. The fact that the newly revised Company Law of 2006 persists in maintaining the existence of the Party Committee in the Chinese company structure may thus serve to undermine other efforts, such as the share ownership reform, aimed at getting the State out of business management. It may also serve to make much more difficult the 'cultural shift' that, according to the IIF Equity Advisory Group, is needed within Chinese companies if the 'new' corporate governance structure is to be successfully adopted.[89]

III IMPROVING THE QUALITY OF FINANCIAL DISCLOSURE: NEW ACCOUNTING STANDARDS

Proper accounting regulations and standards, together with requirements for regular and accurate reporting by listed companies, are an important means of protecting the rights of shareholders and creditors, as well as promoting better financial management practices in listed firms. A body of scholarly analysis now exists dealing with the rapid development of Chinese accounting standards and practices since 1978.[90] What the evidence now suggests is that there has been a great deal of convergence between the formal standards applicable to corporate accounting and disclosure in China and internationally-accepted accounting principles. A significant gap still remains, however, between theory and practice when it comes to the actual realization of accounting and disclosure principles by individual listed Chinese companies.

A A Significant Degree of Formal Convergence

The current mainland Chinese accounting system applicable to all listed Chinese companies has a three-level structure. First, there are the basic rules and principles to be followed in the keeping of accounts as set out in legislation, including the *Securities Law* and the *Accounting Law*. This legislation forms the basis for the *Accounting Regulations for Joint Stock Limited Enterprises* (1998 version), together with the *Chart of Accounts and Accounting Statements for Joint Stock Limited Enterprises* also issued in 1992, and amended in 1998.[91] At the third level, since 1993, the Ministry of Finance has obtained funding from the World Bank to develop a series of accounting standards aimed at harmonising Chinese with international reporting practices. The first formal accounting standard was issued by the MoF in 1997 and, by the end of 2003, 16 detailed standards had been issued, broadly in line with International Financial Reporting Standards. For enterprises listed overseas, a number of additional rules and notices issued by the MoF are aimed at bringing reporting requirements even further into line with international practice.[92]

Most recently, on 15 February 2006, the MoF formally issued 38 specific Basic Accounting Standards for Business Enterprises (ASBEs) that became effective on 1 January 2007 and now apply to all listed Chinese companies. The new ASBE standards will bring Chinese accounting practices largely in line with International Financial Reporting Standards, with some exceptions.[93]

For companies with shares listed both in the PRC and overseas, PRC law requires that if the requirements of the overseas stock exchange differ from

PRC regulations, the more rigorous regulations should be followed. In the case of H-share companies, the legal and accounting requirements of both mainland and Hong Kong laws must be complied with, and two sets of accounts must be prepared, in both the original listing prospectus, and in all annual and interim reports. One set of accounts must be prepared in accordance with PRC GAAP, while the second set of accounts must comply with generally accepted Hong Kong accounting standards (Hong Kong GAAP or International Accounting Standards).

Within Hong Kong, the disclosure of financial information in the listing documents, annual reports and other documents issued by listed corporations is governed by three main sources. First, there is the Hong Kong *Companies Ordinance* (the Companies Ordinance) which contains a number of important disclosure provisions. The Schedules to the Ordinance in particular spell out detailed requirements in relation to matters to be specified in prospectuses (Third Schedule), the form and content of annual returns (Fifth Schedule) and the keeping of accounts (Tenth Schedule).

The second important source of guidance for Hong Kong-listed firms on reporting and disclosure obligations are the Listing Rules. Chapter 4 of the Listing Rules sets out the basic principles and requirements for accountants' reports prepared for inclusion in company listing documents and circulars.[94] In addition, Chapters 14 and 14A provide further detailed requirements in regard to 'Notifiable Transactions', details of which must be disclosed by the company through public announcements and circulars, while Appendix 16 sets out the minimum financial information that listed issuers must include in preliminary announcements of results, interim reports, annual reports, listing documents and circulars. More specific requirements regarding disclosures in company annual reports are stipulated in Appendices 7a, 7b and 7i of the Listing Rules (ie. The Listing Agreement). There are certain minor deviations in the requirements for disclosure in annual reports depending on the place of incorporation of issuers. Appendices 7a, 7b and 7i are applicable to issuers incorporated in Hong Kong, outside Hong Kong and in the Mainland, respectively. The differences are mainly related to the additional disclosure requirements applied to issuers incorporated outside Hong Kong, in order to maintain the same level of disclosure as if they were incorporated in Hong Kong.

Finally, there are the Statements of Standard Accounting Practices (the SSAP) issued by the Hong Kong Institute of Certified Public Accountants (HKICPA). In 1993, the HKICPA decided that International Accounting Standards (IAS) would serve as the basis for the development of all new standards. Prior to 1993, HKICPA standards were based largely on those from the UK. Since 1993, firms can satisfy HKEx listing requirements by preparing financial statements that comply with either International or existing HKEx accounting standards. It is worth noting that, due to the legal requirements imposed by its New York listed presence, Shanghai Petro is the only one of the nine H-share companies examined in Chapter 5 to prepare accounts in accordance with the IAS. All the other eight prepare their second set of accounts in accordance with the Hong Kong GAAP. At the time of writing, the Hong Kong Institute of Certified Public Accountants (HKICPA) has issued a number of new and revised Hong Kong Financial Reporting Standards and Hong Kong Accounting Standards which are effective for accounting periods beginning on or after 1 January 2005. Along with their Hong Kong listed counterparts, the nine companies focused on here are in the process of assessing the impact of, and beginning to implement, these new standards.

Right from the birth of the H-share market, investors and professional intermediaries have been regularly confronted by accounting difficulties and uncertainties. Especially in the early years, there was a lack of precedent for dealing with accounting questions unique to the State-owned Chinese firm. In addition, continued regulatory reform in both Hong Kong and the mainland has occasionally brought about some unintended consequences.[95] Regional differences in taxation treatment in China have sometimes served to compound such uncertainties, as well as reflecting tensions and inconsistencies between regional and central taxation practices.[96]

B The Need for Ongoing Communication and Regular Reporting Requirements

Investors and analysts rely on being able to compare the performance of different companies over the same period of time, and also need to be able to compare the performance of a single company over separate periods of time. Such comparisons require consistent accounting treatment of similar variables both across companies and across different accounting periods in respect of the same company. But in the context of a rapidly developing economy and legal system where reforms are continually being made, such consistency has been extremely difficult, if not impossible, to achieve.

By the time that China's state-owned enterprises listed in Hong Kong released their first annual reports, the communication problems between company management, foreign investors, financial analysts and reporters had already become evident. While Shanghai Petrochemical and Guangzhou Shipyard were praised for their efforts in attempting to clear up uncertainties and maintain positive relations with investors, smaller-scale Kunming Machine Tool and Beiren Printing Machinery were criticized for having released hardly any news of corporate development since their listing.[97] Analysts noted the need for H-share enterprises to ensure more regular information disclosures through announcements, reports or analysis, especially for the benefit of foreign shareholders and creditors.[98]

An initial issue here is the regularity of company reporting of income levels and business earnings.[99] The value of requiring listed companies to publish quarterly as well as half-yearly reports has been questioned by some who argue that the extra compliance costs involved generally outweigh any benefits gained. This is not, however, the view reflected in the rules of most modern markets. Indeed, as at the end of 2005, Hong Kong remains the last substantial market in Asia not to require its main-board listed companies to report quarterly, and gives them one of the longest periods in the world to report their results: a full four months after the year end,[100] or three months for the half-year results.[101] This compares with the mainland situation where, in January 2002, partly in response to a number of high-profile cases of securities fraud involving false and misleading reporting practices, the CSRC promulgated new rules requiring *all* listed companies to produce quarterly reports as well as annual and interim reports.[102] In other words, PRC-listed companies are subject to more frequent reporting requirements than are their Hong Kong-listed counterparts.[103]

In light of the time periods between regular (half-yearly) reports, the Hong Kong Rules governing the ongoing disclosure obligations of listed firms become particularly important. In addition to receiving regular corporate reports in a consolidated form, investors and analysts need to be appraised of price-sensitive developments affecting the firm immediately they occur. Hence the requirements under the HK Listing Rules for company announcements to be issued in respect of price-sensitive information and notifiable transactions.

1 On-going disclosure requirements: price-sensitive information

The Hong Kong Main Board Listing Rules require issuers to make timely public disclosure of price-sensitive information. Under paragraph 2 of Appendix 7 of the Main Board Rules (the 'Listing Agreement'), an issuer must keep the exchange, members of the issuer and other holders of its listed securities informed, as soon as reasonably practicable, of any information relating to the group (including information on any major new developments in the group's sphere of activity that are not public knowledge) that (i) is necessary to enable them and the public to appraise the position of the group; (ii) is necessary to avoid the establishment of a false market in its securities; and (iii) might be reasonably expected materially to affect market activity in, and the price of, its securities.

To help listed companies and their directors determine whether information is material and should properly be disclosed to the public, the Hong Kong Stock Exchange published a comprehensive *Guide on Disclosure of*

Price Sensitive Information in 2002. This includes guidance on particular situations and issues as well as explaining the principles and criteria used by the Exchange in assessing whether a particular company has complied with its listing rule obligations in relation to price-sensitive information. A second Guide on disclosure obligations for companies in different sectors emphasizes that whether or not information is price-sensitive and needs to be disclosed very much depends on the individual circumstances of the firm. Individual chapters of the Guide thus provide comprehensive sector-by-sector guidance on information which should be disclosed by listed companies operating, inter alia, in the Iron and Steel Industry (Chapter 8), the Petrochemical Industry (Chapter 9) and the Industrials sector (Chapter 16). The mainland securities markets provide similar guidance in the form of detailed regulations that, for example, provide a list of events that fall under the definition of 'significant event'. The mainland regulations also spell out the explanation that is required when significant differences exist between actual operation results and profit forecasts.[104]

2 On-going disclosure requirements: connected transactions and other notifiable transactions

Listed companies are required under Chapter 14 of the Hong Kong *Listing Rules* to disclose publicly details of any major transaction, very substantial transaction or other disclosable transaction, as defined in Chapter 14 of the *Listing Rules*. Similar rules are contained in Article 67 of the mainland *Securities Law* (2006), which requires listed companies to issue an 'ad hoc' report whenever there occurs 'a major event that could have a relatively large effect on the trading price of a company's shares and investors are not yet aware thereof'.[105]

The term 'disclosable transaction' includes both 'share transactions' and 'Connected transactions'. A 'connected transaction' is any transaction between a listed company or any of its subsidiaries and a connected person, or an acquisition or realization by a listed company or any of its subsidiaries of an interest in a company, a substantial shareholder of which is, or is proposed to be, a director, chief executive or controlling shareholder of the listed company or any of its subsidiaries or an associate of such director, chief executive or controlling shareholder of the listed company or its subsidiaries.

Regulatory oversight of transfers of valuable assets between connected parties has also been strengthened on the mainland. In late August 2003, the CSRC and the State-owned Assets Supervision and Administration Commission (established in March 2003) of the State Council issued a new Circular on *Several Issues Concerning the Regulation of Cash Flows Between Listed Companies and Their Affiliates and Security Provided to*

Outside Parties by Listed Companies.[106] In relation to cash flows between listed companies and their controlling shareholder and other affiliates, the Circular emphasizes that listed companies must not, directly or indirectly, provide funds to a controlling shareholder (or other affiliate) by inter alia:

- lending funds to the controlling shareholder/affiliate;
- providing entrusted loans to an affiliate through a bank or non-banking financial institution;
- entrusting a controlling shareholder or another affiliate to carry out investment activities; or
- repaying debts on behalf of a controlling shareholder or another affiliate.

The Circular required all listed companies to conduct an internal investigation into, and submit reports on, the status of cash flows and appropriations of funds between the listed company and its controlling shareholder and other affiliates. A report on the results of the investigation was required to be submitted to the CSRC by the end of September 2003, and a copy of that report included as a significant item in the listed company's next Annual Report. Certified accountants acting as auditors for listed companies must in future issue a special explanation whenever the company's funds are appropriated by the controlling shareholder or other affiliate of the listed company in one of the ways listed above, and a company announcement must be issued in respect of the same.

The introduction of ASBE 36 on 1 January 2007 has also served to expand the definition of 'related party' for the purpose of reporting obligations. ASBE 36 now provides that, if two parties are subject to joint control or significant influence from the same party, they are regarded as related parties. Previous Chinese GAAP did not consider them as related parties.[107] The new ABSE 36 also provides that a statement in a company report that related party transactions were conducted at fair value is only allowed if the reporting enterprise is able to provide supporting evidence.

C Voluntary Disclosure by State-owned Enterprises Listed on the Stock Exchange of Hong Kong

The compliance record of H-share companies in respect of compulsory ongoing disclosure obligations appears at least as good as that of other companies listed on the Hong Kong exchange. Indeed, as Ferguson, Lam and Lee suggest, it may even be better than average, at least as far as voluntary disclosure of market-relevant information is concerned.[108] Ferguson et al. examined the proposition that, in order to compensate for this perceived greater uncertainty in the eyes of investors, H-share firms are likely voluntarily to disclose additional financial and strategic information as a means of enhancing corporate image and improving the marketability of their shares. The authors hypothesized that, for H-share firms, the benefits of disclosing additional (voluntary) financial and strategic information (enhanced corporate image, improved marketability of shares and lower capital costs) should outweigh the costs of such disclosure (increased exposure to competitive and political costs via disclosure of proprietary information as well as the cost of preparing and disseminating such information). Consistent with these predictions, they find the following:

- H-share firms voluntarily disclose significantly more financial and strategic information than other firms listed on the SEHK. H-share firms thus appear sensitive to the information demands of competitive international capital markets;
- Red-chip firms disclose significantly less information than H-share firms, but do not differ from local SEHK firms in the level of overall disclosure; and
- State-ownership alone does not appear to drive disclosure policies. H-share firms disclose significantly more information than Red-Chip firms despite the fact that both are majority-owned by the state.

What Ferguson, Lam and Lee also find, however, is that 'H-share firms voluntarily disclose significantly less information on the PRC exchanges than on the SEHK. Although the presence of substantially higher costs and lower benefits of disclosure could explain these differences, their magnitude suggests that disclosure by H-share firms on the SEHK may also reflect the effects of state-encouraged disclosure policies.'[109] In any event, the authors' findings in relation to the greater levels of disclosure provided by H-share companies appear to confirm observations made by other commentators. In May 1994, for example, analyst Nick Moakes of SG Warburg, observed that 'Far from being impenetrable, the results published by the H-share companies listed to date are more revealing than those of Hong Kong counterparts'.[110] What this points to is the important influence of market discipline and market culture in the maintenance of corporate disclosure and reporting standards.

D The Role of the State, the Market and the Accounting Community in Maintaining the Integrity of Corporate Disclosure

Major accounting oddities and corporate governance scandals have recently emerged in developed markets like America (Enron), Australia (HIH) and

Hong Kong. The mainland Chinese markets, however, seem to have had far more than their fair share. When the State Auditing Administration checked 1290 state-owned enterprises in 2001, it found that 68 per cent, or around 877, had misstated their financials.[111] Four years later, the Shanghai Securities News reported that about 107 out of more than 1000 listed firms had been involved in 177 corruption cases in 2005, from accusations of falsifying earnings to crimes by executives, up from 56 firms and 111 cases in 2004.[112] Nor has exposure to the discipline of the Hong Kong market (via an H-share listing) rendered mainland firms immune from accounting and reporting irregularities. In August 2002, for example, the CSRC announced that it had identified six areas of improper accounting practices at Tianjin Capital Environmental Protection.[113] The CSRC also pointed out that the chairwoman and general manager of Tianjin Capital, Ma Baiyu, was also vice-chairwoman of the parent company.[114]

The response by the Chinese authorities to continued flouting of the rules was to launch a sweeping crackdown on market corruption in 2001,[115] and to increase the powers of the State Assets Commission to monitor the management of state assets by individuals and enterprises.[116] Penalties for violations of information disclosure and other requirements of the exchange listing rules have been significantly increased.[117] In addition to criminal law provisions covering counterfeit, fraud, embezzlement etc., a number of provisions of the PRC *Accounting Law* (Revised) 2000[118] set out civil penalties for breach of the standards and practices set out in that law. Fines which can be imposed under the *Accounting Law* for non-criminal breaches of its provisions range up to 50 000 RMB for individuals and 100 000 RMB for units.

More recently, Article 69 of the new *Securities Law*[119] has strengthened the civil liabilities of listed companies, their directors, supervisors, managers, underwriters and sponsors for market misrepresentation,[120] while article 193 of the amended Law now imposes hefty new penalties for failure to comply with reporting and disclosure obligations. What the studies of market culture by Puxty et al. suggest, however, is that state-imposed rules and sanctions, no matter how stringent in theory, are unlikely to be effective in the absence of a market culture that values integrity in corporate disclosure (a topic which is further discussed in Chapter 6).

IV THE CHANGING OWNERSHIP STRUCTURE OF LISTED CHINESE FIRMS

The state in its various guises is currently the dominant shareholder in nearly all listed Chinese firms, including H-share firms.[121] This dominant

State presence in the market has gradually been reduced over recent years, but remains large enough to seriously compromise the independence of company management. Moreover, many of the state-controlled parent entities of listed firms are in financial trouble, with heavy debt burdens. This is because when an SOE is restructured and obtains listing for the productive, commercial parts of its organisation, it is typically the parent company that retains control over the loss-making social welfare functions of the original SOE. As controlling shareholder, the parent SOE therefore has a strong incentive to nominate directors and supervisors willing to approve various forms of co-operation and assistance between parent and listed subsidiary. The presence of significant business and financial links between parent and listed subsidiary thus remains a prevalent feature of Chinese corporate life. In many cases, for example, the listed company depends on the parent company and its other controlled entities to distribute products or supply raw materials. Senior managers often hold positions in both the listed and unlisted parts of the group. As recognised by CSRC spokesmen, large loans from the listed company to the parent organisation are also common.[122] In other cases, listed companies have purchased mainland-based assets, often of dubious value, from parent organizations.[123] As the World Bank has noted, this type of interdependence between listed companies and their parent firms creates fertile ground for conflicts of interest to arise.[124]

The problem is further compounded by the fact that most non-State shareholders in China are individual Chinese citizens who have neither the experience nor the motivation necessary to regularly attend shareholders' meetings or monitor the performance of company management. So far as foreign holders of H-shares are concerned, geographical distance and lack of familiarity with the on-ground operations of Chinese firms also mean that few are able to scrutinize the decisions and actions of management with any degree of effectiveness. And this remains the case despite the presence of international financial institutions, multinational corporations and professional personnel (lawyers, accountants, market researchers and investment advisers) in Hong Kong able to make credible market intelligence readily available to shareholders. Corporate governance rules and disclosure standards can do little to alleviate the problems which arise under the existing ownership structure of most Chinese firms. The high degree of (state) ownership concentration, and the non-tradability of such a large proportion of the shares issued by Chinese firms, imply a low contestability of control[125] and hence lack of exposure to the market discipline imposed by the presence of takeover threats in more 'efficient' markets such as the US and UK.

Three areas of reform, each of which is serving to alter the ownership structure of listed Chinese firms, have, however, recently begun to take effect. These are (i) reforms which facilitate the greater presence of institutional shareholders; (ii) reforms which facilitate the introduction of significant foreign equity-partners into listed firms and (iii) reforms aimed at turning non-tradable state-owned shares into freely transferable equity.

A Institutional Investors in the Chinese Market

The role of both local and foreign institutional investors as shareholders with stakes in listed Chinese firms has also been given a major boost by a number of recent reforms. A number of new laws have helped to promote the growth of local institutional investors as important stakeholders in corporate equity ownership. The *Interim Measures on the Administration of Securities Investment Funds* was promulgated in October 1997, and the first five contractual closed-end funds were launched in 1998. The first contractual open-end fund was launched in 2001 and the number of funds has grown since then. By the end of 1993, there were 34 fund management companies (including eight Sino-foreign joint ventures) managing 54 closed-end and 56 open-end securities investment funds. As China's domestic and foreign-invested funds, including funds with significant growth potential such as the 124.1 billion yuan National Social Security Fund, are allowed into the market, they are likely to strengthen the presence of an independent, minority shareholder voice in corporate decision making.[126]

Insurance companies and banking institutions are other possible sources of institutional investment in listed Chinese companies. As yet, however, their role remains limited. The model adopted for China's financial sector when the economy began to move from state-run socialism to a marketized economy was borrowed from America, or more accurately, from the American model prior to the Glass–Steagall reforms of the early 1990s. Embedded in this model is the notion that the banking and securities markets should be kept separate. The result was fragmentation of China's financial services sector into separate industries, each with different roles and governed by different regulatory systems.[127] This system serves to promote stability and protect the interests of small depositors, in particular, by isolating insurance and banking institutions from exposure to the risks of securities market investment and speculation. The degree of separation required between banks and non-banking financial institutions was spelt out legally at the national level by the Commercial Bank Law of 1995. Under this law, dealing in stocks is expressly forbidden for all Chinese banks. Also forbidden is investing in trusts and investment businesses or real estate, or indirectly investing in non-bank financial institutions.[128]

A key issue for China now is the extent to which banking institutions should be allowed to participate directly, or through their subsidiaries, in securities markets. The desire to protect the traditional deposit-taking functions of banks from potential losses in the course of securities activities is understandable.[129] On the other hand, the fact that commercial banks are prohibited from investing in non-banking financial institutions means that they cannot supplement their creditor rights with ownership stakes in client firms. Holding shareholder stakes in debtor firms is one way for banks to exercise a greater restraining influence over the spending practices of client corporations. In addition, when commercial banks are permitted to engage in providing securities management advice, this can lead to significant proxy voting by such banks.[130]

After the 1995 *Commercial Banking Law* came into effect in July 1995, some of the pre-existing ties that existed between banking and non-banking financial institutions remained, and were not finally severed until after the Asian financial crisis, when the PBOC issued a regulation expressly discouraging commercial bank investments in non-bank financial institutions. The trust companies that had originally been set up by the four State Owned Commercial Banks became the legal predecessors of the Asset Management Companies, set up in 1999 and now owned by Treasury, and their securities operations were spun off and merged into new entities independent of their previous bank owners. The four Asset Management Companies were established to manage and sell off 1.4 million yuan of bad loans, mostly owed by SOEs, at the four biggest state-owned banks.[131]

In 2001, the People's Bank of China (PBoC) began to relax the strict separation between different sectors of the financial industry. The *Provisional Regulations on Intermediary Businesses of Commercial Banks*,[132] together with an April 2002 PBoC Circular,[133] now provide that, following PBoC approval, banks may engage in a number of intermediary financial services business, including the following:

- payment and settlement-type intermediary services;
- bank card services;
- agency-type intermediary services including securities agency and insurance agency services;
- security/guarantee services (including negotiable instruments and standby letters of credit);
- loan commitments;
- transactional services (including derivatives; swaps and forwards);
- fund custody services (including custody services associated with closed and open-ended securities investment funds and other funds; and
- consultancy and advisory services, including cash management services to assist enterprises in better management of funds.

Although the prohibition on cross-industry investment for Chinese banks remains in place, recent signs are that the strict separation between the banking, securities and insurance sectors of the financial industry is gradually being relaxed even further. The CBRC has indicated its view that qualified commercial banks should be allowed to take limited share ownership stakes in trust and investment companies, and also issue their own fund management companies.[134]

So far as insurance companies are concerned, they were not permitted to invest in securities at all, but were restricted to investments in bank deposits and government and financial bonds. This remained the case until 1999, when the China Insurance Regulatory Commission (CIRC) and the CSRC jointly decided that insurance firms could invest in select corporate bonds (as of April 1999), and in securities investment trusts (as of October 1999).[135] This still meant, however, that China's enormous insurance industry, with accumulated total assets of more than Rmb 1.1 trillion (as at July 2004), and with an ever-growing need for diversified investment channels, was precluded from investing directly in China's stock markets. It was not until late 2004 that this need, and the equally pressing need to find a potential source of long-term funds to promote the healthy growth of the securities markets, finally prompted the Chinese authorities to give the green light for insurance company purchases of ordinary domestically listed shares and other domestic securities. The *Administration of Stock Investments by Insurance Institutional Investors Tentative Procedures* (the Tentative Procedures) were jointly promulgated by the China Insurance Regulatory Commission (CIRC) and the CSRC jointly promulgated on 24 October 2004.[136] Subject to certain restrictions, insurance institutional investors may now directly purchase most renminbi common stock in the primary market or trade it in the secondary market, and can also purchase convertible corporate bonds and other investment products stipulated by the CIRC.[137]

Institutional investors are different from small, individual shareholders, as they have the sophistication and resources to process and utilize the information that is publicly available. They also have the incentive to make use of, and act upon, that information as their investment policies are strictly driven by financial considerations – in the case of stocks, the expectation of share value maximization. Thus, institutional investors are most likely to scrutinize the quality of information flow from companies, and to take part in decision making at the shareholder meeting level. Where possible, they are also most likely to participate actively in corporate control contests. Consequently, the institutionalization of financial assets, especially corporate stocks, increases the role of the market in imposing discipline upon managers, and plays an important role in restricting the ability of (state-controlled) block holders to exercise control.

Finally, it should also be mentioned that, even without access to shareholder rights, creditors such as banks and other financial institutions can influence the governance of listed enterprises through the signals they send to other stakeholders. If such stakeholders perceive the banks as having strong credit analysis skills and the right incentives for making credit decisions, then the award of credit alone can be a powerful signal. In the past, observers viewed loans by SOCBs as a signal of continued government support for an enterprise, but the abolition of the mandatory loan quota system, and the introduction of requirements for all commercial banks (including state-owned commercial banks) to lend strictly according to commercial considerations, served to change completely the environment in which such expectations operated. In addition, the credit ratings industry, beginning to take a stronger foothold, and banks now have much better access to corporate credit-rating information. For example, in some locations PBOC offices have published lists of loan-defaulting companies in the inter-bank computer network. These lists are now forming the basis for a national credit bureau available for banks' reference when extending loans. By the end of 1999, the database already covered borrowers in 301 cities. When a listed defaulter begins to apply for new bank or trade credit, the firm's existing creditors and the financial authorities both have an interest in seeing legal action taken against the defaulting firm. In some cases PBoC branches have acted by prohibiting any new bank lending to listed defaulters.[138]

B The Introduction of Significant Foreign Investor Involvement in Listed SOEs

Foreign institutional investors are also being allowed, even encouraged, to enter the Chinese securities markets as institutional shareholders. On 1 November 2002, the CSRC, Ministry of Finance and the State Economic and Trade Commission (SETC) issued a joint Circular on *Issues Relevant to the Transfer of State-owned Shares and Legal Person Shares in Listed Companies to Foreign Investors* (the Joint Circular).[139] The Joint Circular reversed the 1995 ban on the trading of legal person and state shares to foreign investors, and expressly allows foreign institutional investors to enter the domestic share market through direct portfolio investment, through takeovers and merger and acquisition transactions and through participating in the reorganization of unlisted SOEs.

The Qualified Foreign Institutional Investor (QFII) scheme, which came into effect on 1 December 2002, was designed to allow foreign institutional investors to invest in China's A-share markets.[140] The *Provisional Measures on Administration of Domestic Securities Investments of Qualified Foreign*

Institutional Investors (the 2002 Provisional QFII Measures) established a scheme whereby approved foreign institutional investors (fund managers, insurance companies, securities companies and other asset management companies) could invest a minimum of US$50 million and up to a maximum of US$800 million in Rmb-denominated A shares and convertible bonds listed on China's domestic exchanges.[141] By the end of 2003, 12 foreign institutional investors had been licensed as QFIIs with total investment quota of USD 1.7 billion, and 11 banks (including four overseas banks) were licensed as QFII custodians.[142]

The 2002 Provisional QFII Measures were superseded by *New Measures for the Administration of Securities Investment in China by Qualified Foreign Institutional Investors* (New QFII Rules) which became effective on 1 September 2006.[143] The New QFII Rules are designed to attract long-term investment in China's domestic securities market, and so favour longer-term investors such as foreign fund management companies and insurance companies, as a matter of policy. The qualifying criteria for fund management companies, insurance companies and other categories of long-term institutional investors have been lowered,[144] while the criteria applicable to foreign securities companies and commercial banks have been maintained.[145]

Under the 2002 Provisional QFII Measures, a QFII was required to appoint a PRC custodian and open one Rmb special account and only one securities account with a PRC Clearing House.[146] Proprietary investments of a QFII through its QFII quota had to be commingled in the same account with assets of the QFII's customers and other investors investing through the QFII's quota. The New QFII Rules go some way towards addressing the custody risks involved in such an arrangement,[147] and address the need to segregate assets between the QFII and its customers by allowing each QFII to hold multiple securities sub-accounts with a PRC Clearing House that correspond to respective multiple Rmb accounts.[148] The new QFII Rules also recognize the interests of underlying investors investing through QFIIs, by providing that QFIIs may appoint the actual beneficiary investors to exercise shareholder rights with respect to underlying investments, and that, as nominee for beneficiary investors, a QFII may use its votes in part and may cast its votes in different ways according to the interests of the underlying beneficiary investors.[149]

The 2002 Provisional QFII Measures imposed a rather stringent lock-up period of at least 12 months before repatriation of amounts invested by QFIIs was allowed.[150] The New QFII Rules contain no specific requirements with respect to repatriation, but instead provide that remittance, repatriation and any lock-up period should be as adjusted by SAFE based on the economic and financial situation of the PRC, foreign exchange balance of payments and according to arrangements set by the PBoC. This allows SAFE to adopt a more flexible and pragmatic approach with respect to repatriation arrangements. For example, as at the beginning of 2007, it seems that the lock-up period may be reduced to three months for open-ended investment funds and 'long-term capital' investment bodies (pension funds, insurance funds and mutual funds).[151]

Approved applicants are issued with a 'securities investment licence' (SIL), following which an application can be submitted to SAFE for an investment quota. The 2002 Provisional QFII Measures then required that QFIIs disclose all of their interests in listed companies, taking into account both domestic (A-shares or B-shares) and overseas shares (H-shares) of the same company, as well as interests in convertible bonds and depository certificates. Strict limits on the extent of foreign investment in any single Chinese firm were imposed.[152] These limits have now been revised to refer to individual offshore investors who invest through QFIIs (rather than the combined interests managed by the QFII), as follows:

1. Each underlying offshore investor investing through a QFII may not hold more than 10 per cent of the total outstanding shares in one listed company (but excluding strategic investment by such offshore investor in accordance with the 'Regulations on Strategic Investment in Listed Companies by Offshore Investors'); and
2. All offshore investors may not hold more than 20 per cent of the total outstanding shares in one listed company.[153] Moreover, any proposed investment must not violate China's *Industrial Catalogue for Foreign Investments*, which lists industries closed to foreign investment.[154]

This opening up of the domestic market should help to improve the overall quality of corporate governance in China's listed companies, if only because foreign institutional investors are more likely than small individual shareholders to take an active interest in corporate management decision making.

Outside of the QFII context, other Chinese listed firms are forging strategic partnerships with leading multinational enterprises in the relevant industry area. For example, with the introduction of Anheuser Busch as a strategic partner in 2002–2003, Tsingtao Brewery became the first Chinese listed firm ever to transform itself from a majority state-controlled firm, to a firm with majority foreign ownership. The concept of foreign strategic investor was formally introduced into Chinese law by the *Measures for the Administration of Strategic Investment in Listed Companies by Foreign Investors* (the Strategic Investor Circular) issued on 31 December 2005.[155] The Strategic Investor Circular allows strategic foreign investors to acquire tradable A-shares in listed firms that have reformed their share capital structure under the September 2005 regulations (discussed below). It goes much further than the QFII programme which allowed only a limited number of qualified foreign institutions to purchase tradable A-shares legally. Foreign investors without QFII status could only acquire a stake in a listed company by privately purchasing non-tradable state holdings.[156]

The Strategic Investor Circular subjects foreign investors to much lower entry requirements and fewer investment restrictions than QFIIs. The foreign strategic investor must acquire a minimum of 10 per cent of the shares of the target company, and must comply with the *Foreign Investment Industrial Guidance Catalogue*, as well as ceiling percentages set out in any industry-specific regulations. However, foreign strategic investments can only be made in those few listed companies that have fully implemented share-segregation reform. Moreover, shares acquired by the foreign strategic investor under the Circular, whether by private share transfer or private placement, are subject to a three-year lock-up period (compared with the much more flexible lock-up arrangements recently introduced for QFIIs), although the Ministry of Commerce may approve a shorter lock-up period. Ministry of Commerce approval is also required if and when the foreign investor wishes to exit the listed company after the three-year lock-up period.

Under the Strategic Investor Circular a general takeover offer is required only if the acquisition of shares results in the foreign investor obtaining 'effective control' over the listed company in which the investment is made.[157] This is different from the 30 per cent shareholding trigger for a general offer requirement under the 2006 *Securities Law* and the even more recent *Measures for the Administration of the Takeover of Listed Companies* (2006 Takeover Code).[158]

Article 14 of the Strategic Investment Circular provides that payment for the acquisition must be made in foreign currency and no other form of payment is mentioned, leaving uncertain the degree of flexibility which would be allowed in regard to forms of payment.[159] More recently, however, the *Provisions on the Merger or Acquisition of Domestic Enterprises by Foreign Investors*[160] (the 2006 M & A Provisions) and the 2006 Takeover Code both expressly allow the acquirer of listed shares to pay the price for those shares in cash, securities or a combination of cash and securities.

The 2006 M & A Provisions also provide a framework for the anti-trust regulation of foreign investor acquisitions,[161] and specifies which mergers with anti-trust implications require government approval. For example, an anti-trust examination is required if the foreign investor has an annual sales volume of RMB 1.5 billion or more in the Chinese market, or where the transaction causes any party to the merger to acquire a 25 per cent share of the relevant market in China. The M & A Provisions demonstrate the authorities' concern with excessive market concentration, and their desire for foreign investment not to restrict the development of domestic industry or cause the disappearance of domestic brands.[162]

So far as the Strategic Investor Measures are concerned, the introduction of the strategic investor concept is undoubtedly a significant development which should encourage merger and acquisition activity in the PRC securities markets, where such activity has so far been notably lacking.[163] Its full effect cannot be known, however, until a greater proportion of PRC-listed firms have implemented share-segregation reform to transform their non-circulating shares into listed and freely tradable shares. And this, in turn, cannot happen for at least another four or five years, because of the restrictions imposed on the trading of previously non-tradable shares (state and legal person shares), when these shares are listed as part of the reform process. It will be the combination of share-reform, improved takeover rules and strategic investment that will bring about fundamental change, rather than any single one of these, but, of the three, share-reform is the precondition for new takeover rules and strategic investment rules to succeed – a topic to which I now turn.

C Reforming China's Share-ownership System: Floating Two Trillion Yuan Worth of Non-tradable Shares

As early as 1999, the Chinese government began issuing a series of reforms aimed at enabling the flotation of over two trillion yuan worth of non-tradable shares held by state-controlled entities.[164] The long-term aim has been to bring about the eventual integration of tradable and non-tradable shares by reclassifying non-tradable shares and allowing them to be transferred. It is this process, above all, which will be most significant in altering the ownership structure of listed Chinese firms. The first trial to convert non-tradable shares to listed circulating shares was launched by the CSRC in December 1999. Two pilot companies were chosen for the trial, China Jialing Industrial and Guizhou Tyre Company. In both cases, the non-tradable shares of the company were offered for sale at ten-times their respective average earnings per share for the preceding three years, but the price of the listed shares of the two companies plunged after the announcement of the trial, and the trial was eventually abandoned when offerings of non-tradable shares were not fully subscribed to by investors.[165]

After the failure of the first trial, the State Council issued the Administration of Reduction of State Share Holdings to Raise Funds for Social Security Tentative Procedures (the Reduction of State Holdings Tentative Procedures) to launch a modest programme to reduce state share ownership in June 2001. Section 5 of the Reduction of State Holdings

Tentative Procedures required that SOEs launching IPOs sell 10 per cent of their state-owned shares to public investors at the listing price. Major indexes on the Shanghai and Shenzhen Stock Exchanges fell substantially in October 2001, following the announcement. On 22 October 2001, the CSRC announced that Section 5 of the Reduction of State Holdings Tentative Procedures would be suspended while a new proposal for reducing state-owned shares was developed.[166]

In January 2002, the Development Research Center of the State Council unveiled a new proposal to grant holders of tradable shares of PRC listed companies the right to purchase non-tradable shares in such a company at 'fair value' (which may be less that the market price of the tradable shares). Even though the PRC government emphasized that this was merely a proposal, its existence contributed to the perception that implementation of a plan to sell non-tradable shares was imminent and thus contributed to a significant downward trend in the relevant indices. From January 2002 to the end of June 2002, the Shanghai Composite Index dropped by 39 per cent and the Shenzhen Composite Index fell by 44 per cent. In June 2002, the State Council announced a halt to the sale of state-owned shares on domestic stock markets.[167]

On 1 February 2004, with market expectations already prepared for the announcement, China's State Council issued new *Guidelines on Promoting Reform, Opening-up and Steady Development of China's Capital Market* which made clear the government's determination to resolve the split share structure.[168] A special workforce on share reform was established, composed of representatives of the SCRC, the State-owned Assets Supervision and Administration Commission of the State Council and the Ministry of Finance. By the end of 2004, the aggregate shares of China listed companies were 714.9 billion, of which 454.3 billion, or 64 per cent, were still non-tradable.[169]

The CSRC promulgated the Issues Relevant to Pilot Reform Projects regarding the Separation of Equity Ownership and Trading Rights of Listed Companies Circular (the Separation Circular) on 29 April 2005. The Separation Circular sets out a procedure by which listed companies participating in the pilot programme (trial companies) may apply for a percentage of the non-tradable shares held by their controlling shareholders to be reclassified as tradable shares. The Circular provides, among other things, for (i) a selection of the trial companies; (ii) information disclosure requirements for the trial companies; (iii) procedures for the extraordinary meeting of shareholders to adopt plans to reclassify non-tradable shares as tradable shares; and (iv) lock-up restrictions on the sale of non-tradable shares that have been reclassified as tradable shares. The requirement for share reclassification plans to be approved by an extraordinary meeting of shareholders is particularly important in protecting the rights of tradable shareholders. According to the Circular, holders of non-tradable shares of the pilot companies are responsible for coming up with a proposal for floating their non-tradable shares, and the proposal must be approved, not only by two-thirds of all shareholders who voted at the special shareholders meeting, but also with the approval of two-thirds of the holders of tradable shares. During the special shareholders meeting, the company has to provide on-site voting, telephone voting, Internet voting and voting through trading terminals to encourage maximum participation by tradable shareholders.[170]

The lock-up provisions are important for controlling the downward pressure on share prices that occurs when the supply of tradable shares in the Chinese market is suddenly increased through the conversion of non-tradable shares. Non-circulating shares (state and legal person shares) that are listed on a domestic stock exchange following shareholder approval of a share-reform proposal are known as G-shares (from *gai ge*, the Chinese word for reform). Section 5 of the Circular provides for the gradual release of G-shares into the stock market after being reclassified as tradable shares. The first rule is that that no such shares may be sold or transferred through the stock exchange within 12 months of the reclassification taking place. The second rule applies to holders of G-shares with more that 5 per cent of the total issued share capital in a trial company. Such a holder may not sell, through the public stock exchanges (i) more than 5 per cent of the company's total outstanding shares within 12 months after the end of the first 12-month lock-up period; or (ii) more than 10 per cent of the company's total outstanding shares within 24 months after the first 12-month lock-up period. The third rule enshrined in Section 5 is that, when total sales of G-shares by any holder through public transactions over a stock exchange reaches 1 per cent of the total outstanding shares of a company undergoing share reform, the selling shareholder must make a public announcement of such a fact within two business days of its occurrence.

The Circular also requires the close involvement of sponsors and stock exchanges in the planning and process of share reclassification. All companies undergoing share reform must engage sponsors to conduct due diligence, issue recommendations in connection with share reclassification plans, and assist in the implementation of such plans. Each sponsor is required to designate three representatives for such an engagement. The role of the stock exchanges under the Circular is to review application documents submitted by share reclassification trial companies, and to monitor sales of the reclassified shares. Stock exchanges and securities depositary and clearing entities are also instructed to adopt practice guidelines to govern the pilot programme. To this end, the Shanghai Stock Exchange,

Shenzhen Stock Exchange and China Securities Depository & Clearing Corporation jointly issued, on 8 May 2005, the *Pilot Reform Projects Regarding Separation of Equity Ownership and Trading Rights of Listed Companies Operational Guidelines.*[171]

With the ground laid by the Separation Circular, the CSRC announced just before the start of trading on 9 May 2005 that four listed companies had been selected for participation in the pilot programme. The four companies include the Shanghai Zi Jiang Enterprise Group, Sany Heavy Industry, Tsinghua Tongfang and Hebei Jinniu Energy Resources Company. These companies had a combined market capitalization of about US$2.4 billion, or about 1 per cent of China's total.[172] News of the event sent the Shanghai and Shenzhen Stock Exchanges into a string of new six-year lows. Although the proposed reclassification plans published by the four selected trial companies offered various cash and/or stock compensation packages to their tradable shareholders, the market reacted negatively as investors again feared substantial dilution of their tradable equity. Within two weeks of the start of this first pilot programme, the Shanghai Composite Index and the Shenzhen Composite Index tumbled by 7.5 per cent and 7.9 per cent, respectively.[173]

A further list of 42 listed companies was chosen for participation in the second Pilot Reform Project,[174] and the non-tradable share flotation scheme involving these companies was completed at the end of August 2005. A total of 45 out of the 46 companies participating in these two share reform projects successfully accomplished the flotation of their non-tradable shares, with the only exception being the one company that did not gain enough votes from the floating shareholders for the re-classification proposal to proceed. Apart from this exception, official reports indicate that an average of over 60 per cent of tradable shareholders actually voted at the special shareholders' meeting held by each of the participating 46 companies, with an average of over 90 per cent of those votes being in favour of the flotation proposal. This compares with a much lower average of about 10 per cent of tradable share holders who typically vote at Chinese company shareholders' meetings.[175]

A period of consultation followed the conclusion of the second Pilot Reform Program, after which the two domestic stock exchanges issued additional disclosure rules in relation to share reform proposals, and the CSRC revised the *Operational Guidelines on the Reform of Non-Floating Shares*.[176] Share reform was formally extended to all listed companies on 4 September 2005, when the CSRC issued the *Administration of Listed Companies Stock Right Allocation Reform Method*,[177] the provisions of which substantially reflect those of the Circular.

The process of transforming a large number of non-tradable shares into tradable shares inevitability creates a conflict of interest between the holders of tradable (floating) and non-tradable shares. The core of the issue is that non-tradable shareholders do not need to concern themselves about share price movements on the open securities exchange. If a listed corporation wants to release additional shares onto the market, the share price will usually go down. This is of grave concern for the holders of listed shares, but not at all for the non-tradable shareholders. A chief challenge in managing future non-tradable share conversion schemes will thus be to ensure that the interests of tradable shareholders are not significantly harmed by equity dilution as the tradable share market expands. In order to minimize the negative impact of equity dilution, compensation packages, usually in the form of additional shares (although cash compensation is also permitted), were attached to the share-reform proposals put forward by the 46 companies taking part in the Pilot Reform Projects. Despite this, however, the negative reaction by tradable shareholders to the reform initiative indicates that they remain concerned about the sufficiency of their compensation packages, especially in light of the continued expansion of tradable shares along with an expected continued fall in share prices.

The problem of market dilution and inadequate compensation for existing tradable shareholders has been further compounded by traditionally different pricing between tradable and non-tradable shares. Although both non-tradable and tradable shares have the same par value, there are distinct trading methods and prices between the two categories of shares, with the costs of obtaining tradable shares being much higher.[178] Non-tradable shares, by their nature, have rarely been transferred, and, when they have been, the transfer has typically been at a substantial discount to the tradable shares of the company. The lower value of non-tradable shares is due partly to the additional administrative hurdles and expenses (transaction costs) incurred during the transfer of non-tradable shares, and partly to the comparatively limited supply of, and higher demand for, tradable shares in China.[179]

In an effort to bolster confidence in the market, and to make future share-reform proposals more palatable, the CSRC issued the *Issues Relevant to Increases in the Holding of Public Shares by the Controlling Shareholders of Listed Companies after the Reform Regarding the Separation of Equity Ownership and Trading Rights Circular* (the Controlling Shareholder Circular) on 16 June 2005. The Controlling Shareholder Circular specifically allows majority shareholders to further their control through purchases on the open market. The specific recognition of major state-backed purchasing power as presence in the market appears to be aimed at reassuring investors that the State has not abandoned share prices to the vagaries of private demand and supply altogether.

Also on 16 June 2005, the CSRC promulgated the *Buyback by Listed Companies of Their Public Shares Procedures (Trial Implementation)* (the Buyback Procedures). By paving the way for share buybacks to occur more easily and more readily, the Procedures are also aimed at maintaining confidence in the market. The Buyback Procedures allow for listed companies to conduct supervised share buybacks with shareholder approval, in order to reduce the registered capital of the company. Buybacks can be conducted by collective bid (through the tradable share market) or by direct offer. The Buyback Procedures also provide that all creditors of the company must be notified of the buyback plan, which must not damage creditors' interests.[180] Creditors are entitled to require the company to repay the debt owed or provide corresponding security within 30 days from the date on which a share buyback notification is received. Share buybacks can help to bring about the orderly reduction of the total amount of Chinese corporate equity, thereby limiting the price-dampening effect of releasing a large amount of previously non-tradable shares onto the market. Moreover, both the Buyback Procedures and the Controlling Shareholder Circular provide avenues for tradable shareholders to obtain cash in return for selling their shares. This is likely to be a preferable option, in the eyes of many, to being handed additional, but increasingly worthless, equity in the form of a share-reform compensation package.

On 17 June 2005 the State-owned Assets Supervision and Administration Commission of the State Council (SASAC) clearly stated in its *Reform Regarding the Separation of Equity Ownership and Trading Rights of State-controlled Listed Companies Guiding Opinion* that the controlling shareholder of a state-controlled listed company should determine the minimum shareholding in such a company after the integration of tradable and non-tradable shares. Non-tradable shareholders are concerned that this rule may see them losing control over the company. The Buyback Procedures and the Controlling Shareholder Circular, however, provide market-based mechanisms for alleviating this concern. As tradable shares are purchased and cancelled through share buybacks, the proportion of shares owned by the state-controlled or corporate non-tradable shareholder will increase, and can be maintained through the tradable market in accordance with the Controlling Shareholder Circular.[181]

The key to the impact of the new Buyback Procedures and Majority Shareholder Increase Rules may lie in the ability of listed firms to implement different types of share ownership change in conjunction with each other. By improving the inherent value of each tradable share, share buybacks help tradable shareholders seek better prices for shares they still hold after the buyback is complete. Under the Controlling Shareholder Circular, tradable shareholders can use this improved bargaining position when negotiating with controlling shareholders wanting to increase their holding of tradable equity. The Controlling Shareholder Circular ensures that majority shareholders intending to increase their equity holding in a listed company must first provide advance notice of such intention by making a public announcement – a requirement which also helps protect the interests of tradable shareholders. Moreover, controlling shareholders that do purchase additional shares on the tradable share-market cannot re-sell them within six months of completing such a purchase. Both of these rules appear aimed at helping to stabilize the market as the share-reform process continues.

By the beginning of 2007, two of the nine case-study companies (Beiren Printing Machinery and Dongfang Electrical Machinery) examined in Chapter 5 had successfully implemented share-segregation reform procedures to transform their state-owned non-circulating shares into circulating shares, subject to certain lock-up restrictions, and at the same time to compensate existing holders of listed A-shares through a direct transfer of equity. In two other cases (Sinopec Shanghai Petrochemical and Sinopec Yizheng Chemical Fibre) share-reform proposals have, however, been actively opposed and defeated by domestic ordinary shareholders, thus demonstrating the controversial nature of the whole share reform process.[182]

NOTES

1. World Bank (Stoyan Tenev and Chunling Zhang), *Corporate Governance and Enterprise Reform in China* (International Financial Corporation, World Bank Group, 2002) 7.
2. OECD, *Principles of Corporate Governance* 2004, available at the OECD website http://www.oecd.org/.
3. For other definitions along the same lines, see On Kit Tam, *The Development of Corporate Governance in China* (Edward Elgar, 1999) 18–19.
4. John Gillespie, 'Transplanted company law: an ideological and cultural analysis of market-entry in Vietnam' (2002) 51 *International & Comparative Law Quarterly* 641.
5. See generally On Kit Tam, *The Development of Corporate Governance in China* (Edward Elgar, 1999) and G.J. Wen & D. Xu (eds), *The Reformability of China's State Sector* (World Scientific, 1997).
6. See, for discussion, Hing Lin Chan, 'An alternative to privatization: the listing of H-shares in Hong Kong' (1996) 9:3 *International Journal of Public Sector Management* 40–50.
7. See, eg., Roman Tomasic and Jian Fu, 'Legal regulation and corporate governance in China's top 100 listed companies' (2006) 27(9) *The Company Lawyer* 278–287; On Kit Tam, *The Development of Corporate Governance in China* (Edward Elgar, 1999); G.J. Wen & D. Xu (eds), *The Reformability of China's State Sector* (World Scientific, 1997); World Bank, *China's Emerging Capital Markets* (FT Financial Publishing Asia Pacific, 1997); Ron Duncan & Yiping Huang (eds), *Reform of State-Owned Enterprises in China: Autonomy, Incentive and Competition* (NCDS Asia Pacific Press, 1998).
8. Issued on 29 March 1999 as 3710/99.03.29. Translated in June–July 1999) 13(6) *China Law & Practice* 50–57.
9. Point No 11 of the Joint Opinion.

10. Point No 1, 2 and 11 of the Joint Opinion.
11. Point No 3 and Point No. 6 of the Joint Opinion.
12. Issued by the NPC on 27 October 2005. For discussion, see Jean-Marc Deschandol and Charles Desmeules, 'One hesitant step forward: new company law brings mixed feelings' (December 2005/January 2006) 19(10) *China Law & Practice* 13.
13. Ji Chen and Stephen C. Thomas, 'The ups and downs of the PRC securities market', (2003) 30:1 *The China Business Review* 36, at 38.
14. Chao Xi, above, n. 177, 102.
15. *Regulatory Opinion on Standardising Shareholders' General Meetings of Listed Companies*, issued by the CSRC on 18 May 2002.
16. *Guidelines for Corporate Governance of Listed Companies* jointly promulgated by the CSRC and the SETC on 7 January 2002.
17. *Strengthening the Protection of the Rights and Interests of Public Shareholders Several Provisions*, Issued by the CSRC on, and effective as of, 7 December 2004. Translated in (June 2006) 20(5) *China Law & Practice* 64–69. See also *Company Law* (2006) Articles 99–108.
18. *PRC Company Law (Amended)* [2330/05.10.27] PRC President's Order No. 42. Promulgated on 27 October 2005 and effective as of 1 January 2006. Translated (December 2005-January 2006) in 19(10) *China Law & Practice* 21–71.
19. See Articles 49–50 and article 70.
20. This compares with 25 per cent under the 1994 *Company Law*.
21. Article 103 of the *Amended Securities Law* (2006). The 3 per cent threshold compares with 5 per cent under the 1994 *Company Law*.
22. Article 98.
23. Article 151.
24. Article 71.
25. *PRC Company Law* (Amended) 2006, article 16.
26. Compare *Company Law* 1994, article 89.
27. *PRC Company Law* (Amended) 2006, article 143.
28. 'Corporate governance and investigation powers of the securities and futures commission', Speech presented by Mr Mark Dickens, Executive Director of the SFC to the Law Society of Hong Kong, 19 November 1998 (accessed December 2002, at http://www.hkse.com.hk/speeches/md981119.htm).
29. PRC *Company Law* (Amended) 2006 articles 16 and 122.
30. Jean-Marc Deschandol and Charles Desmeules, 'One hesitant step forward: new company law brings mixed feelings' (December 2005/January 2006) 19(10) *China Law and Practice* 13, 14.
31. *PRC Company Law* (Amended) 2006, article 106.
32. Shanghai Petrochemical Circular relating to Proposed Amendments to the Articles of Association dated 21 May 2003 and available through the Hong Kong Stock Exchange website at http://www.hkex.com.hk/.
33. Shanghai Petrochemical, 2005 *Annual Report* 29, noting that 'Mr Rong Guangdao is the chairman and president of the company'.
34. For shareholder figures see Guangzhou Shipyard 2005 *Annual Report* 13, and for details of the 2004 AGM attendance figures see 2005 *Annual Report* 15.
35. Craig Anderson and Bingna Guo, 'Corporate governance under the new company law (Part 2): shareholder lawsuits and enforcement' (May 2006) 20(4) *China Law & Practice* 15. See also Hongchuan Liu and Zili Ren, 'Halfway to effective shareholder protection' (March 2003) 17(2) *China Law & Practice* 29–32.
36. Craig Anderson and Bingna Guo, 'Corporate Governance under the New Company Law (Part 2): Shareholder Lawsuits and Enforcement' (May 2006) 20(4) *China Law & Practice* 15, 20; citing *Circular on Temporary Dismissal of Securities-related Civil Remedies Cases*, issued by the Supreme People's Court on 21 September 2001.
37. Hongchuan Liu and Zili Ren, 'Halfway to effective shareholder protection' (March 2003) 17(2) *China Law & Practice* 29–32; citing *Questions Concerning the Acceptance of Civil Tort Dispute Cases Arising from Misrepresentation in the Securities Market*

Circular, issued by the Supreme Court on, and effective as of, 15 January 2002. See also C. Anderson and Bingna Guo, above, n. 301.
38. C. Anderson & Bingna Guo, above, n. 301, 16.
39. Bei Hu, 'Company trio get suspended jail terms for fraud', *South China Morning Post* (Hong Kong) 15 November 2002.
40. Hongchuan Liu and Zili Ren, 'Halfway to effective shareholder protection' (March 2003) 17(2) *China Law & Practice* 29, 30.
41. Ibid.
42. Ibid.
43. Liu & Ren, above, n. 305, 31–32.
44. C. Anderson & Bingna Guo, above n. 301, 16.
45. See also article 150 of the new *Company Law* 2006.
46. See also article 113 of the new *Company Law* 2006.
47. C. Anderson & Bingna Guo, above, n. 301, 17.
48. Article 152.
49. C. Anderson & Bingna Guo, above, n. 301, 17.
50. Ibid.
51. Translated (May 2006) in 20(4) *China Law & Practice* 35.
52. Liu and Ren, above, n. 302, 31–32.
53. C. Anderson and Bingna Guo, above, n. 301, 20.
54. See further, Alice de Jonge, 'Red chip boom – H-share bust: solving cross-border insolvency problems in Hong Kong and the PRC' (1998) *LawAsia* 1.
55. PRC *Company Law* (Amended) 2006, article 109.
56. (October 2002) *Asiamoney* 36. Available at http://www.asiamoney.com.
57. CSRC, *Inspection of Listed Companies Procedures* 3710/2001.03.19. Available at the *China Law & Practice* website, New Law Digest 4 June 2001 (http://chinalawandpractice.com/).
58. Issued by the CSRC on 16 August 2001. Cited as the *Establishment of Independent Director systems by Listed Companies Guiding Opinion* in Charles Qin, New Guidance on Corporate Governance, Business Law Bulletins (March 2002) *China Law & Practice*, available at http://www.chinalawandpractice.com. Hereafter cited as the PRC *Independent Director Guidelines*.
59. Leung, et al., above, n. 65.
60. See eg. PRC *Company Law* (Amended) 2006, article 52.
61. Article IV of the PRC *Independent Director Guidelines*; and HKEx *Listing Rules*, Appendix 14, articles 7 and 12.
62. PRC *Independent Director Guidelines* article I(2).
63. Article VII of the *Independent Director Guidelines*, see also Hong Kong *Listing Rules*, Appendix 14, Code of Best Practice, article 9.
64. World Bank (2002) above, n. 1, 82.
65. According to executive search firm Bo Le Associates, the average salaries of senior managers in Beijing and Shanghai are still lower than those in Hong Kong, but the gap is narrowing rapidly: Toh Han Shih, 'Mainland salaries for executives to top HK', *South China Morning Post* (Hong Kong) 24 November 2003.
66. According to the National Bureau of Statistics, by late 2003 there was only one Chinese MBA graduate for every 22 foreign-invested companies in China, and one Chinese master's degree holder for every 1.5 foreign-invested firms: Toh Han Shih, 'Mainland salaries for executives to top HK', *South China Morning Post* (Hong Kong) 24 November 2003.
67. IIF Equity Advisory Group, *Corporate Governance in China: An Investor Perspective (Task Force Report)* (Institute of International Finance Inc, March 2006) 7.
68. See HKEx *Listing Rules*, Rule 3.10(1).
69. Mark O'Neill and Hui Yuk-Min, 'Lianhua Supermarket delays HK listing', *South China Morning Post* (Hong Kong) 20 May 2003. See also Peggy Sito, 'Supermarket chain cleared for listing', *South China Morning Post* (Hong Kong) 31 May 2003.
70. Leung et al., above, n. 65, 17.

71. Ibid.
72. For discussion, see David Webb's newsletter, 'Listing Rules Review Part 2: Board Games', 21 February 2002, available at http://www.Webb-site.com/ (archives).
73. Bei Hu, 'Independents shunned by China firms', *South China Morning Post* (Hong Kong) 7 February 2004.
74. Tsingtao Brewery, 2001 *Annual Report* 29.
75. Tsingtao Brewery, 2002 *Annual Report* 28–29.
76. Steven Shi & Drake Weisert, 'Corporate governance with Chinese characteristics' (February 2003) 13(2) *Company Secretary* 10, 13, pointing out that 'most listed companies in China lack an incentive mechanism that ties the management team's performance to its compensation'.
77. Tsingtao Brewery, 2001 *Annual Report* 29.
78. Robert J. Shiller, *Irrational Exuberance* (Scribe Publications Pty Ltd, 2000) 23–24.
79. See further Steven Shi & Drake Weisert, 'Corporate governance with Chinese characteristics' (February 2003) 13(2) *Company Secretary* 10, 13.
80. Under article 108 of the Mandatory Articles.
81. IIF Equity Advisory Group, above, n. 332. Cai ShuMo and Deng YingXia, 'Corporate governance: obstacles and new developments', *South China Morning Post* (Hong Kong) 12 April 2002.
82. Article 106 of the Mandatory Provisions and article 52 of the new *Company Law* 2006.
83. IIF Equity Advisory Group, above, n. 332, 8.
84. Ibid.
85. Guanzhou Shipyard had 6356 employees on the payroll as at 31 December 1994 (Guangzhou Shipyard, Annual Report 1994, 2) and only 4088 employees by the end of 2005 (Annual Report 2005, 24).
86. Rong Guangdao, who was then Deputy Secretary of the Communist Party Committee of Shanghai Petrochemical, was elected Chairman of the board of the Company in 2005. The previous year, Deputy Secretary of the Communist Party Committee and Secretary of the Communist Party Discipline Supervisory Committee of the Company, Dai Shuming, had been elected to the position of Chairman of the Supervisory Committee of Shanghai Petrochemical.
87. Dongfang Electric Machinery, 2003 *Annual Report* 11–12. Zhu Yuanchao, Chairman of the Company, was Secretary to the Party Committee and Head of DFEW. Li Hongdong, Chairman of the Supervisory Committee of the Company, was Deputy Secretary of the Party Committee and Secretary to the Discipline Committee and Chairman of the Labour Union of DFEW.
88. Chao Xi, 'Transforming Chinese enterprises: ideology, efficiency and instrumentalism in the process of reform', in John Gillespie & Pip Nicholson (eds), *Asian Socialism & Legal Change: The Dynamics of Vietnamese and Chinese Reform* (2005) 91, 106–107.
89. IFF Equity Advisory Group, above, n. 332, 7.
90. See for example Allen Huang and Ronald Ma, *Accounting in China in Transition: 1949–2000* (World Scientific Publishing, Accounting and Business in Asia, vol. 2, 2001) 66; Shanghai University of Finance and Economics and the University of Texas at Dallas, 1987 *Accounting and Auditing in the People's Republic of China*, Center for International Accounting Development, University of Texas, Dallas, TX; Zhu and Chen, *International Accounting Comparison and Development* (Publishing House of Southwest University of Finance and Economics, Chengdu, 1992); Blake and Gao, 1995 *Perspectives on Accounting and Finance in China*, (Routledge; Tang, Y.W., Cooper, B.J. and Chow, L., *Accounting and Finance in China: A Review of Current Practice*, 3rd edn, Longman, 1996).
91. Before 1992, Chinese companies applied accounting rules on an industry-by-industry basis. The 1992 Accounting Regulations were issued to rectify this situation. See, further, Howard Gensler (ed.), *China Tax and Accounting Manual* (Asia Law and Practice, 1998), 2, 9. See also Y.W. Tang, B.J. Cooper and L. Chow, *Accounting and Finance in China: A Review of Current Practice*, 3rd edn, Longman, 1996) paras 15.01–15.02. See also Ji Li, Kevin Lam and Jane W. Moy, 'Ownership reform

amongst state firms in China and its implications' (2005) 43(4) *Management Decision* 568–588.

92. For example, the *Response regarding Certain Accounting Issues for Joint Stock Limited Enterprises Listed in Hong Kong* and the *Notice regarding Profits Distribution by Joint Stock Limited Enterprises Listed Overseas*, which, in essence, provides that the distributable profit of such a company shall be deemed to be the lesser of the retained profits determined in accordance with overseas' accounting regulations and PRC accounting regulations (Howard Gensler (ed.) *China Tax and Accounting Manual* (Asia Law and Practice, 1998) 14; further noting that such a rule is aimed at restraining company management from seeking to stretch beyond the limits of financial prudence the amounts distributed to shareholders.
93. For a detailed comparison of the new Chinese ASBEs with International Financial Reporting Standards (IFRS) see Deloitte China, Comparison of IFRSs and New Chinese Accounting Standards (August 2006) available at http://www.iasplus.com/country.china.htm.
94. See also Chapter 9 of the Hong Kong *Listing Rules*.
95. Take, for example, the accounting consequences of unifying China's official and swap market exchange rates in 1994: Renee Lai, 'Accountants' society queries Guangzhou Shipyard's 1993 report', *South China Morning Post* (Hong Kong) 25 August 1994. See also GSI Annual Report at 81, and Renee Lai, 'Exchange Rate gain will not reflect in profit', *South China Morning Post* (Hong Kong) 24 August 1994. See also Gareth Hewett, 'Guangzhou Shipyard lifts profit', *South China Morning Post* (Hong Kong) 6 August 1994. Another example was the unintended accounting consequences of China's switch from the Industrial and Commercial Consolidated Tax (ICCT) to the value-added tax (VAT) in January 1994: Gareth Hewett, 'H-share profits face VAT wipeout', *South China Morning Post* (Hong Kong) 7 August 1995. See also 'Different approaches taken by companies', *South China Morning Post* (Hong Kong) 10 August 1995. More recently, each of the nine H-share firms examined here is facing the prospect of being required to pay back taxes after enjoying a preferential 15 per cent tax rate ever since they were listed. The tax benefit officially expired at the end of 1995 but was extended to 1997. A tax notice issued in 1998 failed to indicate a clear expiry date, so none of the nine firms has ever paid the full tax rate, or made provision for doing so in its annual accounts: Enoch Yiu, Charlotte So and Eric Ng, 'Huge back taxes loom on state-controlled companies: earnings to suffer once provisions are made, says expert', *South China Morning Post* (Hong Kong) 7 July 2007.
96. Foo Choy Peng, 'costs squeeze Shanghai profits', *South China Morning Post* (Hong Kong) 25 September 1995. Headlines such as 'H-share profits face VAT wipeout' also served to increase investor awareness of the risks and uncertainties inherent in the H-share market, and themselves had an impact on the market as the H-share index continued to decline; see Christine Chan, 'Tax worries panic H-share investors', *South China Morning Post* (Hong Kong) 17 November 1995. See also Renee Lai, 'Analysts play down fear on interest costs for H shares', *South China Morning Post* (Hong Kong) 8 November 1995.
97. Renee Lai, 'China companies' acid test', *South China Morning Post* (Hong Kong) 26 April 1994.
98. Ibid.
99. One early issue was the fact that the Hong Kong stock exchange rules did not require newly listed companies to announce interim results if the closing date for submitting such accounts fell before the actual date of listing. The HKEx was also forced to grant waivers on submitting audited interim accounts to Tsingtao Brewery, Shanghai Petro, Beiren Printing and Guangzhou Shipyard because of the delay in their flotations after 30 June. Nor were they even used to the practice of preparing interim reports, since listed companies in China were only required to announce yearly results: Kerry Wong, 'Listing loophole causes anxiety', *South China Morning Post* (Hong Kong) 14 November 1993.

100. See also Article 66 of the PRC *Securities Law* 2006 which also requires listed companies to file annual reports within four months (120 days) of the end of each financial year, and to issue a public announcement regarding the Report.
101. David Webb, Webb-site.com, '2005 Christmas Pick–regulatory note', 15 December 2005. Compare the US situation where the US Securities and Exchange Commission requires quarterly filing of reports and imposes accelerated periodic report filing requirements on all large domestic public companies (from 90 days to 60 days for annual reports, and from 45 to 35 days for quarterly reports with effect from 15 December 2002 (http://www.sec.gov/rules/final/33-8128.htm).
102. HSBC *China Supplement*, distributed with December 2002 edition of *Asiamoney* (Euromoney Publications (Jersey) Ltd, 2002) 19.
103. Chris Wright, 'China takes note of governance', *China Supplement* December 2002 edition of *Asiamoney* (Euromoney publications (Jersey) Ltd, 2002, at 20.
104. Tang Yun-Wei, Barry J. Cooper and Lynne Chow, *Accounting and Finance in China: A Review of Current Practice*, 3rd edn (Longman, 1996) para. 15.24.
105. Amended PRC *Securities Law*, above, n. 198.
106. Issued and effective as of 28 August 2003; translated in vol. 17, no. 8, *China Law & Practice* (October 2003) at 62–67.
107. ASBE 36 expressly acknowledges that state-controlled entities are not to be regarded as related parties simply because they are State-controlled. State-controlled entities, however, are not exempted under IAS 24.
108. Michael J. Ferguson, Kevin C.K. Lam and Grace Meina Lee, 'Voluntary disclosure by state-owned enterprises listed on the Stock Exchange of Hong Kong' (2002) 13(2) *Journal of International Financial Management and Accounting* 125–152, 127.
109. Ibid. 128.
110. Gareth Hewett, 'H-shares offer more disclosure', *South China Morning Post* (Hong Kong) 31 May 1994.
111. HSBC China Supplement, above, n. 367, 19.
112. Reuters, 'China takes aim at corporate abuses with jail' 26 December 2005. Reuters website accessed at http://in.today.reuters.com on 27 December 2005.
113. Formerly Tianjin Bohai Chemical Industry Corporation. See Hui Yuk-Min, 'Watchdog finds governance faults at Tianjin Capital', *South China Morning Post* (Hong Kong) 23 August 2002.
114. Ibid.
115. Reuters, above, n. 377.
116. Mark O'Neil, 'Mainland tries to rein in blatant asset stripping', *South China Morning Post* (Hong Kong) 29 December 2003.
117. Cai Shumo and Deng Yingxia, 'Corporate governance: obstacles and new developments', *South China Morning Post* (Hong Kong) 12 April 2002.
118. Promulgated by the Ministry of Finance on 31 October 1999, effective as of 1 July 2000. Discussed in Tang Yun Wei, Barry J. Cooper and Lynne Chow, *Accounting and Finance in China: A Review of Current Practice*, 3rd edn (Longman 1996) para. 4.14.
119. Compare Article 63 of the 1998 PRC *Securities Law*.
120. Hongchuan Liu and Zili Ren, 'Halfway to effective shareholder protection' (March 2003) 17(2) *China Law & Practice* 29–32.
121. See above at n. 9.
122. Bloomberg, 'Motorcycle firm avoids expulsion', *South China Morning Post* (Hong Kong) 1 September 2003; quoting the assistant to the chairman of the CSRC as saying, in November 2002, that 'About 676 Chinese publicly traded companies [including H-share firms] are together owed 100 billion yuan by their parents'.
123. Kathy Wilhelm, 'Casinos by another name' (8 March 2001) 164(9) *Far Eastern Economic Review* 46, 47.
124. World Bank (2002) above, n. 1, 82–83.
125. Ibid. 83.
126. Bei Hu, 'Citigroup seeks QFII licence', *South China Morning Post* (Hong Kong) 21 March 2003.

127. In relation to American financial regulation and its reform, see further Dr Thomas F. Huertas, 'A market paradigm', *International Financial Law Review* Special Supplement August 1993, 3–5, and Warren F. Cooke and Lynn Stofan Kaplan, 'United States', *Asian Financial Law Review* Special Supplement 1991, 207–224.
128. World Bank (1997) above, n. 13, 40.
129. Ibid.
130. World Bank (2002) above, n. 1, 62.
131. The four Asset Management Companies are Huarong Asset Management Corporation, China Cinda Asset Management, Great Wall Asset Management and China Orient Asset Management. As at the end of 2004 the four AMCs had recovered about 122 billion yuan in cash from bad loans since 1999. Sales of NPLs also appear to be accelerating as the big four state-owned banks try to clean up their books before selling shares to the public: Bloomberg in Beijing, 'Big Four's bad-debt sales reach 605b yuan', *South China Morning Post* (Hong Kong) 30 December 2004.
132. *Commercial Bank Intermediary Services Tentative Provisions* (Order [2001] No. 5 of the People's Bank of China.
133. Translated as *Relevant Questions in Implementing the 'Commercial Bank Intermediary Services Tentative Provisions' Circular*, issued by the People's Bank of China on 22 April 2002 in (June 2002) 16(5) *China Law & Practice* 39. See also Philip Gilligan & Athena Wong, 'New rules on intermediary services offered by commercial banks' (June 2002) 16(5) *China Law & Practice* 51.
134. 'Banks to get green light for fund biz', XinhuaNet 11 November 2004; available at http://www.cei.gov.cn/ce/. See also 'China lifts barrier on local bank fund units', XinhuaNet 12 November 2004.
135. Chinese insurance companies were thereafter allowed to invest up to 30 per cent collectively and 10 per cent individually in securities funds.
136. *Administration of Stock Investments by Insurance Institutional Investors Tentative Procedures* (3910/04.10.24, Order of the CIRC [2004] No. 12) Promulgated by the CIRC and the CSRC on, and effective as of, 24 October 2004, translated in vol. 18(10) *China Law & Practice* 39–53.
137. Articles 11 and 12. See also article 14 for those stocks in which Insurance firms may not invest. Stocks in a listed company held by an insurance company shall not attain 30 per cent of the said listed company's renminbi common stock (article 13). The Tentative Procedures also authorize the CIRC to enact other stipulations governing the exact proportion of an insurance institutional investor's stock investments (article 13). According to senior officials of the CIRC, for the time being the proportion shall be 5 per cent of an insurance investor's total assets (calculated according to the cost price) at the end of the previous year: Xu Guojian, Lu Guoming & Pek-Siang Tee, 'Stock market access paves the way for new utilization of insurance Funds' (December 2004/January 2005) 18(10) *China Law & Practice* 54–56, 54.
138. World Bank (2002) above, n. 1, 64.
139. *Issues Relevant to the Transfer of State-owned Shares and Legal Person Shares in Listed Companies to Foreign Investors Circular* [3710/02.11.01]. Issued by the CSRC, Ministry of Finance and the State Economic and Trade Commission on, and effective as of, 1 November 2002. Translated (December 2002) in 16(10) *China Law & Practice*. For discussion, see FDI, 'Foreign Investors Allowed to Invest in Trust and Securities', available through the China Economic Information Network at http://www.ce.cei.gov.cn/.
140. Translated as *Administration of Securities Investment in China by Qualified Foreign Institutional Investors Tentative Procedures* [3700/02.11.05]. Jointly promulgated by the CSRC and the PboC on 5 November 2002, effective as of 1 December 2002. Translated (December 2002) in 16(10) *China Law & Practice*. See also Shanghai Stock Exchange, Securities Transactions by Qualified Foreign Institutional Investors Implementing Rules 3700/02.12.01/SH; Shenzhen Stock Exchange, Securities Transactions by Qualified Foreign Institutional Investors Implementing Rules 3700/02.12.01/SZ in New Law Digest – 22 December 2002 16(10) *China Law & Practice*. For discussion see 'The

missing piece of the puzzle: new QFII rules open a share market' (December 2002) 16(10) *China Law & Practice*.

141. Ibid. For more discussion see Lehman, Lee & Xu, vol. 1, no. 10 *China Law Digest Newsletter*, 13 December 2002 (chinalawdigest@lehmanlaw.com), received via email on 13 December 2002. See further Thomas E. Jones, 'Trailblazing developments in state sector and capital markets', *South China Morning Post* (Hong Kong) 9 December 2002.

142. CSRC, *China's Securities and Futures Markets* (April 2004), at 27. The first five foreign financial institutions to be approved under the QFII scheme were Citigroup, Goldman Sachs, Morgan Stanley, Nomura Securities and UBS. Both Citigroup and UBS had made their first purchases in the China market by mid-2003. For further details, see 'QFII updates', vol. 4., no. 4., *Hong Kong Securities* (July–August 2003) at 28. CSRC, *China's Securities and Futures Markets* (April 2004), p. 7. Available from the CSRC website at http://www.csrc.gov.cn.

143. *Measures for the Administration of Securities Investments in China by Qualified Foreign Institutional Investors*, 3700/06.08.24(1). Promulgated by the CSRC, People's Bank of China and State Administration of Foreign Exchange on 24 August 2006, and effective as of 1 September 2006; translated in (November 2006) in 20(9) *China Law & Practice* 28–34. Discussed in Taylor Hui and Vivien Teu, 'China QFII rules revised – significant developments for foreign fund managers' (November 2006) 20(9) *China Law & Practice* 16–18.

144. Taylor Hui and Vivien Teu, 'China QFII rules revised – significant developments for foreign fund managers' (November 2006) 20(9) *China Law & Practice* 16–17, 16–18.

145. Securities assets managed by QFII applicants that are securities companies or commercial banks must not be less than US$10 billion. Lehman, Lee & Xu, vol. 1, no. 10 *China Law Digest Newsletter*, 13 December 2002 (chinalawdigest@lehmanlaw.com), received via email on 13 December 2002. See also Taylor Hui and Vivien Teu, above, n. 144, 16.

146. Lehman, Lee & Xu, vol. 1, no. 10 *China Law Digest Newsletter*, 13 December 2002 (chinalawdigest@lehmanlaw.com), received via email on 13 December 2002.

147. Taylor Hui and Vivien Teu, above n. 144, 17.

148. Ibid.

149. Ibid.

150. Lehman, Lee & Xu, vol. 1, no. 10 *China Law Digest Newsletter*, 13 December 2002 (chinalawdigest@lehmanlaw.com), received via email on 13 December 2002.

151. Taylor Hui and Vivien Teu, above, n. 144 citing a set of questions and answers issued by the CSRC (CSRC Q&A) on 27 September 2006.

152. Under the 2002 Provisional QFII Measures, each QFII could not hold more than 10 per cent of the outstanding shares in any one listed company, and the total shares held by all QFIIs in a single listed company could not exceed 20 per cent of the total outstanding shares of the company.

153. Taylor Hui and Vivien Teu, above, n. 144, 18.

154. The current catalogue, which took effect on 1 April 2002, excludes foreign firms from taking large or controlling stakes in strategic industries such as military facilities, airlines and civil airport construction and airport operation firms. See, further, Peggy Sito, 'New SOE rules considered short of foreign needs', *South China Morning Post* (Hong Kong), 5 November 2002; Bei Hu, 'Door opens to foreign investors', *South China Morning Post* (Hong Kong), 8 November 2002 and Geoffrey Baker, 'New avenue for M & A transactions', *South China Morning Post* (Hong Kong) 28 October 2002.

155. Also known as Circular 28, the Strategic Investor Circular was jointly issued by the Ministry of Commerce (MOFCOM) the CSRC, the State Administration of Taxation, the State Administration of Industry and Commerce and the State Administration of Foreign Exchange on 31 December 2005, and effective on 30 January 2006. The Strategic Investor Circular actually followed another Circular, the *Matters Relevant to the Administration of Foreign Capital Involved in the Reform of the Division of Equity Interests of Listed Companies Circular* issued in October 2005, which introduced the concept of foreign 'strategic investors'.

156. *Matters Relevant to Foreign Investment in Listed Companies Several Opinions*; jointly issued by the Ministry of Foreign Trade and Economic Cooperation (MOFTEC) and the CSRC on, and effective as of, 8 November 2001 (3710/01.11.08). Translated (December 2001/January 2002) in 15(10) *China Law & Practice* 93.
157. Article 9.
158. Promulgated by the CSRC on 31 July 2006 and effective as of 1 September 2006 (3700/06.07.31). Order of the CSRC No. 35. Translated (November 2006) in 20(9) *China Law & Practice* 40–73. See also Qiang Li, 'The new M & A code and the new takeover rules: impact on future M & A transactions', *China Law Update* Capital Markets (CCH Hong Kong Limited, 2007).
159. Article 36. Discussed in Deschandol and Desmeules, above, n. 121; especially at note 11.
160. Issued by the Ministry of Commerce, the State Assets Supervision and Administration Commission of the State Council, the State Administration of Taxation, the State Administration for Industry and Commerce, the China Securities Regulatory Commission and the State Administration of Foreign Exchange on 8 August 2006 and effective as of 8 September 2006. Discussed in Volume 3 Issue 1 *M & A Review* (*Asialaw* Supplement January 2007) 11–14, also discussed in 'China legal briefs' (September 2006) 20(7) *China Law & Practice* 14. The 2006 M & A Provisions replace the earlier 2003 *Interim Provisions for Foreign Investors to Merge Domestic Enterprises* promulgated by the Ministry of Foreign Trade & Economic Cooperation and four other government agencies in 2003. Similar provisions have also been promulgated for unlisted SOEs – the *Using Foreign Investment to Re-organise State-Owned Enterprises Tentative Provisions*. Jointly promulgated by the State Administration for Industry & Commerce, the State Economic & Trade Commission, the Ministry of Finance and the State Administration of Foreign Exchange on 8 November 2002, and effective on 1 January 2003.
161. David Yu & Wayne Cehn, 'Controls on foreign acquisitions of Chinese enterprises' (January 2007) 3(1) *Asialaw M & A Review* 11–13, further noting that China does not yet have a systematic and integrated anti-trust regulatory system. On 7 June 2006, the State Council of the People's Republic of China approved, in principle, a draft Anti-trust Law of the People's Republic of China; however this draft law has yet to be submitted to the Standing Committee of the China National People's Congress for its consideration. It remains uncertain whether the law, which has been under debate for many years, will be promulgated in 2007 as planned.
162. Thus a foreign investment proposal that would alter the control of a prominent Chinese brand or a firm with more than 2000 staff must undergo an anti-trust investigation and obtain the approval of the investigating authorities: 'Ministry of Commerce approves M&A share swaps' in 'China Legal Briefs' (September 2006) 20(7) *China Law & Practice* 14. See also David Yu & Wayne Cehn, 'Controls on foreign acquisitions of Chinese enterprises' (January 2007) 3(1) *Asialaw M & A Review* 11–13.
163. See discussion below in Chapter Six.
164. China Economic Quarterly, *South China Morning Post* (Hong Kong) 22 November 2004.
165. Michael G. DeSombre and Weiheng Chen, 'Unloading state-owned shares: another trial under new rules' (June 2005) 19(5) *China Law and Practice* 17.
166. Ibid.
167. Ibid.
168. Ibid.
169. Christophe Han and Wayne Chen, 'Accelerating reform in China's equity market: share buybacks and majority shareholder share increases', July/August 2005 19(6) *China Law & Practice* 17.
170. 'Fair shares' (November 2005) *Company Secretary* 18, 19.
171. DeSombre and Chen, n. 165.
172. Ibid.
173. Ibid.

174. Han and Chen, n. 169.
175. 'Fair Shares' (November 2005) *Company Secretary* 18, 19, quoting Tong Daochi, Deputy Director-General of the CSRC's Department of Listed Company Supervision. The 10 per cent figure is supported by Annual reports of the nine H-share companies examined in Chapter Five.
176. Ibid.
177. Deschandol and Desmeules, above n. 176; especially at note 3.
178. Han and Chen, n. 169.
179. DeSombre and Chen, above n. 165.
180. See also articles 178 and 186 of the 2006 *Company Law*.
181. DeSombre and Chen, above, n. 165. See also article 143 of the *Company Law* 2006.
182. See also Bei Hu, 'Shenzhen expands state share sales', *South China Morning Post* (Hong Kong) 10 February 2004, noting the role of local (municipal and provincial level) governments in the share reform process.

5. Nine case studies: the story of nine vanguard firms in China's H-share market

I INTRODUCTION

The chronological examination in Chapter 2 of the way in which the first nine candidates were introduced to the H-share market provided an opportunity to examine a number of issues related to timing: political, legal and financial. Politically, the timing of an IPO may, for example, tend to indicate official favouritism bestowed upon an individual company and/or the locality in which it is based. Financially, timing of an IPO may, deliberately or otherwise, coincide with times of positive or negative market sentiment, positive or negative market trends and/or positive or negative economic circumstances generally. Particularly in a newly emerging market, timing may affect the degree of regulatory clarification available in respect of legal issues to do with the way in which a particular IPO is conducted. Conversely, lack of legal clarity may affect timing, with officials more inclined to delay IPOs involving a greater degree of regulatory and legal complexity, while giving the green light to others.

The chronological pattern is continued in this chapter, enabling an exploration of similar issues of timing and the way in which events and circumstances coincide to affect the fortunes of companies and stocks. This chapter tells the story of the first batch of H-share companies, beginning in 1993 with the first to be launched onto the market (Tsingtao) and ending in 2007, nearly 12 years after the last of the first batch (Dongfang Electrical Machinery) had been successfully launched.

As we follow the story of these nine firms, what soon becomes obvious is the pervasive influence of the state in almost every aspect of decision making affecting the way in which individual companies develop. The many and varied ways in which the State can and does make its presence felt in business life in China were touched upon in the previous chapter, and are worth re-emphasising here. First, there is the ownership factor. As with nearly all listed Chinese companies, the nine firms examined here all have around 50 per cent of their equity in the form of non-tradeable A-shares controlled by the State. As the major shareholder in all of these firms, the State exerts a considerable influence in determining the composition of the company's Board of Directors and Supervisory Committee. This influence is further strengthened and supported by the State's role in appointing personnel to official positions in State agencies that may also be important in determining the business direction of an enterprise. For example, State administrative authorities are responsible for approving all proposals for expansion, diversification, change of business direction or alteration of share capital submitted by individual enterprises under their supervision. State agencies are also responsible for administering government policies designed to promote and support certain business choices (such as takeover or investment decisions) at the expense of other alternatives. Tsingtao Brewery, for example, enjoyed a considerable amount of government financial and administrative support during many years of continued expansion and growth.

II TSINGTAO BREWERY COMPANY LIMITED

A Introduction

In 1993, Tsingtao Brewery Company Limited ('Tsingtao') was the largest beer manufacturing, distributing and marketing operation in China.[1] It now owns 50 breweries and three malting mills in 18 Chinese provinces and cities. Its products are distributed to over 50 countries worldwide,[2] and Tsingtao Beer is one of the most widely consumed beers in China and among the best-known Chinese beers in the international market. As a study of SOE management in China, Tsingtao is interesting, mainly because of the apparently very successful mixture of active government support, combined with foreign capital and the involvement of a foreign 'partner'.

B The Listing

Tsingtao H-shares were listed on the HKEx on 15 July 1993, making Tsingtao the first-ever mainland-incorporated enterprise to 'go public' successfully in the international marketplace.[3]

The issue of 317 600 000 H-shares included a placing of 45 000 000 H-shares, under a special arrangement made with Anheuser-Busch International Holdings, Inc. ('A-B Holdings' – later to become Anheuser-Busch Companies, Inc.),[4] the world's largest brewery. The arrangement gave A-B Holdings 5 per cent of the total registered capital of Tsingtao.

The H-share issue was followed by the issue of publicly available A-shares in mainland China which were listed on the Shanghai Stock Exchange on 27 August 1993.[5]

By the end of 1993, when added to the 5 per cent of total share capital controlled by A-B Holdings, foreign investors with H-shares held a 38.54 per cent[6] interest in Tsingtao, while domestic individual holders of tradable A-shares held a total of 11.11 per cent of registered capital. The State, however, remained by far the largest holder of equity interest in the Company. The State, in the case of Tsingtao, is represented by the Qingdao State-Owned Assets Bureau (later the Qingdao State-Owned Assets Supervision and Administration Commission) as the holder of 399 820 000 State shares or 44.42 per cent of the Company's share capital in 1993. Also essentially non-tradeable were the 53 330 000 PRC legal person shares issued by Tsingtao, comprising 5.93 per cent of total share capital and owned primarily by state-controlled 'legal persons' such as the Bank of China Shandong Province Branch (3.25 per cent of total share equity), and the People's Construction Bank of China, Qingdao Branch (2.12 per cent of total equity).[7]

C Subsequent Performance

In 1994, international brokerage Warburg forecast healthy rises in profit levels for Tsingtao over the next few years.[8] In fact, however, profit levels fell in the year ended December 1995. Another brokerage, Salomon Brothers, put a sell recommendation on Tsingtao shares in 1995, forecasting poor results and fund-raising exercises that would dilute earnings. This was sound advice, as Tsingtao, along with all the other H-shares, had a disastrous 1995. In early 1995, Tsingtao shares traded at $3.425, but by the same time in early 1996 they were worth only $2.525, underperforming the Hang Seng index by 37.96 per cent. 1995 also saw the company's net profit down 9.6 per cent, to 97.79 million yuan.[9] Earnings per share for year ended 1995 was down 9.2 per cent, to 10.9 fen.[10]

Despite these initially poor results, Tsingtao has not only survived, but prospered, as one of the main beneficiaries of government policies and government financial support. In particular, the central government's 'seize the large and discard the small' policy has supported Tsingtao's ambitious expansion programme through a series of takeovers. The policy was launched in 1994–95 when, faced by an increasing number of failing and inefficient SOEs, Beijing began a massive rationalization drive designed to concentrate reforms on big state-owned enterprises through mergers and acquisitions. Rationalization was to take place in all major industries, including the beer market.[11]

The mainland economy had long been characterized by the dominance of small state-owned firms, owned and operated by more than 40 central government ministries and four different layers of regional governments: province, municipality, county and village. These firms generally enjoy a captive market, protected by local government authorities which also act as industry regulators. With better companies unable to drive poorer competitors in neighbouring provinces out of the market, all have suffered from high unit costs and an inability either to take advantage of economies of scale or to invest in research and development. This has been just as true of the mainland beer market as any other. Thus, in 1992, China had a total of 813 beer breweries, with no single brewery commanding any more than a small percentage of the national market. The ten largest breweries in 1992 accounted for only 14.22 per cent of total beer production,[12] with Tsingtao brewery, the largest producer, occupying only 2.3 per cent of the domestic market.[13] By 2005, the picture was dramatically different. There were only 530 breweries in China,[14] and the top ten breweries accounted for much higher concentration – 61 per cent – of the total national production.[15] By 2005, Tsingtao Brewery controlled about 13 per cent of the national market.[16]

Focusing on those existing enterprises large enough to survive in the new economic environment, the national government soon selected Tsingtao as a major player in its 1990s rationalization drive. In 1996, the government earmarked preferential loans for 300 state-owned enterprises,[17] and in 1997 a second list of 212 state-owned enterprises that would receive government support was published. Tsingtao Brewery was on both lists, being amongst 1000 state-owned enterprises selected by Beijing to form the backbone of the State's continued participation in the economy. The national government's strategy of sponsoring industry rationalization was designed to place minimal financial pressure on beneficiary companies. Nolan is just one writer who has emphasized the importance of mergers in China's industrial sector policies as a vehicle to develop economies of scale.[18]

As a beneficiary of the government's *Zhuada* (grasp the big) policy enunciated in 1997 at the 15th Congress of the Chinese Communist Party, Tsingtao was able to acquire debt-ridden breweries, like bankrupt brewer Rizhao Brewery and the highly-geared Beihai Brewery, virtually free of charge throughout the late 1990s.[19] Debt-ridden breweries acquired by Tsingtao were granted favourable debt-repayment terms by government-owned creditors, and effectively exempt from interest payments.[20] Tsingtao was also allowed to retain its preferential profits-tax rate of 15 per cent[21] (as compared to the standard enterprise income tax rate of 33 per cent), a privilege which it still retained in 2006.[22] Throughout Shandong Province and elsewhere, municipal governments have also stepped in to provide 'certain financial incentives', when Tsingtao has rescued loss-making breweries in the local area.[23]

Tsingtao launched a new holding company to steer its merger and acquisition drive in early July 1997. The proposal was for the Qingdao Municipal State-owned Assets Administration Bureau (the Bureau) to transfer its 44.42 per cent of Tsingtao to the Tsingtao Brewery Group Company Limited (the Holding Company) which was wholly-owned by the Bureau.[24] The aim was for the Holding Company to buy loss-making breweries, bring them back to profitability and then inject them into the listed arm. In line with this plan, several breweries were originally earmarked for the holding company to purchase. In the case of Shandong-based Beihai Brewery, a letter of intent to acquire was even signed between Tsingtao Brewery Group and Beihai. But it was soon realized that the Beihai acquisition, and plans for others like it, would violate exchange rules under which a parent company may not compete with its listed arm in the same industry.

A solution was soon found. While 'certain technical problems'[25] were worked out with the national government authorities, the municipal government passed new regulations, the *Measures for the Delegation of Management of State-Owned Assets in Qingdao Municipality* under which the Bureau could appoint the Holding Company to hold and manage on the Bureau's behalf the State shares owned by the Bureau for a term of four years from 1 January 1997.[26]

At the provincial level, the Shandong government implemented a number of policies in the late 1990s designed to support the development of the eight largest concerns in the province seen to offer the most promise of prospering. For example, Tsingtao was also amongst the 14 state-owned enterprises selected by the Shandong government for government assistance in lobbying for foreign partners during the Shandong Foreign Trade and Economic Co-operation Fair held in Hong Kong in mid-September 1997. This was followed by other, similar, events, including the inauguration in 1999 of the Qingdao Beer Festival, a jointly funded effort that proved beneficial for both the company's coffers and the local economy.[27] Perhaps the most recent symbol of the closely-shared interests of the firm and the state is the selection in 2005 of Tsingtao to be one of a handful of privileged 'sponsors' of the Beijing 2008 Olympic Games, giving an immediate boost to the company's prospects for the short-term future.[28]

Despite all this support for its buying spree, loss-making enterprises purchased by Tsingtao have not always been easy or even possible to turn around. Jardine Fleming is just one brokerage which has warned investors to be sceptical of the supposed benefits of merger-and-acquisition-based expansion.[29] In making a 'sell' recommendation for Tsingtao stock in 1997, the brokerage pointed to the firm's poor record in turning round loss-making enterprises, and stated that no medium-term benefits could be expected from the acquisition of ailing breweries like Rizhao and Beihai. Moreover, a more serious problem has been that much of the expansion has been funded by a rapidly escalating gearing ratio: according to one analyst when placing a sell-rating on the stock in September 1998, Tsingtao's gearing had by that stage increased to 92 per cent.[30]

While rapid expansion has led to a rise in income receipts for the company, as well as in its asset portfolio, rescuing bankrupt breweries has often been costly, despite state support for Tsingtao's expansion drive. In 1995, for example, the Xian Hans Brewery and Beverage Factory was teetering on the brink of collapse, with a debt-gearing ratio of 97 per cent. Enter white-knight Tsingtao. In December 1995, a joint venture agreement was entered into under which the Xian-based factory would contribute its remaining productive assets and Tsingtao would contribute cash of RMB 82.5 million (around HK$76.7 million) to create Tsingtao Brewery Xian Company Limited as a new joint venture enterprise, with Tsingtao holding a majority 55 per cent interest in the new firm.[31] During its first full year of operation, the Xian-based joint venture operated with a debt gearing of 75 per cent and suffered losses of RMB 24 million, of which RMB 17 million was interest expenses.[32] Its new subsidiary became a major drag on Tsingtao, which itself saw its 1996 profits plunge by over 70 per cent.[33]

In the face of declining profits and dubious proposals for injecting cash into joint venture projects with failing state-owned enterprises, questions have arisen regarding the use to which much of Tsingtao's income has been put. Less than two years after the company was listed, for example, analysts were expressing concern about the use of funds raised from share listings to make loans to ailing state-owned enterprises and for 'white-knight' rescues of state-owned firms. A tongue-in-cheek financial quiz published at the end of 1995 asks, 'Which Chinese company decided to use its $1.1 billion listing proceeds to make loans to financially ailing Chinese state-owned companies, contrary to statements in its listing prospectus? (a) all of them; (b) Tsingtao Brewery; (c) the Outer Hongqiao Economic Zone Wig Company.'[34]

The correct answer is, of course, Tsingtao. To test the truth of the implied allegation made here, let us turn to the company's listing prospectus. This document would have the investor believe that most of the proceeds raised by the proposed share issue would be used for expansion projects in nominated factories owned by the company. A year later, Tsingtao's 1993 Annual Report reveals what the money[35] was really used for:

> (1) RMB 213,000,000 and US$14,000,000 [was] used to repay loans. (2) A total amount of RMB 126,300,000 [was] applied to the improvement of

> infrastructure and technology projects. (3) RMB 240,000,000 and US$65,000,000 [was] deposited in banks for lendings (*sic*).[36]

In other words, by the end of 1993, over half of the listing proceeds were in the hands of state-owned banks for lending to other mostly state-owed enterprises. Later Annual Reports reveal that much of the money was used to inject new capital into ailing firms (mostly controlled by municipal governments) being taken over by Tsingtao. Millions of yuan were also advanced as loans to Tsingtao subsidiaries, which by the end of 1999 numbered more than 27.[37]

By the late 1990s, Tsingtao was suffering from a phenomenon characteristic of all too many listed Chinese SOEs – a significant triangular debt problem existing throughout the Tsingtao Group. Triangular debt arises when enterprises both rely on credit from suppliers, and provide credit to customers, each creditor becoming increasingly unable to pay its own debts as the recoverable value of its trade receivables decreases. In the case of Tsingtao, the problem has been caused by the company's policy of supporting related firms through direct loans and a lenient policy on credit sales to regular and related customers.[38] Triangular debt had started to become obvious by 1996, when the company was forced to nearly double its provision for bad debts to RMB 15.973 million.[39] Later years also saw the company forced to write off significant amounts of bad debts owed mainly by related firms and state-run business partners.[40] By the end of 2001, the company was forced to take a number of measures to deal with the problem:

- Provision for, and write-off of, bad and doubtful debts;[41]
- Debt restructuring agreements;[42]
- Acquisition agreements;
- Waiver of interest charges;[43]
- Guarantees between related companies;[44]
- Transfer of assets between related companies and to other creditors as security for debts owed;[45]
- Regular renewals of short-term bank loans;[46]
- The transfer of account receivables at net book value as part of the consideration to acquire subsidiaries.[47]
- Debt forgiveness;[48]
- Accepting fixed assets in settlement of accounts receivable from customers;[49] and
- Court-run liquidation auctions to sell assets of bankrupt firms.[50]

By 2001, the Group had 322 577 000 in net accounts receivable, of which it was forced to write off more than half (RMB 170 929 000) as provision for bad debts in light of the aging profile of amounts due.[51] A significant proportion of the accounts receivable came from credit sales, typically to related and associated firms within the Tsingtao Group. Total sales to related and associated companies amounted to RMB 71 619 000 in 2001. Of this amount, sales to related companies under the same key management personnel as the Tsingtao Group accounted for RMB 67 491 000.[52]

Expansion through mergers and acquisitions continued over the next few years. By the end of 2005, Tsingtao held direct and indirect equity investments worth over RMB 1.7 billion in 71 (unlisted) subsidiary operations.[53] Between them, these subsidiaries also received over RMB 2.7 billion in unsecured loans,[54] more than half of which was interest-free, and most of which was 'regarded as quasi-capital contributed by' Tsingtao.[55]

D Recent Ownership Changes and the Introduction of a Significant Foreign Partner

Along with other H-shares, Tsingtao was affected by a sluggish consumer market and increased competition within China during the late 1990s, and the Hong Kong share price of the firm fell considerably in the early half of 1999.[56] The response from Beijing came at the Communist Party Congress in September 1999 when reforms were proposed to relax then-existing Company Law restrictions on state-owned companies repurchasing their own shares abroad.

By December 1999, Tsingtao had been named as one of a number of pilot H-share firms approved to carry out the first experimental share buyback plans. Publicly, it was claimed that only companies that were in a sound financial position would be permitted to buy back some of their B- or H-shares. Market observers commented that 'Approval for Tsingtao Brewery's share buy-back plan indicated the authorities' support for improving the image of overseas-listed state-owned companies in international markets.'[57] In November 1999, the Company embarked on a 'two-week presentation tour in Asia and the United States, capitalizing on the . . . announcement that it [would] pioneer a share buy-back scheme for state-companies overseas'.[58] One media commentator described the scheme as a move 'aimed at arousing foreign investors' interest at a time when Beijing plans to float more state firms' assets on the domestic and international equity markets to finance state-sector reforms', and at 'a time when H-shares [were] languishing at rock-bottom lows'.[59]

At the firm level, the ground for a possible share buyback plan was laid on 14 December 1999 in Qingdao, when the company held an Extraordinary Shareholders' Meeting, a PRC Shareholders' Extraordinary Meeting and a Foreign Shareholders' Meeting. It was at these meetings that the Tsingtao Board of Directors was granted a general mandate to approve new share issues up to 20 per cent of the issued H-shares of the company, or to carry out share repurchase plans for up to 10 per cent of issued H-shares.[60]

The benefits of a share buyback for listed enterprises were recognized both by the company and by commentators. As well as providing the company with more flexibility in international financial markets, '[s]hare buy-backs can boost a company's per share earnings and value if the repurchased shares are being cancelled, thus stabilizing the share price'.[61] As Tsingtao chairman Li Guirong noted, share buybacks 'would allow the company to reduce its aggregate registered capital, while raising net asset value and earnings per share'. It would also 'allow the company to operate in line with international standards'. Commentators and analysts also took comfort from the statement made by Tsingtao Board Secretary Yuan Lu that 'the company had no plans to raise funds through the issue of new shares'.[62]

But the denial turned out not to be true. The share repurchase scheme never took place. Instead, Tsingtao did precisely what Ms Yuan Lu had claimed it had no plans to do – it increased the share capital of the company and issued a whole new batch of A-shares, which were listed in March 2001.

By a special resolution passed on 28 February 2001, the authorized ordinary share capital of the Company was increased from RMB 900 000 000 to RMB 1 000 000 000 by the creation of 100 000 000 A-shares of RMB 1 each. In February 2001, the newly-created A-shares were sold to the public via a public offering and placement of shares with institutional investors at a price of RMB 7.87 per share. Most of the newly-issued shares were listed in Shanghai on 7 March 2001, and the remaining 3 416 368 shares held by institutional investors were listed on 7 June 2001.[63]

The foreign-owned share capital of the company was also increased, in the form of a deepening of the relationship with A-B Holdings. On 21 October 2002, Tsingtao entered into a Strategic Investment Agreement with Anheuser-Busch Companies, Inc. (A-B Holdings), and agreed to issue an aggregate of approximately USD182 million convertible bonds to A-B in three tranches. The first Tranche of Convertible Bonds was fully converted into 60 000 000 new overseas-listed foreign shares by late 2003, bringing the total share capital of Tsingtao to 1 060 000 000 shares, and giving A-B Holdings an economic interest of 9.9 per cent in the firm. The 2002 strategic investment agreement also laid the ground for the conversion of the second tranche of convertible bonds into 134 000 000 additional new overseas-listed shares, and conversion of the third tranche of convertible bonds into 114 219 178 foreign invested shares, both within seven years. Conversion of the second and third tranches actually took place in early

2005, resulting in the issue of a total of 248 219 178 new H-shares on 11 April 2005. Some of the new H-shares went to A-B Jade Hong Kong Holding Co. Ltd. ('A-B Hong Kong'), the controlling subsidiary of A-B Holdings, and the remainder (91 575 342) went to the trustee Law Debenture Trust (Asia) Limited.[64]

Following the conversion of all three tranches of convertible bonds into a total of 308 219 178 new H-shares, the registered capital of the company rose to 1 308 219 178 shares. Of this total, the Qingdao State-Owned Assets Administration Office now holds 399 820 000 shares; PRC holders of domestically-listed tradable shares hold 200 000 000 shares; legal-person A-share holders own 53 330 000 shares; and foreign-owned shares comprise a total of 655 069 178 shares[65] (see Table 3 in Appendix 1). In other words, by the beginning of 2006, directly state-controlled equity (non-tradable A-shares) in the company had fallen to 30.56 per cent, and foreign-controlled (H-share) equity had risen to 50.07 per cent.[66] It looks as though Tsingtao Brewery has thus been transformed from a majority state-owned enterprise, to a majority foreign-owned company, but a closer look at the arrangement under which the trustee company Law Debenture Trust (Asia) Limited holds 91 575 342 H-shares reveals that Tsingtao cannot really be called a 'foreign-controlled' firm at all. Law Debenture Trust (Asia) Limited holds 91 575 342 H-shares (7 per cent of total equity) under an arrangement (section 317 Agreement[67]) whereby it exercises the voting rights associated with those shares,

> under the written instruction of the State-Owned Assets Supervision and Administration Commission of Qingdao (the Qingdao SASAC), while the financial interest including the dividends, profit distribution and payments delivery of those shares are processed under instructions of A-B [Holdings].[68]

In other words, while A-B Holdings retains economic rights to 27 per cent of Tsingtao's equity, its voting interest in the firm is 20 per cent. The Qingdao SASAC's voting interest is 37.6 per cent. It remains uncertain, therefore, whether recent changes in the ownership structure of Tsingtao will actually serve to bring about transformation in the composition and priorities of the company's management team.

E Changing Management Structure

When the company began trading on 15 July 1993, Tsingtao's board of directors comprised nine directors, of whom six were executive directors. The six executive directors each held prominent management positions in the company, including the Chairman, who was also the General Manager.

Of the three non-executive directors, two came from the state-controlled banking sector and had significant connections and experience in local branches of state-controlled banks.[69]

A management reshuffle took place in mid-1996, when four new directors were nominated by the controlling shareholder Qingdao State-Owned Administration Bureau (as it then was) and successfully elected at the AGM on 24 June 1996. Businessman Peng Zuo Yi, a former general manager of Qingdao Dayang Food Group, a Sino-foreign joint venture, was appointed vice-chairman and general manager, replacing Shao Rui Qi, who returned to working for the government. Qingdao Planning Commission Party secretary Li Gui Rong was appointed chairman, replacing Liu Deyuan, who retired.[70]

By the end of 2001, only one member of the 1993 Board of Directors – Liu Ying Di who was very young by Chinese standards, only 37, in 1993 – was still a Director of the company. The 1993 Supervisory Committee had been completely replaced by 2001, and had grown from three members to six. The Board of Directors in 2001 comprised seven members, of which only three were executive directors holding concurrent management positions. The non-executive directors all held senior positions in local political and business interests, such as the Qingdao State Assets Administration Bureau, the Qingdao Municipal Economic Commission, the Bank of China (Shandong Province) and Qingdao University. Of the six members of the Supervisory Committee, two held senior management positions in the company, two held senior positions in the Qingdao Discipline and Inspection Committee, one was the head of a local accounting and audit firm and one was director of a local law firm.[71]

Following the 2003 conversion of the first tranche of convertible bonds issued to A-B Holdings into 60 000 000 overseas-listed shares, A-B Holdings, with 9.91 per cent of total equity, became entitled to nominate one non-executive director and one supervisor to the board and supervisory committee of Tsingtao, respectively. Then, at the Extraordinary General Meeting held in August 2003, shareholders were asked to amend the company's Articles of Association to provide for a Board of Directors of ten, of whom at least half would be external (ie. non-executive) directors. At least one-third of the board would comprise independent directors, with at least one of the independent directors to be an accounting professional. The supervisory committee would grow to eight supervisors (later seven),[72] with the Chairman of the supervisory committee to be elected by at least two-thirds of the committee. Five (later four) of the supervisors would be shareholder representatives elected by shareholders in general meeting, and three supervisors would be elected to represent staff and workers of the company.

When A-B Holdings further increased its shareholding in April 2005, it became entitled to nominate one additional director to the Tsingtao Brewery board of directors, giving A-B Holdings two seats on Tsingtao's board.[73] By the end of 2005, Tsingtao's board of directors comprised 11 members, including the Chairman, the vice-chairman and three executive directors nominated by the Qingdao SASAC, two non-executive directors nominated by A-B Holdings,[74] and four independent directors nominated by the board. In the eight-member Supervisory Committee, three supervisors are elected by, and represent the interests of, company staff, A-B interests are represented by Frances Zheng (Finance Director of Anheuser-Busch Asia), and three supervisors are external supervisors. In addition to the participation of A-B representatives during Board and Supervisory Committee meetings, the A-B representatives are also active on the Special Committees of the company (the Strategy and Investment Committee, the Audit and Finance Committee and the Human Resource and Corporate Governance Committee). Tsingtao has also established five Best Practice Exchange Groups with A-B to exchange experience in enterprise system efficiency and quality control. So far, it seems that Tsingtao is placing itself in an excellent position to benefit from the management experience and technique of its international partner.

At the same time, however, the State is clearly not going to relinquish its final say and control over the Tsingtao group any time soon. In line with the government's 'five separations' policy,[75] the controlling interest of the State shareholder is currently represented on the Board of Directors only in an indirect manner, with three executive directors of the board nominated by the Qingdao SASAC, plus a Chairman of the board who previously held senior positions in various sections of the Qingdao government.[76] Here we see the State protecting both its economic interests in the future prosperity of the firm, and its obvious political interest in the maintenance of widespread personal linkages throughout Chinese business.

III SHANGHAI PETROCHEMICAL COMPANY LIMITED & YIZHENG CHEMICAL FIBRE COMPANY LIMITED

A Introduction

The Chinese government has long had a strong interest in the country's petroleum, petrochemicals and petrochemical industries, having identified these industries as amongst the key sectors in economic development. Not surprisingly, therefore, two of the initial companies selected for the first listing abroad came from the petrochemical sector. Since its establishment in 1993, Shanghai Petrochemical Company Limited (Shanghai Petro) has been one of the largest petrochemical enterprises in China, and one of the largest PRC producers of ethylene, an essential intermediate petrochemical product used in the production of synthetic fibres, resins and plastics. Ever since it was established in 1993, Yizheng Chemical Fibre Company Limited has been one of the largest manufacturers of chemical fibre and its raw materials in the PRC and one of the largest polyester manufacturers in the world. The two companies have recently been brought under the control of a single government-controlled umbrella organization, the China Petroleum & Chemical Corporation (Sinopec Corp), and their names have been altered to reflect this. Given the similarities of interests and coincidences of fortune in the past ten-year history of these two firms, they are dealt with together in the following case study.

B The Issue

Shanghai Petro was registered as a joint stock company on 29 June 1993 with a total equity of 6.55 billion shares, of which Sinopec Corp, its promoter and state-controlled parent organization, held four billion non-circulating state shares, an amount which remains unchanged in 2007. Originally representing 61.07 per cent of Shanghai Petro's total equity, Sinopec Corp's interest in the listed firm declined to 55.56 per cent of total equity, following a new issue of H-shares in 1996–1997.

In July 1993, Shanghai Petro became the first company organized under the laws of the PRC to make a global equity offering. A total of 1.68 billion H-shares were issued, of which 840 million were sold in a Hong Kong offering, while the remainder were sold in a global offering and listed as ADRs on the New York stock exchange. Shanghai Petro thereby became the first Chinese company with shares listed internationally in both Hong Kong and New York. The company's first batch of H-shares began trading on 26 July 1993.

The 1993 global H-share offering was followed by the issue and sale of 150 million non-tradable legal person A-shares to mainland corporate shareholders, and 720 million tradable A-shares to individual mainland shareholders. The tradable A-shares of the company were issued and listed on the Shanghai stock exchange in several batches during late 1993 and early 1994. The original number of legal person and tradable A-shares of Shanghai Petro remains unchanged in 2007.

In all, 650 million additional H-shares were issued in global offerings in late 1996 and early 1997, bringing the total number of overseas-listed foreign shares to 2.33 billion, and the total share equity of the company to

7.2 billion.[77] These figures remain unchanged in 2007. A share reform proposal to convert all of Shanghai Petro's non-tradable and unlisted legal person shares into tradable A-shares was put to a domestic shareholders meeting in October 2006, but failed to attract the necessary two-thirds support of the ordinary holders of tradable A-shares who voted at the meeting.[78] The share-reform proposal included compensation payable as a transfer of 3.2 shares from Sinopec to existing holders of tradable A-shares for every 10 shares held – a transfer that would effectively have reduced Sinopec Corp's holding in Shanghai Petro from 55.56 per cent to 52.36 per cent.[79] This compensation was not enough, however, to prevent the price of domestically-listed Shanghai Petro A-shares from declining rapidly in the days following release of the share-reform proposal.[80]

Yizheng Chemical Fibre Company (Yizheng) was established as a joint stock limited company on 31 December 1993 following a reorganization of the national textile industry. The reorganization occurred when the central government Textile Ministry transferred its 70 per cent interest in the Yizheng Joint Corporation of Chemical Fibre Company (YJC) to the newly established Textile Council. The Textile Council is an industrial association of the major textile companies in China set up to assume certain of the administrative responsibilities of the Textile Ministry. It prepares plans and forecasts for the textile industry, but has no policy-making authority. In 1993 it had no significant investments other than its shareholding in YJC. This shareholding became a 100 per cent interest as a result of the reorganization of all polyester production units and ancillary production lines of YJC. As part of the reorganization, The China International Trade and Investment Corporation (CITIC) which had held a 30 per cent interest in YJC, exchanged its interest in YJC for a direct shareholding in the newly formed Yizheng. Since that time, CITIC has held its 30 per cent share in Yizheng on behalf of the State.

By 1994, therefore, Yizheng was 30 per cent owned by CITIC and 70 per cent owned by the YJC, which, in turn, was wholly owned by the Textile Council. YJC was later renamed the Yihua Group Corporation ('Yihua').

At the time of its incorporation, Yizheng had registered share capital of RMB 2 057 340 000. A revaluation of the fixed assets of the company was then conducted by the State-owned Assets Administration Bureau, as part of the 1993 restructuring of the textile industry described above.[81] The revaluation led to a rise in the capital value of the company to RMB 2.4 billion A-shares, of which YJC held 1.68 billion shares and CITIC held 0.72 billion.[82] Then, in January 1995, Yizheng completed a public issue of 200 million A-shares at an issue price of RMB 2.68 per share.[83]

As noted in Chapter 2, Yizheng's H-shares were issued in two tranches; the first batch of 1 billion H-shares being listed on the HKEx on 29 March

1994, and the second batch of 400 million H-shares being listed in April 1995.

In 1995, therefore, Yizheng's share capital comprised a total of four billion shares of par value RMB 1 each, of which Yihua Group Corporation ('Yihua') (formerly Yizheng Joint Corporation of Chemical Fibre Industry) owned 1680 million shares, or 42 per cent of total share equity; and CITIC controlled 720 million shares, or 18 per cent. Tradable domestically-listed shares comprised 200 million A-shares, or 5 per cent of the company's equity, and Hong Kong-listed foreign capital H-shares comprised 1400 million shares or 35 per cent of equity.[84] This equity structure remained in place in early 2007. A share reform proposal which would have reduced the proportion of shares controlled by state-owned legal person shareholders (Yihua and CITIC) to a total of 58.4 per cent was voted upon at a Class Shareholders Meeting of holders of A-shares of the Company in November 2006, but failed to attract the required support of two-thirds of the ordinary shareholders (holders of circulating A-shares) who voted at the meeting. Active opposition by individual holders of tradable A-shares ensured that the state-owned shares of Yizheng would remain non-tradable.[85]

C Subsequent Performance

Neither Shanghai Petro nor Yizheng have ever made a secret of their expansionist ambitions. With the petrochemical sector designated as one of the key industries for China's future development, government macroeconomic policies designed to control excessive growth in other areas of the economy have had little effect on either company.[86] Further government assistance in the early years, especially, came in the form of official limits on polyester imports.[87]

Both Shanghai Petro and Yizheng suffered, along with the rest of the petroleum and petrochemical industries of Asia, in the wake of severely depressed economic conditions brought about by the Asian financial crisis of 1997. By the first half of 1998, especially, overseas polyester manufacturers, particularly in Taiwan and South Korea, were dumping their products at extremely low prices onto the PRC domestic market. Prices for domestic polyester products deteriorated even further than they already had in the depressed conditions, and most domestic polyester manufacturers suffered losses. At the same time, prices for raw materials of polyester such as PTA, ethylene glycol ('MEG') and paraxylene ('PX') also continued to deteriorate, partly owing to the slump in crude oil prices, partly as a result of new production capacities coming on stream, and partly because of depressed demand from manufacturers of polyester products.[88]

Hard times in the late 1990s did not, however, curb the government's taste for allowing, indeed encouraging, both Shanghai Petro and Yizheng, as well as other members of the national petrochemical industry, to continue in their plans for expansion, consolidation and integration. Both Shanghai Petro and Yizheng were granted a preferential income tax rate of 15 per cent by the PRC Tax Bureau for most of the 1990s. In addition, the Beijing authorities, in 1997, directed a national reorganization to further strengthen the local petrochemical industry in the face of economic pressures and increasing competition from abroad.

D Industrial Reorganization

When Yizheng acquired the FCF Group of companies under the management of Foshan Chemical Fibre Complex, on 1 August 1995, it obtained control of a number of subsidiaries mostly, but not all, operating in related areas. Then, in November 1997, a reorganization of China's petrochemical industry began that would take place over two main stages. As part of the first rationalization stage of the rerform, and pursuant to the government's broader *zhuada* (grasp the big) policy of 1997, Yizheng became part of the country's biggest ever merger in the petrochemical sector when a number of large-scale chemical producers in the Nanjing area (Jinling Petrochemical Corporation, Yangzi Petrochemical Corporation, Yihua Group Corporation, Nanjing Chemical Industrial Group and Jiangsu Petroleum Group) were grouped together into a new, larger entity, the China Eastern United Petrochemical (Group) Company Limited ('CEUPEC').[89] The 1680 million state-owned legal person shares of Yizheng held by Yihua were transferred to CEUPEC, which thereby became the largest shareholder in Yizheng.[90]

The establishment of CEUPEC was a prelude to the broader reorganization of the entire PRC petroleum and petrochemical sector planned for 1998, which would involve a process of vertical integration to establish two extra-large-scale petroleum-petrochemical groups nationally.[91] Two national petrochemical giants would be created: the China National Petroleum Corporation (PetroChina) would be dominant in the northern and western regions of the country, while the China Petroleum Corporation (Sinopec Corp) would be the leader in southern and eastern provinces.

In 1998, the State Council approved the reorganization of China Petrochemical Corporation (CPC), an investment organization controlled by the State. Sinopec was a wholly-owned subsidiary of CPC. Pursuant to the reorganization of CPC, all CEUPEC subsidiaries, including Yizheng, became directly owned subsidiaries of Sinopec, and CEUPEC was dissolved. Sinopec Corp thereby replaced CEUPEC as the holder of 1680 million state-owned A-shares, or 42 per cent of Yizheng's equity. At the same time, an agreement was entered into between Sinopec, CEUPEC and Yihua relating to the change of the shareholder of the 42 per cent state-owned shares of the company.[92] Pursuant to this agreement, Yihua, a wholly-owned subsidiary of Sinopec after the reorganization, became the holder of the 1680 million state-owned A-shares of the Yizheng. Consequently, Yihua became the largest shareholder of Yizheng.[93] At the time of writing, Yizheng's immediate parent is still Sinopec (also the immediate parent of Shanghai Petro), and the company's ultimate holding company is China Petrochemical Organisation (CPC), also the ultimate holding company of Shanghai Petro.

As part of the first stage of restructuring, there was also a major reorganization of the central government's organizations. The State Bureau of Petroleum and Chemical Industry (SBPCI) was established under the State Economics and Trade Commission as an administrative body to take over the government (social) functions previously performed by PetroChina and Sinopec. The role of SBPCI was to oversee the restructuring of subordinate enterprises within PetroChina and Sinopec and to formulate re-employment programmes for workers made redundant through the restructuring process. This freed PetroChina and Sinopec to be established as totally independent companies with complete operational independence from the State Council. The State Council empowered PetroChina and Sinopec to make their own investment decisions, including forming joint ventures with foreign companies and arranging their own financing. Prior to restructuring, all major investment decisions and large-scale borrowings needed the approval of relevant government authorities.[94]

A further reorganization of the China Petrochemical Corporation (CPC) took place in 2002. Following the reorganization, China Petroleum & Chemical Corporation ('Sinopec Corp') was established on 25 February 2000 as a joint stock limited company in the PRC, wholly owned by CPC, which retained its status as a state-controlled investment organization under the direction of the State-owned Assets Supervision and Administration Commission of the State Council. With effect from that date, CPC either by itself or through its wholly-owned subsidiaries transferred to Sinopec Corp a number of its best and most valuable assets, including controlling interests in Shanghai Petro, Yizheng, Beijing Yanhua and Zhenhai Refining.[95] The asset injection was required to make Sinopec Corp attractive for investors when it (Sinopec Corp) was listed on the Hong Kong stock exchange later in the year.

Sinopec Corp was listed on the Hong Kong Stock Exchange and its H-shares began trading on 19 October 2000. CPC, on behalf of the State, retained a 67.92 per cent interest in the newly listed entity. One result of the reorganization leading up to the listing was that both Shanghai Petro and Yizheng were formally renamed, to insert the word 'Sinopec' as a prefix. Thus, these two H-share subsidiaries of Sinopec Corp are now known as Sinopec Shanghai Petrochemical Company Limited and Sinopec Yizheng Chemical Fibre Company Limited, respectively. As at the time of writing in 2005, Sinopec Corp owned 42 per cent of Yizheng and 55.56 per cent of Shanghai Petro. As further explained below, while Sinopec Corp owns less than a 51 per cent majority interest in Yizheng, the Sinopec Group effectively controls the board of Yizheng, and has the power to govern its financial and operating policies. Moreover, the State-controlled CITIC holds 18 per cent of Yizheng's total issued share capital. The largest foreign shareholder in both Yizheng and Shanghai Petro is the nominee company, HKSCC nominees, with 33.63 per cent of total share capital of Yizheng,[96] and 26.61 per cent of Shanghai Petro's total share capital.[97]

In the wake of the 2003 upswing in the petrochemical industry, CPC continued to sell assets to its Hong Kong listed arm, Sinopec Corp. Such asset injections have usually been looked on favourably by the government and stock exchange authorities as a means of arranging things so that listed state-controlled firms are no longer in direct competition with their parent companies. When Sinopec was listed in Hong Kong in 2000, some of CPC's assets were excluded from the listed vehicle as they were either too small in operating scale or under construction. Since then, several more assets have been transferred from parent to listed company, Sinopec Corp. In 2003, for example, the Sinopec Group parent company sold two crude oil refineries – Xinjiang-based Tahe Petrochemical and Shaanxi-based Xian Petrochemical – to the listed vehicle.[98]

The mainland petroleum and petrochemical sector have now been consolidated to the stage where almost the entire industry now comes under two national umbrella groups. The PetroChina group now controls most of the industry in the northern part of the country, while China Petroleum and Chemical (Sinopec Corp) now controls most of southern China. Smyth and Zhai have examined the reasons for China's restructuring of the petrochemical sector, and argue that 'China's approach to reforming its petrochemical sector is well founded'.[99] They discuss the main motives behind the reforms as being the desire to ensure unification of upstream and downstream industries, and thus to bring about economies of scale and scope, and also the desire to separate (profitable) production sections of the industry from the (generally unprofitable) service parts of the sector. The annual reports of both Shanghai Petro and Yizheng reflect this pre-occupation with separating principal business from auxiliary operations.[100]

Following industry restructuring, both PetroChina and Sinopec Corp have become responsible for both downstream and downstream production in their respective geographic areas, and together they dominate China's oil and petrochemical sector,[101] as well as extending into associated income-earning areas such as transport, trading and finance. Thus, for example, by becoming part of the Sinopec family, Yizheng gained connections to a whole host of potentially useful 'relatives', including raw material suppliers like Sinopec Yangzi Petrochemical Company Limited and Sinopec Zhenhai Refining & Chemical Company Limited,[102] as well as financial service providers such as Sinopec Finance and CITIC Industrial Bank.[103]

As Smyth and Zhai point out,

> One of the main rationales for economic integration between upstream and downstream enterprises is to eliminate unnecessary internal competition between petrochemical enterprises in the same geographic area, and to generate economies of both scale and scope. Prior to restructuring, disputes between firms in upstream and downstream industries resulted in an inefficient use of resources due to the central price setting for crude oil. . . . Upstream and downstream industries fought not only for state funding but also for price setting of crude oil, refined products and petrochemicals. One party's gain in the battle at high government levels was often another party's loss. In the end the government had to be responsible for all policy-related losses.[104]

After the restructuring, mergers between what were previously separate plants operating in the same geographic area enabled advantage to be taken of economies of scale. The creation of larger, competitively stronger operations reflects, in particular, the government's desire to strengthen the Chinese sector against the onslaught of cheap foreign imports and foreign competition in the wake of WTO accession. In addition, vertical integration of diverse operations under a single umbrella has also helped to create economies of 'scope'. For example, members of the Sinopec group are able to benefit from economies of relative advantage between different members of the group, by sharing different parts of various production processes, for example, and by being able to streamline operations from the supply of raw material to production process to retail distribution and marketing.

There are two main criticisms which have been made of the way in which China's petrochemical sector (and other sectors as well) has been reformed. The first is that 'the restructured CNPC [PetroChina] and Sinopec are too diversified to compete in overseas markets';[105] the second, and arguably more serious, concern is that 'the relationship between the government, CNPC, Sinopec and the state-owned banks continues to be too close'.[106] The argument is that 'as long as state enterprises including those in the oil sector remain in the hands of the state and dominate the economy, it is hard to make them truly competitive'.[107]

One thing ensuring that China's petrochemical sector is gradually being opened up to the impact of global market forces is the series of price reforms initiated by the government in 1998 aimed at linking domestic oil prices with international (Singapore) prices. It is true that the process of price reform has been slow, and only the crude oil price has really been liberated from state control to any extent, as government controls over refined oil prices will not be lifted until 2007 (the deadline date under China's WTO commitments for the industry to be opened to global competition).[108] Even as late as December 2006, however, stringent controls remained on domestic prices of petroleum products, following a year of continuous rises and record highs in international crude oil prices. The mismatch between domestically controlled prices of petroleum products and the increasing cost of international crude, caused significant losses for oil refining firms in particular. In order to alleviate the impact of policy-driven price controls on the prices of Shanghai Petro's products, the Chinese government decided to grant a one-off (taxable) compensation payment of RMB 282.14 million to the company in the 2006 financial year.[109]

Nevertheless, China does appear committed to implementing its WTO undertakings. The creation of giant integrated oil companies able to compete globally seems to be part of preparing for the opening of the market, and a natural response to the increase in size of PetroChina and Sinopec Corp's international competitors, all of which were merging into ever-larger organizations (eg. the EXXON-Mobil and BP-Amoco mergers). As explained by Nolan (writing more generally about the Chinese government's Zhua-da reforms), the 'best policy was not passively to sell off individual plants to private buyers attempting to construct a textbook, perfectly competitive structure of small business in open competition with other countries' established firms. It would take a long time for large firms to emerge through the spontaneous play of market forces in the teeth of open competition from long established multinational corporations. In the meantime . . . this would lead to efficiency losses stemming from failure to take advantage of economies of scale at the plant level as well as economies of "scope" arising from multi-plant operation.'[110]

The point remains, however, that both Shanghai Petro and Yizheng are members of a very large group of companies, and one which appears more likely to grow in size than to shrink.[111] And this, in turn, increases the number and likelihood of connected operations between members of the Sinopec group of companies. Partly this is the inevitable result of the fact that China's oil and petrochemical industry is subject to extensive regulation by the PRC government. The number of companies that are permitted to conduct sales and purchases of crude oil-related raw materials are limited, and the transactions involving sales and purchases of such raw materials are also subject to the State Plan. Accordingly, Shanghai Petro's options in allocating its raw materials purchases are limited and are governed by the relevant State regulations and measures.[112] These regulations and measures are promulgated by the PRC government and dictate the transaction value, the volume and all other terms and conditions under which the company conducts its purchases of crude oil-related raw materials.[113]

When combined with the heavily consolidated nature of China's oil and petrochemical sector, the effect of government regulation in the oil and petrochemical sector is to ensure that most of Shanghai Petro's business transactions are effected with parties that are related in one way or another. Business partners tend to be either other Sinopec group companies or the company's own subsidiaries. In accordance with government policy, to the extent that Shanghai Petro has followed a strategy of diversification, it has invested in related diversification, that is, in enterprises that are in industries related in some way to the petrochemical industry. Ever since it was listed, the subsidiary and associated operations of Shanghai Petro have been, and still are, mostly companies involved in the trading or production of petrochemical products. The company itself sells most of its products, especially its intermediate petrochemical products, to customers in Eastern China, within the context of a broader Chinese economy that is 'currently predominated by state-controlled entities'.[114]

For both Shanghai Petro and Yizheng, the sheer size and number of connected transactions remains undeniable – far larger than most other Chinese corporate groups. The value of connected transactions appears to have stayed relatively stable over the 12 or so years since listing. Year-on-year comparisons for the purpose of estimating the degree of change in connected transactions are hard to make. For example, the 1995 Annual Report for Shanghai Petro details only the raw figure for total related purchase, sale and other transactions, without providing any indication of what proportion of the total these amounts account for. By 2005, accounting practices had altered so that connected transactions are presented under different categories from those used ten years earlier, and an extra column has been added to reveal the percentage of total amount of transactions of the relevant type that was connected.

What we do learn by examining the 2005 Interim Report for Shanghai Petro, however, is that over 50 per cent of the amount spent by Shanghai Petro in purchasing goods during the first half of 2005 went to connected parties, while over 40 per cent of money earnt from sales of goods and services came from connected parties. These percentages represent ongoing transactions under periodic agreements entered into with connected parties since the birth of the company as a joint stock enterprise, and are thus likely to be representative of the average level of connected transactions during the life of the company. Yizheng's Annual Reports and other documents reveal a similar history of continuing connected transactions ever since it was first registered as a limited liability company. Yizheng's connections extend even into the financial sector, thanks to the significant influence over the company's financial and operating decisions exerted by CITIC. Moreover, as already suggested above, apart from transactions with CPC and their fellow CPC subsidiaries, both Shanghai Petro and Yizheng conduct regular business activities with entities directly or indirectly owned or controlled by the PRC government and numerous government authorities and agencies.

After the implementation of newly amended Hong Kong Listing Rules on 31 March 2004, certain waivers from announcement, reporting and shareholder approval requirements previously granted to both Shanghai Petro and Yizheng in respect of their ongoing connected transactions became no longer valid. Under Chapter 14A, both companies became subject to announcement and independent shareholder approval requirements in respect of their major continuing connected transactions. In Circulars sent to shareholders in mid- and late 2005, both Shanghai Petro and Yiheng have provided estimates of continuing connected transactions for the years ending 31 December 2005, 2006 and 2007. What these estimates reveal is the impact of recent significant expansion in the companies' operations, resulting in rapidly rising figures for purchases of raw materials from connected parties.[115] The figures also reveal a rising income from sales of petrochemical and petroleum products to connected parties for Shanghai Petro,[116] but falling income from sales of polyester products for Yizheng.[117] This suggests that Shanghai Petro's immediate future prospects remain more certain than those of Yizheng, and that Yizheng will be forced to earn more of its sales income from sales to unconnected parties in an increasingly competitive domestic market and from export sales to overseas markets.

E The Future

So far as the broader Chinese petroleum and petrochemical sector is concerned, the emergence of PetroChina and Sinopec as broadly-integrated giant operations oriented towards expansion and consolidation has been well-timed. The years 2003 and 2004 have seen an upswing in the petroleum and petrochemical industries following the unstable conditions brought about by the 11 September 2001 incident in New York and other factors adversely affecting the world and US economies. Both international and, in particular, domestic, demand for petrochemical products have been strong, and sales of petrochemical and petroleum products have grown. One of the main drivers of strong domestic demand for refined oils like diesel and petrol has been the rapid growth in private car ownership in China, and a boom in fixed asset investment requiring transport of bulk commodities such as cement, coal and steel.[118] The time seems ripe to maximize the gains to be obtained through the Hong Kong-listed Sinopec Corp and, in particular, to invest in things such as research and development, technology and capital equipment upgrades, as well as workplace health and safety and environmental measures. A number of Sino-foreign joint ventures in the petrochemical sector, such as the multi-billion dollar Secco joint venture between BP and Shanghai Petrochemical,[119] together with increasing foreign ownership levels in the Chinese petrochemical sector,[120] should help to provide access to foreign technological, management and other expertise that will assist in ensuring that such investments succeed. Shanghai Petro also maintains a range of technology development units, including a Petrochemical Research Institute, a Polyester Fibre Research Institute and an Acrylic Fibre Research Institute.[121]

On the other hand, however, the price of Shanghai Petro's major raw material, crude oil, is likely to continue to rise. Since Shanghai Petro purchases its major raw materials through Sinopec Corp from overseas sources, and also exports a proportion of its petroleum products directly through Sinopec Corp, rising crude oil prices on the world market will affect profitability.[122] So also will the change in the exchange rate brought about with the partial floatation of the yuan in mid-2005. The recent acceleration in China's expansion of its crude oil refining capacity, substantially to cope with rapidly growing demand, appears set to continue, at least for the short-to-medium term.[123] In the context of growing demand, however, prices for intermediate petrochemical and petroleum products especially are likely to maintain growth along with the crude oil price. As Shanghai Petro's 2004 Annual Report notes, despite the presence of a degree of uncertainty due to unstable international crude oil prices, increasing pressure on inflation and intensifying market competition, general growth in both demand and prices for the company's products increased dramatically in 2004, and is expected to continue to rise at least in the short term. Moreover, the company has been able to rely on the competitive advantage from its vertical integration to adapt its product mix, and increase the capacity of its key upstream plants.[124]

The situation appears less rosy for Yizheng. While Shanghai Petro gets over half of its income from supply of petroleum products and intermediate petrochemicals (such as PX, MEG and PTA), Yizheng's major source of income is sales from polyester products, further down the processing chain. In other words, Shanghai Petro specializes in the supply of the very same raw materials Yizheng needs for its productive activities. In the case of both petroleum and intermediate petrochemicals, there is a shortage of supply in relation to demand both domestically and internationally, and the resulting strong price situation is reflected in Shanghai Petro's historical record in its 2004 operating results.[125] In the case of downstream textile industry companies like Yizheng, however, profit margins are being squeezed by a number of factors, including increasing prices of polyester raw materials and intensified competition and oversupply in the domestic Chinese polyester sector. Although prices for polyester products did rise in 2004, they did not rise anywhere near as much as raw material prices, and many Chinese polyester producers either stopped production or reduced output in 2004. Nor are compressed profit margins being much improved by the ending of the WTO Multifibre Agreement on 1 January 2005. While the ending of the global textile quota system is generally expected to be a boon for the Chinese export sector in the longer term, its effect on the local petrochemical industry in the short-to-medium term is less clear. In 2005 both the US and the EU refused to allow access to huge inventories of polyester and other fibre products which spent months piling up in the ports awaiting import clearance. Yizheng was also affected by an adverse EU anti-dumping finding against it, also in 2005.

A final point is that market risk is not the only risk to which operations in the petrochemical sector are exposed. A far more serious set of risks may be the increasing level of environmental risks to which so much of China's economy is becoming exposed. PetroChina's chemical blast in Jilin province in late 2005 and the subsequent contamination of a major river were a recent reminder of the risks involved.[126] The inadequacy of insurance coverage of mainland oil and petroleum sector firms is one of the most alarming aspects of these risks. Sinopec's filing to the US stock exchange reveals that it does not carry business interruption and third-party liability insurance. The 2004 Annual Reports of Shanghai Petro and Yizheng contain no mention of insurance coverage.

F Changing (or Unchanging) Management Structure

Perhaps not surprisingly, given the strategic and economic importance of the petroleum sector, it is the two petrochemical sector companies which appear to have been slowest to ensure compliance with the Hong Kong stock exchange Listing Rules requirement that at least one-third of the board must be 'independent', as that term is legally defined. For example, when Shanghai Petro's H-shares first began trading on 26 July 1993, there were seven executive directors and eight non-executive directors, only two of whom appear to have been truly independent in the sense of having no former or current connection to the company.[127] There were three members of the Supervisory Committee. All three had lengthy prior employment in various positions within the company. Ten years later, at the end of 2003, the situation remained basically the same: management dominated by directors and supervisors, with interests closely aligned to those of the parent company and the Chinese government. There were 15 members on the board of directors, seven of whom were executive directors holding concurrent senior positions within the firm. There were also four non-executive directors, all of whom held positions in the parent company Sinopec, plus four directors who qualified as 'independent'.[128]

In the case of Yizheng, the company's board of directors also remains controlled by representatives from the Sinopec group. At the end of 2005, there were 14 directors on the board, of whom three hold current positions within CITIC, four hold current positions within Yihua, two come from previous positions within Yihua, one comes from Sinopec and four are labelled 'independent'. Three directors are noted in the 2004 Annual Report as receiving special subsidies from the State Council.[129] Of the five members of the supervisory committee, two are non-executive and labelled as 'independent'. Both of the 'independent' supervisors hold current management positions within one of China's 'big-four' state-owned banks.[130]

IV GUANGZHOU SHIPYARD INTERNATIONAL COMPANY LIMITED

A The Issue

Guangzhou Shipyard International Company Limited (GSI) was registered as a joint stock limited company on 7 June 1993,[131] following the reorganization of the State-owned Guangzhou Shipyard. Its principal activities include shipbuilding, container manufacturing, ship repairing, large-scale steel structure and terrestrial machinery.

Upon incorporation, the total share capital of GSI was 494 677 600, of which China State Shipbuilding Corporation (CSSC), a State Council subsidiary, held 210 800 080 unlisted state-owned shares, representing 42.613 per cent of the total share capital. This represented a deviation from previous practice of the Chinese Government to maintain a majority stake in originally state-owned assets after any public listing.[132]

In July 1993, 145 million GSI H-shares were offered to the public at $2.08 each,[133] while the remaining 12.398 million H-shares were privately placed (at the same issue price) with two Hong Kong-based business partners of GSI: Civet Investment Co (Hong Kong) and Vincent Leader.[134] The public issue was 76–77 times oversubscribed,[135] and the H-shares were listed and began trading in Hong Kong on 6 August 1993.[136] The issue price of the H-shares, at about 9.5 times prospective earnings on a pro-forma fully-diluted basis, was by far the lowest offered by a mainland state-owned enterprise.[137]

The company's A-shares were offered in Shanghai in October 1993, and were listed and began trading in Shanghai on 28 October 1993. Following the conversion of 28 396 400 employee shares to listed shares in 1994, GSI's equity amounted to a total of 210 800 080 non-tradable State-owned shares, 126 479 500 A-shares listed in Shanghai, and 157 398 000 Hong Kong-listed H-shares, comprising 31.82 per cent of GSI's total share capital.[138]

Shortly after its H-shares were floated, GSI received government support in the form of a special permit to export and import on its own account, allowing the shipbuilder to control its own foreign currency reserves.[139] This was in anticipation of GSI's change of status to a Sino-foreign joint stock limited company which occurred on the PRC on 21 October 1994.[140] Like all of its pioneer H-share counterparts, GSI was permitted by the central authorities to retain its specially-granted 15 per cent profits-tax rate following the alteration of status.[141]

B The Structure of the Group and the Significance of Related Party Transactions in GSI's Operations

In 1994, GSI held direct controlling interests in five principal subsidiaries, operating in areas that included container manufacturing, ship dismantling, furniture manufacture and advertisement production and design.[142] The company also held minority share interests in five associated companies all operating in related industry areas.[143] In 1998 the GSI Group had expanded to include a total of 11 controlled (majority owned) subsidiaries of GSI,[144] but by the end of 2005, this had fallen back again to controlling interests of 51 per cent or more in eight subsidiary operations (plus indirect controlling interest in a further three operations).[145]

Right from the beginning there was a cosy relationship between GSI and its subsidiaries (the GSI Group) and CSSC, the state-owned parent organization of the GSI Group.[146] One feature of this relationship was the 'comprehensive service agreement' between GSI and Guangzhou Shipyard for the continued supply by Guangzhou Shipyard of the social services to which GSI employees had grown accustomed under the central planning system (including medical care, primary and secondary education, staff accommodation and retirement support services). This agreement has been renewed regularly since 1993, and was still in existence in late 2005, although the annual amounts payable appear to be declining steadily.[147] More important for the longer-term future of GSI, and as the original GSI listing prospectus makes clear, the operations of GSI and its subsidiaries are largely dependent upon a series of connected transactions involving both the provision of products and services by the GSI Group to the CSSC Group, and the purchase by GSI and its subsidiaries of products (especially steel and steel products) and services from other entities in the CSSC Group.[148] This was partly the inevitable result of the way in which assets were divided when GSI was originally split off from Guangzhou Shipyard. At the time of GSI's H-share listing, equipment relating to the supply of water and electricity was included in the assets of GSI Group, instead of remaining in the CSSC Group. This formed the basis for a long-term relationship in which the smooth operations of the CSSC Group remain reliant upon the continued supply of water and electricity utilities by GSI and its subsidiaries.[149]

As discussed further below, China's shipping industry firms were badly hit by the effects of the 1997 Asian financial crisis. Government measures to overcome the effects of the crisis included moves to restructure several major industries, including the petroleum sector (as shown above) and the shipbuilding sector. Thus, in January 1998, China State Shipbuilding Corporation announced that it was planning to create three large groups through mergers and acquisitions based on operations in Dalian, Shanghai and Guangzhou,[150] all of which would come under the supervision of the central government's State-owned Assets Supervision and Administrative Commission (SASAC). As GSI was the largest shipyard in southern China and CSSC's only Hong Kong-listed vehicle, it would lead the restructuring exercise.[151] The reorganization of CSSC took place in 1999, and two new umbrella SOEs were established: the China State Shipbuilding Corporation and the China Shipbuilding Industry Corporation. The newly-incorporated China State Shipbuilding Corporation (CSSC), founded on 1 July 1999, became the new representative holder of the state-owned shares of GSI, which remained at 42.613 per cent of GSI's total equity. The respective proportions of listed A-shares and H-shares also remained unchanged.[152] The reorganization of CSSC in part represented a move to centralize CSSC's management of state-owned assets under the supervision of the SASAC. Thus it is the SASAC which is described as the 'actual controller' of GSI in the company's Annual Reports between 2000 and 2005.[153] The central government authority in charge of the industry affairs of GSI, however, is the Commission of Science Technology and Industry for National Defence (CSTIND).

At the time of its initial listing in 1993, the Hong Kong Stock Exchange granted a waiver to GSI with respect to the continuing connected transactions on the basis that those transactions would be on normal commercial terms or on terms no less favourable than terms available to third parties. In 1993, the total value of connected transactions between the GSI Group and other members of the CSSC Group amounted to RMB 151 537 000 (1994 = 204 380 000).[154] Just over ten years later, in 2004, GSI formalized its continuing connected transactions in the form of a written Framework Agreement which was approved at the company's Annual General Meeting of that year in accordance with new rules governing 'non-exempt' continuing connected transactions under Rule 14A.35 of the Hong Kong Listing Rules.[155] In compliance with the Listing Rules, transactions conducted under the Framework Agreement are subject to annual cap amounts for the three years to 31 December 2006. In March 2005, a review of the annual caps revealed the likelihood that the value of connected transactions undertaken in 2005 was likely to exceed the amounts approved in a 2004 'Framework Agreement'.[156] A circular was sent to shareholders seeking approval for revised caps on the annual value of the various categories of connected transactions under the Framework Agreement.[157] Another circular seeking approval for a Second Supplemental Agreement to further revise annual caps outlined in the Framework Agreement was sent to shareholders on 17 November 2006.[158]

A new Framework Agreement for continuing connected transactions was signed with CSSC for the period 1 January 2007 to 31 December 2009. Transactions under the 2007–2009 Framework Agreement can be classified into two main categories: (1) products and services provided by the GSI Group to the CSSC Group; and (2) products and services provided by the CSSC Group to the GSI Group. In both categories, the value and nature of continuing connected transactions is expected to continue expanding for the period 2004–2009. Key features of the Framework Agreement are the following:

1. The value of electrical and mechanical engineering equipment, metallic materials and ship-building equipment GSI Group purchases from the CSSC Group appears considerably greater than the value of electrical and mechanical engineering equipment and metallic accessories supplied by GSI Group to the broader CSSC Group. This may be because GSI Group purchases, but does not supply, ship-building accessories and equipment.[159]
2. The value of labour, design and technology services supplied to CSSC Group used to be noticeably less than the value of labour and design and technology services purchased, but in this area the respective values of services supplied and purchased appear to be converging.[160]

3. CSSC Group provides financial services (deposits and loans) to the GSI Group.[161] In addition, when purchasers of ships require GSI to deliver a performance guarantee issued by a bank, CSSC provides the third-party guarantee to the bank to secure the performance guarantee. CSSC also provides corporate guarantees to banks granting loans to members of the GSI Group. The bank guarantee fees payable by GSI Group are set at lower than market rates.[162]
4. A final feature of the GSI–CSSC relationship is the sales agency fee (commission) of 1 per cent paid by GSI Group to the CSSC Group when vessels are sold through CSSC Group. The 1 per cent commission is in line with international vessel-sales practice. GSI Group also procures certain material via the CSSC Group, mainly foreign-produced equipment and steel accessories for ship-building which have to be imported mainly through an import-agency subsidiary of the CSSC Group located in Hong Kong.[163]

C Changes in Management since 1993

When its shares began trading on 6 August 1993, there were 19 members of the Board of Directors of GSI, including 14 executive directors and five non-executive directors, only one of whom could be said to have been independent.[164] By 2004, the official size of the board had shrunk to 12, of which 11 positions are recorded in the 2004 and 2005 Annual Reports as filled, leaving one apparent vacancy. Four of the directors whose biographical details are recorded are classified as independent non-executive directors, while the remaining seven all have extensive years of experience within the CSSC group and hold positions within GSI itself or within CSSC. Moreover, the continuing presence of the Party in business in China remained apparent in 2004, with the chairman of the board being a former secretary of the Party Committee of GSI.[165]

In addition to the introduction of independent directors on the board in compliance with the 'one-thirds' rule[166], a number of other important changes occurred in the corporate governance structure of GSI between 1994 and 2006. First, while in 1994 the positions of chairman and general manager of the company were held by a single individual,[167] in 2004 and 2005, the positions of chairman of the board and company CEO were held by different appointees.[168] Second, in 2004, four special committees were set up under the board, each with defined terms of reference to monitor specific areas of the company's business. The four committees are the Audit Committee, the Emolument and Examination Committee, the Strategy Committee and the Nomination Committee.[169] Third, and finally, a system of cumulative voting for the election of company directors was introduced when GSI's articles of association were amended at an extraordinary meeting of shareholders held on 11 December 2006. Under the new system:

> where a general meeting of shareholders elects more than two directors, each share held by shareholders shall have the same number of votes as the number of directors proposed to be elected. Shareholders may cast all or any of their votes in favour of one or more of the candidates. At the end of the voting, the candidates with the highest percentage of votes shall be elected.[170]

D Expansion and Diversification and the Significance of Policy Sticks and Carrots

Right from its emergence onto the market GSI made no secret of its plans for diversification, 'utilising its resources and expertise in shipbuilding' and expansion.[171] Aspects of the expansion policy included a number of major bridge-building contracts[172], the establishment of a joint venture enterprise, 'Guangzhou United Steel Structure International Limited', with Havens Steel Company of the United States in November 1994[173]; and establishment of a number of other local joint ventures.[174] At the local level, the Guangzhou municipal government did its part in supporting GSI's expansion plans by granting the company land use rights to large tracts of industrial-zoned lands in Guangzhou.[175]

Policy-related changes in government taxation rules were important motivating factors for much of GSI's business strategy and focus in the later 1990s. For example, a new taxation system was introduced in 1995 that imposed a new value-added tax on domestically consumed products. Since most of the ships built by the company's shipbuilding division had been, and were, for domestic consumption, the most effective way for the company to minimize the impact of the new tax was to expand its export-oriented container manufacturing section. Local customers in the shipbuilding market were also more likely to receive relatively easy credit payment terms, and to expose GSI's balance sheet to a greater degree of risk. Even as early as 1993, outstanding and dubious debts owed by local customers presented a major risk to GSI's future company profits. As early as 1993, the GSI balance sheet was already weighed down by just one local customer based in Shanghai that had failed to pay RMB 252 million owing as at 30 June.[176] An additional progress payment on ships being built for the same customer of about 249 million yuan was due by the end of the year. If overdue progress payments were not received, the impact on profits for the group would be severe. But GSI directors were quoted as saying that mainland officials had instructed a bank to lend the customer the required amount, and so they were confident that the entire 252 million yuan would be settled by the end of the year.[177] The following year, 1994, saw a further

287 per cent rise in accounts receivable, mostly from one major customer, Haixing Shipping.[178]

GSI Group's steel structure operations also continued to expand in 1995. As well as avoiding the effect of the VAT, steel structure projects earned, and were expected to continue earning, higher profit margins than either of the company's core shipbuilding or container making businesses.[179] At the same time, the company also reduced the size of its ship-breaking business as a result of high import tariffs on scrapped steel and falling prices of construction steel in China.[180]

Expansion and diversification continued into 1995[181] and the late 1990s, with national government support and under the guidance of the eighth and ninth five-year plans. Under the eighth five year plan, GSI's state-owned parent company, the CSSC, committed itself to several shipyard expansion projects which would see the injection of almost US$750 million into the shipbuilding industry, identified by Beijing as a key element in the country's modernization.[182] The focus was on expanding capacity to meet export demand for ships by producing larger ships (350 000 dwt or more)[183] and by upgrading facilities to match international standards for delivery time and quality management.[184] In mid-1996, the company made maritime history with the launch of a 39 800 tonne cargo vessel, the biggest launched in south China up to that date.[185] Container manufacturing and related steel-structure construction operations also expanded,[186] and diversification continued as the company moved into terrestrial machinery operations and new products, such as aluminium high-speed boats and elevators.[187] The point here is the way in which expansion and diversification was pursued with government support and encouragement, and to an extent that analysts were already suggesting was risky.

By early 1996, several brokerages were recommending that GSI was a stock to be sold rather than held, citing rising material costs and a cut in the VAT rebate, both of which would curtail the company's profits. Brokers also noted that the coming into operation of the proposed joint venture with Havens Steel of the US had been postponed until 1997, slicing 22 million RMB off GSI's 1996 projected net earnings.[188] Their pessimism was borne out when the company reported a plunge of 44.7 per cent in net profit to 101.3 million RMB for 1995 from the previous year.[189] 1996 saw a second year of even larger falls in total profit levels: a fall of 67.3 per cent from 1995 levels to a total of 39.8 million yuan, while earnings per share fell to 6.73 fen from 20.47 fen.[190] Again, the profit decline occurred despite a continued rise in total turnover.[191] The profit decline was explained by reference both to the loss of foreign exchange earnings as a profit item under Hong Kong Accounting Rules, and to Beijing's lowering of export tax rebates from 17 per cent to 14 per cent in late 1995, then from 14 per cent to 9 per cent at the beginning of 1996.[192] The cut in tax rebates reportedly cost the company up to 40 million yuan for the 1996 financial year.[193]

Two developments, rebate-cuts and declining container export sales, were related. The government's decision to cut tax rebates for exporters to shore up state coffers increased traders' export costs, and total exports fell as a result. Dwindling exports meant fewer ships called at Chinese ports, and this, in turn, meant that demand for GSI containers also declined.[194] The lowering of prices for both shipbuilding and containers, and the fall in both production and sales volume, represented other major factors in the downward movement of GSI profit.[195]

One bright spot in 1996 was the fact that more of GSI's turnover was beginning to come from overseas sales.[196] Also in 1996, GSI was placed on a list of 300 enterprises approved by the Central Bank to receive preferential working capital loans from state banks as part of the government's policy of 'propping up the state sector'.[197] That most of the other nine pioneer H-share companies were also lucky enough to find themselves on the same list almost goes without saying.[198] In the case of GSI, the company received working loans from the Industrial and Commercial Bank of China worth 60 million yuan in 1996. It was also able to refinance about 90 million yuan of its more than 200 million yuan in outstanding loans at lower interest rates. The company obtained loans at a 10 per cent annual interest rate, compared to between 12 per cent and 13 per cent previously, precisely because it was on the government's list of SOEs chosen for state support.[199] GSI would continue to benefit from a number of government policies under the new 1996–2000 ninth five-year plan.[200] In 1997, for example, the government-owned policy bank, Export-Import Bank of China (Eximbank), assisted by providing export credit loans, and the state-owned People's Insurance (Property) Co of China assisted by providing export-credit insurance.[201]

Cost-cutting measures were implemented in 1997 in an effort to improve the situation, including a 10 per cent cut in company staff levels and measures to shorten the shipbuilding period.[202] Another measure was to reduce the business volume of its container building division by 20 per cent in 1997, to minimize the damage inflicted by harsh price-cutting competition.[203]

In late 1997, the Asian financial crisis hit, and markets around the region plummeted. Hong Kong markets were no exception, and the H-share index fell, along with other regional market indexes. As the impact of the crisis took hold, new contract signings for GSI came to a virtual standstill, and the company did not get any substantial new work after the crisis hit until late in April of 1998, when it finally managed to win a 50 million yuan crane manufacturing contract. Possibly to help distance the company from the crisis and its effects in investors' minds, the company's chairman Hu Guoliang stated publicly that the slowdown in contract signings was 'not unusual' and had *not* been caused by the regional crisis. He stated that the financial crisis had had little impact on the company as its customers were 'mostly based in Europe and the mainland'.[204] Certainly it remains true that the GSI saw attributable profit recover almost 20 per cent to 39.68 million yuan in 1997 from 1996.[205]

The company insisted in January 1998 that it already had fixed 'orders on hand of more than US$400 million to be delivered to 2000, accounting for two-thirds of its ship-building capacity', and making it less vulnerable in the short term to increasing competition from shipyards in South Korea and Japan.[206] Despite such protestations however, by September 1998, GSI was forced to seek yet another export-credit loan from Eximbank, this time for 1.2 billion yuan. By that stage, Eximbank bank had extended a total amount in export-credit loans of 1.8 billion yuan since 1995 to support the company's export-producing operations.[207] Beneficial interest rates for the loans were set at 1.5 percentage points to two percentage below the level charged by Chinese commercial banks.[208]

In December 1998, Beijing acted yet again to protect and shore up mainland shipyards as they struggled to fend off the effects of the strong yuan and rising competition. Because domestic shipyards like GSI were badly hit by the advantage that the post-crisis currency declines bestowed upon Japan and South Korea exports, the State Council and the Ministry of Communications acted to curb the increasing tendency by mainland shipping firms to switch their orders abroad.[209] An order was issued for all domestic shipping companies to buy locally built vessels, not foreign ones, and, in a move apparently aimed at overcoming the export-dampening effect of the strong yuan, the Ministry of Finance and State Tax Bureau announced that the export tax-rebate would be allowed to rise back to its pre-1995 levels, from 9 per cent to 14 per cent for shipping products declared exported on or after 1 June 1998, then again from 14 per cent to 16 per cent in respect of shipping products declared exported on or after 1 October 1998, and to 17 per cent for shipping products exported on or after 1 January 1999.[210] However, none of this assistance came in time to prevent a further fall in company profits for 1998, down to RMB 19.032 million for year ended 31 December 1998, less than 50 per cent of 1997 profit levels.[211]

E The GITIC Bankruptcy and its Impact on GSI

In 1994, a large proportion of the funds raised by GSI during its listing were placed as trust deposit investments in the government-controlled Guangzhou International Trust and Investment Corp (GITIC) and other provincial government-owned non-banking financial institutions connected to GITIC. GSI's Annual Report for 1994 indicates that amounts of RMB 195 244 000 yuan and RMB 66 570 000 were held as deposits made with trust and investment corporations for interest income in 1993 and 1994, respectively.[212] The deposits were classified as a current asset in the company's balance sheets for the year.[213]

By the end of 1997, this sum had risen to RMB 505 881 000 held by the company as interest-bearing deposits with trust and investment corporations. Again classified as a current asset, these deposits are described as 'interest bearing and mature within one year'.[214] No indication is given that any difficulties might be encountered in recovering these deposits. This sum can be considered as relatively large for a company that reported total earnings attributable to shareholders of RMB 39 678 000 for the same year.[215]

As a result of its strategy of holding such large sums as deposits with trust and investment corporations, the company was severely hit by the bankruptcy of GITIC and its related institutions in 1998.

It was in August 1998 that GSI, along with several other Hong Kong-listed mainland enterprises, finally confirmed what many had suspected: it was having difficulties collecting deposits from various non-bank financial institutions, including GITIC, reflecting the seriousness of liquidity problems facing many mainland financial institutions.[216]

In October 1998, GITIC became the first State-owned financial institution to go bankrupt in China. The GITIC case involves the largest ever amount of assets in a Chinese bankruptcy case. On 6 October 1998, the PBOC issued a notice stating that GITIC was unable to pay its matured debts and that, in order to protect the lawful rights of its creditors, the PBOC had closed GITIC and revoked the financial licences of GITIC and its branches. According to the Notice, the PBOC set up a liquidation to carry out GITIC's closure liquidation. During the liquidation process, all outstanding debts owed to and by GITIC would be placed under the custody of the BOC and the management of GITIC's securities businesses would be entrusted to Guangfa Securities Company, one of the leading securities firms in China. On the same date, the BOC issued a notice which, among other things, stated that the period of registration of rights and liabilities of GITIC would be from 6 October 1998 to 6 January 1999.[217]

The three-month liquidation process found that GITIC was insolvent. GITIC's board of directors decided that GITIC and three of its over 200 subsidiaries – GITIC Shenzhen Company, Guangdong International Leasing Company and Guangxin Development Enterprise – would apply for bankruptcy. On 11 January 1999, GITIC filed a petition for bankruptcy with the Guangdong Provincial High People's Court. On the same date, the

Court issued a notice to the creditors of GITIC inviting them to attend the Court on 16 January 1999. On 15 January, the Court issued a public notice of acceptance of the bankruptcy petition and, the following day, the Court issued a separate public notice of bankruptcy, stating that the Court declared GITIC bankrupt in accordance with the first paragraph of Article 3, Article 8 and Article 23(1) of the *Enterprise Bankruptcy Law* on the grounds that (1), the management of GITIC was disorganized; (2), GITIC's liabilities substantially exceeded its assets; and (3), GITIC was unable to pay its huge debts on time.

KPMG Huazhen Accounting and two law firms were appointed to handle the clean-up of the bankrupt trust, to clear the debts and oversee investment projects of GITIC and its subsidiaries, and to collect money from GITIC's debtors.

By the end of 1998, the situation was so unclear as to precisely how much of the GITIC-related monies would be unrecoverable that no appropriate provision could be decided upon. In particular, much depended upon the outcome of legal actions initiated against both the Guangzhou Economic and Technology Development Zone International Trust and Investment Company (GETDZITIC) and the Guangzhou Foreign Economic and Trade Trust and Investment Company.[218] Until the situation became clearer, no provision for doubtful debts was made in the 1998 Annual Accounts.[219]

In 1999, a meeting of GITIC creditors was held at which the financial advisor reported the estimated value of realizable assets of GITIC represented approximately 20 per cent of its liabilities (including contingent liabilities) and a debt restructuring was proposed. Shortly afterwards, GITIC's proposal that a debt restructuring should take place was approved in principle by the Bank of China, with the support of the Guangzhou municipal government, GITIC's controlling shareholder. The debt restructuring proposal outlined plans for all of GITIC's debt obligations to be met over a period of time through a combination of cash injections by the Guangzhou municipal government, sales of assets, and swaps of its liabilities to depositors with equities or financial instruments of a joint venture company proposed to be set up. A written proposal was presented for comment to the creditors, proposing to repay the principal amounts, due to non-banking creditors and individual depositors over ten years and five years, respectively.[220]

By the end of the 1999 financial year, GSI's overdue deposits with GITIC totalled RMB 422 781 000. GITIC's debt restructuring plan had not yet been finalized, and with no settlement forthcoming, and little information available, the company was forced to write off the interest receivables of RMB 33 290 000 for 1999 completely, as the sum was clearly not going to be recovered. Media reports were that the national government was concerned about the financial crisis that had by now developed in Guangdong province as a result of the GITIC collapse. The national government had also, it was reported, loaned a total amount of RMB 38 billion to the Guangdong provincial government to help resolve the issue.[221]

In respect of sums owing from GETDZITIC (RMB 55 000 000), GSI obtained a favourable court judgment in the legal proceedings for recovery of the amount due, and in 1999 also lodged an application for enforcement of the judgment. During the course of execution of the judgment, the court presented certain assets of GETDZITIC for settlement of the debts and, by the end of 1999, GSI was considering the offer. No information being available regarding the financial status of GETDZITIC, no assessment could be made as to the ultimate recoverability of the amount due, and GSI was forced to accept the likelihood of a significant proportion being unrecoverable.[222]

GSI also obtained a favourable court judgment in respect of amounts owing (RMB 10 000 000) from Guangzhou Foreign Economic and Trade Trust and Investment Company (GFETTIC) in 1999, and submitted an application for execution of the judgment. But GSI was notified by the court that its application for execution of the court judgment would have to be suspended, in order not to adversely affect the progress of GFETTIC's financial restructuring, which was taking place at the time. Again, GSI was forced to accept the likelihood of a significant proportion of its claims against GFETTIC not being met.[223]

An assets swap arrangement which had been previously agreed with the Guangdong Overseas Trust and Investment Company (GOTIC) for settlement of amounts owing to GSI failed, and never took place. As a result, GSI initiated legal action against GOTIC for recovery of both overdue principal and interest receivable (totalling RMB 10 000 000).[224] An application for execution of the court judgment was also accepted, and a total sum of RMB 1.05 million (RMB 1 500 000) had in fact been recovered by the end of the 1999 financial year. Even though the legal action against GOTIC was for recovery of both principal and interest, a decision was taken that the interest receivable amount of RMB 3 142 000 should be fully written off in the 1999 financial year.[225]

In light of the uncertain situation regarding the real risk of non-recoverability from GITIC, GETDZITIC, GFETTIC and GOTIC, the directors of GSI finally decided, rather arbitrarily it would seem, to make provision for non-recovery representing 10 per cent of the total outstanding balances due from the trust and investment corporations as at the end of the 1999 financial year. Price Waterhouse Coopers, the international auditors of the GSI accounts, were highly sceptical about the adequacy of the 10 per cent provision for non-recovery, and expressed their disagreement about the sum in a qualified opinion outlined in their report to shareholders. 'In our opinion,' say the auditors, 'the provision is unlikely to be adequate and a higher provision should have been made'.[226] The Chinese auditors express their disagreement with the 10 per cent figure less vigorously, saying only that 'the adequacy of 10 per cent provision to the trust deposits in non-banking financial institutions and its impact on the profit of the year is not able to be determined'.[227]

GSI's Annual Report for 2000 records the intervention of CSTIND, which 'was concerned and assisted the Company by requesting related government bodies to treat the Company as overseas creditors when considering repayments or asset swap arrangements'.[228] The intervention, however, proved unhelpful, and the board was forced to make a total provision for non-recovery of 80 per cent 'based on the prudence principle'. Taking into account the 10 per cent provision already factored into the 1999 accounts, the additional provision required for current year 2000 was 70 per cent or RMB 295 946 700. Similar figures for doubtful recovery provision are given for deposits with the bankrupt Guangdong Overseas Chinese Trust and Investment Company (GOTIC), Guangzhou Foreign Economic and Trade and Investment Company (GFETIC) and the Guangzhou Economic and Technology Development Zone International Trust and Investment Company (GETDZITIC).[229]

In 2001, the company was forced to take out additional bank loans to finance ongoing operations. The total amount of long-term liabilities increased by 48.23 per cent during the year as a result.[230] On the positive side, further progress was made in recovering the company's losses as creditor when, on 18 July 2001, GSI came to an agreement with GITIC for partial settlement of trust deposits by auctioning a property located in Huizhou city, Guangdong. By the end of November, GSI had received, from the proceeds of this auction, cash amounting to RMB 12 850 000. In return, the GSI Board of Directors agreed to offset RMB 25 700 000 worth of overdue trust deposits due from GITIC.[231]

Also in 2001, the Guangzhou Foreign Economic and Trade Trust and Investment Company (GFETTIC) repaid RMB 8 675 500 of amounts due through an asset swap arrangement. The ownership of certain assets (including properties located in Changchun city and one property located in Guangzhou) was transferred to GSI. The GSI Board of Directors also agreed to write off the remaining balance due from GFETTIC of RMB 1.32 million in the company's 2001 accounts.[232]

By the end of 2001, total trust deposits with GITIC and two GITIC-related non-banking financial institutions amounted to RMB 456.537 million, with total non-recovery provision of RMB 382.414 million.[233] As at 31st December 2004, the Company's trust deposits with non-banking financial institutions amounted to a total of RMB 444.5 million, of which trust deposits at GITIC amounted to RMB 397.07 million with accumulated special non-recovery provision of RMB 325.37 million.[234] The Company's trust deposits at GETDZITIC amounted to RMB 47.43 million. A full provision for bad debt in respect of that deposit was made in 2000.[235]

After a loss-making year in 2001, the company gradually returned to profitability in 2002–2005.[236] A debt-restructuring agreement was entered into with GITIC on 31 January 2005 under which a number of shops located in Urumqi worth about RMB 110 million would be transferred to GSI, in settlement of a principal amount of RMB 220 million plus interest owing.[237] All remaining trust deposit debts with GITIC were settled by a Framework Agreement entered into on 20 February 2006, pursuant to which GITIC agreed to transfer an assortment of compensatory assets to GSI.[238]

By the end of 2005, despite a declared profit attributable to shareholders of RMB 135 011 000 (up from RMB 60 945 000 the previous year),[239] the company remains under pressure from increases in exchange rate risk, rising prices of steel and other raw material inputs, and shortages of power supply. Strategies adopted to cope with these risks included the signing of a long-term supply agreement with the company's major materials suppliers, working-day-hour adjustments to cope with temporary power shortages, and the establishment of a working party to look at measures for locking-in exchange rates and adjusting payment receipt timelines.

V BEIREN PRINTING MACHINERY CORPORATION LIMITED

A Introduction

In 1993, there were four major manufacturers of printing machines in China, only three of which were engaged in production of offset presses: Beiren Group Corporation (BGC), the parent organization of Beiren Printing Machinery (Beiren), with 78 per cent of the market; Shanghai Renmin Machinery Factory, with 13 per cent; and Hunan Printing, with 9 per cent market share.[240] Clearly the printing industry leader in China, BGC, was the obvious choice for a listing in Hong Kong.

As was the case with all early H-share listings, Beiren was created as the productive arm of BGC, the state-owned parent organization. When Beiren was registered and approved as a joint stock limited company in mid-July 1993,[241] it had taken over productive assets from BGC which included a multi-colour offset press factory, a single/double colour offset press factory, a foundry and gear workshop, a sheet-fed machine factory and what was originally the BGC supply division. It also took over a reputation. In 1990, BGC had been accredited as a 'Category 1' enterprise under an annual accreditation process for identifying the leading firms nationwide. The accreditation programme was discontinued in 1992, by which time there were 191 'Category 1' enterprises in China, with eight in Beijing. In 1993, therefore, BGC could claim to be the only 'Category 1' enterprise in the Chinese printing industry. After taking over BGC assets, Beiren became the largest manufacturer of offset presses in China, producing 61 different models. It also inherited over 300 regular customers located throughout China, including printers of books, magazines, newspapers, notes, certificates and packaging materials, and also exported a small proportion of its products to customers in Southeast Asia and the Middle East.[242]

According to a now familiar pattern, a close and long-term financial relationship between listed company and parent SOE was established in 1993–4 and still remained in existence over ten years later, in 2005.[243] The overall effect of a number of long-term contracts set up when Beiren was established as a newly corporatized entity in 1993 has been to ensure a yearly flow of income from Beiren, the listed company, into the parent state-owned organization. Three contracts are significant:

(a) Contract dated 14 July 1993, whereby BGC granted to Beiren rights to the trademark 'Beiren' at a fee payable quarterly of Rmb 15 000 or 1 per cent of sale proceeds from products using the 'Beiren' trademark during the relevant period, whichever is higher.[244]
(b) Agreement dated 18 June 1994 whereby BGC granted to Beiren rights to use the Beiren factory area, roads and facilities for 50 years at an annual fee of Rmb 2 million with the term calculated from 1 January 1993.[245]
(c) Agreement dated 14 July 1993, whereby Beijing Yan Long Import and Export Company, another controlled subsidiary of BGC, agreed to provide export sale agency services for Beiren products at a fee equal to 3 per cent of annual export turnover of products marketed by Beijing Yan Long.[246]

B Share Capital Structure and Shareholders

Beiren's issue and listing of both H-shares (in July–August 1993) and A-shares (in March–April 1994) left H shareholders with 100 million shares or 25 per cent of the company's total equity, individual holders of A-shares with 50 million shares or 12.5 per cent of the company's equity and BGC, the state-owned parent of the company with 62.5 per cent of total equity.[247] Supervisory authority over BGC and its subsidiaries was, and still is, exercised by the Beijing Municipal government, mainly through the Beijing Industrial Machinery Bureau. At the national level, supervisory control is exercised by the State Electrical and Mechanical Department.

The shareholding structure just outlined remained unchanged until late 2002, when Beiren issued (22 million) additional A-shares during the period 26 December 2002–7 January 2003. The 22 million new A-shares were listed and began trading on the Shanghai Stock Exchange on 16 January 2003. Following this expansion in its share capital and consequent dilution of the parent-organization's interest, BGC's interest, as the controlling shareholder of Beiren, was reduced to 59.24 per cent of total equity. A-shares listed and traded in Shanghai comprised 17.06 per cent of total equity and H-shares listed in Hong Kong comprise 23.70 per cent of total equity.[248]

In March 2006, a share segregation reform proposal for Beiren was approved by the SASAC of Beijing Municipal Government and by an extraordinary meeting of A-share shareholders.[249] The effect of the share segregation reform proposal was to transform all state-owned non-circulating shares of Beiren into circulating (tradable) shares, subject to a 12-month lock-up period and strict limits on the number of those shares able to be traded in the two years following the lock-up period. To compensate for the potential share-value diluting effect of this transformation, 27 360 000 state-owned legal person shares were transferred free of charge to existing holders of tradable A-shares listed on the Shanghai Stock Exchange and the number of freely tradable A-shares (ie. not subject to restriction or lock-up) was increased by this amount.[250] The total equity of Beiren remained at 422 million shares, but the interest held by BGC as the controlling shareholder was reduced to 52.76 per cent.[251]

One interesting thing about the shareholders' meeting at which the share reform proposal was approved is the extent of shareholder participation. Of a total of 33 750 holders of ordinary tradable A-shares who could have attended the meeting, 1333 actually participated, 84 shareholders attended in person or by appointing the Board as their proxies, while 1249 shareholders participated by registering their vote on the Internet.[252] Moreover, this was no rubber-stamp vote for board decision making: one or more shareholders holding a total of 1 661 173 A-shares actually voted against the share reform resolution.[253] Unlike the fate of a similar share-reform proposal put forward by Yizheng Chemical Fibre, however, this opposition was not enough to defeat the proposal.

C Management Structure and Composition

Not surprisingly, there is significant state-interest representation on the board and supervisory committee of Beiren. When its shares began trading on 6 August 1993, there were 11 members on the First Beiren Board of Directors, nine of whom were executive directors. Both the non-executive directors had had long careers in government ranks, and had extensive connections within government circles at both municipal and State levels.[254] There were three members on the Supervisory Committee, all of whom had been employed within Beiren Group Corporation ranks for 25 years or more. Ten years later, in 2003, the company's management personnel were still closely connected to state interests and organizations. In 2005, the fifth Board of Directors of Beiren still had 11 members on it, and the number of those claiming to be 'independent non-executive directors' had grown to four.[255] But there were still five executive directors holding senior positions within the Company on the board. Moreover, the Chairman of the Beiren board, Zhu Wuan, held a concurrent position as Chairman of BGC, the parent organization, while Lu Changan, Vice Chairman of the Beiren board, was General Manager of BGC. The Supervisory Committee remained the same size as in 1993 and, again, all three supervisors had several years of employment within BGC ranks.[256]

Although limited in extent, improvements have been made to the internal corporate governance structure of Beiren. First, the board has set up four special committees: the Strategic Development Committee, the Audit Committee, the Remuneration and Monitoring Committee and the Nomination Committee.[257] With the exception of the Audit Committee, which met four times in 2005, however, each Committee met on only one occasion during the year, which raises questions about their effectiveness.[258] A second development related to corporate governance, and, in particular, to the protection of minority shareholder rights, was the amendment to the company's articles of association approved at the 2006 Annual General Meeting which made it possible, although not mandatory, for a cumulative voting system to be used in future elections of directors and supervisors.[259] The extent to which this possibility will actually affect the future composition of Beiren's management team, however, remains to be seen.

Another proposal put to the Annual General Meeting held in mid-2006 was to grant to the directors of the company both a general mandate to issue new H-shares of the company (in an amount not exceeding 20 per cent of the total number of H-shares in issue), and a mandate to repurchase up to 10 per cent of the H-shares of the company. Of a total of 35 505 shareholders who could have attended this meeting, only 12 did so.[260] The 12 shareholders who attended represented 75.94 per cent of the total shares carrying voting rights of the company.[261] What is interesting about this meeting is that, instead of the usual rubber stamp in favour of all resolutions put, there was opposition to allowing the directors to issue new H-shares. One or more shareholders with 17 655 000 shares (representing 5.51 per cent of Beiren equity), voted against the resolution.[262] There was no opposition to any other resolution, including the H-share repurchase mandate, which passed unopposed at the AGM and both the extraordinary general meetings of class shareholders.[263] Unlike the repurchase mandate, the resolution to grant the board a general mandate to issue new H-shares was not made conditional upon the approval of class shareholders' meetings.[264]

D Company Performance since Listing

Beiren, like the other companies examined here, has also participated in the Government's drive to 'seize hold of the large, release the small' through a process of acquisition and expansion.[265] By 2005, Beiren had expanded from being a single company with five operating divisions[266] to being a group holding company with a total of 11 controlled subsidiary operations.[267] Expansion has been pursued despite some significant weaknesses within Beiren's accounts. For example, Beiren is yet another victim of the parlous state of China's state-owned banking and financial corporations. As at the end of 2002, Beiren had 10 million Rmb worth of already-overdue fixed deposits placed with financial institutions in the PRC, all of which suffered from 'internal problems that make repayment unlikely'.[268] The 2002 Accounts therefore show a sum of Rmb 4 844 000 in provision for the estimated non-recoverable portion of these deposits.[269] Early concerns were also expressed about the recoverability of long-term investments made by the company in other speculative non-core assets, such as real property.[270]

Another weakness in the Beiren accounts is the significant proportion of the company's assets taken up by inventories. That inventories account for 56.8 per cent of current assets is only partly due to the nature of the machinery manufacturing industry, which requires a relatively longer production period.[271] Continued expansion and increased reliance on debt financing in 2005[272] appears less justifiable than it might otherwise be in the increasingly harsh environment in which Beiren has been operating since 2002. On the one hand, increased market competition has kept prices of machinery sold by Beiren down, while, on the other hand, costs of the company have increased.[273] Profit attributable to shareholders fell from Rmb 102 023 000 in 2004 to Rmb 61 585 000 in 2005[274], and net profits are expected to fall again (this time by more than 50 per cent) in the 2006 financial year.[275]

Yet Beiren is far from being in danger of failure, or even decline. Its parent organization, BGC, is 'One of the 520 Enterprises that Are Mainly Supported by the Chinese Government'.[276] Beiren is the largest printing machinery manufacturer in China and, under the Beijing Municipal Government's 'master plan', has been allowed to relocate (in 2003) to the Beijing Economic and Technological Development Zone.[277] Beiren continues to receive various forms of direct and indirect government support, including a preferential profits tax rate of 15 per cent,[278] and, in 2006, newly-imposed high-technology machinery import controls provide a better environment for sales of domestically produced high-end machinery.[279] In June 2006, Beiren established a new joint venture company with Mitsubishi Heavy Industries Ltd for the manufacture and sale of high-speed multicolour sheet-fed printing machines, under licence from MHI.[280] With demand for printing increasing in the lead up to the 2008 Beijing Olympic Games and the 2010 Shanghai World Expo, the future looks bright – something which even Bill Gates appears to have noticed.[281]

VI MAANSHAN IRON & STEEL COMPANY LIMITED

A Introduction

Maanshan Iron & Steel Company Limited (Maanshan) and its subsidiaries ('the Group') were established on 1 September 1993, as part of the reorganization of Maanshan Iron and Steel Company ('Original Magang'). Upon completion of the reorganization process, Maanshan took over the principal iron and steel business undertakings (with the exception of the mine sites and other operations unrelated to iron and steel production) and two subsidiaries of Original Magang, together with the related operating assets and liabilities. The consideration for the net assets acquired was satisfied by the issue of 4 034 560 000 State A-shares to Original Magang, under its new name of Maanshan Magang Holding Company ('Holding'). Holding retained assets and liabilities related to the mining operations and the provision of social services such as medical, housing, education and catering.[282] Following the reorganization, Holding continued to come under the leadership and administration of the Anhui Provincial Government – a relationship of mutual support and dependency established in the 1980s – and to a lesser extent the Maanshan Municipal Government. It also remains subject to the administration of the Ministry of Metallurgic Industries of the PRC.[283]

The share capital of the Company was increased to RMB 6 455 300 000, divided into 4 722 370 000 A-shares and 1 732 930 000 H-shares on 9 October 1993.[284] The Company's H-shares of nominal value RMB 1.00 each were offered for subscription in Hong Kong and by private placements to international investors, at an issue price of HK$2.27 from 20 October 1993 to 26 October 1993. The 1 732 930 000 newly issued H-shares were listed on The Stock Exchange of Hong Kong Limited on 3 November 1993.[285]

The private placement to international investors was achieved through the establishment of a GDR programme, through which Maanshan was able to raise capital, although without getting a full listing outside Hong Kong.[286]

The Company's A-shares of RMB 1.00 each were offered for subscription by individual citizens of the PRC at an issue price of RMB 3.45 from 6 November 1993 to 25 December 1993. The total of 687 810 000 A-shares issued included an amount of 87 810 000 legal person shares (unlisted and non-tradable), plus 410 000 000 individual shares and 190 000 000 employee shares. Individual shares were listed on the Shanghai stock exchange in two batches, on 6 January 1994 and 4 April 1994. All employee shares were listed on 6 September 1994.[287]

By the end of 1995, the total issued share capital of Maanshan was 6 455 300 000. Holding was the controlling shareholder representing the State, and owning 62.52 per cent of total equity. Legal person A-shares comprised 1.36 per cent of total equity, individual A-shares comprised 9.29 per cent of total equity and H-shares represented 26.85 per cent of total equity.[288]

Ten years later, in 2005, Maanshan's total share capital remained unchanged at 6 455 300 000 shares. The only change was that, in September 1988, Holding had been restructured into a new entity now known as Magang (Group) Holding Company Limited ('New Holding'). By mid-2003, New Holding owned 4 082 330 000 A-shares or 63.26 per cent of total equity. The number of State A-shares owned by New Holding remains unchanged at 62.52 per cent of total equity, but in addition New Holding now owns 47 770 000 legal person shares representing 0.74 per cent of total share capital.[289]

B Performance Subsequent to Listing

Edward Steinfeld has conducted a detailed study of the problems inherent in a number of reforms carried out in China's state-owned steel industry enterprises, including the drive to corporatize firms like Magang. In his examination of the fate of Maanshan in the years following its listing as a 'public' corporation, Steinfeld demonstrates the way in which 'Maanshan, within a year of its debut on the Hong Kong stock exchange, began facing financial irregularities within the firm, a growing tax debt to the state, and rising levels of short-term liabilities.'[290] He shows how, over the years since 1993, '[o]wnership restructuring has by no means prevented the firm from engaging in inter-enterprise lending, overproduction and ill-advised expansion'.[291]

The essence of the problem lies in the extent of government involvement in all aspects of Maanshan's ownership, personnel and management. First, there is the problem of interwoven, cross-cutting lines of regulatory authority over the firm in an environment where 'attempts to describe "who has authority over what" are inevitably hampered by the lack of generalizable rules'.[292] The decreasing importance of the national government's State Plan in controlling output allocation over the years since 1993 has meant that the national Ministry of Metallurgic Industries has ceased to have much authority over Maanshan. At the same time, however, provincial officials in Anhui Province have mostly had neither the means nor the expertise to understand or monitor the activities of such a large firm as Maanshan. What is clear, however, is that a number of governments at different levels have seen fit to extract value from Maanshan. 'Both central and provincial tax agencies have levied a range of circulation, sales and natural resources taxes' upon Maanshan and its subsidiaries, while the municipal government has also collected a range of somewhat ad hoc fees from Maanshan for such things as infrastructure improvements, utilities usage and public services.[293] In essence, the situation has been one where 'Ma'anshan (*sic*) Iron and Steel, as the single largest state enterprise in the area, [has] served as [a convenient] cash cow for its city government'.[294]

The problem of extensive government involvement is also indicated through the existence of a series of long-term financial linkages established as part of the reorganization process from which Maanshan emerged. Of those linkages established in 1993 and still in existence in 2003, two are particularly significant:

1. Under a Service Agreement entered into between Maanshan and Holding on 14 October 1993, Maanshan and Holding have provided and continue to provide each other with certain services. The Agreement was designed to ensure that Maanshan employees would continue to receive necessary social services from Holding after the 1993 reorganization was completed. The agreement was effective from 1 September 1993, officially expiring on 31 December 2003. Under the service agreement, the service fees to be paid would equal (i) the State price of the agreed service; or (ii) in the absence of a State price, the

market price for the agreed service; or (iii) in the absence of either a State price or a market price for the agreed service, the actual cost attributable to the party providing the service.

2. A Sale and Purchase of Ore Agreement was entered into between Maanshan and its holding company, also on 14 October 1993. Under the agreement, which also remained in force until 2003, all the iron ore and limestone produced by Holding must first be offered to Maanshan at a price to be agreed after consultation between the two parties, provided that such price should not be higher than the prevailing domestic market price.[295] In essence, what these two Agreements have established is a mechanism to ensure a continual flow of funds from the listed firm into the State-owned Holding company.

Maanshan's new corporate form since 1993 has failed dismally to alter the system of incentives that have led to overproduction, ill-advised expansion and overreliance on debt financing. From an original number of two subsidiaries upon establishment in 1993–94, and three by the end of 1995, the size of the Maanshan Group had grown to eight subsidiaries of the company by end of 2002 and, on 29 January 2003, the company injected Rmb24 854 930 to purchase a 70 per cent interest in a new sino-foreign joint venture Company Anhui Masteel K. Wah New Building Materials Co. Ltd.[296] Expansion and investment continued into 2005, when the Maanshan Group invested a total of Rmb 5379 million in projects under construction.[297] In order to support these projects, the Maanshan Group also contributed RMB 402.7 million to establish four new joint ventures in China, with a commitment to providing a further 34.7 million capital in two of those joint ventures.[298]

Expansion and investment in new facilities has taken place despite shortages of raw materials and other resources[299] that have left a significant percentage of steel production capacity sitting idle, and despite central government directives seeking to rein in overinvestment in heavy industries. Beijing has sought to clamp down on excessive fixed assets investment by banning new projects that are deemed small-scale, low-quality, environmentally unfriendly or involving old technology.[300] One mechanism for discouraging overproduction of lesser quality steel products was the cancellation in 2005 of the Export VAT Refund Policy for primary steel products such as pig iron steel billet and steel ingot.[301] The National Development and Reform Commission also promulgated the 'Iron and Steel Industry Development Policies' on 20 July 2005, in an effort to enhance the overall technological standards of the domestic iron and steel industry. The Policies provide support for Maanshan's research and development, design and high-technology projects and also impose more stringent environmental protection standards on iron and steel facilities.[302]

In the case of Maanshan, expansion has also been pursued despite significant weaknesses in Maanshan's financial situation. The first of these weaknesses arises from the fact that Maanshan was yet another victim of the fall-out from the GITIC bankruptcy. The company has been forced to write off most of the significant sum due from long-overdue fixed deposits placed with GITIC and two members of the GITIC group (China Venturetech Investment Corporation and CITIC Ningbo Inc). It has also had to contend with the failure of SEG International Trust and Investment Corporation, which by 2003 was in the process of business suspension and rectification under the supervision of People's Bank of China. This means that no attempt can be made to recover the deposit placed with SEG unless and until the suspension has been lifted. In addition, Maanshan has been forced to renegotiate extended terms of repayment of an overdue deposit placed with Shenzhen Leasing Co. Ltd. By 2003, total overdue fixed deposits placed with these five financial institutions amounted to Rmb 202.18 million, of which Maanshan was forced to make a provision of Rmb 175 million for non-recoverable amounts in its 2002 Annual Accounts.[303]

Related to the above is the Maanshan Group's high gearing ratio and reliance on bank loans for both working capital and new construction. By the end of 2005, the Maanshan Group's gearing ratio was 52.09 per cent,[304] with a total amount of working capital and construction loans borrowed by the Group of Rmb 8762 million.[305]

C Changing (or Unchanging) Firm Management

A further aspect of State involvement in the management and control of Maanshan is de facto state control over personnel appointments. 'Prior to 1992, Magang's general manager and eight to ten vice-managers were all appointed by the provincial government, with the apparent approval of the MMI, while the party secretary and vice-secretary were appointed by the organization department of the provincial party committee.'[306] When Maashan's shares began trading on 3 November 1993, it had a board of directors with nine members, six of whom were executive directors holding senior management positions within the firm. Of the three non-executive directors, two were from senior-level provincial government circles. The newly-incorporated enterprise also had a Supervisory Committee with three members, one of which was elected to represent employees of the company, another of whom was the President of the Company's trade union.[307]

Ten years later, in mid-2003, the company's articles of association had been amended to ensure that 'External Directors shall account for more than one-half of the composition [of the Board of Directors of Maashan] and Independent Directors shall account for more than one-third.' The amendment made in late 2002 was needed to ensure compliance with the government's January 2002 *Standards for Governance of Listed Companies*,[308] and the August 2001 *Guiding Opinions on the Establishment of the Independent Director System by Listed Companies*.[309] Partly as a result of the new amendments, the firm's board of 12 directors included four independent directors by mid-2003. The four independent directors had also formed an Audit Committee in accordance with the 'Rules for the Office of Independent Director' and 'Regulations for the Office of the Audit Committee'.[310] The eight executive directors were all senior company officials: six were deputy general managers of Maanshan and two were deputy general managers of Holding. The Supervisory Committee in mid-2003 comprised eight supervisors, four of whom were independent supervisors.

By the end of 2005, a new ten-member board comprised ten directors, of whom five were executive directors, one was a (connected) non-executive director and four were independent directors. There were five supervisors on the supervisory committee, three of whom were Company employees and two of whom were independent.[311] The key point here is that, despite the presence of independent directors and supervisors, it remains the case that control over the management of Maanshan remains substantially with individuals whose nomination and appointment has been instigated and approved by the controlling state-owned shareholder. This result is virtually assured by the terms of the recent amendments made to the company's Articles of Association as regards the election and nomination of directors.

The newly-inserted Article 98 of the Articles provides that 'Directors be nominated by the Board of Directors, the Supervisory Committee or shareholders interested in more than 5 per cent of the Company's shares in separate or aggregated holdings', while 'Independent Directors shall be nominated by the Board of Directors, the Supervisory Committee or shareholders interested in more than 1 per cent of the Company's shares in separate or aggregated holdings.' When one realizes that, apart from Holding, the only other shareholder of Maanshan able to control more than 1 per cent of total share equity (and related voting rights) is HKSCC (Nominees) Limited, with 1 582 258 977 circulating H-shares, or 24.5 per cent of total equity by mid-2003 (25.409 per cent in 2005),[312] it becomes obvious where control over the nomination process really lies. Even in the case of HKSCC, the power of its presence as registered shareholder of Maanshan is significantly diluted by the fact that it holds those shares on behalf of a diverse and multiple number of clients.

VII KUNMING MACHINE TOOL COMPANY LIMITED: LATER RENAMED JIAODA KUNJI HIGH TECH CO LTD

A The Listing

The predecessor of Kunming Machine Tool Company Limited (KMT) was Central Machine Plant (KMT Plant) established in 1939 as a manufacturer of machine tools under the Nationalist government's Resources Commission. It was renamed Kunming Machine Plant in 1953 when it was brought under the supervision of the PRC government's First Ministry of Machinery Industry. By 1993, it was one of China's leading manufacturers of machine tools, mainly for the local market.[313]

On 18 October 1993 the major productive assets of KMT Plant, including its design, research and development units and manufacturing and trading operations relating to machine tool products and accessories, precision measuring equipment and precision transducers were injected into KMT, which was formally registered and established as a joint stock company on 19 October 1993. In return for the assets and liabilities which KMT Plant contributed to it, KMT issued 102 397 700 State shares which were held by Kunming Kun Ji Group Company (Kun Ji) on behalf of the Yunnan Provincial Government.[314] At the time of the reorganization, a long-term (five-year renewable) relationship was established between KMT and Kun Ji, pursuant to which KMT would provide water, electricity and other utility services to Kun Ji, while Kun Ji would provide social services (eg. education and medical services) to KMT employees, as well as transport services for KMT products. A trade-mark licence and sales agency agreement was also signed.[315] The overall effect of this relationship was to ensure an overall flow of payments from the listed firm to the State-owned parent.[316]

KMT became a public subscription company on 2 November 1993 with a total approved equity of 245 007 400 shares of par value RMB 1. Approval was given for KMT to issue 65 000 000 H-shares, which make the KMT issue the sixth and smallest such issue for 1993. The shares were listed in Hong Kong on 7 December 1993 at an issue price of $1.98.[317] The shares had earlier soared in the 'grey market' (illegal in Hong Kong) to nearly twice that amount, and their price on the official market also rose rapidly. The rapid appreciation in price was probably inevitable, given the pricing of the issue which, on a weighted average basis, was as low as 8.9 times 1993 forecast earnings.[318] On a comparable basis, this represented a 70 per cent discount on the issue price of Tsingtao Brewery shares six months earlier.[319]

The Company issued 60 000 000 A-shares in the PRC, also during 1993.[320] By the end of 1994, then, the total share capital of KMT stood at

245 007 400 shares, of which 102 397 700 shares, or 41.79 per cent of the Company's total equity, comprised State-owned shares controlled by the Yunnan Provincial People's Government. In addition, there were 17 609 700 legal person shares, or 7.19 per cent of the company's total equity, which were controlled by the Kunming Jinghua Company – a controlled subsidiary of the Yunnan People's government.[321]

B Subsequent Performance

Following the pattern set by its newly-listed H-share counterparts, KMT was enthusiastic in its pursuit of expansion during the years following its Hong Kong listing. Growth in output quantity was pursued at the expense of new product development and quality, leading to inventory obsolescence and increasing inventory balances.[322] Thus it was that, when the economies of Asia were hit by the effects of the 1997 financial collapses of newly floated regional currencies in Thailand and Indonesia, KMT found itself in immediate difficulties. Cheaper imports of machine-tool goods and parts into China put intensified competitive pressures on KMT, and the company made significant losses in both 1998 and 1999.[323] Other financial weak points included a significant weight of non-recoverable trade receivables, plus 'serious infrastructural constraints' imposed by the difficulties of transport between Kunming City in the western province of Yunnan and the rest of China.[324] By the year 2000, the Yunnan Government was forced to explore ways of restructuring the company to keep it alive as a viable, and preferably much more competitive, entity.

C Restructuring for Survival

A large part of the problem was that KMT operated as a traditional machine tool producer whose modes of production and products were, by the late 1990s, rapidly becoming obsolete and outdated. As a means of introducing much-needed improved technology into the company, the decision was made to bring in Xian Jiaotong University Industrial (Group) Incorporated (Jiaotong Group), a wholly-owned subsidiary of Xian Jiaotong University. On 5 June 2001, the Yunnan Provincial Government transferred a total of 71 052 146 shares, representing 29 per cent of the company's equity, to Jiaotong Group, and KMT was renamed Jiaoda Kunji High-Tech Company (Jiaoda Kunji).[325] The involvement of the Provincial Government was now represented by a much smaller 12.79 per cent of total share equity.[326] The largest part of the listed company's equity (29 per cent) would henceforth be controlled by Jiaotong Group, the wholly-owned subsidiary of Xian Jiaotong University, which is, in turn, under the direct control of the State Owned Assets Supervision and Administration Commission of the State Council.[327] In other words, substantial control over Jiaoda Kunji was effectively shifted from the Provincial Yunnan government to the national government in Beijing.

The hope behind the restructuring of Kunming Machine Tool was that the involvement of Jiaotong Group would help to transform the company from a traditional machine-tool producer into Jiaoda Kunji, a high-technology designer, developer and supplier of information technology products (digital machine tools, precision equipment etc) and technology services. Thus an important part of the restructuring plan was the fact that it also included a 'Disposal Agreement'. This provided a mechanism for Jiaoda Kunji to off-load its accumulated inventory of outdated spare parts and components, together with some of its no longer productive properties, to the Yunnan government. In return, the company received a payment of Rmb 91 581 000.[328] The Rmb 91 581 000 was then used to make the following purchases:

1. First, the newly-named Jiaoda Kunji would acquire three major assets of Xian Jiaoda Resources Technology Joint Stock Company Limited (Jiaoda Resources), an 83.80 per cent owned subsidiary of Jiaotong Group. The three assets purchased from Jiaoda Resources were an 80 per cent equity interest in Xian Ser Turbo Machinery Equipment Company Limited (Xian Ser), plus the automatic machinery department and the intelligence electrical Department of Jiaoda Resources.
2. Second, Jiaoda Kunji would purchase a total of 90 per cent equity interest in Shaanxi Hengtong Intelligence Machine Company Limited (Hengtong) from the five major shareholders of Hengtong.
3. Third, Jiaoda Kunji would purchase from Jiaotong Group technological know-how in the form of laser prototyping and manufacturing technology plus controllable centrifugal energy conservation compressor technology. The newly-acquired technology could then be licensed to Xian Ser and Hengtong, the two new subsidiaries of Jiaoda Kunji. Xian Ser was granted the licence to the controllable centrifugal energy conservation compressor technology, while Hengtong became licensee of the laser prototyping and manufacturing technology.

The asset restructuring process was designed, from the start, to provide a way of not only saving the ailing KMT from what appeared almost inevitable failure, but also to allow it, with significant government assistance, to strengthen its competitiveness through the acquisition of productive high-technology assets. The acquisition of new assets would also be beneficiaries of the State Torch Plan, a programme launched by the State

Science Technology Commission in the PRC, which provides preferential tax treatment and special loans to finance new ventures in high technology. This is part of the 11th national five-year plan beginning in 2006, under which the turbo machine industry, along with the digital machine and other related industries, are to benefit from state policy assistance.[329] Taxation policies and incentives form an important part of this assistance. For example, for the period 1 January 2006–31 December 2008 (and in the case of Jiaoda Kunji ever since 2003) the Ministry of Finance grants a 50 per cent rebate of all value added tax (VAT) paid on numerical control machine products. In the case of Jiaoda Kunji, this rebate is estimated to be worth RMB 10 million per year from 2007 to 2009.[330]

Political negotiations over the future of control over Jiaoda Kunji did not end with the 2001 Asset Restructuring. On 16 September 2005, Jiaotong Group signed an agreement with Shenyang Machine Tool (Group) Company Limited (Shenyang Group) under which Jiaotong Group would transfer its 29 per cent of equity in Jiaoda Kunji to Shenyang Group.[331] The transfer of this equity was eventually completed over one year later, on 1 December 2006, when Shenyang Group became the registered owner of state-owned legal person shares representing 29 per cent of the total issued share capital of Jiaoda Kunji.[332] Shenyang Machine Tool Group is China's largest machine tools manufacturer and has been expanding rapidly over recent years, mostly through acquisitions and mergers. Shares of Shenyang Group amounting to 49 per cent of the company's total equity were sold to more than 40 strategic investors, mostly from overseas, in a November 2006 share placement.[333] Shenyang's municipal government, the majority state-owned shareholders of the firm, retained a 51 per cent stake in the firm after the sale.[334] The consequence of this is that control over the state-owned shares in Jiaoda Kunji is now shared between the Yunnan Provincial Government and the Shenyang Municipal Government. The company's name was changed for a second time in 2007, to Shenji Group Kunming Tool Company, with the new name taking effect as of 29 June 2007.

What now remains to be seen is whether or not the authorities of the Provincial-level Government in Yunnan and the Municipal-level government in Shenyang can effectively cooperate to maximize both management autonomy and management's incentive to act in the best interests of the company and its shareholders. On the one hand, the State can conceivably exercise its supervisory and supportive roles more efficiently when it becomes involved in business decision making 'at the coal face'. On the other hand, however, the presence of the State in business decision making can introduce an unfortunate political element into crucial personal and business relationships. And this, in turn, can generate conflicts-of-interest for management that arise despite the presence of laws meant to ensure 'good corporate governance'.

The other ingredient in the ever-changing recipe of Jiaoda Kunji's equity ownership has been the introduction of a share-reform proposal in early 2006. The proposal was revised soon afterwards (following a period of consultation), effectively increasing the amount of compensation available to holders of tradable A-shares of the company.[335] The first step in the revised share-reform proposal was an increase in the total capital equity of the company with every shareholder to be allocated 1.5606 shares for every 10 shares held. The result of this new issue was to give state-owned and legal person holders of non-tradable shares a total of 18 728 355 new shares. All these new shares would then be transferred to holders of tradable A-shares as compensation for transforming all non-tradable shares of the company into tradable shares.[336] The equity capital increase and share-reform proposals were approved by a special majority of voting shareholders on 22 December 2006.[337] If and when the share-reform process is completed as approved, the total equity of Jiaoda Kunji will increase to 283 243 255 shares. The proportion of total equity controlled by Shenyang Group would decline to approximately 25.1 per cent, while the percentage of total equity directly or indirectly controlled by the Yunnan Provincial Government would decline, from 19.98 per cent to 17.29 per cent.

D Management Changes since 1993

When its shares began trading on 7 December 1993, KMT's board of directors had eight members. One of the non-executive directors, Sun Xiaoliang, was also an independent non-executive director of Dongfang Machine Tool, a man who came with extensive senior-level experience in national government organs.[338] The Supervisory Committee comprised three members. Over the years since 1993, the management of Kunming Machine Tool has typically included at least one person both employed and nominated by the Provincial government-controlled Kunming Kunji Group Company.

It is often claimed that China has no effective takeover market – that there is no way of keeping management accountable through the threat of takeover. Yet, in the case of the ailing Kunming Machine Tool Company, a total management change and introduction of new blood was achieved as an important part of the wholesale restructuring of the company which took place in 2001. The new 11-member board was led by the President of Jiaotong Group, and comprised eight executive directors plus three independent non-executive directors.[339] The supervisory committee grew to four members and grew again, to five members by, 2005. By December 2005 there were still two non-executive directors holding concurrent positions within Xian Jiaotong University or its Industrial Group subsidiary (Jiaotong Group), the most substantial shareholder in Jiaoda Kunji between 2001 and 2005.[340] The number of independent directors had grown to four.[341] Two members of the Supervisory Committee also held concurrent senior positions within Xian Jiaotong University Industrial (Group) Incorporated, and two others held senior positions within Kunming Kunji Group Company. The Chairman of the Supervisory Committee was the General Manager of Yunnan Province State-Owned Assets Operating Company.[342]

Six new directors and four new supervisors were elected shortly after the introduction of Shenyang Group as the majority holder of state-owned shares in the company. Voting for the new members of management was held at the first extraordinary meeting of the company to be held on 28 February 2007. Shenyang Group, still at this stage controlling 29 per cent of total equity, nominated two independent directors, Liu Minghui and Chen Ying, as candidates for the board, plus one internal candidate, Wang Xing. The Yunnan State-owned Assets Operation Company Limited, controlling 12.8 per cent of total equity, nominated three internal candidates for board positions, while Kunming Jinghua Company, representing 7.19 per cent of total issued share capital, nominated one candidate. The two candidates for independent directorships nominated by Shenyang Group were the only candidates for the two independent director positions vacant, and so were almost certain to be elected. But there were only four positions vacant for non-independent directors, and five candidates were nominated. Likewise, there were only four vacant positions on the company's supervisory committee, for which five candidates were nominated – two by Shenyang Group, two by the Yunnan SASAC and one by Kunming Jinghua Company.[343]

VIII TIANJIN BOHAI CHEMICAL INDUSTRY (GROUP) COMPANY LIMITED: LATER RENAMED TIANJIN CAPITAL ENVIRONMENT PROTECTION CORPORATION LIMITED

A The Listing

By the end of 1995, following completion of Tianjan Bohai's H-share and A-share issues, the total share capital of the newly listed entity comprised 1 330 000 000 shares, of which 63.09 per cent were state shares owned by the Municipal Government's Tianjin Bohai Chemical Industry Group Corporation (Bohai Corporation); 2.89 per cent were legal-person shares owned by other PRC State-owned enterprises; 8.46 per cent of the total issued share capital were A-shares listed on the Shanghai Stock Exchange and 25.56 per cent were H-shares listed in Hong Kong and mostly controlled by the HKSCC.[344] This equity structure remained unchanged for seven years, until the end of 2000.

In 1995, the primary business focus of the newly-listed enterprise was the production of chemical products such as soda ash, PVC, caustic soda, agricultural chemicals and other organic and inorganic chemicals using salt. The major business assets of Tianjin Bohai and its subsidiaries (the Group) included three large chemical plants producing caustic soda, PVC, soda ash, ammonium chloride, sodium bicarbonate, calcium chloride and other chemical products,[345] together with a supplies and sales company providing sale and other agency services to the Group and a finance company providing financing and related services to members of the Group.[346]

B Subsequent Performance

The Tianjin Bohai Group was, from the beginning, burdened by heavy loan costs and the heavy carrying cost of its three large and ageing chemical product plants (mainly depreciation expenses but also maintenance costs). Gradual downsizing and upgrading fewer, more valuable assets may have seemed advisable, but it was never to be. Instead, production grew, inventory accumulated and the existing chemical product plants became increasingly outdated. For a while, intra-group lending helped ailing parts of the Group to survive, and growing credit-sales helped to get rid of some of the inventory. Indeed, survival almost seemed possible in the context of a steadily growing Chinese and Asian economy – until the Asian economic crisis of 1997 changed everything.

In fact, not only Tianjin Bohai but the entire PRC chemical industry was devastated by the Asian financial crisis and the collapse of key Asian currencies. Chinese chemical product manufacturers just could not compete when cheap imports from Indonesia, Thailand, South Korea and elsewhere in the region brought about a rapid decline in market prices for their products. In the case of Tianjin Bohai, the Group recorded losses of Rmb 616.9 million in 1998 and Rmb 374.2 million in 1999.[347] A further loss of approximately Rmb75.4 million was incurred during the first half of 2000. Something had to be done.

C Restructuring for Survival

It was in the early months of 2000 that the Tianjin Municipal Government began conducting negotiations over ways to restructure Bohai Corporation and transform the operations of its various subsidiaries, including its listed arm, Tianjin Bohai. The final arrangement agreed upon involved a number of steps.

The first step was to transfer majority ownership in Tianjin Bohai from Bohai Corporation to the Tianjin Municipal Investment Company Limited (TMICL), another wholly-owned arm of the municipal government. No consideration would be paid. Bohai Corporation would simply transfer its 63.09 per cent interest in the listed Tianjin Bohai to TMICL, and TMICL would become the new controlling shareholder of the listed company.

The second step would be for Tianjin Bohai and its subsidiaries to get rid of the Group's heavy burden of deteriorating financial assets, including trade debts, other receivables, loan receivables and long-term investments totalling approximately Rmb305.2 million (approx. HK$285.2 million) by the end of 1999. These financial assets would be purchased by the Tianjin Huaze (Group) Co. Ltd. (Tianjin Huaze), a State-owned enterprise of the Tianjin Municipal Government. The cash consideration paid would be equivalent to the book value of the assets disposed of (ie. Rmb305.2 million), despite their deteriorating real market value.

The third step would be for Tianjin Bohai to exchange its existing ailing business assets, for several new and far more lucrative assets. The whole business focus of the listed entity would be transformed, and the company would change its name to Tianjin Capital Environmental Protection Company Limited (Tianjin CEP). The newly-named enterprise would be primarily engaged in the operation and development of two new sewage water processing plants, together with the operation and development of a major city road, the South-eastern Half Ring Road, with its 16 toll stations.

Tianjin Bohai would transfer to TMICL its existing business assets, including its three chemical plants, its supplies and sales company and its finance company, together with payment of the Rmb305.2 million received from Tianjin Huaze. In exchange, TMICL would transfer two large sewage treatment plants based in Tianjin (the Dongjiao sewage treatment plant and the Jizhuangzi sewage treatment plant) to Tianjin Bohai. TMICL would also transfer to Tianjin Bohai ownership and operation rights in the Tianjin South-eastern Half Ring Road and its 16 toll stations.

The two sewage treatment plants transferred to Tianjin Bohai would come together with a 30-year Sewage Water Processing Agreement, under which the Tianjin Sewage Company would pay the newly-named Tianjin CEP for processing an agreed annual minimum volume of sewage water.[348]

The road and toll stations would come together with a road repair and maintenance agreement under which the Tianjin Urban Road & Bridge Construction Company would provide repair and maintenance services to the new owner of the South-eastern Half Ring Road, in return for fees set by the Tianjin Urban Construction Bureau.

The new premises of Tianjin CEP would be based in a building located in the Nankai District of Tianjin, owned by TMICL and leased to its new majority-owned subsidiary in return for an agreed annual rental. The whole process was completed by the end of 2000, making Tianjin Bohai the first-ever H-share company to undergo a fundamental change in its core business.[349]

D Changes in the Company's Management Structure

When its shares began trading on 17 May 1994, there were 19 directors on the board of Tianjin Bohai, including 11 executive and eight non-executive directors. The non-executive directors included several significant personalities from provincial financial and investment enterprises, as well as from provincial government organs, including the chairman of the government-owned Tianjin Trust and Investment Corporation. There were also two labour union representatives on the board.

The Supervisory Committee in 1994 comprised 13 supervisors, nine of whom were elected at shareholder general meetings, four to be representatives of the Tianjin Bohai (Group) employees. Four supervisors held 'political' posts within the company, indicated by titles such as 'political officer' or 'senior political officer'.

The restructure and change of direction of Tianjin Bohai at the end of 2000 resulted, not unexpectedly, in a total replacement of the management of the company. As in the case of Kunming Machine Tool, this demonstrated that management of SOEs in China are not immune from the threat of being replaced if they do not perform to shareholder expectations. The new controlling shareholder of Tianjin CEP was clear from the outset about its intention to replace all existing directors and supervisors. At the Extraordinary General Meeting of the company held to approve the restructure, the TMICL nominated and secured the election of six new executive directors and six new supervisors who would take charge of the newly restructured organization from the moment the restructuring was complete. The new board of directors of Tianjin CEP comprised nine members, including six executive directors and three independent non-executive directors. Four of the executive directors came from previous positions held within TMICL, the State-controlled majority shareholder. Two of the executive directors have held previous positions within Tianjin municipal infrastructure project management divisions.

The new Supervisory Committee of Tianjin CEP following the 2000 restructure comprised six supervisors, five of whom were elected from amongst those nominated by TMICL, and one of whom was nominated by Tianjin CEP employees. All six supervisors came from previous positions held within Tianjin municipal infrastructure project-development divisions.[350] In other words, the State's obvious interest in the future prosperity of the firm was manifested through the personal linkages it retained with the decision-making leadership of the listed enterprise. Nor is this surprising, given the role that Tianjin CEP looks set to play in the future economic, social, environmental and political development of the municipality and the region.

IX DONGFANG ELECTRICAL MACHINERY COMPANY LIMITED

A The Listing

Dongfang Electrical Machinery Company Limited (Dongfang) was the last of the first batch of nine mainland companies to be listed on the HKEx. The company was formally established as an incorporated entity on 29 December 1993, following the reorganization of the former Dongfang Electrical Machinery Works (DFEW),[351] a wholly-owned subsidiary of China Dongfang Electric Corporation (DFEC). Under the State planning system, the operations of DFEW were partially financed by the national government through DFEC by way of loans. DFEC acted as coordinator for receiving government loans and advances specifically designated for funding operations of its subsidiaries. Following the reorganization of DFEW, these government loans were transferred to Dongfang under a demerger agreement between DFEW and Dongfang, with interest charged at market rates.[352]

The demerger agreement between DFEW and Dongfang was signed to effect the division of assets and liabilities of the original DFEW between the new DFEW and Dongfang.[353] According to a, by now, familiar pattern, productive facilities related to the manufacturing of electric power-generating equipment and motors and to scientific research and development were assigned to Dongfang, while those operations relating to the provision of social services and facilities to employees remained with DFEW. In return for the land-use rights and assets received from DFEW, Dongfang issued 220 million A-shares of par value 1 Rmb each to DFEW.[354] A long-term (10-year) service agreement was entered into for Dongfang to supply utility services, office space, communication services and various supplies needed for DFEW to carry out its service obligations owed to Dongfang. DFEW in return provides Dongfang with staff welfare services, including staff quarters (accommodation), child care, education and training service, medical services, pension fund and security services. DFEW also provides cleaning and sanitation services for Dongfang premises, office space and office-supply procurement services, as well as printing, packaging and distribution services for the marketing and delivery of Dongfang's products.[355]

Following the demerger process which was completed by May 1994, the total approved share capital of the newly incorporated entity was 450 million shares of par value 1 Rmb each.[356] A total of 170 million Dongfang H-shares were issued on 30 May 1994 at a final price of Rmb 3.17 per share payable as HK$2.83 per share;[357] 112.5 million H-shares were issued in a public offering in Hong Kong that opened on Thursday 19 May and closed on Tuesday 24 May 1994.[358] The remaining 57.5 million shares were reserved for an international placement, which was 13 times oversubscribed.[359] Dongfang's H-Shares were listed and began trading on 6 June 1994.

Dongfang's issue of 60 million A-shares (23 million of which were employee shares) took place on 4 July 1995, at an issue price of Rmb 4.10.[360] The shares were listed for trading on the Shanghai Stock Exchange on 10 October 1995. Following the completion of the H-share and A-share listings, DFEW, the State-owned parent company of DFEM, was left with 220 million non-circulating state shares, or 48.89 per cent of total share capital.[361] Tradable A-shares listed in Shanghai comprised 13.33 per cent of total equity, and the 170 million Hong Kong-listed H-shares comprised 37.78 per cent of share capital, nearly all of which (168 939 799 shares as at end of 2005) is controlled by HKSCC Nominees Limited on behalf of its customers.[362]

The hierarchy under which Dongfang was controlled was simplified in early 2006 when DFEW transferred all of its state shares to DFEC at nil consideration. Following that transfer, Dongfang came under the direct control of DFEC, with DFEW no longer holding any of its shares.[363] Shortly following the transfer of DFEW's 48.89 per cent of Dongfang equity to DFEC, a share segregation reform proposal was approved and implemented. The aim of the share segregation reform proposal was to transform all of the non-tradable shares owned by DFEC into tradable shares, subject to certain trading limitations. To compensate for the potentially depressing effect of this transformation on share-value, a total of 16 200 000 shares were transferred from DFEC to holders of listed Dongfang A-shares. The result of this transfer was that the shareholding of DFEC decreased from 48.89 per cent to 45.29 per cent, whilst the total issued share capital of Dongfang remained at 450 million shares.[364] The share segregation reform also opened the way for DFEC to trade a limited proportion of its non-circulating shares following a 12-month lock-up period. The state-owned legal person shares of Dongfang can then be traded on the Shanghai Stock Exchange subject to two conditions:

1. The number of state-owned legal person shares so traded shall not exceed 5 per cent of the total issued share capital of the Company for 12 months of trading and not exceed 10 per cent of total issued share capital of the Company for twenty-four months of trading.
2. The selling price of such shares should not be lower than 150 per cent of the closing price of A-shares on the trading day immediately preceding the date of the announcement of segregation reform (Rmb 23.39 per A-share).

B Performance Subsequent to Listing

In 1994, Dongfang had plans to use Rmb 160 million of the money raised during its A-share issue for capital inputs into joint venture projects with foreign investors, including Siemens of Germany, for the production of large-scale hydro-turbine generator sets and steam turbine generators.[365] Joint venture negotiations continued until 1999 but finally fell through in the face of poor domestic market conditions for hydro and steam turbine generators.[366] In 2001 and 2002, the company was forced to ask shareholders for permission to use the Rmb 160 million allocated to foreign partnerships as ordinary working capital instead.[367] Joint venture negotiations were renewed in 2005 with French company Jellmont SA.

One reason Dongfang was suffering from insufficient working capital in 2001 – 2002 was because it too had been caught up in the endemic problem of 'triangular debt' plaguing the Chinese financial system. While the company has not been forced to write off bad debts to the extent that other listed companies like Guangzhou Shipyard have, it has not been immune from corporate failures amongst its debtors. For example, in the mid-1990s, Dongfang placed 156 milion yuan as entrusted deposits with China Construction Bank's Chongqing sub-branch for on-lending to a third party which then defaulted on payment. A writ filed by Dongfang against the Bank in May 1998 was withdrawn on 12 June 1998 following intervention by the People's Bank of China.[368] The company also become involved in several other legal actions attempting to recover and secure overdue debts in 1999 and 2000. By the end of 2005, the company's accounts revealed a bad and doubtful debt provision of Rmb 108 322 000[369] and the company's overall gearing ratio was 79.92 per cent.

The other main reason for poor performance in 1999 was market-related. There was an oversupply of steam turbine generators and AC and DC motors in the domestic market on which Dongfang had mostly relied for its sales.[370] While significant investment has been made in improvements to technology, the company only recently began to establish its first joint venture partnership with an overseas firm (Jellmont SA) that could offer even greater improvements to technological capacity.[371] Only limited success has been achieved in exploring the international market, mostly in Southeast and South Asia.[372] Although Dongfang has reduced its workforce by around 12 per cent since 1994, this is less than its H-share counterparts.[373] Instead, Dongfang has focused on using its workforce to achieve continual increases in production volume and output.[374]

In 2006, 12 years after its appearance on the market, Dongfang is one of the biggest power-generating equipment manufacturers in the PRC. DFEM is known for its specialization in manufacturing hydro turbine and steam turbine generators. Partly because of this, it has benefited from its ability to win contracts as a supplier and participant in the government's ambitious Three Gorges Dam project. The company has expanded in all areas, including its market share, the size of the group it controls and its range of activities.[375] In terms of its size, by 2005 it had four major subsidiaries specializing in production of A/C and D/C motors, other power-generating machinery and the provision of technical consultancy and engineering services, as well as in the design, manufacture and sale of environmental equipment and other special equipment.[376] In terms of its range of activities, in 2001 DFEM formally expanded its business scope to include, inter alia, contracting outboard power-generating equipment, machinery and electric appliances and sets of projects, domestic international bidding and provision of labouring services for the same, production and sale of wind-driven power-generating equipment and insulated products.[377]

C Changes in Company Management

In 1994, when DFEM went public, its board of directors had 14 members, eight of whom were executive directors holding senior positions within the firm.[378] Of the six non-executive directors, three came from senior positions within DFEW, the parent firm,[379] while two came from senior positions within the PRC government.[380] All three supervisors on the supervisory committee came from more than ten years' experience at the original DFEM and held senior positions within the firm.[381]

Since that time, the Company's Articles of Association have been amended, first to allow for more flexibility in the size and composition of the board of directors and supervisory committee (in December 1999),[382] and secondly (in December 2002) to provide for the inclusion of at least one-third independent directors on the board.[383] Dongfang has also established several board committees aimed at improving its internal management structures and operations, including a Strategic Development Committee, an Assets Management Committee and an Audit and Review Committee that is independent in that it must have a majority of independent directors.[384]

What Dongfang has yet to achieve, however, is more complete independence from its controlling shareholder, DFEW. In 2003, for example, the Chengdu Securities Administration Office of the CSRC issued a 'Notice of Rectification' following an inspection tour of the company. One problem identified by the Notice was that the Chairman of Dongfang was also the Head of DFEW, the controlling shareholder of the company.[385] This situation was not rectified until a new board of directors began its three-year term of office on 28 December 2005. The new board, being the fifth board of directors since the incorporation of the company, comprises nine directors, of which three are independent directors. Five of the executive directors on the Dongfang board, as well as all of the supervisors on the three-member Supervisory Committee, come from previous positions at senior level within DFEW.[386] One might therefore question the extent to which company management is truly independent from the parent company.

Two other features are also noticeable. First, a majority of company management (including independent directors) have significant Party connections: for example, holding a senior position within the Party Committee of Dongfang, DFEW or another organization.[387] Second, only one member of senior management as at the end of 2005 is female. Previous years have also been notable for the lack of women in senior management, with a maximum of no more than two women in senior positions at any one time.

X CONCLUSION

In this chapter, I have explored the fate of the nine debutante H-share firms over the decade which has passed since the birth of the H-share market in 1993, a decade which has seen the formal recognition of Western-style, free-market principles in China's highly regulated state-owned industrial sector. In 2004, all nine firms examined are leading stocks amongst the 78 H-share enterprises now listed on the HKEx. What the story of these firms reveals is that all nine of the firms have several features in common that, as later chapters will demonstrate, can be seen as characteristic of the broader H-share market as a whole. These features include the following:

1. An overreliance on government support provided both directly (through government involvement in corporate restructuring, government grants and tax relief policies and government contracts) and indirectly. This has both an upside, when government involvement assists the efficient and speedy implementation of business plans made at corporate level, and a downside, when it results in corporate obedience to government policy directives, without regard for the interests or views of minority shareholders.
2. Second, nearly all have followed a programme of persistent growth and expansion even at times of market decline and despite other considerations making such expansion both ill-advised and costly. Expansion has, moreover, been driven by Boards that, at least until very recently, have lacked any real independence from the state-controlled parent organization of the firm.
3. Third, all have suffered, to varying degrees, from the financial problems and inefficiencies which plague China's corporate world. In particular, nearly all have been forced to write off significant sums of money placed with government-controlled investment and financial organizations and/or have written off large sums in bad and doubtful trade receivables and/or depreciated inventory. Financial vulnerability, in turn, has ensured that companies become even more dependent on government support and intervention.
4. Fourth, all boards of directors have been dominated to different degrees by individuals who also represent state interests and/or have strong state/Party connections. It is through such domination that communication channels are established between government and firm – a necessary precondition for the benefits and downsides of government involvement in business. This has also led to the situation, or at least the perceived situation, where conflicts of interest can, and do, operate to the detriment of both the firm and its non-state shareholders and creditors.

The actual experience of how H-share enterprises are managed shows just how difficult it is proving to be for China's SOEs to escape from the legacy of a highly-regulated past. Despite the presence of free-market language throughout the laws and regulations which now govern share-holding companies in China, it is the State's political preoccupations and policy objectives that have in practice determined the business strategy and decision-making outcomes of firms where the State remains the dominant shareholder. While recent reforms are slowly eroding the extent of state equity ownership as a means of controlling decision making in listed firms, the influence of the state through the personal connections of firm management, the presence of the Party Committee in the firm, and policy-driven financial support for selected enterprises all remain significant.

NOTES

1. The company was in fact the earliest beer manufacturer in China, and can trace its roots back to 1903, when its predecessor, Tsingtao Brewery Factory, was first established. The reorganization of the state-owned Tsingtao Brewery Factory in 1992–1993 led to the birth of Tsingtao as a joint stock company with an authorized total share capital of 900 million shares of RMB 1 each: Tsingtao Brewery *H-share Listing Prospectus*, dated 29 June 1993, 71.
2. Tsingtao Brewery, 2005 *Annual Report*, 3.
3. The public issue in Hong Kong met with a positive market response and was oversubscribed approximately 110.5 times: Tsingtao Brewery, 1993 *Annual Report*, 4.
4. Under the special placement arrangement, China Development Finance Co (HK) Ltd, acting as agent of Tsingtao, entered into an agreement with A-B Holdings for the placing of 45 000 000 H-shares at a price equal to the issue price under the new H-Share issue (HK$2.8 per share): Tsingtao Brewery, *H-share Listing Prospectus*, dated 29 June 1993, 15.
5. The tradable A-shares were issued at an issue price of RMB 6.38 per share, and the issue raised approximately RMB 638 000 000: Tsingtao Brewery, 1993 *Annual Report*, 4.
6. Apart from A-B Holdings, the largest foreign shareholder was HKSCC Nominees Limited, with 35.88 per cent of total listed share capital at 31 December 1995: Tsintao Brewery 1995 *Annual Report* 22. The total number of holders of H-shares at the end of 1995 was 1172, considerably fewer than the 75 178 holders of Tsingtao Shanghai-listed tradable A-shares: 1995 *Annual Report*, 21.
7. See Tsingtao Brewery, *H-share Listing Prospectus*, dated 29 June 1993, 30, and see 1995 *Annual Report*, 22.
8. S.G. Warburg Research, Company Update, Hong Kong dated 6 October 1993 'Tsingtao Brewery (168.HK)'.
9. Tsingtao Brewery, 1995 *Annual Report*, 37. The company's Consolidated Profit and Loss Account prepared according to Hong Kong GAAP shows Profit Attributable to Shareholders for 1995 of RMB 97 787 000, down from RMB 108 164 000 in 1994.
10. Tsingtao Brewery, 1995 *Annual Report*, 37.
11. The programme, which was generally welcomed as a viable way of reinvigorating the ailing state sector, saw Shangdong province, where Tsingtao Brewery is located, allocated a quota of 300 million yuan for enterprises to settle interest payments for the companies they purchased: Renee Lai, 'Joint venture perfect tonic for ailing brewery', *South China Morning Post* (Hong Kong) 11 September 1997.
12. Tsingtao Brewery, H-share Listing Prospectus dated 29 June 1993, 25. Total national production of beer in 1992 was approximately 10 050 000 tonnes.
13. In 1993, despite being the largest brewery in terms of production in the country, Tsingtao occupied only 2.3 per cent of the domestic market: 1993 *Annual Report*, 8. See also 2001 *Annual Report*, 3.
14. 'China's brewing industry gears for expansion', 7 October 2004, *Breaking News on Food and Beverage in the Asia Pacific*, available at http://www.ap-foodtechnology.com/news/printNewsBis.asp.
15. Tsingtao Brewery, 2005 *Annual Report*, 9. Total production was 306.2 million hl: 2005 *Annual Report* 39.
16. 'Anheuser lifts Tsingtao stake to 27%', China Daily/HK Edition, 12 May 2005; available at http://www.chinadaily.com.cn/english/. See also figures provided in 2005 Annual Report 2005, 39.

17. In the case of Tsingtao, the loans came from Bank of China and China Construction Bank (both of which held shares in Tsingtao and were represented on the Board) 'in accordance with the central bank's policy of propping up the state sector': *South China Morning Post* (Hong Kong) 11 July 1996. See also 1996 *Annual Report*, 34.
18. Nolan, P., 'Large firms and industrial reform in former planned economies: the case of China' (1996) 20(1) *Cambridge Journal of Economics* 1–29.
19. See Tsingtao Brewery, 1997 Annual Report, 33. For details of continuing acquisitions in 1999, see 1999 *Annual Report*, 43–45.
20. For discussion, see Renee Lai, 'Tsingtao in brewery-takeover talks as part of Shangdong Acquisition drive', *South China Morning Post* (Hong Kong) 16 January 1998.
21. 1997 *Annual Report*, 54, citing approval document dated 18 April 1994 issued by the State Administration for Taxation, and confirmation of preferential tax rate from the Qingdao Ministry of Finance on 23 March 1997. But see discussion above, n. 95 regarding doubts raised recently regarding preferential tax rate entitlements claimed by the inaugural nine H-share firms.
22. See 2005 *Annual Report*, 102.
23. See 1999 *Annual Report*, 87–93, noting financial incentives provided by the municipal governments of Xuecheng, Rongcheng, Maanshan, Huangshi, Anqiu, Yingcheng, Zhuhai and Wuhu. See also Renee Lai, 'Tsingtao in brewery-takover talks as part of Shandong acquisition drive', *South China Morning Post* (Hong Kong) 16 January 1998.
24. See Tsingtao Brewery, *Company Announcement*, dated 10 July 1997. To enable the transfer of shares to take place without legal complications, the HKEx granted a waiver from the obligation under the Hong Kong *Code on Takeovers and Mergers* to make a mandatory offer to all shareholders.
25. 1998 *Annual Report*, 20.
26. The appointment gave the Holding Company full rights (including voting rights) to deal with State shares as though it owned them: 1998 *Annual Report*, 20. See also Renee Lai, 'Tsingtao poised to swallow two breweries in Shandong', *South China Morning Post* (Hong Kong) 5 November 1997; Lana Wong, 'Tsingtao Brewery launches holding company to steer acquisition drive', *South China Morning Post* (Hong Kong) 9 July 1997, and Lana Wong, 'Tsingtao in bid to benefit listed arm', *South China Morning Post* (Hong Kong) 28 August 1997.
27. For discussion, see 'Mass consumption', *South China Morning Post* (Hong Kong) 24 October 1999, noting that 'The beer festival is strongly supported by the Shandong government.'
28. 2005 *Annual Report* 2005, 10.
29. 9 November 1997, 'Tsingtao Brewery Co recommendation: sell', under major headline 'Amoy set for property killing', *South China Morning Post* (Hong Kong) 9 November 1997.
30. Stewart Oldfield, 'Tsingtao under pressure', *South China Morning Post* (Hong Kong) 20 September 1998.
31. 1995 *Annual Report*, 44. The new firm was incorporated on 27 December 1995.
32. Renee Lai, 'Tsingtao subsidiary in debts reshuffle', *South China Morning Post* (Hong Kong) 4 August 1997.
33. 1996 *Annual Report*, 37–42. See also Renee Lai, 'H shares feel pressure', *South China Morning Post* (Hong Kong) 26 April 1997; Renee Lai, 'Tsingtao sees earnings dip as costs squeeze profit margin', *South China Morning Post* (Hong Kong) 17 April 1996, and Renee Lai, 'Tsingtao subsidiary in debts reshuffle', *South China Morning Post* (Hong Kong) 4 August 1997.
34. *South China Morning Post* (Hong Kong) 31 December 1995.
35. The total raised was HK$889 000 000 and RMB 638 000 000.
36. 1993 *Annual Report*, 9. By the end of 1997, there was still approximately RMB 100 million from the 1993 listing proceeds which remained deposited in Chinese state-owned banks: 1998 *Annual Report*, 12. See also Charles de Trenck, 'The growth of

China's key conglomerates' in Charles De Trenck et al., *Red Chips and the globalisation of China's enterprises* (2nd revised edn, 1998) 43–80. De Trenck notes that some of the harsher critics of China equities have 'pointed to companies such as Tsingtao Brewery as examples of companies that had squandered the funds they had raised from international investors. The criticism leveled at Tsingtao was that it had taken funds earmarked for investment in new capacity and re-invested them as high-interest-bearing loans to other companies'.

37. The Tsingtao Brewery 1999 *Annual Report*, 83, reveals that Tsingtao held RMB 448 128 000 worth of unlisted shares in its 27 principal subsidiary enterprises (up from RMB 131 220 000 in 1998) and had advanced loans to its subsidiaries totalling RMB 397 581 000 (up from RMB 31 735 000 in 1998). For a list of subsidiaries, see 1999 *Annual Report* 83–86.
38. The company's 2001 *Annual Report*, 114, describes its policy regarding the granting of credit as follows: 'Credit is granted to customers according to specific review of the circumstances of each customer with credit period not more than one year.' By 2001, the Tsingtao Group had 322 577 000 in net accounts receivable, a significant proportion coming from credit sales to associated firms and firms within the same Group. Of the total receivables owing, the Group was forced to write off more than half, RMB 170 929 000, as provision for bad debts in light of the aging profile of amounts due: 2001 *Annual Report*, 85–86, 113. Other accounting strategies used to work bad and doubtful debts out of the Group's balance sheets included debt-restructuring arrangements; acquisition agreements; arrangements to accept fixed assets in lieu of payment and regular renewals of short-term bank loans.
39. 1996 *Annual Report*, 42. The figure given for bad-debt provision in 1995 is RMB 7.823 million. See also Renee Lai, 'H shares feel pressure', *South China Morning Post* (Hong Kong) 26 April 1997.
40. See eg. Tsingtao Brewery, 2001 *Annual Report*, 114–117.
41. Ibid.
42. Ibid., 114, notes that 'As at 31 December 2001, the Group and the Company had reached an agreement with a customer and a related company in connection with an aggregate receivable balance aged between one to four years due from them, totalling RMB 105,000,000.'
43. Ibid., 116, notes that 'Pursuant to debt restructuring agreements or acquisition agreements of certain subsidiaries, the interest charge on the Group's and the Company's loans of approximately RMB 185,993,000 (2000: RMB 241,265,000) and RMB 83,732,000 (2000: RMB 97,790,000) respectively were waived.'
44. Ibid., 116 notes that 'Loans of the Group and the Company amounting to approximately RMB 1,499,850,000 (2000: 2,031,505,000) and RMB 637,080,000 (2000: 1,419,258,000), respectively are guaranteed by a related company. In addition, loans of the Group amounting to approximately RMB 125,000,000 (2000: RMB 244,000,000) are guaranteed by the minority shareholders of a subsidiary. . . . Approximately RMB 385,000,000 of the Group's loans are guaranteed by the Company.'
45. Ibid., 117 notes that 'Approximately RMB 158,900,000 (2000: RMB 77,190,000) of the Group's loans of the Group are secured by the following assets:
    (a) All assets of Xian Company . . . and
    (b) Building, plant and machinery and motor vehicles . . .'
46. Ibid., 117 notes that 'Most of the bank financing of the Group is in the form of short-term bank loans, as a result the Group has net current liabilities of approximately RMB 2,035,276,000 (2000: RMB 1,152,110,000) as at 31 December 2001. The Board of Directors of the Company is confident that the Group will be able to renew these short-term facilities upon their maturity . . .'.
47. Ibid., 129, notes that Tsingtao's major non-cash transactions during 2001 included the use by the company of the net book value of receivables of approximately RMB 24 658 000 as part of the consideration to acquire subsidiaries.
48. Ibid., 129 notes that, in 2001, the Tsingtao Group 'was exempt from the settlement of payment of liabilities totalling RMB 9,439,000'.

49. Ibid., 129 notes that in 2001, Tsingtao 'agreed to allow certain customers to settle the accounts receivable due from them totalling RMB 14,408,000 with fixed assets of equivalent book value'.
50. In March 2002, Tsingtao appointed an independent third party to participate in an open auction held by the Xiamen Municipal Court. The auction resulted in the acquisition by Tsingtao of all the assets of Xiamen Yincheng Company Ltd at a total cash value consideration of approximately RMB 166 030 000. A new Tsingtao subsidiary, Tsingtao Brewery (Xiamen) Co Ltd was established and all of the acquired assets were injected into it: 2001 *Annual Report*, 133.
51. 2001 *Annual Report*, 113.
52. 2001 *Annual Report*, 85–86.
53. 2005 *Annual Report*, 82–86.
54. 2005 *Annual Report* 2005, 82, gives figure for Loans to subsidiaries of RMB 2 735 123 000 for 2005 (RMB 2,345,371,000 for 2004) and notes that loans to subsidiaries were entrusted loans arranged through the Bank of Communications and the Industrial and Commercial Bank of China. All these entrusted loans were unsecured and due to reach maturity within one year. Entrusted loans amounting to RMB 1.555 150 000 (2004: 1 428 320 000) were interest free, while the remaining balances were interest bearing at rates ranging from 2 per cent to 5.02 per cent.
55. Ibid.
56. 1999 *Annual Report*, 12.
57. *South China Morning Post* (Hong Kong) 4 November 1999.
58. *South China Morning Post* (Hong Kong) 2 November 1999.
59. *South China Morning Post* (Hong Kong) 4 November 1999.
60. Tsingtao Brewery, 1999 *Annual Report* 1999, 27.
61. *South China Morning Post* (Hong Kong) 2 November 1999.
62. *South China Morning Post* (Hong Kong) 29 October 1999.
63. The issuance raised net proceeds of approximately RMB 757 729 000 after deducting related issue expense of approximately RMB 29 271 000: 2001 *Annual Report*, 21.
64. 2005 *Annual Report*, 17.
65. A-B Holdings therefore now owns a total of 261 643 836 Tsingtao H-shares through its fully-owned subsidiary A-B Hong Kong.
66. 2005 *Annual Report*, 17.
67. Under section 317 of the Hong Kong *Securities and Futures Ordinance*, each party to the agreement (Qingdao SASAC and A-B Holdings agreement dated 21 October 2002) is taken (for the purposes of the duty of disclosure) to be interested in any shares comprised in the relevant share capital in which any other party to the agreement is interested apart from the agreement: Tsingtao Brewery, 2005 *Annual Report*, 20.
68. 2005 *Annual Report*, 19. Parenthesis added.
69. Zhang Zhen Duo was deputy manager of the Shandong Branch of the Bank of China, and Yu Fu Zhong was General Manager of the Industrial and Commercial Bank of China, Qingdao Branch.
70. 'Shake-up likely at Tsingtao', *South China Morning Post* (Hong Kong) 4 June 1996; 'Entrepreneur to join Tsingtao management', *South China Morning Post* (Hong Kong) 25 June 1996. See also Tsingtao Brewery, 1996 *Annual Report*, 33.
71. 2001 *Annual Report*, 39–42.
72. As proposed in *Circular to Shareholders*, 'Proposed Amendments to the Articles of Association, The Order of Meeting for the Shareholders' General Meeting, The Order of Meeting for the Board of Directors and the Order of Meeting for the Supervisory Committee and Notice Convening the Annual General Meeting' dated 15 May 2006. See especially original article 128, renumbered as article 133, and original article 129, renumbered as article 134.
73. See further 'Tsingtao and Anheuser-Busch Strengthen Strategic Alliance: Anheuser-Busch Increases Economic Interest in Tsingtao to 27 Percent', 11 April 2005, at http://anheuser-busch.com/press_room/2005/Tsingtao_041105.html.

74. Stephen Burrows (Chief Executive Officer and President of A-B Holdings) and Mark F. Schumm.
75. This policy states that all publicly listed SOEs must be completely separated from their controlling state-shareholder (in this case, the Qingdao State-owned Assets Administration Office) in all important aspects: business, staff, assets, organization and finance.
76. Chairman of the board Li Gui Rong previously served as Deputy Director and Director of the Qingdao Municipal Planning Commission, while executive director Sun Yu Guo (a Qingdao SASAC nominee) was a former Deputy Department Head in the Finance Bureau of Qingdao and then Department Head in the Qingdao SASAC. Vice-Chairman of the Board, Jin Zhi Guo is a former General Manager of the firm. The national government's interests are also (indirectly) represented on the Supervisory Committee in the person of Chen Jun, General Manager of CITIC Wantong Securities Company and former Assistant to the Director of the Department of Business Development of *People's Daily*: 2005 *Annual Report*, 47.
77. Shanghai Petro, 1996 *Annual Report*, 29, noting that 'Pursuant to the resolutions for the issue of new H Shares passed at the 1995 AGM and the separate Class Meetings of A shareholders and H shareholders, on 22 August 1996, the Company entered into an agreement with Peregrine Capital Limited and Peregrine Brokerage Inc. for the global offering of 500 000 000 new H Shares at a price of HK$2.075 per share. The amount raised would be used to finance the capital expenditure programme of the Company and to provide for working capital. On 6 January 1997, the Company signed a similar agreement with Peregrine Capital Limited and issued 150 000 000 new H Shares to international (excluding US) investors at a price of HK$2.28.'
78. *Overseas Regulatory Announcement on the Voting Results at the Relevant Shareholders' Meeting for the Holders of A-Shares Relating to the Share Reform*, dated 8 November 2006, further noting that a total of 6505 holders of listed and tradable A-shares voted at the meeting, representing 44.7776 per cent of the total tradable A-shares of the company, and 6.6201 per cent of the total A-shares of the Company. A total 164 ordinary shareholders attended the meeting in person, while 6241 voted on-line. The total number of listed tradable A-shares represented by shareholders who voted at the meeting was 322 399 014, of which less than half, only 127 692 708 shares were used to vote in favour of the share-reform proposal. Ordinary holders of listed A-shares who voted against the share-reform proposal represented 179 146 268 shares, while those who abstained represented 15 560 038 shares.
79. *Share Reform Announcement* (Overseas Regulatory Announcement) made pursuant to Rule 13.09(2) of the HKEx *Listing Rules*, dated 12 October 2006, further noting that a total of 230 400 000 shares would be transferred from Sinopec Corp to holders of listed tradable A-shares. Shares retained by Sinopec Corp. would be subject to trading restrictions as follows: during the first 12 months following the implementation of the share reform proposal no more than 360 000 shares (5 per cent of total company equity) held by Sinopec Corp. could be traded; during the 24 months following the implementation of the share-reform proposal a total of no more than 720 000 shares (10 per cent of total company equity) could be traded, while the remaining 3 049 600 000 shares (42.36 per cent of total equity) would become freely tradable only once 36 months had elapsed from the day the share reform proposal had been implemented. Holders of Social Legal Person shares, including Shanghai Kangli Industrial & Trading Co Ltd, would be able to freely trade their shares (amounting to total of 2.08 per cent of company equity) after a lock-up period of 12 months after the date of the share reform implementation.
80. See Overseas Regulatory Announcement pursuant to rule 13.09 of the HKEx Listing Rules following three days of significant consecutive decline in the trading price of Shanghai Petro's Shanghai-listed A-shares dated 26 October 2006, available on the HKEx website at http://www.hkex.com.hk.
81. Yizheng, 1993 *Annual Report*, 33.
82. Yizheng, 1993 *Annual Report*, 11.

83. 87 per cent of the issue was subscribed for by the public in the PRC, with the balance taken up by the underwriting syndicate. Trading on the Shanghai Stock Exchange began on 11 April 1995.
84. Yizheng, 1996 *Annual Report*, 24.
85. *Announcement of the Voting Results at the Shareholders' Meeting of A-Share Market Relating to the Share Reform Scheme* dated 8 November 2006, noting that the total number of holders of tradable A shares of the company and the shareholder representatives who attended the Meeting in person or by way of on-line voting was 2090, representing 42 817 902 shares of the company and accounting for 21.41 per cent of the aggregate tradable A-shares of the company and 1.65 per cent of the aggregate shares held by the relevant shareholders of A-share market of the company. Only two holders of tradable A-shares actually attended the meeting in person, while 2088 holders of tradable A-shares participated in the meeting by way of on-line voting. Of the total votes represented by tradable A-shares, only 56.27 per cent voted in favour, which was less than the required two-thirds vote in favour required.
86. Yizheng, 1994 *Annual Report*, 15.
87. Yizheng, 1994 *Annual Report*, 15.
88. Yizheng, 1998 *Annual Report*, 8.
89. Smyth and Zhai provide a slightly different version of the creation of the China Eastern United Petrochemical Group. According to their 2001 article, the group was formed when 'four large-scale chemical producers in Nanjing – Jinling Petrochemicals, Yangzi Petrochemicals, Yizheng Chemical Fibre and Nanjing Chemical Fibre – were merged': Russell Smyth & Zhai Qingguo, 'Reforming China's large-scale state-owned enterprises: the petrochemical sector' (2001) 5(2) *Asia Pacific Journal of Economics and Business* 82–104, 90. There is no mention of either Yihua Group Corporation or the Jiangsu Petroleum Group, and the authors do not mention that CEUPEC was ever dissolved.
90. Yizheng, 1997 *Annual Report* 2, 22–23. See also Russell Smyth & Zhai Qingguo, 'Reforming China's large-scale state-owned enterprises: the petrochemical sector' (2001) 5(2) *Asia Pacific Journal of Economics and Business* 82–104, 90.
91. Yizheng, 1997 *Annual Report* 10.
92. See also *Notice relating to the Change of the shareholder of the State-owned A-shares of Yizheng Chemical Fibre Company Limited*, issued by Sinopec in 1998.
93. Yizheng, 1998 *Annual Report* 47.
94. Russell Smyth & Zhai Qingguo, 'Reforming China's large-scale state-owned enterprises: the petrochemical sector' (2001) 5(2) *Asia Pacific Journal of Economics and Business* 82–104, 89.
95. See Beijing Yanhua <0325>, Shanghai Pechem <0338>, Yizheng Chem <1033> and Zhenhai Refin <1128>, jointly issued announcement dated 25 February 2000, available through the HKEx Website at http://www.hkex.com.hk/listedco/listedconews/sehk/20000228/.
96. The largest foreign shareholders in Shanghai Petro were HSBC Asset Management (Hong Kong) Limited, JP Morgan Chase & Co and Alliance Capital Management LP, with 8.87 per cent, 5.05 per cent and 5.00 per cent of total H-share capital, respectively. Sinopec Shanghai Petrochemical Company Limited and ABN-AMRO Asia Corporate Finance Limited, *Continuing Connected Transactions*, Circular to shareholders dated 13 May 2005.
97. Shanghai Petro, 2004 *Annual Report*, 40.
98. Eric Ng, 'Sinopec lifts refining target on demand surge', *South China Morning Post* (Hong Kong) 20 January 2004. See also Eric Ng, 'Sinopec parent ponders injection of assets', *South China Morning Post* (Hong Kong) 25 September 2003.
99. Smyth & Zhai, above, n. 94, 83.
100. See eg. Shanghai Petro, 2004 *Annual Report*, 18.
101. Smyth and Zhai note that 'The two companies account for about 90% of crude oil production, 75% of the output of natural gas and 95% of oil-refining capacity. Between them, CNPC [PetroChina] and Sinopec account for about 90% of the ethylene cracking

capacity. Their joint capacity within ethylene is 90% within polyethylene, 80% within polypropylene and 60% in synthetic resin': Smyth and Zhai, above, n. 94, 89, citing P. Nolan, *China and the Global Business Revolution* (2001, Palgrave) 470.

102. 48 per cent of the company's purchases of raw materials in 2005 came from fellow Sinopec group companies Yangzi and Zhenhai. A circular to shareholders seeking approval for new caps on continuing connected transactions for years ending 31 December 2005, 2006 and 2007 indicates that total value of purchases of raw materials from connected parties is expected to rise from 2 251.097 million RMB in 2002 to 11 231 million RMB in 2008.
103. Sinopec, CPC and CITIC as well as other groups and enterprises controlled by Sinopec, CPC or CITIC are all considered to be related to Yizheng: Yizheng, 2005 *Interim Report* 14.
104. Smyth and Zhai, above, n. 94, citing Fereidun Fesharaki & Kang Wu, 'Restructuring and innovation' (1998) 3 *China Petroleum* 24–25 (in Chinese).
105. Smyth and Zhai, above n. 541, 83.
106. Smyth and Zhai, above n. 541, 96.
107. Smyth and Zhai, above n. 541, 96 citing Feireidun Fesharaki & Kang Wu, 'Revitalizing China's petroleum industry through reorganization: will it work?' (1998) 96(32) *Oil and Gas Journal* 33–34.
108. Eric Ng, 'Mainland refiners count down to 2007', *South China Morning Post* (Hong Kong) 6 September 2004.
109. *Announcement of Receiving a One-off Compensation by Sinopec Shanghai Petrochemical Company Limited*, dated 26 December 2006.
110. Smyth and Zhai, above, n. 94, 99, citing P. Nolan, 'Large firms and industrial reform in former planned economies: the case of China' (1996) 20(1) *Cambridge Journal of Economics* 1–29, 9.
111. Eric Ng, 'Refining growth goes into overdrive', *South China Morning Post* (Hong Kong) 18 September 2004.
112. Including *Measures for the Administration of Ningbo-Shanghai-Nanjing Pipeline Network*, *Notice on Pipeline Crude Oil Price for Ningbo-Shanghai-Nanjing Area* in 2004, *Measures for Crude Oil Administration (for Trial Implementation)* and *Letter Concerning Adjustment to Commission Standards on Foreign Trade Agency for Crude Oil Import*.
113. Sinopec Shanghai Petrochemical Company Limited and ABN-AMRO Asia Corporate Finance Limited, 'Continuing Connected Transactions', *Circular to Shareholders*, dated 13 May 2005, 32.
114. Yizheng, 2005 *Interim Report*, 41.
115. Worth 11 912 million RMB in 2002, and estimated to be worth 26 300 million RMB in 2007 for Shanghai Petro. Worth 2 251.097 million RMB plus 41.89 million RMB in 2002 and estimated to be worth 11 231 million RMB plus 57.7 million RMB in 2008 for Yizheng.
116. Worth 8100 million RMB in 2002, and estimated to be worth 20 540 million RMB in 2007. See also Eric Ng, 'Sinopec units sign supply contract', *South China Morning Post* (Hong Kong) 13 November 2003. See also 2005 *Interim Report* 18, which notes that upwardly-revised caps for Shanghai Petro's continuing connected transactions were approved by independent shareholders at an extraordinary general meeting held on 28 June 2005.
117. Sale of polyester products to connected parties is given as 908.181 million RMB for 2002, and estimated to be 400 million RMB in 2008.
118. Eric Ng, 'Sinopec lifts refining target on demand surge', *South China Morning Post* (Hong Kong) 20 January 2004.
119. Established in late 2001 with total registered capital of US$901,440,964. Shanghai Petro owns 20 per cent, while BP and Sinopec Corp own 50 per cent and 30 per cent of the equity interest of Secco, respectively. See also Smyth and Zhai's discussion of the difficulties presented for Secco and other joint ventures by China's long approval processes: Smyth and Zhai, above, n. 94, 83–84.

120. In 2000, BP, Shell, EXXON and ABB purchased more than $US1.5 billion worth of H-shares in Sinopec Corp, accounting for 50 per cent of the total issued H-shares. These companies have also signed an agreement with Sinopec to build 500 gas stations: Smyth and Zhai, above, n. 94, 84, citing *China's economic times* (*Zhongguo jingji shibao*) 5 July 2001, accessible at http://images.chinainfobank.com/report/wto/file/che07.htm (in Chinese).
121. Shanghai Petro, 2004 *Annual Report*, 31.
122. Shanghai Petro, 2005 *Interim Report*, 7.
123. Eric Ng, 'Refining growth goes into overdrive', *South China Morning Post* (Hong Kong) 18 September 2004.
124. Shanghai Petro, 2004 *Annual Report* 3.
125. Shanghai Petro, 2004 *Annual Report* 63, 53.
126. See Shi Jiangtao and Josephine Ma, ' "Serious pollution" of river after blast finally admitted', *South China Morning Post* (Hong Kong) 24 November 2005; Eric Ng, 'Oil majors choose risk over insurance', *South China Morning Post* (Hong Kong) 28 November 2005; Mark O'Neill, 'PetroChina braces for legal and financial fallout from spill', *South China Morning Post* (Hong Kong) 7 December 2005 and Shi Jiangtao, 'Vice-mayor of spill city kills himself', *South China Morning Post* (Hong Kong) 8 December 2005.
127. For example, one of the non-executive directors held the position of chairman of the trade union of the company, having joined the company in 1973. Another non-executive director, Gu Chuanxun, was the former Vice Mayor of Shanghai Municipality and Chairman of Changjiang Economic Joint Development Company, a company engaged in economic cooperation projects along the Yangtse (*Chang Jiang*) river. His connections to Shanghai Petro lasted until his retirement in 1988: Shanghai Petro, *H-share Listing Prospectus* 49.
128. Shanghai Petro, 2003 *Annual Report* 50. See also data provided in Appendix 1 of this book.
129. Yizheng, 2004 *Annual Report* 38–42. See also tables provided in Appendix 1.
130. One is Director of Bank of China, Shanghai Branch, and the other is the Head of Internal Auditing Bureau of Industrial and Commercial Bank of China, Chengdu Branch.
131. GSI, 1994 *Annual Report*, 111.
132. Carrie Lee, 'Hurdles cleared by Guangzhou shipyard', *South China Morning Post* (Hong Kong) 18 June 1993.
133. The company's H-share prospectus was released on Tuesday 20 July 1993, and the public offer for GSI H-shares in Hong Kong opened on Wednesday 21 July 1993. The offer, sponsored and underwritten by Peregrine Capital and four other underwriters, closed on 26 July 1993: Carrie Lee, 'Shipyard offer to kick off next week', *South China Morning Post* (Hong Kong) 16 July 1993.
134. Civet Investment Co and Vincent Leader agreed to subscribe for 9.9 million and 2.49 million H-shares, respectively.
135. Wong Joon San, 'Shipyard set to list in Shanghai', *South China Morning Post* (Hong Kong) 25 October 1993.
136. Ray Heath, 'Shipyard's major unit faces 20pc dip in profit', *South China Morning Post* (Hong Kong) 21 July 1993.
137. But this did not stay the case for long: the light-duty truck maker Qingling Motors Co listed its H-shares at about nine times prospective earnings in August 1994: Renee Lai, 'Rock-bottom price for Qingling designed to lure', *South China Morning Post* (Hong Kong) 21 July 1994. See also GSI, *H-share Listing Prospectus* 4, 87.
138. The largest foreign holder of GSI H-shares for the 10 years between 1994 and 2005 was HKSCC Nominees Limited, with approximately 29 per cent of total equity: GSI, 2005 *Annual Report* 14.
139. 'Guangzhou Shipyard beats forecast', *South China Morning Post* (Hong Kong) 6 April 1994. See also GSI, 1994 *Annual Report* 23.
140. GSI 1994 *Annual Report* 2.
141. The GSI *H-share Listing Prospectus*, dated 19 July 1993, 95, notes that, pursuant to a notice issued by the State Tax Bureau, profits earned by the Company would

be taxed at 15 per cent (effective as of 1 January 1993), instead of at the usual income tax rate applicable to joint stock limited companies of 33 per cent. See also GSI, 1994 *Annual Report* 109–110, noting that a government special order issued in late 1994 and applicable to all of the nine companies examined here ensured that the tax rate applicable to GSI was not affected when GSI amended its registration status with the State Administration for Industry and Finance on 21 October 1994.

142. 1994 *Annual Report* 89–90.
143. 1994 *Annual Report* 91.
144. 1998 *Annual Report* 119–120.
145. 2005 *Annual Report* 40–41, 113–115. GSI's Annual Report for 2005 reveals majority controlling interests in eight subsidiary operations, including one Sino-foreign joint venture steel construction firm and one Hong Kong-registered trading business, plus indirect holdings in a further three companies, also including one Hong Kong registered general trading operation.
146. GSI, *H-share Listing Prospectus*, dated 19 July 1993, 80–82.
147. Ibid. 80. See also 1994 *Annual Report* 103 and 2005 *Annual Report* 192. Figures given are service fees of RMB 11 982 000 and RMB 23 830 000 for 1993 and 1994, respectively; and RMB 7 330 000 and RMB 7 328 000 for 2004 and 2005, respectively.
148. GSI, *H-share Listing Prospectus*, dated 19 July 1993, 80–82. The CSSC Group comprised approximately 40 corporate entities in 2005: 2005 *Annual Report* 116.
149. See 'Continuing connected transactions, change of domestic auditors and notice of postponement of extraordinary general meeting', *Circular to Shareholders* dated 8 December 2006, 29. The 8 December Circular indicates that provision of utilities (primarily water and electricity) from GSI Group to CSSC Group was worth RMB 2.30 million and RMB 3.12 million in 2004 and 2005, respectively, and expected to continue rising, as indicated by the annual caps set for 2008 and 2009 of RMB 7.25 million and RMB 8.33 million, respectively.
150. Renee Lai, 'Guangzhou Shipyard confident of surviving regional turmoil', *South China Morning Post* (Hong Kong) 21 January 1998.
151. Ibid., citing announcement from CSSC company secretary Wang Wenhui.
152. 1999 *Annual Report* 10, 34.
153. 2005 *Annual Report* 14–15.
154. 1994 *Annual Report* 40, 102–103.
155. See 'Information for 2003 Annual General Meeting (Amendments to Articles of Association, Continuing Connected Transactions and Resignation and Appointment of Directors and Supervisors)', *Circular to Shareholders* dated 30 April 2004, 19–23.
156. Ibid., setting out details of the *Framework Agreement for connected transactions of an operating nature*, entered into between GSI and CSSC on 19 April 2004, approved by Independent Shareholders on 25 June 2004. The Framework Agreement was amended by the *First Supplemental Agreement* on 31 March 2005, and the amendment was approved by Independent Shareholders on 27 May 2005. Details of a *Second Supplemental Agreement* dated 26 October 2006 were set out in a company Circular to shareholders dated 17 November 2006.
157. The total value of steel materials and accessories, utilities (water and electricity), and labour services provided by the GSI Group to other entities in the CSSC Group amounted to RMB 21.23 million in calendar accounting year 2004, and was expected to rise to RMB 77.9 million in 2006. In the other direction, the value of steel, ship building accessories and ship equipment purchased by GSI and its subsidiaries from the CSSC Group in 2004 was RMB 146.45 million, and was expected to rise to a value of RMB 469.5 million in 2006; while the value of labour services provided by other members of the CSSC Group to GSI and its subsidiaries in 2004 was RMB 24.36 million and was expected to be worth RMB 88.9 million in 2006.
158. 'Continuing connected transactions, amendments to Articles of Association and Purchase of Directors and Officers Liability Insurance', *Circular to Shareholders*, dated 17 November 2006.

159. Provision of electrical and mechanical engineering equipment and metallic accessories from GSI Group to CSSC Group was worth RMB 3.61 million in 2004, RMB 4.13 million in 2005, and expected to rise, as indicated by the annual caps set for 2008 and 2009 of RMB 210.21 million and RMB 110.93 million, respectively. Purchase by GSI Group from CSSC Group of (i) electrical and mechanical engineering equipment and metallic materials and (ii) ship-building accessories and equipment for use on ships was worth approximately RMB 146.43 million and RMB 158.61 million in 2004 and 2005, respectively, and expected to rise, as indicated by annual caps set for 2008 and 2009 of RMB 635.67 million and RMB 689.01 million, respectively: *Circular (Continuing connected transactions, change of domestic auditors and notice of postponement of extraordinary general meeting)*, dated 8 December 2006, 27–28 and 32–34.
160. Labour and design and technology services supplied by GSI Group were worth RMB 15.30 million and RMB 15.33 million in 2004 and 2005, respectively, and expected to rise, as indicated by annual caps set for 2008 and 2009 of RMB 148.57 million and RMB 158.19 million, respectively. The value of labour and design and technology services purchased by GSI Group was approximately RMB 24.38 million and RMB 71.40 million for 2004 and 2005, respectively and expected to rise, as indicated by annual caps set for 2008 and 2009 of RMB 132.91 million and RMB 152.84 million respectively: *Circular (Continuing connected transactions, change of domestic auditors and notice of postponement of extraordinary general meeting)*, dated 8 December 2006, 30–32, 34–35.
161. *Circular (Continuing connected transactions, change of domestic auditors and notice of postponement of extraordinary general meeting)*, dated 8 December 2006, 36–37.
162. Ibid. 37–38.
163. Monies paid by the GSI Group for sales agency services and procurement of materials amounted to RMB 4.36 million and RMB 3.38 million in 2004 and 2005, respectively, and this amount is expected to continue rising, as indicated by annual caps set for 2008 and 2009 of RMB 18.08 million and RMB 20.79 million, respectively: ibid. 38–40.
164. GSI, 1994 *Annual Report*, 32–35. Three of the non-executive directors held positions within the parent organization, CSSC. One non-executive director was a lawyer from a firm that provided advice on Hong Kong law to the company, and the fifth was a member of the Standing Committee of the National Committee of the Chinese People's Political Consultative Conference and Justice of the Peace, Hong Kong. See also GSI, *H-share Listing Prospectus* dated 19 July 1993, 73–76.
165. 2004 *Annual Report* 16–17. A new three-year term for the board began in May 2005. The new Chairman whose term began on 10 October 2005 was a senior engineer and former vice president of CSSC with no Party connections recorded. In 1993, there were five supervisors on the Supervisory Committee of GSI, all of whom held senior positions within GSI as well as owning GSI shares. By 2004, the influence of the party remained strong on the Supervisory Committee. Three supervisors are named, two of whom are senior political officers within the Party Committee of the Company: 2004 *Annual Report* 17.
166. Refers to the rule that at least one-third of the directors on a company's board must be independent (must comply with the legal definition of the term 'independent director').
167. 1994 *Annual Report* 32. Ren Fuwei was appointed as the chairman and general manager of the Company on 28 May 1993. See also 1994 data in Appendix 1 of this book.
168. 2004 *Annual Report* 16–18. See also 2005 *Annual Report* 16–18 which, interestingly, does not record any position of General Manager. Instead, three 'vice-presidents' are named as 'senior management'. See also tables provided in Appendix 1.
169. 2004 *Annual Report* 26–28.
170. GSI Circular to Shareholders, *Continuing Connected Transactions Amendments to Articles of Association and Purchase of Directors and Officers Liability Insurance*, dated 17 November 2006, Appendix 1: 'Amendments to Articles of Association', 46.
171. 1994 *Annual Report* 10, 18.
172. 1994 *Annual Report* 14. See also Gareth Hewett, 'Guangzhou Shipyard lifts profit', *South China Morning Post* (Hong Kong) 6 August 1994; 'Group nets $9m contract',

South China Morning Post (Hong Kong) 23 December 1995; and Josephine Ma, 'Export rebate cuts may cost Guangzhou Shipyard', *South China Morning Post* (Hong Kong) 31 August 1996.

173. 1994 *Annual Report* 16. Under the original agreement, GSI held a 49 per cent interest in the new joint venture, but increased its equity interest to 51 per cent in 1995.
174. 1994 *Annual Report* 16–18.
175. 'Guangzhou Shipyard pays $17.7m for site', *South China Morning Post* (Hong Kong) 20 April 1994. See also 1995 *Annual Report* 18, noting that assistance was received from the Guangzhou Government to overcome problems related to land procurement and compensation payable to affected farmers. This government assistance enabled agreement to be reached on the use of land in Fangcun District for industrial plant construction, with the land and plant to be leased by the newly established Guangzhou United Steel Structure Limited.
176. Of the RMB 252 million owing in mid-1993, about 89 million yuan had already been outstanding for more than six months: GSI, *H-share Listing Prospectus*, dated 19 July 1993, 97.
177. Ray Heath, 'Shipyard's major unit faces 20pc dip in profit', *South China Morning Post* (Hong Kong) 21 July 1993.
178. Gareth Hewett, 'Caution needed in buying H shares', *South China Morning Post* (Hong Kong) 12 July 1995. See also 1994 *Annual Report* 71, showing accounts receivable (prepared according to Hong Kong GAAP) for the GSI Group of RMB 410 410 000 in 1993, and RMB 601 300 000 in 1994.
179. Renee Lai, 'Shipbuilder in venture with US steelmaker', *South China Morning Post* (Hong Kong) 9 August 1994, quoting Zeng Yixin, director of the company's investment department, who evidenced the Sanshansi Bridge project in Nanhai and the Humen Bridge project in Guangdong as high profit-margin steel structure projects.
180. Renee Lai, 'Mainland taxes force shipbuilder to change focus', *South China Morning Post* (Hong Kong) 12 August 1994.
181. In January 1995, GSI announced that it had taken a 35 per cent stake as one of five partners in a new $10 million joint-venture company which would be engaged in the refurbishment business, utilizing foreign capital, technology, materials and management methods: 'Chinese Press Digest', *South China Morning Post* (Hong Kong) 20 January 1995. GSI also took a 67 per cent stake in the Guangzhou Three Dragon Industrial Trade Development Company Limited – a joint-venture established to undertake large engineering projects (eg. bridges), and to provide equipment leasing and technology consultancy services – together with Guangzhou Municipal Engineering Corporation (a municipal government organ) and Tianjin Modern Industrial Trade Development Company Limited: 1995 *Annual Report* 17.
182. Randall Collis, 'Ageing of global merchant fleet tipped to push mainland up among the giants', *South China Morning Post* (Hong Kong) 3 November 1994.
183. K.K. Chadha, 'Pacific Basin launches ship', *South China Morning Post* (Hong Kong) 12 May 1995. As at the end of 1995, GSI had contracts of shipbuilding on hand with a total tonnage of 477 400 dwt and contract net value of RMB 2.107 billion: Annual Report at p. 21. Orders for six large vessels were secured during 1995, worth RMB 1.1 billion: four cargo ships were for a customer in the Czech Republic and two cargo vessels for a customer in Germany: Annual Report 12–13.
184. Randall Collis, 'Ageing of global merchant fleet tipped to push mainland up among the giants', *South China Morning Post* (Hong Kong) 3 November 1994.
185. 'Record for Guangzhou', *South China Morning Post* (Hong Kong) 3 June 1996.
186. 'Chinese press digest', *South China Morning Post* (Hong Kong) 18 January 1996. 'Shipyard sales increase', *South China Morning Post* (Hong Kong) 17 January 1996. Container manufacturing in 1995 rose 25.4 per cent over 1994 levels, while sales at GSI rose 29.9 per cent in 1995 to 1.97 million yuan, and exports rose 73.7 per cent to US$128 million.
187. Lana Wong, 'Guangzhou Shipyard dives 33 pc', *South China Morning Post* (Hong Kong) 30 August 1996.

188. Nicholas Reynolds, 'Venture delay hits shipyard profits', *South China Morning Post* (Hong Kong) 11 February 1996.
189. Renee Lai, 'Shipyard dives 44pc on turnover', *South China Morning Post* (Hong Kong) 16 April 1996. See also Chairman's Statement in 1995 *Annual Report* 13–14; and see 'Consolidated Profit and Loss Account Prepared under Hong Kong GAAP' for year ending 31 December 1995 showing profit attributable to shareholders of RMB 101 278 000 (RMB 183 084 000 in 1994): 1995 *Annual Report* 87. This decline in profits was made larger than it would otherwise have been, however, by the fact that 1994 profit levels had been artificially boosted by a one-off foreign exchange gain (of RMB 86 237 000) arising from the unification of the Reminbi's official and swap centre exchange rates: 1995 *Annual Report* 87, 100.
190. 'GSI gains plummet as tax changes hurt, building prices fall', *South China Morning Post* (Hong Kong) 12 April 1997. See also 1995 *Annual Report* 87 and 1997 *Annual Report* 76, 91.
191. 1996 *Annual Report* 9 (recording rise in total turnover for 1996 of 19 per cent over 1995 levels). See also Josephine Ma, 'Export rebate cuts may cost Guangzhou Shipyard', *South China Morning Post* (Hong Kong) 31 August 1996.
192. 1996 *Annual Report* 9. The rebate cut was prompted by the state's heavy burden of rebates – 50 billion yuan in arrears – to be paid back to exporters in two years. The company sent its officials all the way to Beijing to seek the national government's permission for at least all those contracts signed before the 1996 changes took effect to receive VAT rebates at 1995 levels, but the bid failed: 'Tax changes hit Guangzhou yard', *South China Morning Post* (Hong Kong) 2 August 1996; Christine Chan, 'H-share to lobby for 17pc rebate', 18 April 1996.
193. Josephine Ma, 'Export rebate cuts may cost Guangzhou Shipyard', *South China Morning Post* (Hong Kong) 31 August 1996.
194. 'Tax changes hit Guangzhou yard', *South China Morning Post* (Hong Kong) 2 August 1996.
195. Ibid. See also Josephine Ma, 'Export rebate cuts may cost Guangzhou Shipyard', *South China Morning Post* (Hong Kong) 31 August 1996, and 'H shares intrigue investors', *South China Morning Post* (Hong Kong) 8 August 1997.
196. Kent Chen, 'GSI share performance fails to reflect strength', *South China Morning Post* (Hong Kong) 19 May 1996. Chen notes that, at a time when most H-share companies were struggling with dwindling order books under the strains of China's credit-tightening policies, GSI could boast shipbuilding contracts on hand at the end of 1995 worth RMB 2.107 billion: 1995 *Annual Report* 21. Chen also points to improving cross-straits relations (following Taiwan's 1996 presidential election), and revived discussions about direct shipping links between China and Taiwan, as a promising sign for contined future demand for ships, containers and ship repairs.
197. In 1995, GSI Group obtained short-term foreign-exchange loans from six foreign banks, and an export credit with an aggregate of RMB 260 million from China Import & Export Bank, all as part of the company's plans for continuing development of new sources of loans to lower the cost of loan capital: 1995 *Annual Report*.
198. Renee Lai, 'Tsingtao in move for loans of $93m', *South China Morning Post* (Hong Kong) 11 July 1996. See also Josephine Ma, 'Export rebate cuts may cost Guangzhou Shipyard', *South China Morning Post* (Hong Kong) 31 August 1996; and see Tsingtao Brewery, 1996 *Annual Report*.
199. 'Tax changes hit Guangzhou yard', *South China Morning Post* (Hong Kong) 2 August 1996.
200. Lana Wong, 'Guangzhou Shipyard dives 33 pc', *South China Morning Post* (Hong Kong) 30 August 1996.
201. In August 1997 the People's Insurance Co provided US$78.9 million in export credit insurance for the sale of five ships to the Islamic Republic of Iran Shipping Line. The *China Daily* reported that an agreement signed on Wednesday 13 August 1997 would cover a $130 million contract for five ships built by GSI: 'China–Iran ship deal', *South China Morning Post* (Hong Kong) 18 August 1997.

202. The total number of staff on the company payroll at the end of 1995 was 6534 (1995 *Annual Report* 3). As at 31 December 1997, the total number of employees on the payroll was 5806 (1997 *Annual Report* 36).
203. Lana Wong, 'Tax rebate cut hits shipbuilder', *South China Morning Post* (Hong Kong) 15 April 1997. See also 'GSI gains plummet as tax changes hurt, building prices fall', *South China Morning Post* (Hong Kong) 12 April 1997.
204. Denise Tsang, 'Shipyard secures crane contract', *South China Morning Post* (Hong Kong) 28 April 1998.
205. Ibid. See also 1997 *Annual Report* 76, 'Consolidated Profit and Loss Account Prepared According to Hong Kong GAAP' showing profit attributable to shareholders of RMB 39.678 million for 1997: up from RMB 33.295 million in 1996.
206. Renee Lai, 'Guangzhou Shipyard confident of surviving regional turmoil', *South China Morning Post* (Hong Kong) 21 January 1998.
207. 'Shipyard gains export credits', *South China Morning Post* (Hong Kong) 22 September 1998, citing loan agreement signed 19 September 1998.
208. 'Shipyard receives $1.1b loans', *South China Morning Post* (Hong Kong) 23 September 1998. The 1998 *Annual Report* reveals that GSI Group received special loan facilities of RMB 140 000 000 from the Construction Bank of China, Guangzhou Branch, to finance construction of 'Ninth Five-Year Plan projects'; 80 000 000 of the loan facility had been utilized by the end of 1998: 1998 *Annual Report* 82, 125.
209. Lana Wong, 'Beijing edict boosts domestic builders', *South China Morning Post* (Hong Kong) 26 December 1998.
210. 1998 *Annual Report* 49.
211. 1998 *Annual Report* 101, 'Consolidated Profit and Loss Account Prepared According to Hong Kong GAAP', showing profit attributable to shareholders of RMB 19.032 million for 1998.
212. 1994 *Annual Report* 93.
213. 1994 *Annual Report* 71.
214. 1997 *Annual Report* 102.
215. Ibid. 76.
216. Eric Ng, 'The week that was', *South China Morning Post* (Hong Kong) 30 August 1998.
217. Jianbo Lou, *China's Troubled Bank Loans: Workout and Prevention*, 22 *International Banking Finance and Economic Law Series* (Kluwer Law International, 2001) 307–8. See also J. Lam, 'The closure of GITIC' (1999) 4 *Journal of International Business Law* 127, and T.K. Chang, 'The Easter is in the red' (March 1999) 43 *International Financial Law Review*.
218. In respect of RMB 55 000 000 in deposits held with GETDZITIC, and RMB 10 000 held with Guangzhou Foreign Economic and Trade Trust and Investment Company, the 1998 *Annual Report* indicates that, by the end of the year, GSI had initiated legal action in respect of both amounts, and the actions had been accepted by the relevant court: 1998 *Annual Report* 122–3.
219. 1998 *Annual Report* 122. In respect of the 1998 amount of RMB 456 077 000 deposited with GITIC itself, no provision was made for non-recovery on the basis that GITIC had announced its intention of debt restructuring, but details of the final restructuring plan had not yet been confirmed. In late 1998, GSI was offered a newly built hotel in Macao as collateral for the overdue GITIC deposits. The true value of the offered collateral appears to have been in debate. An official at GSI said that GSI had been told by GITIC the hotel was worth 600 million yuan, whereas GSI itself thought the hotel was worth only about 200 million yuan: 'Gzitic hotel offered, says firm', *South China Morning Post* (Hong Kong) 1 January 1999.
220. 1999 *Annual Report* 92.
221. 1999 *Annual Report* 92–3.
222. 1999 *Annual Report* 93.
223. 1999 *Annual Report* 93.
224. Joseph Lo, 'Shipyard sues Itics for $483m loans due', *South China Morning Post* (Hong Kong) 26 April 1999.

225. 1999 *Annual Report* 93.
226. 1999 *Annual Report* 74.
227. 1999 *Annual Report* 37.
228. 2000 *Annual Report* 32.
229. 2000 *Annual Report* 32–4.
230. See 2001 *Annual Report* 36, 'Balance Sheet', 31 December 2001, showing opening balance of long-term loans for 2001 of RMB 270 000 000 and a closing balance of long-term loans of RMB 410 000 000.
231. 2001 *Annual Report* 32, 'Significant events'.
232. 2001 *Annual Report* 32.
233. These comprised trust deposits receivable from GITIC amounting to RMB 397 067 000, with non-recovery provision of RMB 325 374 000. Trust deposits receivable from GETDZITIC amounted to RMB 51 380 000, with non-recovery provision of RMB 51 380 000, and deposits receivable from GOCTIC amounted to RMB 8 090 000, with non-recovery provision of RMB 5 660 000, respectively: 2001 *Annual Report* 32.
234. 2004 *Annual Report* 58.
235. On 6 January 2003, the People's Bank of China, Guangzhou Branch, announced the abolition of GETDZITIC, which was in the process of liquidation. By mid-2004, it became obvious that there were no assets remaining in GETDZITIC to repay any of its creditors. One proposal put forward by the liquidation team of GETDZITIC was to assign the book creditor's rights of GETDZITIC to each of its creditors: GSI 2004 *Annual Report* 58. GSI did not agree with this proposal, and requested a full bankruptcy liquidation.
236. See 2002 *Annual Report* 6, showing profit attributable to shareholders for 2002 of RMB 15 020 000, following a loss of RMB 5 160 000 in 2001. See also 2004 *Annual Report* 118, recording profit attributable to shareholders for 2004 of RMB 60 945 000 for 2004, following profit of RMB 24 555 000 in 2003.
237. 2004 *Annual Report* 59. See also Circular to Shareholders, *Discloseable Transaction: GZITIC Debt Restructuring*, dated 25 February 2005. 2005 *Annual Report* 61, notes that GSI had obtained the entire ownership certificate to the real estate involved by the end of 2005, but, as the developer had not yet paid the land grant fees in full, GSI was unable to obtain all of the corresponding land use right certificate. Despite this, GSI issued a certificate of full discharge of trust deposits owing in the principal amount of RMB 227 102 566.
238. 2005 *Annual Report* 61, noting that the compensatory assets include properties located in Hunan Province, Shenzhen and Guangdong, plus 108 golf membership cards and creditor's rights of RMB 10.64 million in Hong Kong Guanghong International Co Ltd. See also Circular to Shareholders, *Discloseable Transaction: GZITIC Remaining Debt Restructuring*, dated 13 March 2006.
239. 2005 *Annual Report* 129.
240. See Beiren *H-share Listing Prospectus*, dated 23 July 1993, i, 14.
241. Beiren H-share Listing Prospectus, dated 23 July 1993, 17, citing approval document *Ti Gai Sheng* (1993) No. 118 dated 16 July 1993.
242. Beiren, *H-share Listing Prospectus*, dated 16 July 1993, 18.
243. There is one exception to this. Under an agreement signed before Beiren's listing, Beiren paid money to BGC for the parent company's provision of housing benefits and living quarters to staff, so the money was classified as an expense in Beiren's accounts. When this agreement was cancelled on 1 April 1995, Beiren began adopting the more common practice of setting aside six to 10 per cent of its profit attributable to shareholders to the statutory public welfare fund. Under Chinese law, the public welfare fund can only be used for capital items for employees' collective welfare and the non-utilized fund must be kept in liquid form (cash): Renee Lai, 'Beiren controversy finally cleared up', *South China Morning Post* (Hong Kong) 12 April 1995.
244. See 2005 *Annual Report* 202.
245. Ibid.
246. 2002 *Annual Report* 97–99. Other relationships created between Beiren and its associated companies by 2005 included a loan guarantee of Rmb 34 million from BGC to

cover short-term loans; lease agreements with associated companies Beijing Monigraf Automatic Systems Company Limited and Beijing Beiying Casting Company Limited, providing Beiren with rental income of Rmb 130 529 for 2005, plus sales to and purchases from these and other associated companies: 2005 *Annual Report* 196–205.

247. Ivan Tong, 'Beiren's parent sends it ready for outside world', *South China Morning Post* (Hong Kong) 23 July 1993. See also Christine Chan, 'Beiren Printing to float six subsidiaries', *South China Morning Post* (Hong Kong) 18 June 1993.
248. 2005 *Annual Report* 12.
249. *Announcement of the Voting Results of the Relevant Shareholders' Meeting of the A Share Market*, dated 20 March 2006, available at http://www.hkex.com.hk.
250. 2006 *Interim Report* 5. Under Beiren's Share Segregation Reform Proposal, BGC was required to allocate 27 360 000 shares to holders of circulating shares. That is, 3.8 shares were to be granted for every 10 circulating A-shares. The required transfer of shares was completed on 31 March 2006.
251. 2006 *Interim Report* 5.
252. *Announcement of the Voting Results of the Relevant Shareholders Meeting of the A Share Market*, above, n. 248, 2.
253. Ibid. 3.
254. The two non-executive directors were Zhang Peng, former deputy mayor of Beijing Municipality, former adviser to Beijing Municipal government and former commissioner of the State Commission of Industries of Beijing Municipality; and Fan Muhan, president of State Printing and Equipment Supply Industry Association, whose former positions in government circles included deputy department head of Dongbei munitions department, deputy supervisor of the State Planning Committee, deputy supervisor of the State Industrial Machinery Committee and supervisor of the State Economic Committee Research Centre: Beiren *H-share Listing Prospectus*, dated 23 July 1993, 31–33. See further tables provided in Appendix 1.
255. 2005 *Annual Report* 21. The two non-exective directors not classified as 'independent' were Yu Baogai, who was the Chairman of the Labour Union of the Company, and Lu Changan, General Manager of BGC. See further tables provided in Appendix 1.
256. 2005 *Annual Report* 26–27. The Chairman of the Supervisory Committee held concurrent positions as Deputy Secretary of the Party Committee, and Secretary of the Discipline Committee of BGC. See further data provided in Appendix 1.
257. 2005 *Annual Report* 39. See further data provided in Appendix 1.
258. 2005 *Annual Report* 39–44.
259. Circular to shareholders, *Proposed General Mandate to issue additional H-shares and to repurchase H-shares; Amendments to the Articles of Association; Adoption of Rules of Procedure for General Meetings, Rules of Procedure for Board Meetings and Rules of Procedure for Supervisory Meetings*, dated 12 May 2006, 18–9, Appendix II, item 19. Under the proposed 'accumulative voting mechanism', each share carrying voting rights would become entitled to 'such number of votes equivalent to the number of director and supervisor candidates', and votes could be pooled in the course of the election of directors and supervisors at the shareholders' general meeting.
260. *Announcement of Resolutions Passed at the 2005 Annual General Meeting, held on 27 June 2006*. Published 27 June 2006 at 10.54 pm on the HKEx website at http://www.hkex.com.hk. Beiren had 35 505 shareholders at the end of 2005, of which 35 397 were holders of A-shares and 107 were holders of H-shares: 2005 *Annual Report* 14.
261. At the meeting, 222 693 799 shares casting votes were A-shares, representing 52.77 per cent of the total shares carrying voting rights, and 97 765 199 were H-shares, representing 23.17 per cent of the total equity of the company. Obviously, BGC, with 52.76 per cent of the total A-shares (the share reform had been completed by this stage) was one shareholder who attended, and so was HKSCC Nominees with H-shares comprising just over 23 per cent of total equity at the time of meeting (23.04 per cent as at the end of 2005: 2005 *Annual Report* 14; and 23.17 per cent of total equity at 30 June 2006: 2006 *Interim Report* 6.
262. *Announcement of Resolutions Passed at the 2005 Annual General Meeting*, above, n. 259.

263. Ibid.
264. Ibid.
265. 2002 *Annual Report* 96; 2005 *Annual Report* 139–140.
266. Beiren, *H-share Listing Prospectus*, dated 23 July 1993, 17–18.
267. 2005 *Annual Report* 139–140. By 2004, the broader BGC Group comprised over 60 subsidiary and branch companies: see BGC website, *About Beiren*, at http://www.eprint.cn/forum/beirenen/index.htm, accessed on 18 January 2007.
268. 2002 *Annual Report* 88.
269. 2002 *Annual Report* 88.
270. Renee Lai, 'Beiren spree on non-core items worries analyst', *South China Morning Post* (Hong Kong) 11 April 1995. Lai notes that Beiren's 1993 accounts reveal an investment of 72.34 million yuan in a property project in Beijing, and that, following its 1993 listing, 'China's Beiren Printing Machinery Holdings . . . spent an additional 30.49 million yuan (HK$27.96 million) on long-term investment in non-core operations, arousing concern about development of its major printing machinery business.'
271. 2005 *Annual Report* 62.
272. As at the end of 2005, Beiren's borrowings from banks and a related company totalled RMB 326 953 000 (RMB 240 037 000 in 2004), most of which was repayable within 12 months. Unsecured bank loans accounted for RMB 285 003 000 of total loans in 2005, of which RMB 34 000 000 was covered by a loan-guarantee from BGC: 2005 *Annual Report* 131.
273. 2005 *Annual Report* 49 (Chairman's Report). See also 2006 *Interim Report* 9.
274. 2005 *Annual Report* 222 (Financial Summary: Results prepared according to Hong Kong GAAP).
275. *Announcement*, 'Estimated results', dated 28 October 2006.
276. Website of Beiren Group Corporation accessed at http://www.eprint.cn/forum/beirenen/index.htm, also available at http://www.beiren.com/EN/About.asp, accessed on 18 January 2007.
277. 2003 *Annual Report* 71, noting that one consequence of the move was that BGC undertook to pay Beiren an amount 'not lower than the net book value' of the property at the original address of Beiren, and 'not lower than the audited expenses for land development when the Company (Beiren) moved out from its premises'. The amount was paid to compensate Beiren for the fact that the land had been included as part of BGC's capital contribution into the company when Beiren was listed in 1993.
278. 2005 *Annual Report* 117, further noting that subsidiary and foreign-invested joint venture Beijing Beiren Fuji Printing Machinery Company Limited is taxed at only 12 per cent, while all other PRC subsidiaries are taxed at the standard domestic rate of 33 per cent.
279. 2006 *Interim Report* 9 (Management Discussion and Analysis).
280. News Release issued 16 June 2006, Mitsubishi Printing Presses, 'MHI to manufacture printing machinery in China in joint venture with Beiren Printing Machinery Holdings', accessed at http://www.mhi-mpp.com/e/releas/e_060616.html. The joint venture was capitalized at 46 million yuan, with MHI owning a 51 per cent share, and Beiren Printing Machinery holding 49 per cent. Zhu Wu-an, Board Chairman of Beiren, was appointed to serve as the first Chairman of the new joint venture, while Yuzura Ichimasa of MHI was appointed to serve as the first General Manager.
281. See Web-site Newsletter, at http://webb-site.com/articles/gatesway.htm, 'Gates' Way to China', dated 9 August 2004, noting Bill Gates' disclosure of a 7.08 per cent H-share equity holding in Beiren, filed with the Stock Exchange on 26 July 2004 and published on 3 August 2004.
282. Maanshan, *H-share Listing Prospectus*, dated 20 October 1993, 38–39.
283. Ibid. 56–7.
284. Ibid. 181.
285. Maanshan, 1995 *Annual Report* 16.
286. Sean Kennedy, 'Morgan pushes Asian ADRs', *South China Morning Post* (Hong Kong) 10 November 1994.

287. 1995 *Annual Report* 16–17.
288. The total number of Maashan shareholders was 254 544, including 1 State shareholder (Holding), 157 A-share legal person shareholders, 247 754 A-share individual shareholders and 6632 H-share shareholders: 1995 *Annual Report* 16–7.
289. 2002 *Annual Report* 33. See also 2005 *Annual Report* 45–6.
290. Edward S Steinfeld, *Forging Reform in China: The Fate of State-Owned Industry* (1998) 125–6.
291. Ibid. 126.
292. Ibid. 139.
293. Ibid. 139–140.
294. Ibid. 140. See also Maanshan, *H-share Listing Prospectus*, dated 20 October 1993, 57.
295. It is interesting to note an Australian connection here. The Sale and Purchase of Ore Agreement also ensured that, during the early years of the Agreement, while the gradual process of lifting government controls over pricing was still occurring in China, and until a market price of iron ore in the PRC was established, the price of sales from Holding to Maashan could be calculated by reference to the price of powder ore of Hammersley, Australia, delivered to the Port of Shanghai: 2000 *Annual Report* 37–8.
296. 2002 *Annual Report* 66–7.
297. 2005 *Annual Report* 18.
298. 2005 *Annual Report* 19–20.
299. 2000 *Annual Report* 12, describing an iron and steel environment in which 'supply exceeded demand due to a rapid increase in iron and steel output', and in which the company was faced with 'substantial increase in prices due to a tight supply of major raw materials and fuel'.
300. Eric Ng, 'Maanshan defies clampdown', *South China Morning Post* (Hong Kong) 14 April 2004; Eric Ng, 'Scarce materials may idle 25pc of new steel output', *South China Morning Post* (Hong Kong) 8 March 2004.
301. 2005 *Annual Report* 21.
302. Ibid.
303. 2003 Annual Report 70–71.
304. 2005 *Annual Report* 20 (Accounts prepared according to Hong Kong GAAP).
305. Ibid.
306. Steinfeld above, n. 289, 139.
307. Maanshan, *H-share Listing Prospectus*, dated 20 October 1993, 61.
308. Document *Zheng Jian Fa* [2002] jointly issued by the China Securities Regulatory Commission and the State Economic and Trade Commission on 7 January 2002.
309. Document *Zheng Jian Fa* [2001] No. 102 issued by the CSRC on 16 August 2001.
310. 2002 *Annual Report* 24–5. See also new Article 104 of the Maanshan Articles of Association as amended in late 2002.
311. 2005 *Annual Report* 28, 38–41. See further data provided in Appendix 1.
312. 2005 *Annual Report* 46 (10 largest shareholders).
313. KMT was one of 18 key machine tool manufacturing enterprises directly under the supervision of the central government. It had 46 per cent of the Chinese large horizontal boring machine market, and was also a presence in the precision measuring equipment market: KMT, *H-share Listing Prospectus*, dated 23 November 1993, 23–4, 29–30.
314. KMT, *H-share Listing Prospectus*, dated 23 November 1993, 24.
315. Ibid. 38–9, 53.
316. For example, in 1998, KMT made payments totalling RmB 1 253 000 to Kun Ji, and received from Kun Ji only RMB 275 000. In 1999, KMT made payments totalling RmB 4 018 000 to Kun Ji, and received only RMB 220 000: 1999 *Annual Report* 84–5. See also KMT, *H-share Listing Prospectus*, dated 23 November 1993, 44, recording payment of RMB 7 million made by KMT to the Yunnan Provincial Government on 20 November 1993.
317. KMT, *H-share Listing Prospectus*, dated 23 November 1993, 3.
318. Ibid. 3–4.

319. Duncan Mount, 'Low issue price ensures sharp rise for Kunming', *South China Morning Post* (Hong Kong) 12 December 1993.
320. The issue included 6 600 000 shares reserved for KMT employees. The employee shares were placed into an escrow account until 3 July 1994, and were listed on the Shanghai Securities Exchange on 24 August 1994: 1999 *Annual Report* 9.
321. KMT, *H-share Listing Prospectus*, dated 23 November 1993, 16.
322. 2001 *Annual Report* 34.
323. The total annual deficit for 1998 was RmB 13 460 000, and for 1999 the total annual deficit was RmB 60 028 000. Loss per share was 10.5 fen (cents) in 1998 and 19 fen (cents) in 1999: 1999 *Annual Report* 14, 64 (Income Statement prepared according to Hong Kong GAAP).
324. Duncan Mount, 'Low issue price ensures sharp rise for Kunming', *South China Morning Post* (Hong Kong) 12 December 1993.
325. 2001 *Annual Report* 12.
326. The other shareholder with 10 per cent or more of total equity was HKSCC Nominees Limited, which by mid-2003 controlled 25.94 per cent of total equity in Jiaoda Kunji.
327. 2001 *Annual Report* 40, citing *Asset Restructuring Agreements* dated 12 November 2001. The other major shareholder was Kunming Jinghua Company with 7.19 per cent of total equity in the form of legal person shares. See also 2005 *Annual Report* 12, 10–1.
328. 2001 *Annual Report* 40, citing *Asset Restructuring Agreements* dated 12 November 2001.
329. 2005 *Annual Report* 35. Since the time of its incorporation in 1993, Kunming Machine Tool (later re-named Jiaoda Kunji) has benefited from a preferential profits tax rate of 15 per cent: 2005 *Annual Report* 113, citing document issued by the PRC State Tax Bureau on 21 October 1993, confirmed by notice issued by the Ministry of Finance and the State Tax Bureau on 18 April 1994. However this preferential tax status now appears to be under threat: see above n. 360.
330. *Announcement*, 'Profit Estimate for January 1 to December 31, 2006', dated 11 January 2007 and published on the HKEx website and in *The Standard* (Hong Kong).
331. 2005 *Annual Report* 12.
332. *Announcement* dated 5 December 2006, confirming share transfer of 71 052 146 state-owned legal person shares in Jiaoda Kunji High-Tech Company Limited. Published on the HKEx website and in the *The Standard* (Hong Kong).
333. 'Shares of Shenyang Machine Tool Group Draws Hot Response', published at http://www.liaoning-gateway.com, dated 21 November 2006, at 24 January 2007.
334. Ibid.
335. *Negotiation Status of Share Reform Proposal and Revised Share Reform Proposal.* Announcement issued pursuant to Rule 13.09 of the HKEx Listing Rules by the Board of Jiaoda Kunji, dated 15 November 2006, published on the HKEx website and in *The Standard* (Hong Kong).
336. Ibid., further noting that, of the 18 728 355 shares, Jiaotong Group would disburse 11 088 398, Yunnan Government would disburse 4 891 787 and Jinghua Company would disburse 2 748 170. Under the share-reform plan, all existing holders of circulating A-shares would receive 2.7 shares for every 10 shares held.
337. *Results of the Relevant Shareholders' Meeting in Relation to A-Share Reform.* Announcement issued pursuant to Rule 13.09 of the HKEx Listing Rules, dated 25 December 2006. The meeting was attended by 492 holders of circulating A-shares, holding 33.04 per cent of the total number of circulating A-shares, or 11.01 per cent of the total number of Jiaoda Kunji A-shares. Only four of the 492 circulating A-share holders attended the meeting in person, while 488 voted through the on-line system; 89.09 per cent of the circulating A-shares with voting rights represented at the meeting voted in favour of the share-reform proposal. Holders of circulating A-shares voting against the share reform proposal included the Yunnan Power Group and individual shareholder Zhu Peifeng. See also *Results of the 2006 Second Extraordinary General Meeting held on 22 December 2006*. Announcement dated 22 December 2006 and published on the HKEx website on that date.

338. KMT, *H-share Listing Prospectus*, dated 23 November 1993, 37.
339. 2001 *Annual Report* 13–19. See further data provided in Appendix 1.
340. 2005 *Annual Report* 14–5. In 2005, Chairman Lei Jinlu was the President and Director of Jiaotong Group. Non-executive director Wang Shangjin was also the Chairman of Xian Ser Turbo Machinery Company Limited; non-executive director Web Peixiong was President of Xian Jiaotong University and non-executive director Luo Guowei was the Deputy General Director of Jiaotong Group. Non-executive director Guo Shangwo was Secretary of the Communist Party Committee of the Group.
341. 2005 *Annual Report* 21. See further data provided in Appendix 1.
342. 2005 *Annual Report* 15–16.
343. *Notice of the First Extraordinary General Meeting of 2007*, dated 11 January 2007. Published on the HKEx website.
344. Tianjin Bohai, *H-share Listing Prospectus*, dated 3 May 1994, 17.
345. Ibid. 85–8.
346. Ibid. 54.
347. Christine Chan, 'Tianjin Bohai sets out on new track', *South China Morning Post* (Hong Kong) 29 December 1999, noting that 'Tianjin Bohai reported the biggest loss among the 41 H-shares last year, as it sank into the red to the tune of 608.5 million yuan (about HK$567.43 million).'
348. The first few such payments were made to TMICL until the transfer of the sewage plants to Tianjin CEP was complete.
349. Christine Chan, above, n. 346.
350. 2001 *Annual Report* 15.
351. Dongfang, *H-share Listing Prospectus*, dated 19 May 1994, 3.
352. Ibid. 65.
353. Ibid. 188–9, citing 'Demerger Agreement' dated 25 February 2004 and effective retrospectively from 28 December 1993.
354. Ibid. 185–8.
355. Ibid. 62–5. A new Agreement signed on 31 December 2003 and covering the three-year period from 1 January 2004 to 31 December 2006 was approved by shareholders at the 2003 Extraordinary General Meeting held on 30 December 2003: 2003 *Annual Report* 24.
356. Dongfang, *H-share Listing Prospectus*, dated 19 May 1994, 188.
357. The price of Dongfang's H-shares represented 11.94 times the company's prospective 1994 earnings on a fully diluted basis, or 11.69 times on a weighted average basis, and was at the lower end of an originally proposed price range of 11.5 times to 13.4 times: Dongfang, *H-share Listing Prospectus*, dated 19 May 1994, 3. This level compares with Tianjin Bohai's price of 12.6 times on a fully diluted basis, and can be considered relatively low by the standards of other H-shares: Renee Lai, 'Dongfang to price shares at lower end', *South China Morning Post* (Hong Kong) 17 May 1994.
358. Renee Lai, 'Dongfang listing likely to do well', *South China Morning Post* (Hong Kong) 19 May 1994.
359. Ibid., noting that most of the shares were placed with investors in Japan, Hong Kong, Singapore and Europe, with only a small portion for US players.
360. 23 million of the new A-shares were reserved for Dongfang employees: Dongfang, *H-share Listing Prospectus*, dated 19 May 1994, 24.
361. Dongfang, *H-share Listing Prospectus*, dated 19 May 1994, 25.
362. Other shareholders holding over 5 per cent of issued H-share capital as at the end of 2005 included the Government of Singapore Investment Corporation Pte Ltd (14 024 000 shares) and HP Morgan Chase & Co.
363. 2005 *Annual Report* 10, citing *Transfer Agreement regarding State-owned Legal Person Shares* dated 10 November 2005, and noting that DFEC was granted waivers from mandatory takeover offer requirements by the CSRC and the Hong Kong Securities and Futures Commission. The transfer of the 220 million state-owned shares held by DFEW to DFEC was completed on 17 February 2006.

364. 2005 *Annual Report* 37 (Significant Events).
365. Foo Choy Peng, 'Electric Trio seek power of the world giants', *South China Morning Post* (Hong Kong) 3 March 1994. See also Renee Lai, 'Analysts see price worry for Dongfang', *South China Morning Post* (Hong Kong) 15 March 1994 and Renee Lai, 'Dongfang to step up output of turbines', *South China Morning Post* (Hong Kong) 11 March 1994, noting that '[w]ith already one-third of China's hydro-electric equipment market, Dongfang Electrical Machinery will push ahead with a four-year expansion plan, backed by proceeds from the issue of shares in Hong Kong and China'.
366. 1999 *Annual Report* 23–4, note 3, reporting that '[d]ue to change in the market of generator equipment and intense competition, the joint venture projects did not make concrete progress and with no capital input' (*sic*).
367. 2002 *Annual Report* 19.
368. 1999 *Annual Report* 43–4 (Material litigation). See also Christine Chan 'Dongfang Electrical recoups most of funds locked in bank', *South China Morning Post* (Hong Kong) 24 April 1999.
369. 2005 *Annual Report* 27, 68.
370. 1999 *Annual Report* 16–7.
371. 2005 *Annual Report* 27–9.
372. By December 2005, Dongfang had signed contracts for construction of power generators in Vietnam, Laos and India: 2005 *Annual Report* 23.
373. The company's workforce actually only declined by around 12 per cent during the ten-year period, from 7804 employees in 1994 to 7083 employees in 2005: Dongfang, *H-share Listing Prospectus*, dated 19 May 1994, 69 and 2005 *Annual Report* 17.
374. 2005 *Annual Report* 3 (Chairman's Statement) and 23, noting increase in production volume of 48.58 per cent compared to 2004.
375. For example, a formal expansion of the business scope of the company to include international activities such as tendering and contracting for overseas power-generating equipment supply and project building was approved at Dongfang's Annual General Meeting for 2000, held on 25 May 2001, and a new business licence was obtained on 15 August 2001 to facilitate the expanded scope of Dongfang's business activities: 2001 *Annual Report* 23.
376. 2002 Annual Report 25; 2005 *Annual Report* 29, 73.
377. 2002 Annual Report 63.
378. Dongfang, *H-share Listing Prospectus*, dated 19 May 1994, 66–7.
379. Liu Shigang was Secretary of the Party Committee and Deputy Factory Director of DFEW; Liu Yiqiao was the Chairman of the factory labour union of DFEW and Zhou Hongxi was the Deputy Factory Director of Dongfang: Dongfang, *H-share Listing Prospectus*, dated 19 May 1994, 67.
380. Sun Xiaoliang came from previous positions in the Ministry of No 1 Machinery Industry of the PRC and from a previous position as Department Head of the State Restructuring Commission of the PRC. He was also a non-executive director of Kunming Machine Tool Company. Xing Yujiu was the Head of the policy restructuring office of the Ministry of Machinery: Dongfang, *H-share Listing Prospectus*, dated 19 May 1994, 67–68.
381. Yang Shijie and Feng Yuming both joined the original DFEW in 1969, while Xiao Shide joined the original DFEW in 1981: Dongfang, *H-share Listing Prospectus*, dated 19 May 1994, 68.
382. *Notice of the Annual General Meeting*, Circular dated 7 November 1999.
383. *Notice of the Annual General Meeting*, Circular dated 7 November 2002, 7.
384. *Annual Report* 2002, at 14. See further data provided in Appendix 1.
385. *Annual Report* 2003, at 29. Citing Notice of Rectification with Time Limit – Cheng Zheng Ban Shang Shi (2003) No. 42 circular issued by the Chengdu Securities Administration Office received by the company on 30 September 2003.
386. *Annual Report* 2005 at 12–17. See further data provided in Appendix 1.

387. For example, in December 2005 Chairman of the Board Zhu Yuanchao was also Secretary to the Party Committee of Dongfang Electrical Machinery Works (DFEW); Director Liu Shigang was also the Vice Secretary to the Party Committee of DEC Group; Director Li Hongdong was also Chairman of the Labour Union of the Company and Deputy Secretary of the Party Committee of DFEW; Independent Director Chen Zhangwu was a member of the Party Committee of Tsinghua University and Independent Director Xie Songlin was member of the 10th National Committee of Chinese People's Political Consultative Conference. Supervisory Committee Chairman Wang Bingyou was a member of the Party Branch and Leader of the Dongfang Disciplinary Team: *Annual Report* 2005, 13–15.

6. Market efficiency in a Chinese context

I INTRODUCTION

Ever since the birth of the H-share market in 1993, as each new batch of SOEs and, later, each individual enterprise, has been approved for listing on the HKEx, policy makers have hoped that corporatization will promote the depoliticization of firm management and personnel relationships, while at the same time increasing the efficiency of asset use, boosting firm profit levels and ultimately increasing revenue from the firm to the state. The underlying premise has been that even partial privatization will improve SOEs' performance, not so much by eliminating monopolistic government ownership per se, but rather because it removes such firms from an environment where the number of government bodies claiming ownership privileges is far too many and the actual financial stakes linking those bodies to the firm far too few. As Steinfeld explains, 'According to this logic, once policy makers provide a clear and decisive answer to the question of *who owns*, enterprise performance will . . . improve.'[1] The theory is that corporatization, by designating shares in the firm and then dividing up those shares amongst a contained group of holders, creates clearly-defined and identifiable owners who have a true interest in maximizing efficiency and firm profitability.

The Hong Kong Stock Exchange is perceived by most as having an effective pre- and post-IPO corporate governance system with higher standards than the domestic mainland stock exchanges. According to a recent IIF Equity Advisory Group Task Force Report, 'Several Chinese companies that have recently listed on the HKEx improved their corporate governance and increased financial transparency prior to their IPO listings.' In addition, the Hong Kong market is usually described as being more 'efficient' than other share markets in the region, including the mainland. An efficient market is said to be one in which share prices reflect readily available and accurate information relevant to the true value of listed firms. It is one in which share prices reflect with relative accuracy the value of corporate operations.

The market liquidity of shares is important for market efficiency. In larger and more liquid markets, market participants have a greater incentive to acquire information about firms, and to act on that information quickly. Thus an efficient stock market is said to be able to reward better corporate governance with lower funding costs. The stock market processes information disclosed by listed companies, but it also creates incentives for acquiring information about firms and, by acting on this information, for disseminating it to other market participants. Efficiently provided information allows company owners to link management incentives with stock prices, which helps align the interests of owners and managers.[2] Efficient stock markets also create incentives to identify poorly-managed companies, facilitate the takeover of such companies, replace their management, and make other changes in the companies' corporate governance.

To what extent does the H-share market demonstrate these characteristics of 'efficiency'? To the extent that efficiency is associated with higher levels of liquidity, neither the mainland Chinese markets nor the H-share market scores highly. Liquidity is a function of free float (the percentage of total corporate equity available to be freely traded) and market turnover. As the World Bank has noted,[3] mainland markets have typically been characterized by a low free float and excessive turnover (volatility). The H-share market, on the other hand, has been characterized by a low free float combined with a much lower level of market turnover, and hence much greater stability. Holdings of freely tradable H-shares have tended to remain relatively stable, remaining in the hands of institutional shareholders whose holdings tend to fluctuate according to factors affecting the market as a whole, rather than individual firm performance. In line with this tendency, individual firms' securities prices have tended to follow the trend for the H-share market as a whole, regardless of actual firm performance. The graphs provided in Appendix 2 of this book illustrate the close correlation between the H-share index value (representing the value of the H-share market as a whole) on the one hand, and individual firm share-price movements on the other, over the period 1993–2000. What this correlation suggests is that investors tend to view all H-share firms as similar, and do not discriminate between individual firms' performance to anywhere near the same extent as they seem to do in so-called 'efficient' markets.

But this does not necessarily mean that shareholders of Chinese firm equities are not concerned about corporate governance or proper transparency. Two further hypotheses therefore need to be tested before we can really say that the H-share market is 'inefficient'. First, it needs to be asked whether or not market prices respond to good reporting standards. Second, it needs to be asked whether or not share prices reflect shareholder concern with corporate governance standards more generally.

II ACCOUNTING STANDARDS, REPORTING TRANSPARENCY AND THE H-SHARE MARKET

One useful way to analyse the regulation of financial reporting is within the theoretical framework developed by Puxty et al., based upon the work of Streeck and Schmitter.[4] The framework is one which recognizes three forces, the state, the market and the 'financial reporting community' in maintaining and enforcing financial reporting standards. For present purposes, these forces can be defined as follows: (a) a financial reporting community is one to which all those subject to financial reporting requirements feel they belong, having some common identity and values; (b) the market is defined as encompassing all those who rely on the integrity and regularity of financial reports, including investors, investment advisors and securities markets (non-state) regulatory personnel.

According to Zhen Ping Hao, '[s]ince 1979 the state, while still very powerful, has begun to allow some of the powers associated with regulating the accounting profession to be shifted to the market and the community'.[5] Reforming the structure, organization and culture of the accounting and auditing professions may prove to be a necessary catalyst for ensuring greater integrity in the accounts and reporting practices of all listed Chinese firms. Just as the presence of an independent company secretary profession is important for the quality of internal decision making in listed firms, so also is the development of an independent accounting profession vital to the development of reporting integrity and firm transparency.

The state and the profession may be more important than the market in maintaining reporting standards amongst listed Chinese firms, but this does not mean that the market has no role to play. As noted above (see Chapter 4), Ferguson et al. found a surprisingly high level of voluntary disclosure amongst H-share firms in 2000. They also found that 'H-share firms voluntarily disclose significantly less information on the PRC exchanges than on the [HKEx].'[6] What this suggests is an important difference in the market cultures of Hong Kong and the mainland, resulting in important differences in the ability of market discipline to maintain good corporate disclosure and reporting practices.

III GOOD CORPORATE GOVERNANCE AND THE H-SHARE MARKET

Cheung et al. have examined the extent to which corporate governance standards are actually reflected in share prices on the Hong Kong stock exchange. In 2004, the authors constructed a database of the 168 largest companies that were stocks of four major indices in the Hong Kong stock market: HIS (Hang Seng Index), HSHKCI (Hang Seng Composite Index), HSCCI (Hang Seng China Affiliated Corporate Index) and HSCEI (Hang Seng China Enterprise Index). The HSCCI and HSCEI constituent stocks are China-related companies; HSCCI accounts for red-chip companies[7] and HSCEI for H-share companies. The authors found that, of their sample, the China-related companies (H-shares and red chips) had on average lower corporate governance index scores. They then went on to find 'a positive and significant relationship between CGI [corporate governance index score] and MTBV [market-to-book-value] . . . for China-related companies'.[8] This finding implies that investors value corporate governance more when firms are China-related. Such a finding also helps to explain the finding by Ferguson et al. that H-share firms appear to find value in improved disclosure and reporting practices so far as the Hong Kong market is concerned.

IV TAKEOVER RULES AND THE MARKET FOR CORPORATE CONTROL

As already noted, the ability of shareholders to respond to market information by selling (or buying) shares is an important part of market efficiency. Downward pressure on share prices, in particular, can indicate a negative reaction by the market to decisions taken by management or other developments affecting a particular firm. The takeover market becomes particularly important in such a situation. By allowing management buyouts and hostile takeovers to occur, the market provides an incentive for directors and managers who want to stay in position to act in the best interests of existing shareholders in the hope of retaining their support. And this, in turn, imposes a discipline upon company managers and directors to act both honestly and in accordance with the interests of the company as a whole. Effective takeover rules are therefore an important method of managerial discipline, and a vital aspect of market efficiency.[9]

A market such as the Chinese one that is characterized by a limited degree of liquidity, however, is also limited in its ability to reflect shareholder feelings expressed through buying or selling behaviour. Such a market provides significant obstacles to the effective operation of takeover rules: indeed, several writers have questioned whether Chinese markets can ever present company management with a realistic threat of hostile takeover. But this doubt can be answered. First, as seen in the cases of Kunming Machine Tool and Tianjin Bohai Chemical, state-owned shareholders appear quite ready to introduce new management blood into poorly performing firms. Second, not only is the Chinese government seeking to turn previously non-tradable equity in freely tradable shares, but takeover rules are also being reformed. That said, however, change, while it is occurring, is slow.

If one discounts those instances (and they may be many) where new management has been introduced following a transfer of non-tradable state or legal person shares, company takeovers in the Chinese market do, in fact, seem rare. Thus, in 2003, while China became the world's largest destination for direct foreign investment, with 9.6 per cent of the world's total investment, mergers and acquisitions (M&A) on the mainland accounted for only slightly over 1 per cent of the world's total. This 1 per cent figure compares to the more than 50 per cent of annual global investment flows generally represented by M&As. An important reason for this lack of takeover activity is that China has traditionally been seen as a difficult M&A market, with complex and ill-defined regulatory schemes. The number of rules, laws and political decisions taken by different ministries or government agencies made obtaining M&A approvals an exhausting process. Moreover, the restrictions and prohibitions on foreign investment in certain sectors, together with the protectionist tendencies of provincial governments, were major deterrents to M&A as a means of entering the market.

The differential pricing of different types of shares – tradable and non-tradable A-shares, B-shares and H-shares, has been a further hurdle to the effective operation of takeover rules, and a number of early takeovers of dually-listed companies were abandoned owing to the difficulties in justifying paying a price to all shareholders representing a premium to the A-share price.[10] The need to do this was partly a result of the mandatory general offer rules under the PRC Securities Law and the Takeover Code,[11] in combination with minimum price requirements originally imposed by the CSRC.[12] Many of the problems that arose under the previous Takeover Code, however, appear to have been ameliorated under the 2006 Takeover Code. Article 35 of the 2006 Takeover Code imposes a minimum price requirement for takeover offers that applies to each class of shares of the takeover target, rather than to all shares of that company.[13] In other words, different prices can be paid for different types of shares in a takeover offer. Moreover, the need to justify such differential pricing is likely to disappear as China gradually eliminates the segregation of shares into different types (as discussed in Chapter 4). Also alleviating some of the difficulties faced by acquirers in takeover offers is the fact that article 36 of the 2006 Takeover Code allows an aquirer to pay the price for taking over a listed company in cash, securities or a combination of cash and securities.[14]

Since the 1990s a series of new measures and reforms have also been introduced, designed to make foreign investor involvement in takeovers and mergers easier.[15] Most recently, new rules relating to foreign acquisitions of domestic firms, the *Measures for the Administration of Strategic Investment in Listed Companies by Foreign Investors* (the Strategic Investor Circular) were issued jointly by six government agencies on 31 December 2005;[16] and the *Provisions on the Merger or Acquisition of Domestic Enterprises by Foreign Investors* (the 2006 M&A Provisions) were issued jointly by the same six agencies on 8 August 2006, effective as of 8 September 2006.[17]

The most recent attempt to make general takeover rules more market-friendly is found in the *Measures for the Administration of the Takeover of Listed Companies* (the 2006 Takeover Code) promulgated by the CSRC on 31 July 2006 and effective as of 1 September 2006.[18] That the introduction of clearer and simpler rules and requirements since 2002 has served to establish a more welcoming legal environment for M&As appears borne out by the figures. In just three years between 2003 and 2006, the situation has changed quite dramatically. The volume of overseas M&A in China increased by 66 per cent over the 12 months from 2005 to 2006, reaching US$46 million.[19]

The Strategic Investor Measures and the 2006 M&A Provisions were discussed above, in Chapter 4. So far as the 2006 Takeover Code is concerned, its provisions serve to both clarify and simplify takeover rules for listed Chinese firms.[20] The Takeover Code also brings China's domestic takeover rules into line with rules in Hong Kong and Western jurisdictions. This is important for companies listed in both mainland China and overseas, as takeovers of cross-listed firms must be conducted in accordance with both domestic legislation and rules in the overseas market where the target company is also listed.

The 2006 Takeover Code vests regulatory oversight of takeovers in the CSRC, and requires the CSRC to establishes a special advisory committee of takeover experts to advise on matters relating to takeovers (article 10). The role of the Stock Exchanges is also clarified: their job is to facilitate and monitor both securities trading activities and compliance with disclosure obligations in takeovers of listed companies (article 11). Part Two of the Takeover Code imposes disclosure obligations on shareholders and 'persons acting in concert' with shareholders that are similar to those found in Hong Kong and in Western markets. Reporting requirements increase as the acquirer[21] increases its stake in the target firm, and different requirements apply to different thresholds (5–20 per cent, 20–30 per cent and more than 30 per cent).

Under the 2006 Takeover Code, a takeover can be conducted by offer or by agreement. The Takeover Code also distinguishes between offers that are compulsory (under the Securities Law)[22] and those which are voluntary. In both cases, acquirers can choose between a general or partial offer. A 'partial offer' must be for at least 5 per cent of the issued shares of the listed target company. When an acquirer, who may be foreign,[23] wants to proceed by offer, an acquisition report must be submitted to the CSRC, which then has 15 days to object to the takeover. In the absence of such objection, the takeover offer may then be launched. The offer can last for between 30 and 60 days following the launch, during which time the terms of the offer cannot be altered (unless CSRC approval is first obtained or the offer is contested).

Following the launch of a takeover offer, the target company's board of directors then has 20 days within which it must (a) examine the status and credit standing of the acquirer and the acquirer's motives for the acquisition; (b) perform an analysis of the terms and conditions of the offer; (c) appoint an independent financial adviser to issue a professional opinion on the offer; and (d) make a proposal to shareholders as to whether they should accept the offer.

Both the board's report and the independent financial adviser's opinion must be published and copies submitted to the local CSRC bureau and the relevant stock exchange. In the case of acquisitions by private agreement, if the agreement results in the acquirer holding a stake of 5–30 per cent of the listed company, the acquisition will be subject to shareholding disclosure requirements. When an acquirer's shareholding reaches 30 per cent of the issued shares of a company, it may only continue to acquire shares of that company by making a partial or general takeover offer. Likewise, to acquire more than 30 per cent of the target company's listed shares by agreement, the acquirer must first proceed by way of offer for those shares in excess of the 30 per cent, unless an exemption is obtained from the CSRC. In the absence of such exemption, a General Offer must be issued before the takeover agreement can be performed.[24]

With a greater percentage of their shares becoming publicly tradable, the Takeover Code makes PRC-listed companies much more vulnerable to hostile takeovers. In particular, the Code severely limits the options open to directors following the launch of a takeover offer and until the offer expires or the acquisition is completed. For example, during the takeover period the target firm may only continue normal business operations and implement resolutions already passed by the shareholders general meeting. Directors of the target company are precluded from taking any action that would have a material effect on the company or its assets,[25] and cannot resign during the takeover offer period.[26]

The 2006 Takeover Code widens the range of circumstances under which an acquirer who is required to launch a takeover offer[27] may apply for an exemption from takeover rules. An acquirer may apply for an exemption from the requirements to issue a general takeover offer where the following applies:

1. the buyer and seller provide evidence that the transfer will not cause a change in the de facto controlling person of the listed company;
2. the listed company faces great financial difficulties, the rescue plan proposed by the acquirer has been approved by the company's shareholders and the acquirer undertakes not to transfer the shares for a minimum three-year period;
3. a private placement of shares with the acquirer causes his or her shareholding to exceed 30 per cent of the company's issued share capital, the acquirer promises not to transfer the shares for a three-year period and the shareholders support the exemption application;
4. there are other circumstances deemed appropriate by the CSRC.[28]

A similar exemption is available for controlling (non-tradable) shareholders that have reduced their shareholding as required under a share-reform proposal, and then seek to repurchase some of those shares through the tradable market. In order to relieve controlling shareholders of the expensive obligation of issuing a general takeover offer, the *Controlling Shareholder Increase Circular* specifies that, if the obligation to make a takeover offer is triggered by an increase of shares within two months of share-reform plan requirements being implemented by a controlling shareholder, then the controlling shareholder is exempted from the obligation.

So far as the price paid for acquired shares is concerned, the Takeover Code ensures that the proposed price for the shares cannot be lower than the highest price paid by the acquirer for the target company's shares in the six months preceding the acquirer's publication of a summarized acquisition report.[29] The share price may be paid in cash, securities or a combination of cash and securities.[30] Where the price is to be paid in non-listed securities, the acquirer must offer shareholders the choice to take cash instead of the securities. However payment is made, a percentage of the price must be deposited with a third party when the takeover offer is first announced.[31]

In contrast to the seemingly bureaucratic nature of much of the Takeover Code are those provisions which establish a broader role for financial advisers. The Takeover Code establishes a responsibility system in which the acquirer must appoint a CSRC-certified 'financial adviser' whose role is to examine, track and supervise the acquirer before, during and for a 12-month period after the acquisition. The emphasis on the financial adviser's role is aimed at reducing the involvement of administrative decision makers, making transactions more market-oriented and increasing the accountability of professional intermediaries. However, the financial consultant's new role as both adviser to, and supervisor of, the acquirer may give rise to conflicts of interest, as the consultant is usually employed by the acquirer to perform a financial due diligence on the target, as well as advise on strategies for the takeover. Under the Takeover Code, the financial advisor must refuse to provide financial advice if he or she believes the acquisition is detrimental to the interests and shareholders of the company.[32]

The changes introduced by the Takeover Code will combine with other recent reforms to bring about a significant increase in the overall level of liquidity in the Chinese securities markets. Market liquidity, as already noted, is an essential ingredient in market efficiency. The extent to which improved market liquidity in the Chinese securities markets will really promote the depoliticization of firm management remains to be seen. Success is most likely to be achieved for those firms which can put the most distance between themselves and their management, on the one hand, and, on the other, the variety of government bodies able to claim oversight privileges.

NOTES

1. Edward S. Steinfeld, *Forging Reform in China: The Fate of State-Owned Industry* (Cambridge University Press, 1998) 124–5.
2. *World Bank* (2002), above, n. 1, 105, citing Ross Levine, 'Financial development and economic growth: views and agenda' (June 1997) 35 *Journal of Economic Literature* 688–726.
3. Ibid. 113.
4. Anthony G. Puxty, Hugh C. Willmott, David J. Cooper and Tony Lowe, 'Modes of regulation in advanced capitalism: locating accountancy in four countries' (May 1987) 12(3) *Accounting, Organizations & Society* 273–291.
5. Zhen Ping Hao, 'Regulation and organization of accountants in China' (1999) 12(3) *Accounting Auditing & Accountability Journal* 286–302 at 289.
6. Michael J. Ferguson, Kevin C.K. Lam and Grace Meina Lee, 'Voluntary disclosure by state-owned enterprises listed on the stock exchange of Hong Kong' (2002) 13(2) *Journal of International Financial Management and Accounting* 125–152 at 128.
7. Stephen Yan-Leung Cheung, J. Thomas Connelly, Piman Limpaphayom and Lynda Zhou, 'Do investors really value corporate governance? Evidence from the Hong Kong market' (2007) 18(2) *Journal of International Financial Management & Accounting* 86–122.
8. Ibid.
9. See Michael Jensen and Richard Ruback, 'The market for corporate control: the scientific evidence' (1983) 11 *Journal of Financial Economics* 5. This view is not without its critics: see Andy Cosh and Paul Guest, 'The long run performance of hostile takeovers: UK evidence', *Working Paper No 215* (ESRC Centre for Business Research, University of Cambridge, 2001) 4–5, 30–1. Available online at http://www.cbr.cam.ac.uk/pdf/WP215.pdf.

10. DeSombre and Chen, above, n. 85, 17.
11. An investor who acquires (whether alone or jointly by agreement with others) shares (whether tradable or non-tradable) representing 30 per cent or more of a company listed on a domestic exchange, and who continues to purchase such shares, must make a general offer to acquire all of the outstanding shares of the target company: article 88 of the Amended Securities Law (2006) and article 24 of the 2006 Takeover Code (*Measures for the Administration of the Takeover of Listed Companies*, translated (November 2006) in 20(9) *China Law & Practice* 40–73).
12. Discussed in DeSombre and Chen, above, n. 85, 17–18. According to DeSombre and Chen, the minimum price payable for tradable shares in a takeover under the pre-2006 Takeover Code regime was 'the greater of either the recent purchase price by the acquirer, or 90% of the 30-day trailing average market price for the shares on the Stock Exchange'. DeSombre and Chen explain that the CSRC was deluged with requests for exemption from this requirement 'because 90% of the market price of the tradable shares [was] generally in vast excess of the purchase price of the non-tradable shares purchased by the acquirer. Potential acquirers . . . apparently indicated to the CSRC that if they [were] to make a general offer for the tradable shares at such a higher minimum price, then they [could not] afford to acquire the non-tradable shares': DeSombre and Chen, above, n. 85, 17–18.
13. Article 35 provides that 'When an acquirer effects a takeover by offer . . . the offer price paid for a class of shares may not be less that the highest price paid by the acquirer to acquire the same class of shares during the six months prior to the date of the alert for the takeover offer. If the offer price is less than the arithmetical average of the daily weighted average price for that class of shares during the 30 trading days prior to the date of the alert, the financial consultant engaged by the acquirer shall analyse the trading in that class of shares during the preceding six months and state whether the stock price is being manipulated, whether there are persons acting in concert with the acquirer that have not been disclosed, whether the acquirer made other payment arrangements when acquiring the company's shares during the preceding six months, the reasonableness of the offer price, etc.: as translated in *Measures for the Administration of the Takeover of Listed Companies*, translated (November 2006) in 20(9) *China Law & Practice* 40–73.
14. *Measures for the Administration of the Takeover of Listed Companies*, above, n. 158.
15. Jean-Marc Deschandol & Charles Desmeules, 'China overhauls takeover code of listed companies' (October 2006) 20(8) *China Law & Practice* 31–34, 31.
16. Also known as Circular 28, the *Strategic Investor Circular* was jointly issued by the Ministry of Commerce (MOFCOM) the CSRC, the State Administration of Taxation, the State Administration of Industry and Commerce and the State Administration of Foreign Exchange on 31 December 2005, and effective 30 January 2006. The concept of foreign 'strategic investors' was actually first introduced by a circular issued in October 2005, titled the *Matters Relevant to the Administration of Foreign Capital Involved in the Reform of the Division of Equity Interests of Listed Companies Circular*.
17. Issued by the Ministry of Commerce, the State Assets Supervision and Administration Commission of the State Council, the State Administration of Taxation, the State Administration for Industry and Commerce, the China Securities Regulatory Commission and the State Administration of Foreign Exchange. The 2006 M&A Provisions are further discussed (in Volume 3 Issue 1) *M&A Review* (*Asialaw Supplement* January 2007) 11–14, and in 'China legal briefs' (September 2006) 20(7) *China Law & Practice* 14. The 2006 M&A Provisions replace the earlier 2003 *Interim Provisions for Foreign Investors to Merge Domestic Enterprises* promulgated by the Ministry of Foreign Trade & Economic Cooperation et al., 2003. Similar provisions have also been promulgated for unlisted SOEs: the *Using Foreign Investment to Re-organise State-Owned Enterprises Tentative Provisions* Jointly promulgated by the State Administration for Industry & Commerce, the State Economic & Trade Commission, the Ministry of Finance and the State Administration of Foreign Exchange on 8 November 2002, and effective as from 1 January 2003.

18. [3700/ 06.07.31]. Order of the CSRC No. 35, translated (November 2006) in 20(9) *China Law & Practice* 40–73. Article 90 repeals four pieces of earlier regulation on corporate takeovers.
19. Mergers and Acquisitions, Lehman Lee & Xu, *China Law Digest Newsletter*, 19 May 2006, http://www.chinalawdigest@lehmanlaw.com.
20. Jean-Marc Deschandol & Charles Desmeules, above, n. 15, 31.
21. See articles 5 and 83 of the 2006 *Takeover Code*, above, n. 18, for definitions of 'acquirer' and 'concerted action', respectively.
22. *Amended Securities Law* 2006, Part Four: Takeover of Listed Companies, articles 85–101.
23. *Matters Relevant to the Transfer of State-owned Shares and Legal Person Shares of Listed Companies to Foreign Entities Circular* (jointly issued by the CSRC, the Ministry of Finance and the State Economic and Trade Committee on 1 November 2002. See also Jean-Marc Deschandol & Charles Desmeules, 'New rules on strategic investments by foreign investors in listed companies' (February 2006) 20(1) *China Law & Practice* 13–15, note 12.
24. Article 47, 2006 *Takeover Code*, above, n. 18.
25. In particular, the target company's board of directors cannot transfer the company's assets, perform investments, provide loans or guarantees, or change the company's business activities: article 33.
26. Article 34.
27. See 'Part Four: Takeover of Listed Companies' (articles 85–101), *Amended PRC Securities Law* (2006) above, n. 22.
28. 'Part Six: Exemption Applications' (articles 61–64), 2006 *Takeover Code*, above, n. 18.
29. Article 35.
30. Article 36.
31. Article 36.
32. Deschandol and Desmeules, above, n. 15, 33.

Conclusion

Corporate governance outcomes are the result of complex interactions between institutions that differ according to the cultural, social and economic conditions in which they emerge. According to Mark Roe, a socialist political system should produce an 'insider' system of corporate ownership and control. An insider system is said to be one where shareholding is said to be concentrated in the hands of blockholders, and where shareholders and creditors are more actively involved in the control of companies. Insider systems, with Japan and Germany being the two 'typical' examples used to illustrate these features, are also said to be characterized by the relative unimportance of the securities market as a source of finance. The principal sources of finance are banks, families, non-financial corporations and the state. Insider systems are typically contrasted with Anglo-American 'outsider' systems,[1] which are characterized by a securities market with dispersed shareholdings, and where shareholders and companies interact on an arm's-length basis, largely determined by market forces.

In light of its Anglo-colonial history and inheritance, the temptation is to categorize Hong Kong amongst those jurisdictions with an 'outsider' system of ownership and control. Recent research on the importance of family-controlled block shareholdings in Hong Kong, however, may tend to cast doubt upon such an automatic categorization. In the Australian context, Alan Dignam and Michael Galanis have revealed features of the Australian system of corporate governance that suggest the listed market there has been mis-characterized as an outsider system, when, in reality, it tends more towards an insider system. It is suggested that a similar investigation carried out in the Hong Kong context, while well beyond the scope of this book, would be a valuable exercise in enhancing understanding of the nature of corporate control and management patterns in that market. For example, in 2004, when Cheung et al. examined the 168 largest companies that were constituent stocks of four major indices in the Hong Kong stock market,[2] they found that, on average, the top five shareholders controlled more than 50 per cent of the company. If this finding was to hold true for Hong Kong main board companies more generally, it would suggest a pattern of concentrated share ownership much more typical of insider systems, and one that belies assumptions based on Hong Kong's Anglo legal origins.

On the mainland side of the border, there are a number of obvious features of China's securities markets which support Roe's theory that socialist political systems are associated with insider systems of corporate ownership and control. These features include the following:

- the presence of a significant blockholder, in this case the State;
- institutional and minority investor powerlessness;
- a strong relationship between management and blockholder, which results in a weak market for corporate control. In this Chinese case, where corporate control has shifted hands, the shift has been from one level of state control to another;
- a historic weakness in public and private securities regulation, which allow the creation and perpetuation of crucial blocks to information flow. In the Chinese context, various forms of media censorship and the lack of a free media generally impose an additional impediment to information flow. Recently strengthened ongoing disclosure rules for listed firms are unlikely to overcome even partially these impediments.

It is a mistake to view the classification of China's system of corporate governance as a matter of purely pedantic inquiry. Most importantly, recognizing that the Chinese system shares features common to insider systems would enable a more appropriate response to corporate governance problems. Chinese corporate governance reforms so far appear to have been based on the assumption that reform initiatives from the UK and the US should be adopted in China in the same way that they have been followed in Hong Kong. If China in fact has an insider system, then adopting reforms which work in the context of an outsider system is either a deliberate strategy aimed at 'converging' China towards an outsider system, or it is misconceived.

There are two major problems with the idea that China is and/or should be 'converging' towards an outsider system of corporate governance. First, as the case studies in this book have demonstrated, regulatory reform alone has not had, and is not having, any convergence effect. If reform was in fact helping to make Chinese firms operate more like those in 'outsider' systems, then one would expect such an effect to be magnified most in the case of H-share firms, as these firms have most exposure to the institutions typical of an 'outsider' market. The nine firms examined in this book, moreover, have been operating as Hong Kong-listed firms longer than any other Chinese firms, and so have had the longest opportunity to adopt corporate governance features typically associated with 'outsider systems'. Yet even these firms, it seems, remain stubbornly the same in the way they actually operate on a day-to-day basis, despite ostensible compliance with regulatory requirements aimed at promoting shareholder protection and market efficiency in 'outsider' systems.

In the case of Tianjin Capital, for example, we see that it was the municipal government, which not only had the incentive, as shareholder, but also the power, to bring about a major turnaround in the nature and direction of the business of the firm. Likewise, in the case of Kunji Jiaoda, the company's major shift in business direction and investment strategy depended, not at all on market support, but on the central government's ability effectively to take control of the firm. Nor did that takeover depend upon, or operate within, the context of market sensitivities. Rather, the central government's ability effectively to 'take over' depended almost solely on the willingness of the Provincial Yunnan government to agree to the takeover plan.

Solutions to corporate failures in outsider systems such as the UK and the US have been based largely on ensuring the accountability of management to shareholders. Such solutions have not solved, and are unlikely to solve, the accountability problem in the Chinese context, because part of the problem is that management is in reality accountable to the state as blockholder. Solutions that increase the accountability of management to shareholders may therefore only increase the accountability of management to the State. This is not necessarily a bad thing of itself, but it does leave behind a significant gap in accountability in situations where the interests of the state blockholder differ from those of arm's-length shareholders, such as small individual shareholders and foreign institutional shareholders. While there are real corporate governance problems in the Chinese listed market, adopting wholesale reform initiatives modelled along Hong Kong/UK/US lines not only runs the risk of failing to solve those problems, but of actually allowing them to get worse under cover of ostensibly greater transparency. That is, regulatory reform can simply serve to disguise the reality of corporate governance in Chinese firms, rather that changing that reality.

One mechanism that may well be more effective than regulatory reform in improving corporate governance in Chinese companies is to encourage the creation of strategic partnerships with foreign multinational companies that have a good track record on governance. The strategic partnership between Tsingtao Brewery and Anheuser-Busch is one example of how this can be done. What the Tsingtao-Anheuser-Busch case reveals is that the introduction of a significant foreign partner into the management of a firm is more likely to be successful in transforming and improving corporate governance in that firm than mere regulatory reform. Similar partnerships are also being forged in the Chinese banking sector, where foreign banks are entering to take a minority strategic stake in state-owned banks. Just as Anheuser-Busch is now represented on the board of Tsingtao Brewery, Chinese banks with strategic foreign partners have added representatives of foreign banks to their boards of directors. Foreign directors have helped improve the quality of board oversight by requesting additional financial information and increasing board discussion on operational and strategic issues.[3]

The benefits of such partnerships appear to have been recognized by the government when it passed the *Administrative Measures on Strategic Investment in Listed Companies by Foreign Investors* at the end of 2005, allowing foreign investors to acquire A-shares of PRC listed companies that have completed the share conversion process (discussed in Chapter 3) as a strategic investor subject to a three-year transfer prohibition period. As the number of such partnerships increases, what may well be revealed is that it is possible to improve corporate governance standards in Chinese companies without need to alter the 'insider' nature of the system in that country. There is simply no need for China to go through what could only be a traumatic transformation of its whole system, assuming it was even possible, from a predominantly insider model to an outsider model. That is not to say that a partial transformation is not happening or would not be beneficial, simply that it is not necessarily so, and that transformation would likely be extraordinarily disruptive.

This raises the other major problem with the argument that China should adopt (or continue adopting) reforms along Anglo-US lines in order to bring about convergence towards an 'outsider' system of corporate control. The strong subtext of such arguments is that insider corporate governance systems are underdeveloped and that the outsider system is the superior model. For example, in an influential series of articles running from 1998 to 2003, La Porta et al. begin with the proposition that weak investor protection has an 'adverse consequence for financial development and growth', and then go on to find that weak investor protection is associated with systems in which public companies have concentrated ownership patterns: ie. with insider systems. Conversely, where there is strong legal protection, an outsider system will emerge that is more likely to facilitate private sector investment. The idea is that insider systems can move towards the superior model only by adopting outsider system shareholder protection norms.

The thesis that the level of legal protection for shareholders is the key factor in determining corporate governance outcomes, a thesis that has been labelled the 'law matters' thesis,[4] is not without its critics. Cheffins, for example, has criticized the work of La Porta et al. for paying little attention to the social, institutional and cultural settings within which insider systems such as the Chinese system have arisen. Moroever, he has argued that they were naïve in assuming that the ideal has been achieved in the outsider system. A further criticism is that La Porta et al. have failed to recognize some of the economically beneficial influences at work within insider systems. For example, as the case studies discussed in Chapter 4 demonstrate, blockholder control, especially when the blockholder is the State, can have positive effects. How else could Kunming Machine Tool and Tianjin Petrochemical have been so efficiently transformed from loss-making enterprises using outmoded production techniques and equipment to produce outmoded products into enterprises with considerable future potential, operating in newly-emerging industry sectors? The restructurings of Kunming Machine Tool Company and Tianjin Bohai Industry Group Company in 1999 and 2000, respectively demonstrate that personal connections can, on occasion, be useful in promoting efficient communications between business and government. Both of these companies were able to undertake a complete reorganization and change of business direction with remarkable ease and speed, not least, it would seem, thanks to the close involvement of local government and good communication channels between business and bureaucracy.

On the other hand, however, blockholder control can also encourage bad management practices. For example, could Tianjin Petrochemical and Kunming Machine Tool have avoided the need to be rescued if they had been better managed in accordance with traditional Western management principles; that is, without the need to satisfy state-imposed production quotas and without other state-imposed incentives to focus on the short-term appearance of success at the expense of longer-term survival?

As Dignam and Galanis have pointed out, there is also the possibility that La Porta et al. have misunderstood the importance of shareholder protection in the emergence of outsider systems. While there can be little doubt about the observation that outsider sytems have strong investor protection, this does not mean that the existence of shareholder protection causes the emergence of an outsider system. Indeed, John Coffee has suggested that the results of La Porta et al. may actually reveal that developed markets are a precondition for the emergence of strong shareholder protection.[5] Thus, taking a snapshot of current shareholder protection in a particular outsider system could be misleading: it may have emerged after the outsider system was already in place. Coffee's point is compelling, given the way outsider systems emerged in the UK and the US. In both countries, the systems emerged without a protective legal environment for shareholders. Rather, the quality control function within the marketplace was fulfilled by the stock exchanges in London and New York, and the brokers attached to them. These private institutions promoted voluntary disclosure and self-dealing rules that provided a certain integrity for the market and those investing in it. Thus, by the time the UK and US had formal legal protection for shareholders, an outsider system had already emerged.

In China, the State has a dominant presence as blockholder in the listed market, and, as block shareholder, engages in self-dealing and rent extraction while protected from the market for corporate control. According to the 'law matters' thesis, this suggests that shareholder protection is weak. However, the level of formal legal protection has been significantly increased over recent years to levels now comparable to those in the UK and the US. Thus the Chinese evidence poses a difficulty for the 'law matters' theory of systems convergence. If Coffee's criticisms are correct, one should look to private sector institutions such as the stock exchanges and their brokers to see if they have failed to carry out similar quality-control activities to those of their UK and US counterparts.

Ferguson, Lam and Lee have found evidence that H-share firms voluntarily disclose significantly more financial and strategic information than other firms listed on the SEHK.[6] This suggests that H-share firms are sensitive to the information demands of significant players in the Hong Kong market: the stock exchange, brokers, analysts and institutional shareholders. The fact that 'H-share firms voluntarily disclose significantly less information on the PRC exchanges than on the SEHK'[7] can also be explained by the failure of the mainland brokerages and other securities institutions to provide the same level of quality control as their Hong Kong counterparts. This failure perpetuates poor quality information disclosure on the mainland exchanges, and is possibly further compounded by the underdeveloped nature of other private market institutions such as institutional shareholders.

One of the major themes to emerge in recent discourse about the regulation of different systems of production has been the 'legal origin' hypothesis. This hypothesis suggests that diversity in national systems of production accords with different 'regulatory styles' between countries. 'Regulatory style' is predominantly influenced by a particular country's 'legal origin'. Expressed very simply, the 'path-dependency' proposition may be put thus: 'the historical legal origin of a country's laws shapes its regulation of . . . markets'.[8]

These ideas have emerged from the work of La Porta, Lopez-de-Silanes, Shleifer and Vishny (and other associates), much of which is concerned with the legal rules operating across nations in relation to various aspects of corporate governance, investor protection and so on. Importantly for present purposes, 'legal origin' theory suggests that 'regulatory style' may broadly be ordered into two major legal families. The first family includes those countries or systems of common law origin, including Britain, the US and Australia, as well as jurisdictions to which the common law has been exported, such as Hong Kong. The other family encompasses legal systems of predominantly civil law origin, including most of Western Europe, but also including areas in Asia where the system has also been incorporated through legal colonization, or where legal developments have been inspired by civil law models.

Mainland China and, in particular, mainland China's system of corporations and securities law, certainly appear to share most, if not all, of the features of the civil law family of legal systems. These include (a) a market that relies mostly on direct supervision by government, and where there is a corresponding lack of private 'contractualized' forms of regulation; and (b) a predominately insider/relational model of corporate governance, characterized by concentrated forms of ownership and control with block-holding of shares, and finance typically obtained through banks and other sources of relational investing.

Concentration of ownership control allows for a more direct form of monitoring and observation of management performance and decision making, and minority, or dispersed, investors are correspondingly less well protected than in the 'outsider' model. Institutional devices supporting this regulatory style include the institutionalization of employee voice in the enterprise, as currently found, for example, in article 118 of the 2006 Chinese Companies Law which mandates employee representation on the Supervisory Committee of all Chinese Companies.

These arguments have important consequences for legal scholars, not least because they invite analysis of convergence and divergence in national systems of regulation. They also invite an examination of the way in which corporate governance operates in light of its 'fit' or 'conformity' with the relevant 'legal family'. If the argument about 'legal origin' is correct, then it would appear that legal origin matters because it can lead to predictions about the future of corporate governance in a particular jurisdiction. In the particular case of Chinese firms listed on the Hong Kong exchange, for example, one might well hypothesize that corporate governance and business decision making within these firms is most likely to reflect the tensions inherent in the differences between the mainland and Hong Kong legal systems, and in fact that each comes from a different legal family. As the case studies in this book demonstrate, however, this hypothesis does not stand up to scrutiny.

Rather than reflecting the tensions between two different legal systems, or the tensions between two different systems of corporate control, the business and strategic decision making that goes on within Chinese firms listed on the Hong Kong Stock Exchange reflects policy decision making within mainland Chinese government circles, and the tensions between different policy objectives at the central and local government levels. To the extent that these policy objectives coincide, as in the case of Kunming Machine Tool, a successful business outcome can be achieved. To the extent that central and local policy objectives conflict, the need to reconcile conflicting objectives more often than not imposes costs.[9]

Understanding corporate governance in large state-owned Chinese firms in light of the tensions between central and regional policy objectives also has consequences for legal analysis of China's further integration into global systems of trade and finance because it highlights the possibility that such integration is occurring at localized levels and not just at the level of the nation state.

Corporate governance practices, and corporate governance law reform in China have been saddled with a number of political burdens. So far as the individual firm is concerned, these burdens include a legacy of local protectionism and the need to mediate often diverging policy aims of various state agencies at local, provincial and national levels. There is also the pervasive influence of the Party in corporate management, and in the creation and timing of corporate governance law reform. In an environment dominated by elderly men who are synonymous with the Party and the State, it is unsurprising that corporate governance law reforms in China have not always provided 'efficient' answers to perceived problems. As Bebchuk and Roe have argued in relation to corporate governance in America,[10] the features which have emerged and survived in Chinese corporate governance have done so first because of the history of problems that have had to be solved along the way (path dependence), but also because of the presence of path-created features which have tended to impede what might otherwise have been chosen as 'efficient' forms of change. In particular, incumbent groups, created because of the path taken, have been both influential and likely to oppose changes tending to unsettle the status quo. Moreover, these groups have been and remain protected by historical institutions (provincial kingdom building, Party hierarchies) that have also tended to block or divert attempts to change the status quo.

Saddled with the burden of strong State and Party involvement in every aspect of corporate life, and with the equally heavy burden of local protectionism and the politics of national–provincial rivalries, corporate governance reform in China has followed a unique path all of its own, and unlike that followed by any other jurisdiction. In this book, legal reforms behind the evolution of China's H-share market have been described through case studies of the first nine mainland firms to be listed on the Hong Kong stock exchange. What emerges is not a story of tensions between ideas of corporate governance from two very different legal systems, nor of covergence as China adopts legal concepts from Anglo-American jurisdictions. Rather, what emerges is a story of individual firms following a path of pragmatic self-interest as they mediate the differing agendas of state agencies that own or control them.

NOTES

1. See Alan Dignam and Michael Galanis, 'Australia inside-out: the corporate governance system of the Australian Listed Market' (2004) 28 *Melbourne University Law Review* 623, and the authors discussed therein.
2. Cheung et al., above, n. 7.
3. World Bank, above, n. 1, 3.
4. Dignam and Galanis, above, n. 1, 643–5.
5. John Coffee, 'The rise of Dispersed Ownership: The role of Law and the State in the Separation of Ownership and Control' (2001) 111 *Yale Law Journal* 1, 25–9.
6. See above, notes 108–110 inclusive.
7. Michael J. Ferguson, Kevin C.K. Lam and Grace Meina Lee, 'Voluntary disclosure by state-owned enterprises listed on the stock exchange of Hong Kong' (2002) 13(2) *Journal of International Financial Management and Accounting* 125–152.
8. Lucian Arye Bebchuk and Mark J. Roe, 'A theory of path dependence in corporate ownership and governance' (November 1999) 52(1) *Stanford Law Review* 127.
9. In the case of Tianjin Capital Environmental Protection, for example, the firm has struggled to reconcile the conflict between the central government's desire to reduce provincial government 'subsidies' to local government-controlled business operations, on the one hand, with provincial government planning objectives based on long-term and substantial support for TCEP on the other: Interview with Financial Secretary Zhu Fan, June 2006. According to Zhu Fan, a Central Government edict placing a financial limit on annual payments made by Provincial governments to support or subsidize their controlled enterprises has forced the Tianjin Municipal government to restructure its agreements with TCEP relating to payments made for sewerage treatment services.
10. Bebchuk and Roe, above, n. 8.

APPENDIX 1

1994

1994 Annual Report (from 1993–1994 prospectus)	Tsingtao Brewery	Shanghai Petrochem	Guangzhou Shipyard	Beiren Printing	Maanshan Iron & Steel	Kunming Machine	Yizheng Chemical	Tianjin Bohai	Dongfang Electrical
Total shares (1000s)	900 000	6 550 000	494 677.58	400 000	6 455 300	245 007.40	3 400 000 (after 1994 A-share issue)	1 300 000	450 000
Equity type (%)									
State-owned shares	44.42	55.56	42.61	62.5	62.5	41.79	60	63.05	48.89
Legal person shares	5.93	2.08	0	0	1.36	7.19	0	2.9	0
Domestically listed	11.11	10	25.57	12.5	9.29	24.49	15	8.5	13.33 incl. 5.1% employee shares
Listed overseas	38.54	32.36	31.82	25	26.85	26.53	25	25.55	37.78
Board of directors									
Total no. of directors	9	15	19	11	10	9	12	19	14
Executive directors	5	7	14	9	5	6	10	11	8
Connected non-executive directors	2	5	3	2	1	3	2	5	5
Independent directors	2	3	2	0	4	0	0	3	1

Chairman = CEO? (Code Prov. A.2.1)	Yes	Yes	Yes	No	No	Yes (Deputy GM)		Yes	Yes (Vice-chair)
Female directors	0	0	0	1	0	0	1	1	1 1
Average age directors	52 yrs 4 m	52 yrs 4 m	51 yrs 2 m	60 yrs	49 yrs 2.5 m	n/a	56 yrs 5 m	46 yrs 9 m	53 yrs 7 m
Elected by Poll vote? (cumulative voting)	No	No	No	No	No	No	No	No	No
No. of board meetings in 1994	6	4	?		4	4		11	4 ?
Board committees									
Audit committee	No	No	No	No	Yes	No	No	Yes	No
Remuneration committee	No	No	No	No	Yes	No	No	Yes	No
Nomination committee	No	No	No	No	No	No	No	No	No
Supervisory committee									
Total no. supervisors	3	3	5	3	5	3	5	13	3
External connected	0	0	0	0	1	0	2	0	0
Independent supervisors	0	0	0	0	2	0	0	0	0
Female supervisors	0	0	0	0	2	0	2	2	1
Supervisors' average age	55 yrs 4 m	48 yrs 8 m	50 yrs 5 m	51 yrs	52 yrs 5 m	48 yrs 8 m	46 yrs 9 m	54 yrs 9 m	46 yrs
Total no. employees	27 085	40 000	6 356	3 699	44 421	3 323	13 633	20 528	7 804

2000

2000 Annual Report (figures for end 2000)	Tsingtao Brewery	Shanghai Petrochem	Guangzhou Shipyard	Beiren Printing	Maanshan Iron & Steel	Kunming Machine	Yizheng Chemical	Tianjin Capital	Dongfang Electrical
Total shares (1000s)	900 000 000	7 200 000	494 677.58	400 000	6 455 300	245 007 400	4 000 000	1 330 658.06	450 000
Equity type (%)									
State-owned shares	44.42	55.56	42.61	62.5	62.5	41.79	60	63.05	48.89
Legal person shares	5.93	2.08	0	0	1.36	7.19	0	2.9	0
Domestically listed	11.11	10	25.57	12.5	9.29	24.49	5	8.5	13.33
Listed overseas	38.54	32.36	31.82	25.5	26.85	26.53	35	25.55	37.78
Board of directors									
Total no. of directors	9	12	11	9	12	9	14	9	11
Executive directors	4	6	4	7	7	5		6	7
Connected non-executive directors	2	2	3	0	2	1		0	3
Independent directors	3	4	4	2	3	3	4	3	1
Chairman = CEO? (Code Prov. A.2.1)	separate	not separate	separate	separate	separate	not separate		not separate	separate
Female directors	0	0	0	1	1	0	5	2	1

Average age directors	49 yrs 10 m	48 yrs 7 m	49 yrs	56 yrs 6 m	51 yrs 4 m	56 yrs 10 m	51 yrs 10 m	46 yrs 9 m	56 yrs 3 m
Elected by Poll vote? (cumulative voting)	No	No	No	No	No	No		No	No
No. of board meetings in 2000	14	4	5	11	5	10		11	6
Board committees									
Audit committee	No	Yes	No	No	Yes	No		Yes	No
Remuneration committee	No	Yes	No	No	No	No		Yes	No
Nomination committee	No	No	No	No	No	No		No	No
Supervisory committee									
Total no. supervisors	6	7	5	3	6	4	5	6	3
External connected	1	2	2	0	2	0		0	0
Independent supervisors	2	2	0	0	0	2		0	0
Female supervisors	2	1	1	1	0	0	0	1	1
Supervisors' average age	49 yrs 10 m	52 yrs 10 m	50 yrs 10 m	50 yrs 4 m	50 yrs 4 m	52 yrs		42 yrs	50 yrs
Total no. employees (end 2000)	n/a	n/a	5055	3672	44454	2460	11906	995	6781

2005

2005 Annual Report (figures for end 2005)	Tsingtao Brewery	Shanghai Petrochem	Guangzhou Shipyard	Beiren Printing	Maanshan Iron & Steel	Kunji Jiaoda High Tech	Yizheng Chemical	Tianjin Capital	Dongfang Electrical
Total shares (1000s)	1 308 219	7 200 000	494 677.58	422 000	6 455 300	245 007	4 000 000	1 330 658.06	450 000
Equity type (%)									
State-owned shares	30.56	55.56	42.61	59.24	62.5	41.79	60	63.05	48.89
Legal person shares	4.08	2.08	0	0	1.36	7.19	0	2.9	0
Domestically listed	15.29	10	25.57	17.06	9.29	24.49	5	8.5	13.33
Listed overseas	50.07	32.36	31.82	23.7	26.85	26.53	35	25.55	37.78
Board of directors									
Total no. of directors	11	12	11	11	10	12	14	9	9
Executive directors	5	6	4	7	5	4		6	5
Connected non-executive directors	2	2	3	0	1	4		0	1
Independent directors	4	4	4	4	4	4	4	3	3
Chairman = CEO? (Code Prov. A.2.1)	No	Yes	No	No	No	No		No	No
Female directors	1	0	0	1	0	1	5	2	0

Average age directors	52 yrs 1 m	48 yrs 7 m	49 yrs	52 yrs	49 yrs 2.5 m	52 yrs 6 m	51 yrs 10 m	46 yrs 9 m	
Elected by Poll vote? (cumulative voting)	No	No	Yes	Optional	No	No		No	
No. of board meetings in 2005	6	4	?	6	9	4		11	11
Board committees									
Audit committee	Yes	Yes	Yes	Yes	Yes	Yes		Yes	Yes
Remuneration committee	Yes	Yes	Yes	Yes	Yes	Yes		Yes	Yes
Nomination committee	No	No	Yes	Yes	No	Yes		No	No
Supervisory committee									
Total no. supervisors	8	7	5	3	5	5	5	6	3
External connected	2	2	2	0	1	3		0	0
Independent supervisors	2	2	0	0	2	0		0	0
Female supervisors	1	1	0	0	2	1	0	1	1
Supervisors' average age	46 yrs 7 m	52 yrs 10 m	53 yrs 5 m	51 yrs	52 yrs 5 m	51 yrs		42 yrs	
Total no. employees	27085	n/a	4088	2944	44421	2484	11906	481	7083

APPENDIX 2

The following figures were generated using daily share-price data (based on the high price for each day) for individual companies between June 1993 and 31 December 1999. These data were purchased from Pacific Basin Capital Markets Research Center, University of Rhode Island. Hang Seng China Enterprises Index ('HSCEI', also referred to as the H-share Index) data were purchased from HSI Services Limited, Hong Kong.

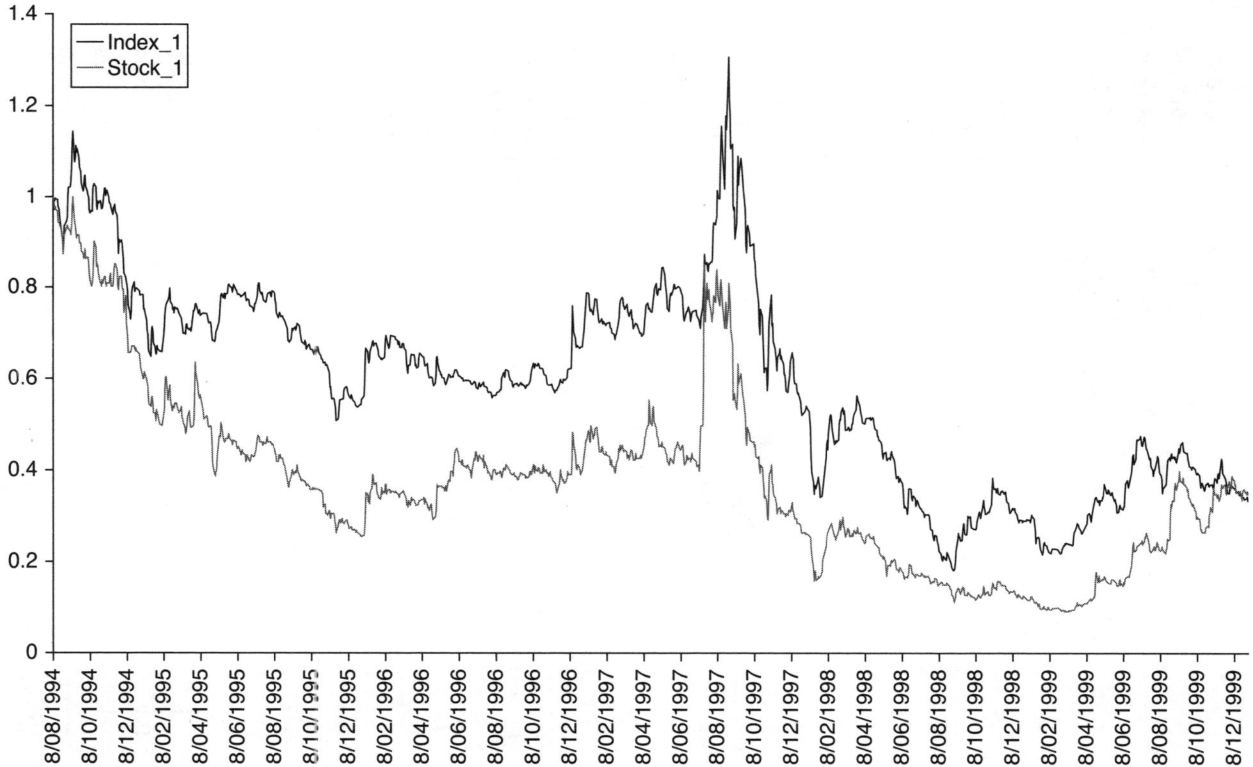

Figure A2.1 Tsingtao Brewery Co. Ltd.

Figure A2.2 Shanghai Petrochemical Co. Ltd.

Figure A2.3 Guangzhou Shipyard International Co. Ltd.

Figure A2.4 Beiren Printing Machinery Holdings Ltd.

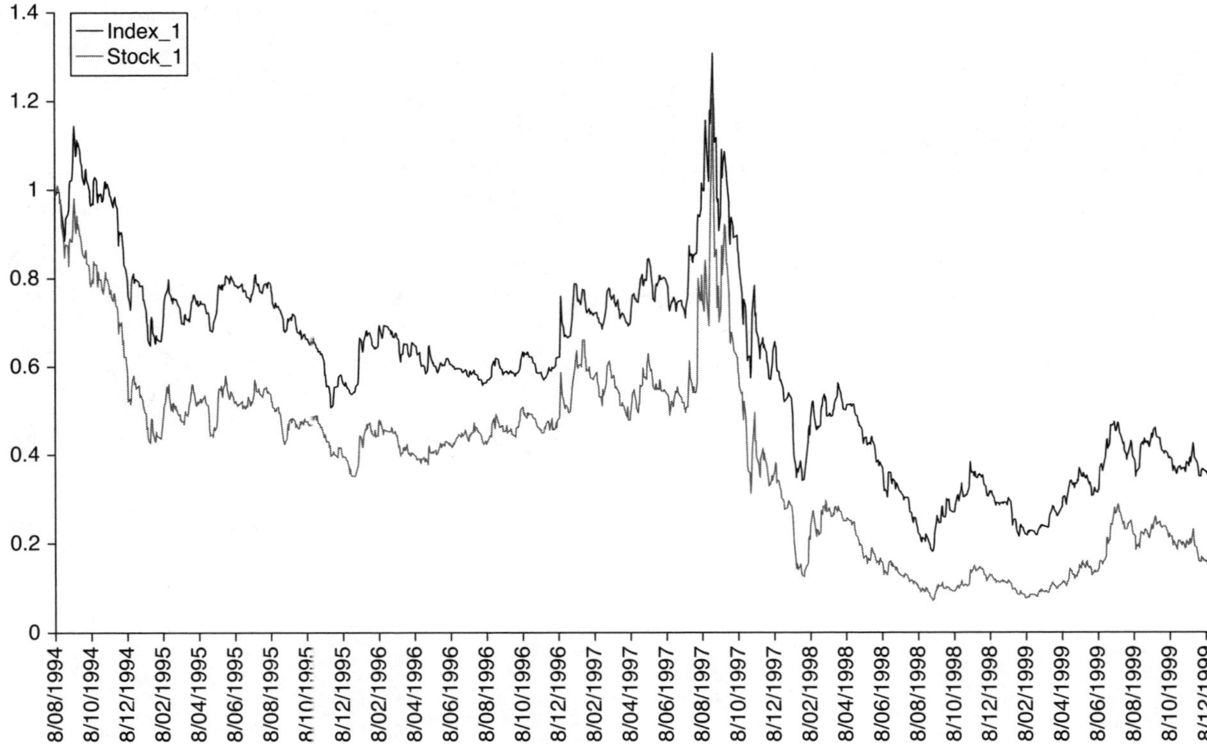

Figure A2.5 Manshaan Iron and Steel

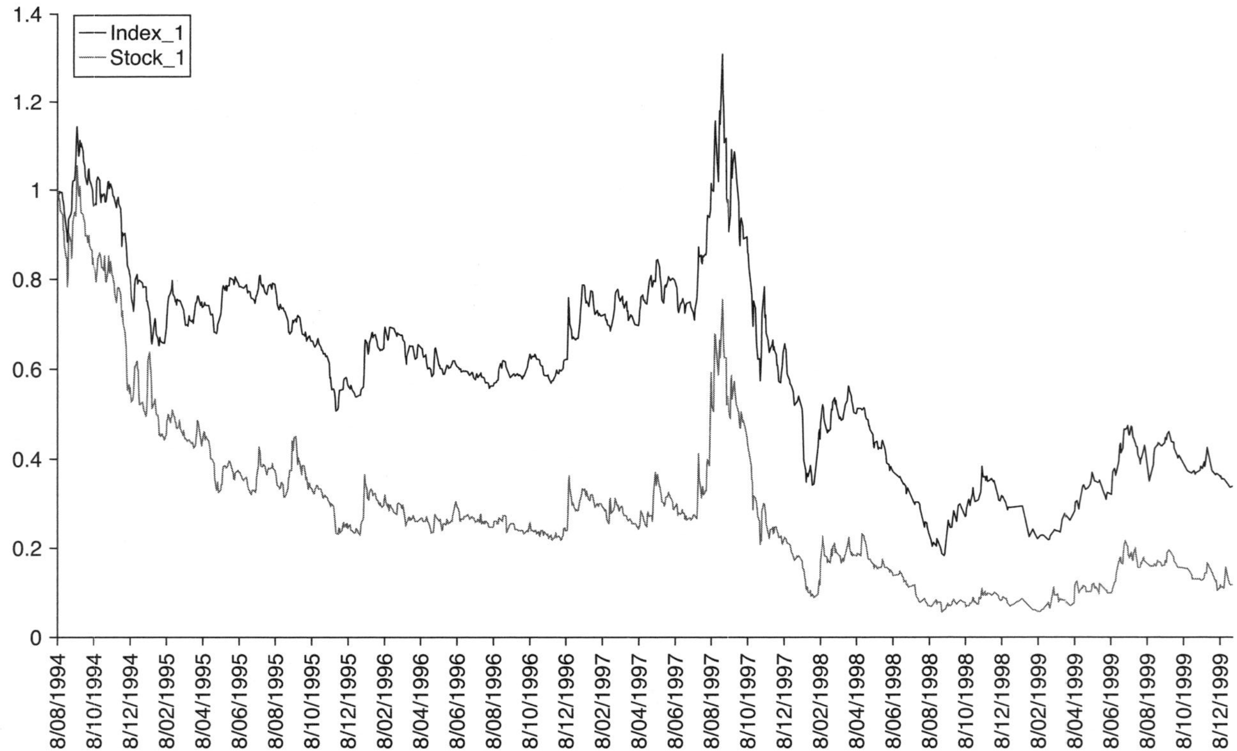

Figure A2.6 *Kunming Machine Tool Co. Ltd.*

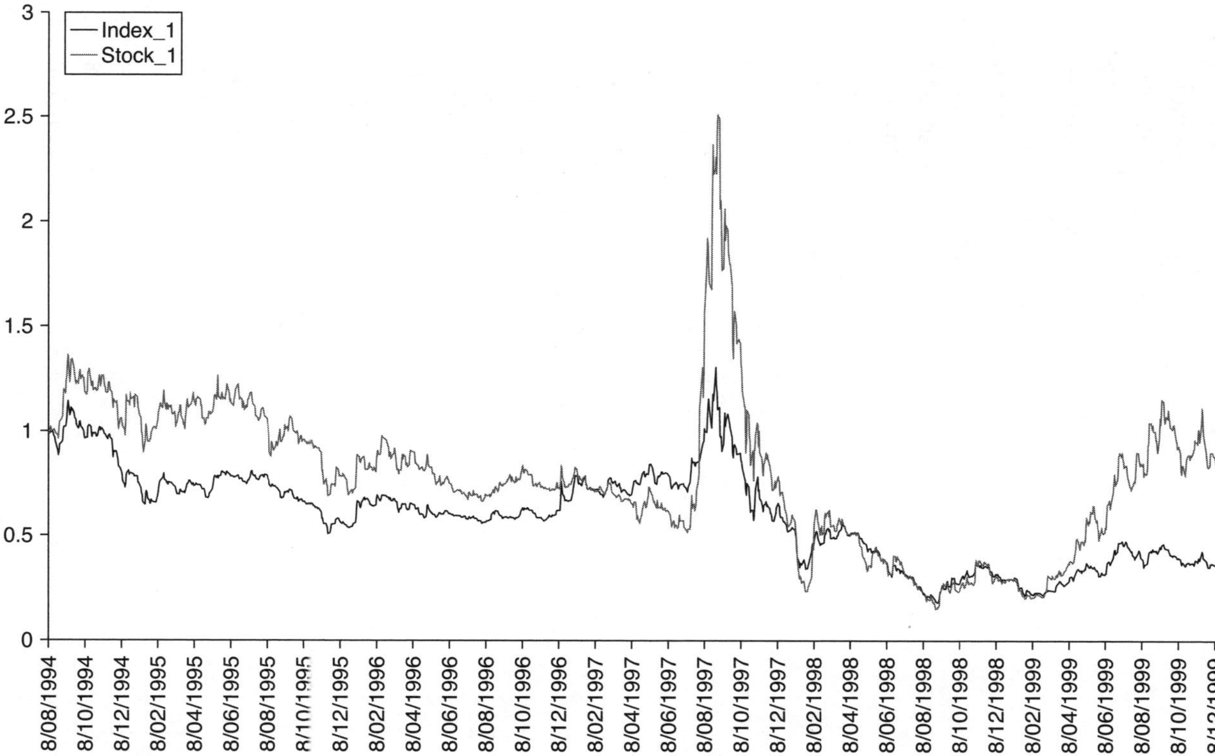

Figure A2.7 Yizheng Chemical Fibre Co. Ltd.

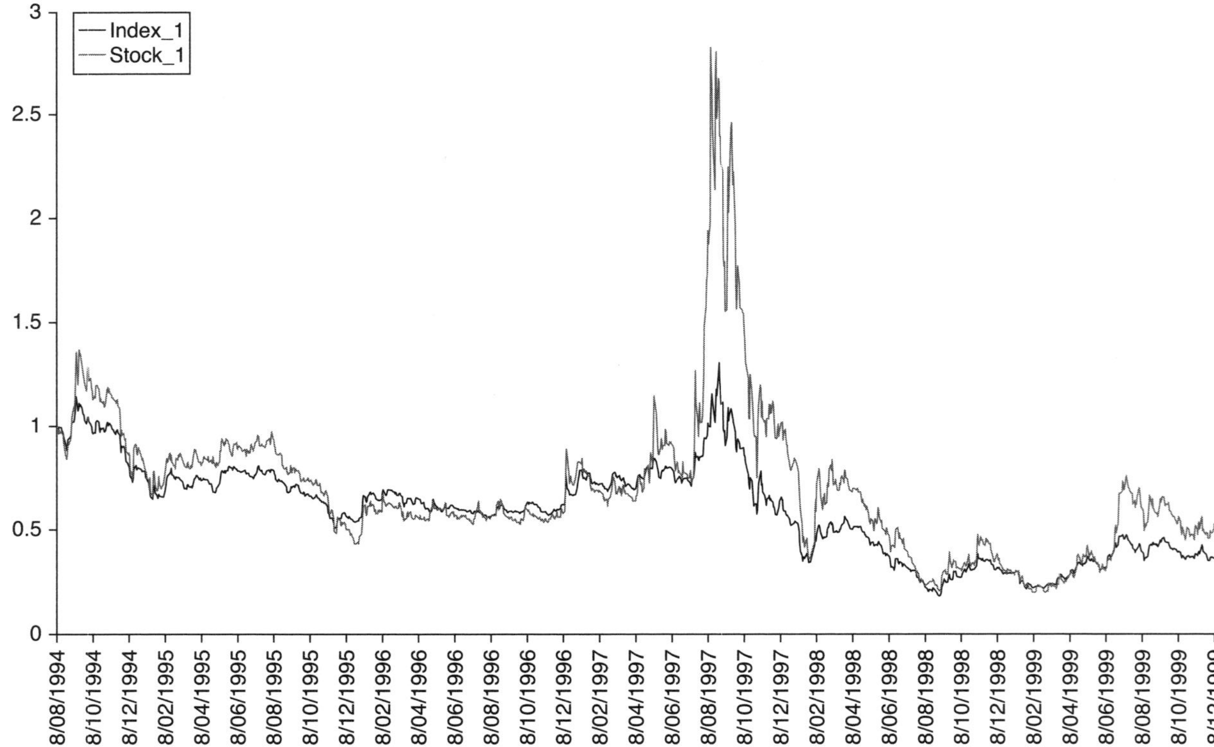

Figure A2.8 *Tianjin Bohai Chemical Industry*

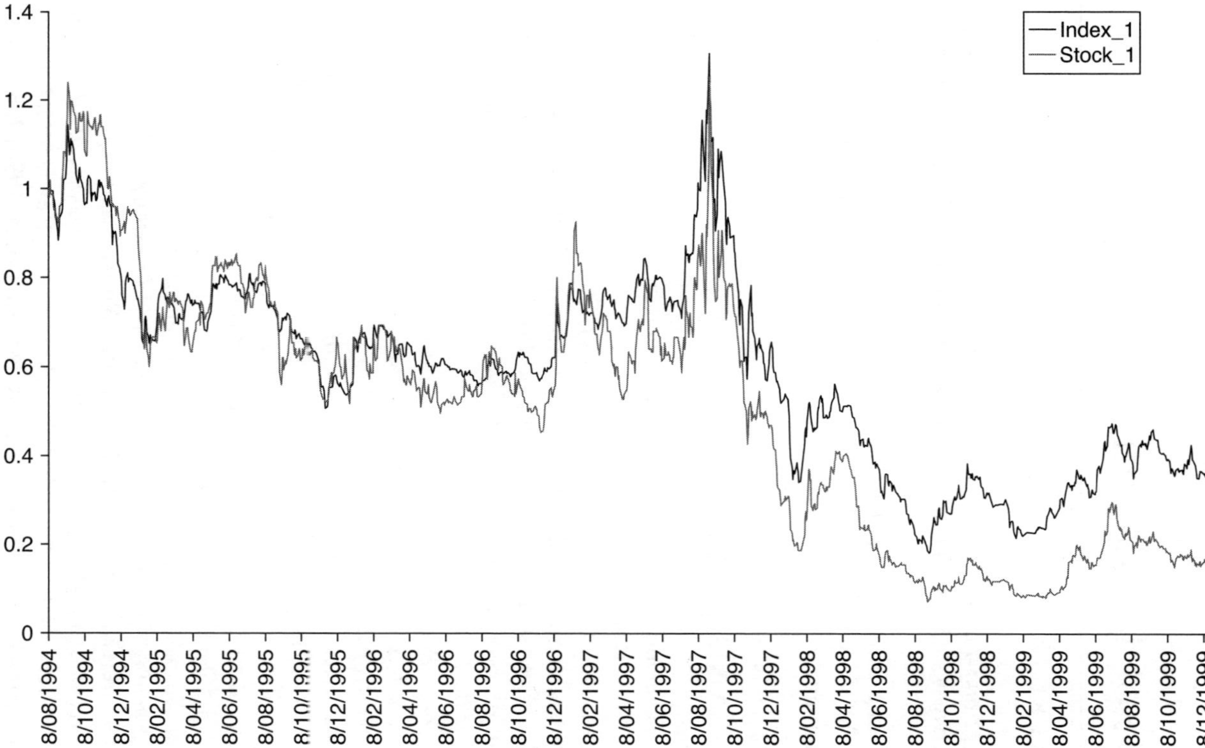

Figure A2.9 Dongfang Electrical Machinery

Table of legislation

HONG KONG:

Securities and Futures Ordinance (Chapter 571) 2003 available online at http://www.sfc.hk/sfc/html/EN/legislation/securities/securities/securities/html/.

Hong Kong Stock Exchange *Listing Rules*. Update No 85. Updated 25 June 2007. Available online at http://www.hkex.com.hk/rule/listrules/listrules.htm.

MAINLAND CHINA

Standard Opinion for Joint Stock Limited Companies issued on 15 May 1992 by the State Restructuring Commission.

Administration of the Issuing and Trading of Shares Tentative Regulations promulgated on, and effective from, 22 April 1993 by Order Number 112 of the State Council. Published as *Provisional Regulations on the Administration of the Issuing and Trading of Stocks* in *China Laws for Foreign Business – Business Regulation*, para. 13-574. Also translated as *Provisional Regulations on the Administration of Issuing and Trading of Shares*, in I.A. Tokley & Tina Ravn (eds), *Company and Securities Law in China* (Sweet & Maxwell Asia, 1998) 179–196.

Provisional Measures on the Prohibition of Deceptive Securities Dealing Activities. Approved 15 August 1993 by the State Council, promulgated 2 September 1993 by the Securities Committee of the State Council. Translated in *China Laws for Foreign Business – Business Regulation*, Para. 13-558 (17,225–17,241).

Notice on Suspension of the Purchase of Overseas Enterprises and Further Strengthening the Administration of Overseas Investment (Guo Fa, 1993, No. 69), referred to in article 4 of the *Notice regarding the Further Reinforcement of Administration on the Issues of Foreign Shares and Listing Overseas*, translated in I.A. Tokley & Tina Ravn (eds), *Company and Securities Law in China* (Sweet & Maxwell Asia, 1998) 256–7.

Accounting Law of the People's Republic of China (originally adopted at the Ninth Meeting of the Standing Committee of the Sixth National

People's Congress on 21 January 1985, as amended at the Fifth Session of the Standing Committee of the Eighth National People's Congress on 29 December 1993. Available in English at Charles D. Paglee, *Chinalaw Web – PRC Accounting Law* (last modified 7 April 1998) http://www.qis.net/chinalaw/prclaw56.htm. Downloaded 6 December 1998.

The Company Law of the People's Republic of China. Adopted at the Fifth Session of the Eighth National People's Congress, promulgated by Order No. 16 of the President of the PRC on 29 December 1993, and effective as of 1 July 1994. Translated in I.A. Tokley & Tina Ravn (eds), *Company and Securities Law in China* (Sweet & Maxwell Asia, 1998) 133–175.

Decision of the Standing Committee of the Nation People's Congress on the Punishment of Criminal Violations of the Company Law. Adopted and promulgated on 28 February 1995 by the Twelfth Session of the Standing Committee of the Eighth National People's Congress. Translated in I.A. Tokley & Tina Ravn (eds), *Company and Securities Law in China* (Sweet & Maxwell Asia, 1998) 176–178.

Special Regulations of the State Council Concerning Floating and Listing of Shares Overseas by Companies Limited by Shares. Adopted 4 July 1994 by the Twenty-second Ordinary Session of the Standing Committee of the State Council, promulgated by the State Council on, and effective from, 4 August 1994. Translated in CCH Asia *China Laws for Foreign Business – Business Regulation* para. 13-552. Also translated in I.A. Tokley & Tina Ravn (eds), *Company and Securities Law in China* (Sweet & Maxwell Asia, 1998) 212–217.

Notice on the Implementation of Essential Clauses in Articles of Association of Companies Listed Overseas, *Zhengweifa* (1994) Document No. 21. Promulgated 27 August 1994 by the Securities Committee of the State Council and the State Commission for Restructuring the Economic System. *Mandatory Provisions in Articles of Association of Companies Listed Overseas*. Translated in *China Laws for Foreign Business – Business Regulation* para. 13-410. Also translated in I.A. Tokley & Tina Ravn (eds), *Company and Securities Law in China* (Sweet & Maxwell Asia, 1998) 218–255.

Listing of Foreign Investment Shares in China by a Company Limited by Shares Provisions. Promulgated on, and effective from, 25 December 1995. Translated in I.A. Tokley & Tina Ravn (eds), *Company and Securities Law in China* (Sweet & Maxwell Asia, 1998) 197–203.

Implementing Rules of the Provisions for the Listing of Foreign Investment Shares in China by a Company Limited by Shares. Issued by the State Council Securities Commission on 3 May 1996. Translated in I.A. Tokley & Tina Ravn (eds), *Company and Securities Law in China* (Sweet & Maxwell Asia, 1998) 204–211.

Administrative Measures on Own-account Securities Business Conducted by Securities Institutions. Promulgated 24 October 1996 by the China Securities Supervision and Management Committee. Translated in *China Laws for Foreign Business – Business Regulation*, para. 13-590 (17,511–17,529).

Notice Regarding the Further Reinforcement of Administration on the Issue of Foreign Shares and Listing Overseas. Issued by the State Council on 21 June 1997. Translated in I.A. Tokley & Tina Ravn (eds), *Company and Securities Law in China* (Sweet & Maxwell Asia, 1998) 256–257.

Administration of Securities Investment Funds Tentative Procedures, promulgated by the State Council on, and effective as of, 14 November 1997. Translated (March 1998) 10(2) *China Law and Practice* 27.

Measures for the Administration of Stock Exchanges. Approved by the State Council on 31 November 1997 and promulgated by the Securities Commission of the State Council 10 December 1997. Downloaded from the Shenzhen Stock Exchange website at http://www.szse.com.cn/sse/en/law/law5.htm on 15 December 2003.

Asset Reorganization by State-owned Enterprises Using Foreign Investment Tentative Provisions (2140/98.09.14). Issued by the State Economic and Trade Commission on, and effective as of, 14 September 1998. Translated (March 1999) 13(2) *China Law & Practice* 25–30.

Further Standardizing Operations and Reform of Companies Listed Outside China Opinion (3710/99.03.29). Issued by the State Economic and Trade Commission and the China Securities Regulatory Commission on 29 March 1999. Translated in *China Law & Practice* June/July 1999, at 50–57.

Circular on Further Improving Methods of Issuing Shares (3710/99.07.28). Issued by the China Securities Regulatory Commission on, and effective as of, 28 July 1999. Translated (September 1999) 13(7) *China Law & Practice* 42.

Public Share Offerings by Listed Companies Tentative Procedures (3710/00.04.30). Promulgated by the China Securities Regulatory Commission on, and effective as of, 30 April 2000. Translated (August 2000) 14(6) *China Law & Practice* 45–49.

Standards for Listed Companies' Shareholders' Meetings Opinion (Amended 2000) (2330/00.05.18). Promulgated by the China Securities Regulatory Commission on, and effective as of, 18 May 2000. Summarized (July/August 2000) 14(6) *China Law & Practice* 5.

Issues Relevant to the Overseas Issue and Listing of Shares by Overseas Companies with Interests in Mainland China Circular, Promulgated by the CSRC on 9 June 2000. Translated (July/August 2000) 14(6) *China Law & Practice* 26–27.

Administration of Offerings of New Shares by Listed Companies Procedures [3710/01.03.28]. Issued by the China Securities Regulatory Commission on, and effective as of, 28 March 2001. Translated (May 2001) 15(4) *China Law & Practice* 24–34.

Issue of Convertible Bonds by Listed Companies Implementing Procedures [3700/01.04.26]. Issued by the China Securities Regulatory Commission on, and effective as of 26 April 2001. Translated (June 2001) 15(5) *China Law & Practice* 43–54.

Questions Relevant to Foreign-funded Companies Limited by Shares Circular [2300/01.05.17]. Issued by the General Office of the Ministry of Foreign Trade and Economic Cooperation on 17 May 2001. Translated (July/August 2001) 15(6) *China Law & Practice* 53–58.

Guidelines for Introduction of Independent Directors on the Boards of Listed Companies (Zheng Jian Fa No. 102 of 2001). Promulgated by the CSRC on 16 August 2001. Translated (October 2001) 15(8) *China Law & Practice* 63.

Notice Regarding B-share Investment by Chinese Citizens promulgated by the CSRC on 19 February 2001: CSRC, *China's Securities and Futures Markets* (April 2004), p. 14. Available from the CSRC website at http://www.csrc.gov.cn.

Matters Relevant to Foreign Investment in Listed Companies Several Opinions (3710/01.11.08). Jointly issued by the Ministry of Foreign Trade and Economic Cooperation and the China Securities Regulatory Commission on 8 November 2001. Translated (December 2001/January 2002) 15(10) *China Law & Practice* 93.

Suspending and Terminating the Listings of Loss-making Listed Companies Implementing Procedures (3710/01.02.22). Issued by the China Securities Regulatory Commission on, and effective as of, 22 February 2001. Translated (April 2001) 15(3) China Law & Practice 62.

Suspending and Terminating the Listings of Loss-making Listed Companies Implementing Procedures (Revised) (3710/01.11.30). Issued by the China Securities Regulatory Commission on 30 November 2001 and effective as of 1 January 2002. Summarized (December 2001/January 2002) 15(10) *China Law & Practice* 8.

Guidance on Initial Public Offering of Shares Procedures (3710/01.10.16). Promulgated by the China Securities Regulatory Commission on, and effective as of, 16 October 2001. Summarized (December 2001/January 2002) 15(10) *China Law & Practice* 8.

Circular on Temporary Dismissal of Securities-related Civil Remedies Cases (3710/01.09.21). Issued by the Supreme People's Court on 21 September 2001 and effective as of 30 September 2001. Summarized in New Law Digest (November 2001) 15(9) *China Law & Practice* 10–11.

Guidelines for Corporate Governance of Listed Companies jointly promulgated by the China Securities Regulatory Commission and the State Economic and Trade Commission on 7 January 2002. Summarized (February 2002) 16(1) *China Law & Practice* 6. Discussed in Charles Qin, 'New guidance on corporate governance' (March 2002) 16(2) *China Law & Practice* 68.

Commercial Bank Intermediary Services Tentative Provisions. Order No. 5 of 2001 of the People's Bank of China. Discussed (June 2002) 16(5) *China Law & Practice* 39.

Relevant Questions in Implementing the 'Commercial Bank Intermediary Services Tentative Provisions' Circular. Issued by the People's Bank of China on 22 April 2002. Translated (June 2002) 16(5) *China Law & Practice* 39.

Questions Concerning the Acceptance of Civil Tort Dispute Cases Arising from Misrepresentation in the Securities Market Circular (3700/02.01.15). Issued by the Supreme Court on, and effective as of, 15 January 2002. Summarized (February 2002) 16(1) *China Law & Practice* 12–13.

Establishment of Securities Companies with Foreign Equity Participation Rules [3700/02.06.01(1)]. Promulgated by the China Securities Regulatory Commission on 1 June 2002 and effective as of 1 July 2002. Translated (July/August 2002) 16(6) *China Law & Practice* 41–48.

Establishment of Fund Management Companies with Foreign Equity Participation Rules [3700/02.06.01(2)]. Promulgated by the China Securities Regulatory Commission on 1 June 2002 and effective as of 1 July 2002. Translated (July/August 2002) 16(6) *China Law & Practice* 31–34.

Matters Relevant to the Transfer of State-owned Shares and Legal Person Shares of Listed Companies to Foreign Entities Circular (3710/02.11.01). Jointly issued by the CSRC, the Ministry of Finance and the State Economic and Trade Commission on 1 November 2002. Translated (December 2002/January 2003) 16(10) *China Law & Practice* 57.

Provisional Measures on Administration of Domestic Securities Investments of Qualified Foreign Institutional Investors. Jointly issued by the CSRC and the People's Bank of China on 5 November 2002 and effective as of 1 December 2002. Translated (December 2002/January 2003) 16(10) *China Law & Practice* 46.

Using Foreign Investment to Re-organise State-Owned Enterprises Tentative Provisions (2140/02.11.08). Jointly promulgated by the State Administration for Industry & Commerce, the State Economic & Trade Commission, the Ministry of Finance and the State Administration of Foreign Exchange on 8 November 2002, and effective as from 1 January 2003. Translated (December 2002/January 2003) 16(10) *China Law & Practice* 101.

Acquisition of Domestic Enterprises by Foreign Investors Tentative Provisions (also translated as *Interim Provisions for Foreign Investors to Merge Domestic Enterprises*) (2300/03.03.07). Promulgated by the Ministry of Foreign Trade & Economic Cooperation, the State Administration of Taxation, the State Administration for Industry and Commerce and the State Administration of Foreign Exchange on 7 March 2003 and effective as of 12 April 2003. Translated (April 2003) 17(3) *China Law & Practice* 27.

Performing the Regulation Function Originally Performed by the People's Bank of China by the China Banking Regulatory Commission (L3600/03.04.26). Effective as of 1 February 2004. Summarized in New Law Digest (May 2003) 17(4) *China Law and Practice.*

Shanghai Municipality, Acquisition of State-owned Enterprises in the Municipality by Foreign Investors Several Opinions Implementing Rules (2300/03.08.04/SH). Issued by the State-owned Assets Supervision and Administration Commission of Shanghai Municipal Government, the Shanghai Foreign Investment Commission and the Shanghai Administration of Industry and Commerce on, and effective as of, 4 August 2003.

Several Issues Concerning the Regulation of Cash Flows Between Listed Companies and Their Affiliates and Security Provided to Outside Parties by Listed Companies Circular (3710/03.08.28). Issued by the CSRC and the State-owned Assets Supervision and Administration Commission of the State Council on, and effective as of, 28 August 2003. Translated in 17(8) *China Law & Practice* (October 2003) at 62–67.

Several Opinions on Promoting the Reform, Opening up and Stable Development of the Capital Markets (3700/04.01.31). Issued by the State Council on 31 January 2004. Translated (September 2004) 18(7) *China Law & Practice* 75.

Standards for Examination and Verification of Share Issues Memorandum No. 17: Examination and Verification Requirements for Fund Raising of Companies Initially Offering Shares to the Public (3710/04.05.11). Promulgated by the Department of Public Offering Supervision of the China Securities Regulatory Commission on 11 May 2004. Summarized in (June 2004) 18(5) *China Law & Practice* 8–9.

Issues Relevant to Regulating Offshore Listing of Subsidiaries of Domestic Listed Companies Circular, issued by the China Securities Regulatory Commission on 21 July 2004 (3710/04.07.21 released on 10 August 2004). *Zheng Jian Fa* [2004] No. 67. Translated (September 2004) 18(7) *China Law and Practice* 37–40.

CSRC, *Circular Concerning Several Issues on Trial Implementation of IPO Pricing Inquiry System (Exposure Draft)*, released by the CSRC on 30

August 2004 (*Zheng Jian Fa Xing Zi* [2004] No. 162). Available at the CSRC website http://www.csrc.gov.cn/. Also translated in its final version as *Circular on Several Issues Concerning the Trial Implementation of an Inquiry System for Initial Public Offerings of Shares.*

Administration of Stock Investments by Insurance Institutional Investors Tentative Procedures (3910/04.10.24, Order of the CIRC [2004] No. 12) Promulgated by the CIRC and the CSRC on, and effective as of, 24 October 2004, translated (2004) 18(10) *China Law & Practice* 39–53.

Network Voting for Shareholders' General Meeting of Listed Companies Working Guide (Trial Implementation) (2300/04.11.29). Issues by the China Securities Regulatory Commission on, and effective as of, 29 November 2004. Summarized (December 2004/January 2005) 18(10) *China Law & Practice* 6–7.

Strengthening the Protection of the Rights and Interests of Public Shareholders Several Provisions (3710/04.12.07; Zheng Jian Fa [2004] No. 118). Issued by the China Securities Regulatory Commission on, and effective as of, 7 December 2004. Translated (June 2005) *China Law & Practice* 64–69.

Handling of the Transfers of Non-tradable Shares of Listed Companies Rules. Issued by the Shanghai Stock Exchange, the Shenzhen Stock Exchange and the China Securities Depository and Clearing Corporation Limited on 15 December 2004 and effective as of 1 January 2005. Translated (March 2005) 19(2) *China Law and Practice* 51–58.

Guiding Opinions on the Reform Regarding the Separation of Equity Ownership and Trading Rights of Listed Companies (3710/05.08.23). Promulgated by the China Securities Regulatory Commission, the State-owned Assets Supervision and Administration Commission of the State Council, the Ministry of Finance, the People's Bank of China and the Ministry of Commerce on 23 August 2005. Summarized (October 2005) 19(8) *China Law & Practice* 7–8.

PRC Company Law (Amended) [2330/05.10.27] PRC President's Order No. 42. Promulgated on 27 October 2005 and effective as of 1 January 2006. Translated (December 2005/January 2006) 19:10 *China Law & Practice* 21–71.

Revised Securities Law [3700/05.10.27]. PRC President's Order No. 43. Promulgated on 27 October 2005 and effective as of 1 January 2006. Translated (February 2006) 20(2) *China Law and Practice* 31–83.

Provisions for the Administration of Registration of the Registered Capital of Companies [2330/05.12.27] Promulgated by the State Administration for Industry and Commerce on 27 December 2005 and effective as of 1 January 2006. Translated (March 2006) 20(2) *China Law & Practice* 59–65.

Measures for the Administrative of the Equity Incentives of Listed Companies (Trial Implementation) [3700/05.12.31]. Issued by the China Securities Regulatory Commission on 31 December 2005 and effective as of 1 January 2006. Translated (April 2006) 20(3) *China Law & Practice* 36–48.

Measures for the Administration of Strategic Investments in Listed Companies by Foreign Investors (3710/05.12.31; Circular 28). Promulgated by the Ministry of Commerce, the China Securities Regulatory Commission, the State Administration of Taxation, the State Administration for Industry and Commerce and the State Administration of Foreign Exchange on 31 December 2005 and effective 30 January 2006. Translated (February 2006) 20(1) *China Law & Practice* 19–29.

Provisions on Several Issues Concerning the Application of the <PRC Company Law> (1) (2330/06.04.28). Promulgated by the Supreme People's Court on 28 April 2006 and effective as of 9 May 2006. Translated (May 2006) 20(4) *China Law & Practice* 35.

Measures for the Administration of Securities Offerings by Listed Companies (3700/06.05.06). Promulgated by the China Securities Regulatory Commission on 6 May 2006 and effective as of 8 May 2006. Translated (July/August 2006) 20(6) *China Law & Practice* 47–63.

Guidelines for the Contents and Formats for Information Disclosures by Companies That Offer Securities to the Public (No. 10): Application Documents for Public Offers of Securities by Listed Companies [2330/06.05.08(1)]. Issued by the China Securities Regulatory Commission on 8 May 2006. Summarized in (June 2006) 20(5) *China Law & Practice* 4.

Guidelines for the Contents and Formats for Information Disclosures by Companies That Offer Securities to the Public (No. 11): Prospectuses for Public Offers of Securities by Listed Companies [2330/06.05.08(2)]. Issued by the China Securities Regulatory Commission on 8 May 2006. Summarized (June 2006) 20(5) *China Law & Practice* 4–5.

Measures for the Administration of Initial Public Offerings of Shares and the Listing Thereof [3710/06.05.17]. Promulgated by the China Securities Regulatory Commission on 17 May 2006 and effective as of 18 May 2006. Translated (July/August 2006) 20(6) *China Law & Practice* 65–76.

Measures for the Administration of the Takeover of Listed Companies (3700/06.07.31; Order of the CSRC No. 35). Promulgated by the China Securities Regulatory Commission on 31 July 2006 and effective as of 1 September 2006. Translated (November 2006) 20(9) *China Law & Practice* 40–73.

Measures for the Administration of Securities Investments in China by Qualified Foreign Institutional Investors [3700/06.08.24(1)]. Promulgated by the China Securities Regulatory Commission, People's Bank of China and State Administration of Foreign Exchange on 24 August 2006, and effective as of 1 September 2006; translated (November 2006) 20(9) *China Law & Practice* 28–34.

Provisions for the Acquisition of Domestic Enterprises by Foreign Investors (2300/06.08.08). Promulgated by the Ministry of Commerce, State-owned Assets Supervision and Administration Commission of the State Council, State Administration of Taxation, State Administration for Industry and Commerce, China Securities Regulatory Commission and State Administration of Foreign Exchange on 8 August 2006 and effective as of 8 September 2006. Translated (October 2006) 20(8) *China Law & Practice* 69–90.

Measures for the Administration of the Offering and Underwriting of Securities (3700/06.09.17). Promulgated by the CSRC on 17 September 2006 and effective as of 19 September 2006. Translated (December 2006/ January 2007) 20(10) *China Law & Practice* 48–61.

PRC Enterprise Bankruptcy Law (2500/06.08.27). PRC President's Order No. 54 of the 10th NPC. Promulgated on 27 August 2006 and effective as of 1 June 2007. Translated (October 2006) 20(8) *China Law & Practice* 39–68.

Bibliography

COMPANY DOCUMENTS

Tsingtao Brewery, *H-share Listing Prospectus*, dated 29 June 1993.

Tsingtao Brewery, *Company announcement*, dated 10 July 1997.

Tsingtao Brewery, *Annual Reports* 1993–2006 inclusive.

Tsingtao Brewery, Amendments to Articles of Association and Notice Convening Annual General Meeting, dated 9 May 2002.

Tsingtao Brewery, *Notice of Extraordinary General Meeting*, dated 26 June 2003.

Tsingtao Brewery, *Circular to shareholders of H-shares of the company*, dated 4 July 2003.

Tsingtao Brewery, Amendments to Articles of Association, General Mandate to Issue Shares and Notice Convening Annual General Meeting, dated 21 April 2004.

Tsingtao Brewery, *Circular to shareholders* dated 15 May 2006.

Tsingtao Brewery, *Announcement and resumption of trading*, dated 30 August 2006.

Shanghai Petrochemical, *H-share Listing Prospectus*, dated 5 July 1993.

Shanghai Petrochemical, *Annual Reports* 1994–2006 inclusive.

Shanghai Petrochemical Circular relating to Proposed Amendments to the Articles of Association dated 21 May 2003 and available through the Hong Kong Stock Exchange website at http://www.hkex.com.hk/.

Shanghai Petrochemical, Circular, *Continuing Connected Transactions*, dated 13 May 2005.

Sinopec Shanghai Petrochemical Company Limited and ABN-AMRO Asia Corporate Finance Limited, 'Continuing Connected Transactions' Circular to shareholders dated 13 May 2005.

Shanghai Petrochemical, Circular, *Continuing Connected Transactions*, dated 11 November 2005.

Shanghai Petrochemical, Share Reform Announcement (Overseas Regulatory Announcement) made pursuant to Rule 13.09(2) of the HKEx Listing Rules, dated 12 October 2006.

Announcement of Receiving a One-off Compensation by Sinopec Shanghai Petrochemical Company Limited, dated 26 December 2006.

Shanghai Petrochemical, *Overseas Regulatory Announcement on the Voting Results at the Relevant Shareholders' Meeting for the Holders of A Shares Relating to the Share Reform*, dated 8 November 2006.

Shanghai Petrochemical, *Notice of 2006 Annual General Meeting and Amendments to the Articles of Association*, dated 30 April 2007.

Yizheng Chemical Fibre, *H-share Listing Prospectus*, dated March 1994.

Yizheng Chemical Fibre, *Annual Reports*, 1994–2006 inclusive.

'Notice relating to the Change of the shareholder of the State-owned A-shares of Yizheng Chemical Fibre Company Limited' issued by Sinopec in 1998.

Beijing Yanhua <0325>, Shanghai Pechem <0338>, Yizheng Chem <1033> and Zhenhai Refin <1128>, jointly issued announcement dated 25 February 2000, available through the HKEx Website at http://www.hkex.com.hk/listedco/listedconews/sehk/20000228/.

Yizheng Chemical Fibre Overseas Regulatory Announcement pursuant to rule 13.09 of the HKEx Listing Rules following three days of significant consecutive decline in the trading price of Shanghai Petro's Shanghai-listed A-shares dated 26 October 2006, available on the HKEx website at http://www.hkex.com.hk.

Guangzhou Shipyard *H-share Listing Prospectus*, dated 19 July 1993 and released on Tuesday 20 July 1993.

Guangzhou Shipyard, *Annual Reports*, 1994–2006 inclusive.

Guangzhou Shipyard, Circular, *Information for 2003 Annual General Meeting (Amendments to Articles of Association, Continuing Connected Transactions and Resignation and Appointment of Directors and Supervisors)*, dated 30 April 2004.

Guangzhou Shipyard, Circular, *Information for 2004 Annual General Meeting (Continuing Connected Transactions, amendment to Articles of Association, appointment of new term and re-election of Directors and Supervisors)*, dated 21 April 2005.

Guangzhou Shipyard, Framework Agreement for connected transactions of an operating nature entered into between the Company (GSI) and CSSC on 19 April 2004 and approved by Independent Shareholders on 25 June 2004. Amended by supplemental agreement on 31 March 2005 approved by Independent Shareholders on 27 May 2005.

Guangzhou Shipyard, April 2004 Framework Agreement with CSSC as set out in the Circular of the Company dated 30 April 2004.

First Supplemental Agreement to the 2004 Framework Agreement, dated 31 March 2005; and Second Supplemental Agreement dated 26 October 2006; as set out in company circulars dated 21 April 2005 and 17 November 2006, respectively.

Guangzhou Shipyard, Circular, 'Continuing Connected Transactions, Change of Domestic Auditors and Notice of Postponement of Extraordinary General Meeting', dated 8 December 2006.

The Second Supplemental Agreement is subject to Independent Shareholders' Approval in the Postponed EGM to be held for approving the 2007 Framework Agreement.

Appendix 1, 'Amendments to Articles of Association', GSI Circular to Shareholders, re 'Continuing Connected Transactions Amendments to Articles of Association (Appendix 1) and Purchase of Directors and Officers Liability Insurance', dated 17 November 2006.

Guangzhou Shipyard, Circular to Shareholders, *Discloseable Transaction: GZITIC Debt Restructuring*, dated 25 February 2005.

Guangzhou Shipyard, Circular to Shareholders, *Discloseable Transaction: GZITIC Remaining Debt Restructuring*, dated 13 March 2006.

Beiren Printing Machinery Holdings (Beiren), *H-share Listing Prospectus*, dated 23 July 1993.

Beiren Printing, *Annual Reports* 1993–2006 inclusive.

Beiren Group Corporation website, available at http://www.beiren.com/EN/About.asp.

Beiren, *Announcement of the Voting Results of the Relevant Shareholders' Meeting of the A Share Market*, dated 20 March 2006.

Beiren, *Announcement in Relation to the Resolutions Passed at the 2006 Extraordinary General Meeting of Holders of Domestic Shares*, dated 27 June 2006.

Beiren, *Announcement in Relation to the Resolutions Passed at the 2006 Extraordinary General Meeting of Holders of H Shares*, dated 27 June 2006.

Beiren Printing: *Announcement of Resolutions Passed at the 2005 Annual General Meeting*, held on 27 June 2006. Published on the Hong Kong Stock Exchange Website at http://www.hkex.com.hk/27 June 2006 at 10.54 p.m.

Beiren, Announcement: Unusual Trading Volume, dated 5 September 2006.

Beiren, Company Announcement, *Estimated Results*, dated 26 October 2006.

Beiren, Company Announcement, *Estimated Results*, dated 28 October 2006.

Maanshan Iron & Steel, *H-share Listing Prospectus*, dated 20 October 1993.

Maanshan Iron & Steel, *Annual Reports* 1994–2006 inclusive.

Maanshan Iron & Steel, Circular, Proposed Amendments to Articles of Association and Notice of Extraordinary General Meeting, dated 15 July 2002.

Maanshan Iron & Steel, Circular, Proposed Amendments to Articles of Association and Notice of Annual General Meeting, dated 16 April 2004.

Maanshan Iron & Steel, Circular, Proposed Amendments to Articles of Association, Proposed Adoption of the Order of Meeting for Shareholders' General Meeting, Order of Meeting for the Board of Directors, Order of Meeting for the Supervisory Committee & Proposed Appointment and Re-election of Directors and Notice of Extraordinary General Meeting, dated 14 July 2005.

Kunming Machine Tool Company (later re-named Jiaoda Kunji High Tech Company Limited), *H-share Listing Prospectus*, dated 23 November 1993.

Kunming Machine Tool Company, *Annual Reports* 1994–2000 inclusive.

Jiaoda Kunji High Tech Company Limited, *Annual Reports* 2001–2006 inclusive.

Jiaoda Kunji High Tech, Announcement on Profit Estimate for January 1 to December 31, 2006, dated 11 January 2007 and published on the HKEx website and in *The Standard.*

Jiaoda Kunji High Tech, Announcement dated 5 December 2006, citing Transfer Registration Confirmation of State-owned Legal Person Shares issued by China Securities Depositaries & Clearing Corporation Limited (Shanghai Branch) Confirming share transfer of 71 052 146 state-owned legal person shares in Jiaoda Kunji High-Tech Company Limited. Published on the HKEx website and in the *The Standard* (Hong Kong).

Jiaoda Kunji High Tech, *Announcement on Negotiation Status of Share Reform Proposal and Revised Share Reform Proposal* issued pursuant to Rule 13.09 of the HKEx Listing Rules by the Board of Jiaoda Kunji dated 15 November 2006, published on the HKEx website and in *The Standard* (Hong Kong).

Jiaoda Kunji High Tech, Announcement on the Results of the Relevant Shareholders' Meeting in Relation to A Share Reform, issued pursuant to Rule 13.09 of the HKEx Listing Rules dated 25 December 2006.

Jiaoda Kunji High Tech, *Results of the 2006 Second Extraordinary General Meeting* held on 22 December 2006. Published on the HKEx website.

Jiaoda Kunji High Tech, *Notice of the First Extraordinary General Meeting of 2007*, dated 11 January 2007. Published on the HKEx website.

Jiaoda Kunji High-Tech, Circular, Share Increase, Amendments to Articles of Association, Appointment of Director, Change of Company Name, And Notices of Annual General Meeting and Class Meetings, dated 14 May 2007.

Jiaoda Kunji High-Tech, Notice of the Second Extraordinary General Meeting of 2007 and Appointment of Supervisor, dated 13 September 2007.

Tianjin Bohai, *Listing Prospectus New issue of 340,000,000 H shares*, dated 3 May 1994. Joint sponsors and lead underwriters Jardine Fleming Securities Limited and China Development Finance Co (HK) Ltd.

Tianjin Capital Environment Protection Company Limited, *Annual Reports* 2000–2006.

Tianjin Capital, Announcement, Discloseable Transaction in Respect of the Hangzhou Qige Sewage Water Treatment Plant and Connected Transaction in Respect of the Guarantee Provided by the Company, dated 21 November 2006.

Dongfang Electrical Machinery, *H-Share Listing Prospectus*, dated 19 May 1994.

Dongfang Electric (DFEM), *Annual Reports* 1994–2006 inclusive.

Announcement of DFEM Extraordinary General Meeting held on 23 December 1999.

DFEM Circular, *Notice of the 1998 Annual General Meeting*, dated 7 November 1999.

Circular, Notice of the 2001 Annual General Meeting, dated 7 November 2002.

DFEM, Circular, *On-going Connected Transactions*, dated 14 November 2003.

DFEM, Circular, *Very Substantial Acquisition and Connected Transaction, Proposed Continuing Connected Transactions, Possible Continuing Connected Transactions, Proposed Amendments to the Articles of Association, Proposed Change of Company Name and Registered Address, Application for Whitewash Waiver, dated 17 May 2007*.

International Materials, Government Reports and Publications

Organization of Economic Co-operation and Development (OECD), Principles of Corporate Governance 2004. Available at the OECD website.

Australian Parliamentary Joint Committee on Corporations and Financial Services, *Corporate responsibility: managing risk and creating value*. Report released on 21 June 2006 and available at http://www.aph.gov.au/Senate/committee/corporations_ctte/corporate_responsibility/.

Slaughter and May, *Review of the Role and Effectiveness of Non-Executive Directors – Higgs Report* (20 January 2003) available at http://www.slaughterandmay.com/.

Stock Exchange of Hong Kong Limited, Consultation Paper on Proposals to Enhance Regulation of Listing, October 2003.

Companies Registry, HKEx, *Non-Statutory Guidelines on Directors' Duties*, updated 20 January 2004, accessed at http://www.hkex.com.hk/ on 16 May 2004.

Stock Exchange of Hong Kong Limited, *Consultation Paper Conclusions*, March 2004.

Stock Exchange of Hong Kong Limited, Exposure Paper of Draft Code on Corporate Governance Practices and Corporate Governance Report, released for public consultation in January 2004.

Stock Exchange of Hong Kong Limited, Conclusions on Exposure of Draft Code on Corporate Governance Practices and Corporate Governance Report 19 November 2004.

Stock Exchange of Hong Kong Limited, Announcement: Amendments to the Listing Rules relating to the Code on Corporate Governance Practices and Rules on the Corporate Governance Report, issued 19 November 2004.

Stock Exchange of Hong Kong Limited, *Code on Corporate Governance Practices*, effective from 1 January 2005 (internal control section effective from 1 July 2005).

Hong Kong Exchanges and Clearing Limited, Feedback Statement on the Consultation on Continuing Listing Criteria and Related Issues, 7 February 2005.

HKEx News Release, HKEx Publishes Consultation Paper on New Structure for Listing Decision-making, dated 18 February 2005.

Mau Kam Shing, Joseph, Company Secretary, Stock Exchange of Hong Kong Limited, *Corporate Governance Report*, 28 February 2005.

Hong Kong Exchanges and Clearing Limited, Exposure Paper: Abolition of Requirement for Main Board Issuers to Publish Paid Announcements in Newspapers and Related Matters, November 2005.

Stock Exchange of Hong Kong Limited, *HKEx Fact Book* 2006.

Conference Papers and Speeches

Leung, Erica, Lily Liu, Lu Shen, Kevin Taback and Leo Wang, 'Financial Reform and Corporate Governance in China', MIT Sloan School of Management, 50th Anniversary Proceedings, June 2002, Cambridge, Massachusetts (http://mitsloan.mit.edu/50th/corgovchina.pdf).

Gumley, Wayne, 'Can corporations law reform save the planet? Seeking a missing link between environmental and economic policies', in Gerald Acquaah-Gaisie & Val Clulow (eds), *Enhancing Corporate Accountability: Prospects and Challenges Conference Proceedings* 8–9 February 2006, Melbourne (Monash University School of Business and Economics, Gippsland & The Department of Business Law and Taxation) 239.

Tomasic, Roman, Andrews and Fu, 'Corporate Governance in China's Listed Companies – Whither the top 100?', Seminar paper for Centre of International Corporate Governance Research (CICGR), 13 December

2005 delivered by Professor Roman Tomasic at Victoria University, Flinders Street, Melbourne.

Qianggui, Jiang (Vice Minister of the State Economic and Trade Commission). 'Speech at the Meeting on Summarizing the Experience of Establishing Modern Enterprise Systems in Listed Companies' (abstract). 27 December 2002. Downloaded from the State Economic and Trade Commission website: http://www.setc.gov.cn.

'Corporate Governance and Investigation Powers of the Securities and Futures Commission', Speech presented by Mark Dickens, Executive Director of the SFC to the Law Society of Hong Kong, 19 November 1998 (accessed December 2002, at http://www.hkse.com.hk/speeches/md981119.htm).

Shuli, Hu, Wei Fuhua and Niu Wenxin (2002), 'An interview with Laura Cha, CSRC vice chair', *Caijing Magazine*, 23 January, obtained through China Online.

Speech by HKEx Chief Executive Paul Chow at the CFO Forum organized by the Hong Kong Society of Accountants on Improving Corporate Governance, 29 September 2003; accessed at http://www.hkex.com.hk/library/speeches/SP031030.htm on 25 November 2003.

'The CSRC to Publicly Soliciting Opinions on Circular Concerning Several Issues on Trial Implementation of IPO Pricing Inquiry System' (*sic*), 30 August 2004, English version, translation provided by Shenzhen Securities Information Co Ltd.

HKEx News Release, 'The Exchange responds to media enquiries on listed companies' compliance with the Independent Non-executive Director requirements', 4 October 2004, accessed at http://www.hkex.com.hk/news/hkexnews/041004news.htm on 21 October 2005.

Paul Chow, Chief Executive Hong Kong Exchanges and Clearing Limited, 'Achievements and New Initiatives', Presentation given on 7 January 2005, Hong Kong.

SECONDARY SOURCES

Books

Allen, Stuart (ed.), *International Capital Markets: A Guide for Asian Business* (Asia Law & Practice, 1996).

Baker & McKenzie, *China Banking & Finance: Essential Legislation* (Asia Information Associates Limited, 2000).

Blake, John and Simon Gao, Perspectives on Accounting and Finance in China (Routledge, 1995).

BNP Paribas Peregrine, *A guide to the Hong Kong and China Equity Markets* (Asiamoney, 2003).

Davies, P.L. *Gower and Davies' Principles of Modern Company Law* (Sweet & Maxwell, 2003).

de Trenck, Charles (ed.), *Red Chips and the Globalisation of China's Enterprises* (revised 2nd edn, Asia 2000 Ltd, 1998).

Duncan, Ron and Huang Yiping (eds), *Reform of State-Owned Enterprises in China: Autonomy, Incentive and Competition* (NCDS Asia Pacific Press, 1998).

East Asia Analytical Unit, Department of Foreign Affairs and Trade, *China Embraces the Market: Achievements, Constraints and Opportunities* (Commonwealth of Australia, 1997).

East Asia Analytical Unit, Department of Foreign Affairs and Trade, *Asia's Financial Markets: Capitalising on Reform* (Commonwealth of Australia, 1999).

Gensler, Howard (ed.), *China Tax and Accounting Manual* (Asia Law & Practice, 2nd edn, 1998).

Gomm, Roger, Martyn Hammersley and Peter Foster, *Case Study Method: Key Issues, Key Texts* (2004).

Goodman, David S.G. and Gerald Segal (eds), *China Deconstructs: Politics, Trade and Regionalism* (Routledge, 1994).

Huang, Allen and Ronald Ma, *Accounting in China in Transition: 1949–2000* (World Scientific Publishing, vol. 2, Accounting and Business in Asia, 2001).

IFF Equity Advisory Group Task Force Report, *Corporate Governance in China – An Investor Perspective* (Institute of International Finance Inc, March 2006).

Itoh, Fumio (ed.), *China in the Twenty-first Century: Politics, Economy, and Society* (United Nations University Press, 1997).

Jenner, W.J.F. *The Tyranny of History: The Roots of China's Crisis* (Allen Lane Penguin Books, 1992).

Lin, Yi-min *Between Politics and Markets: Firms, Competition, and Institutional Change in Post-Mao China* (Cambridge University Press, 2001).

Lou Jianbo, *China's Troubled Bank Loans: Workout and Prevention* (Vol. 22 International Banking Finance and Economic Law Series, Kluwer Law International, 2001).

Nolan, P. *China and the Global Business Revolution* (Palgrave, 2001).

Norton, Joseph, J., C.J. Li and Huang Yangxin (eds), *Financial Regulation in the Greater China Area: Mainland China, Taiwan and Hong Kong SAR* (vol. 14 International Banking, Finance and Economic Law Series, Kluwer Law International, 2000).

Rogers, Benedict and Lotte Pang (eds), *China 2000: Emerging Investment, Funding and Advisory Opportunities for a New China* (Asia Law & Practice, 1999).

Schell, Orville and David Shambaugh (eds), *The China Reader: The Reform Era* (Vintage Books, 1999).

Shanghai University of Finance and Economics and the University of Texas at Dallas, *Accounting and Auditing in the People's Republic of China* (Center for International Accounting Development, University of Texas, Dallas, 1987).

Shaw, Alison (ed.), *The 2003 Guide to Capital Markets in Asia* (Asia Law & Practice, 2002).

Shiller Robert J., *Irrational Exuberance* (Scribe Publications Pty Ltd, 2000).

Steinfeld Edward S., *Forging Reform in China: The Fate of State-Owned Industry* (Cambridge University Press, 1998).

Su, Dongwei, *Chinese Securities Markets: A Research Handbook* (World Scientific Publishing Pte Ltd, 2003).

Tam, On Kit, *The Development of Corporate Governance in China* (Edward Elgar, 1999).

Tang, Yun-Wei, Lyn Chow and Barry J. Cooper, *Accounting and Finance in China: A Review of Current Practice*, 4th edn (Longman, 2000).

Tokley, I.A. and Tina Ravn, *Company and Securities Law in China* (Sweet & Maxwell, Asia, 1998).

Tomasic, Roman (ed., in collaboration with Wang Fuming, Zhao Xudong and Ma Zhong) *Corporate Governance: Challenges for China* (Law Press, China, September 2005).

Wacks, Raymond (ed.), *Hong Kong, China and 1997: Essays in Legal Theory* (Hong Kong University Press, 1993).

Wei, Yuwa *Comparative Corporate Governance: A Chinese Perspective* (vol. 3 Global Trade and Finance Series, Kluwer Law International, 2003).

Wen, G.J. and D. Xu (eds), *The Reformability of China's State Sector* (World Scientific, 1997).

World Bank (Anjali Kumar, Kwang Jun, Anthony Saunders, Susan Selwyn, Yan Sun, Dimitri Vittas, David Wilton), *China's Emerging Capital Markets* (FT Financial Publishing Asia Pacific, 1997).

World Bank (Country Operations Division, China and Mongolia Department, East Asia and Pacific Regional Office), *China's Management of Enterprise Assets: The State as Shareholder* (Report No. 16265-CHA, 5 June 1997).

World Bank (Stoyan Tenev and Chunling Zhang), *Corporate Governance and Enterprise Reform in China*, International Financial Corporation (World Bank Group, 2002).

Wu, Yanrui and Qiang Ye (eds), *China's Reform and Economic Growth* (NCDS Asia Pacific Press, 1998).

Xia Mei, P.D. Grub and Jian Hai Lin, *Re-emerging Securities Market in China* (Quorum Books, 1992).

Yin, Robert K., *Applications of Case Study Research* (2nd edn, Sage Publications, 2003).

Yin, Robert K. (ed.), *Case Study Anthology* (Sage Publications, 2004).

Yin, Robert K., *Case Study Research: Design and Method* (3rd edn, Sage Publications, 2003).

Zhou, Zhongfei, *Chinese Banking Law and Foreign Financial Institutions* (Vol. 21 International Banking, Finance and Economic Law Series, Kluwer Law International, 2001).

Zhu, X.P. and Y.M. Chen (eds), *International Accounting Comparison and Development* (Publishing House of Southwest University of Finance and Economics, Chengdu, 1992).

Chapters in books

Cain, Maureen, 'Gramsci, the state and the place of law', in David Sugarman (ed.), *Legality, Ideology and the State* (Academic Press, 1983) 111.

de Jonge, Alice, 'Solving agency problems in a cross-border environment: ten years of Chinese company listings in Hong Kong', in Russell Smyth, On Kit Tam, Malcolm Warner and Cherrie Jiuhua Zhu (eds), *China's Business Reforms: Institutional Challenges in a Globalized Economy* (RoutledgeCurzon, 2005) 46–61.

Hongchao, Zhu Jiang Xian, James Chen, Feng Wang and Robert Mao, 'Recent developments in China's capital markets', Asia Law and Practice, *The 2003 Guide to Capital Markets in Asia* (Euromoney Publications (Jersey) Limited 2002) 7.

Hunt, Alan, 'Dichotomy and contradiction in the sociology of law', in Piers Beirne and Richard Quinney (eds), *Marxism and Law* (Wiley, 1982) 87.

Koo and Partners, 'Towards better corporate governance: China's continuing struggle', in Ben Maiden (ed.), *The IFLR Guide to Corporate Governance* (Euromoney Institutional Investor, 2001) 44.

Koo and Partners, 'Corporate governance in Hong Kong – the road to reform following the Asian financial crisis', in Ben Maiden (ed.), *The IFLR Guide to Corporate Governance* (Euromoney Institutional Investor, 2001) 52.

Linnan, David, 'Like a fish needs a bicycle: public law theory, civil society and governance reform in Indonesia', in Tim Lindsey (ed.) *Law Reform in Developing and Transitional States* (Routledge, 2007).

Kahn-Freund, Otto, 'Common Law and Civil Law – imaginary and real obstacles to assimilation', in Mauro Cappelletti (ed.) (1978), *New Perspectives for a Common Law of Europe*, at 160.

Wen, Carson and Susan Yu, 'Hong Kong as a gateway to the international capital markets for Chinese enterprises', Asia Law and Practice, *The 2003 Guide to Capital Markets in Asia* (Euromoney Publications (Jersey) Limited 2002) 25.

Xi, Chao, 'Transforming Chinese enterprises: ideology, efficiency and instrumentalism in the process of reform', in John Gillespie and Pip Nicholson (eds), *Asian Socialism and Legal Change: the dynamics of Vietnamese and Chinese reform* (Asia Pacific Press at the Australian National University, 2005) 91–114.

Journal articles

Allen, Annabel, 'IPO fever: will disclosure requirements burst China's bubble?' (June/July 2004) *Asialaw* 16–21.

Anderson, Craig, and Bingna Guo, 'Corporate governance under the New Company Law (Part 1): fiduciary duties and minority shareholder protection' (April 2006) 20(3) *China Law & Practice* 17.

Anderson, Craig, and Bingna Guo, 'Corporate governance under the New Company Law (Part 2): shareholder lawsuits and enforcement' (May 2006) 20(4) *China Law & Practice* 15.

Andrews-Speed, Philip, Stephen Dow and Zhiguo Gao, 'The ongoing reforms to China's government and state sector: the case of the energy industry' (2000) 9(23) *Journal of Contemporary China* 5.

Art, Robert C. and Minkang Gu, 'China Incorporated: the First Corporation Law of the People's Republic of China' (1995) 20 *Yale Journal of International Law* 273.

Arye, Lucian Bebchuk and Mark J. Roe, 'A theory of path dependence in corporate ownership and governance' (November 1999) 52(1) *Stanford Law Review* 127.

Bailes, D. 'Watch your corporation' (1995) 3(1) *Journal of Business Law* 24.

Biddulph, Sarah, 'Through a Glass Darkly: China, Transparency and The WTO' (2001) 3 *Australian Journal of Asian Law* 59.

Black, B. and R. Kraakman, 'A self-enforcing model of Corporate Law' (1996) 109 *Harvard Law Review* 1911.

Blayney, Steven, 'Trust investment companies – a vehicle for a corporate restructuring in China' (March 2001) 15(2) *China Law & Practice* 40–42.

Chan, Hing Lin, 'An alternative to privatization: the listing of H-shares in Hong Kong' (1996) 9(3) *International Journal of Public Sector Management* 40.

Chan, Virginia and Steven Blayney, 'Trends in mergers & acquisitions: the restructuring of domestically listed Chinese companies' (June 2001) 15(5) *China Law & Practice* 55–58.

Chang, T.K., 'The Easter is in the red' (March 1999) *International Financial Law Review* 43.

Chen, Ji and Stephen C. Thomas, 'The ups and downs of the PRC securities market', (2003) 30(1) *The China Business Review* 36.

Cheng, Yuan, 'Listing overseas: what is the real scope of the CSRC Circular?' (July/August 2000) *China Law & Practice* 26–27.

Cheung, Johnny K.W., 'Shortcomings in China's Corporate Governance Regime' (February 2006) 21(1) *China Law & Practice* 27–29.

Cheung, Stephen Yan-Leung, J. Thomas Connelly, Piman Limpaphayom and Lynda Zhou, 'Do investors really value corporate governance? Evidence from the Hong Kong Market' (2007) 18(2) *Journal of International Financial Management & Accounting* 86–122.

China Legal Briefs, 'New takeover rule to boost equity market' (September 2006) 20(7) *China Law & Practice* 14.

China Legal Briefs, 'Ministry of Commerce approves M&A share swaps' (September 2006) 20(7) *China Law & Practice* 14.

China Legal Briefs, 'China securities regulator approves two new IPOs' (September 2006) 20(7) *China Law & Practice* 15.

China Legal Briefs, 'Securities reform lifts investor confidence' (October 2006) 20(8) *China Law & Practice* 13.

Chow, Paul, 'Hong Kong listings' (September 2006) *International Financial Law Review*, at http://www.iflr.com/.

Chua, Eu-Jin, 'China's new Bankruptcy Law: a legislative innovation' (October 2006) 20(8) *China Law & Practice* 17–20.

Clarke, Donald C., 'Regulation and its discontents: understanding economic law in China', (1992) 28 *Stanford Journal of International Law* 283.

Coffee, John, 'The rise of dispersed ownership: the role of law and the state in the separation of ownership and control' (2001) 111 *Yale Law Journal* 1.

de Jonge, Alice, 'Red chip boom – H-share bust: solving cross-border insolvency problems in Hong Kong and the PRC' (1998) *LawAsia* 1.

Delios, Andrew, Zhi Jian Wu and Nan Zhou, 'A new perspective on ownership identities in China's listed companies' (2006) 2(3) *Management and Organization Review* 319.

Deschandol, Jean-Marc and Charles Desmeules, 'One hesitant step forward: new company law brings mixed feelings' (December 2005–January 2006) 19(10) *China Law & Practice* 13.

Deschandol, Jean-Marc and Charles Desmeules, 'New rules on strategic investments by foreign investors in listed companies' (February 2006) 20(1) *China Law & Practice* 13–15.

Deschandol, Jean-Marc and Charles Desmeules, 'New rules on equity offerings: lifting the ban on China's share sales' (July/August 2006) 20(6) *China Law & Practice* 17.

Deschandol, Jean-Marc and Charles Desmeules, 'China overhauls takeover code of listed companies' (October 2006) 20(8) *China Law & Practice* 31–34.

DeSombre, Michael, G. and Weiheng Chen, 'Unloading state-owned shares: another trial under new rules' (June 2005) 19(5) *China Law and Practice* 17.

Dignam, Alan and Michael Galanis, 'Australia inside-out: the corporate governance system of the Australian listed market' (2004) 28 *Melbourne University Law Review* 623.

Doe, Juianne and Carmen Leung, 'Tentative provisions set parameters for SOE buy-outs by foreign capital' (March 1999) 13(2) *China Law & Practice* 21–24.

Liufang, Fang, 'China's corporatization experiment' (1995) 5 *Duke Journal of Comparative & International Law* 149.

Farrar, John H., 'Developing appropriate corporate governance in China' (2001) 22(3) *Company Lawyer* 92–96.

Ferguson, Michael J., Kevin C.K. Lam and Grace Meina Lee, 'Voluntary disclosure by state-owned esnterprises listed on the stock exchange of Hong Kong' (2002) 13(2) *Journal of International Financial Management and Accounting* 125–152.

Fernandez-Stembridge, Leila and Jean-François Huchet, 'What's next for China's SOEs?' (2006) 169(5) *Far Eastern Economic Review* 32.

Fesharaki, Fereidun and Kang Wu, 'Restructuring and innovation' (1998) 3 *China Petroleum*, 24–25 (in Chinese).

Fesharaki, Fereidun and Kang Wu, 'Revitalizing China's petroleum industry through reorganization: will it work?' (1998) 96(32) *Oil and Gas Journal* 33–34.

Fleckner, Andreas M., 'Stock Exchanges at the Crossroads' (April 2006) 74 *Fordham Law Review* 2541.

Fletcher, Stephen and Brian van Langenberg, 'An Overhaul of the SAR's Financial Markets' (April 2003) 4(13) *Company Secretary* 8.

Fung, Eugene T.S., 'Legal implications of foreign listings for PRC enterprises with particular reference to Hong Kong: Part 2' (1996) 17(3) *Company Lawyer* 73–80.

Gao, Xiqing, 'The perceived unreasonable man – a Response to Fang Liufang' [1995] 5 *Duke Journal of Comparative & International Law* 271.

Gillespie, John, 'Transplanted Company Law: an ideological and cultural analysis of market-entry in Vietnam' (2002) 51 *International & Comparative Law Quarterly* 641.

Gilligan, Philip and Athena Wong, 'New rules on intermediary services offered by commercial banks' (June 2002) 16(5) *China Law & Practice* 51.

Gordon, Robert, 'Critical legal histories' (1984) 36 *Stanford Law Review* 65.

Grobowski, John, 'Protecting China's market from anti-competitive foreign investor acquisitions' (June 2003) 1(2) *Asialaw* 27–28.

Gu, Minkang, 'Reform of the "Statutory Representative" under Chinese company law' (2000) 21(6) *Company Lawyer* 192–196.

Guo, Richard Qiang and Yun Zhou, 'Corporate China going private' (July/August 2001) 15(6) *China Law & Practice* 49–51.

Han, Christophe and Wayne Chen, 'Accelerating reform in China's equity market: share buybacks and majority shareholder share increases' (July/August 2005) 19(6) *China Law & Practice* 17.

Han, Christophe, Charles Qin and Andrew Fu, 'New provisions for corporate governance of fund management companies' (October 2006) 20(8) *China Law & Practice* 35.

Hao, Zhen Ping 'Regulation and organization of accountants in China' (1999) 12(3) *Accounting Auditing & Accountability Journal* 286–302.

Henley, Peter, 'Were corporate Tsunami donations made legally?' (2005) 30(4) *Alternative Law Journal* 154.

Ho, Betty M., 'Demutualization of organized securities exchanges in Hong Kong: The Great Leap Forward' (2002) 33 *Law & Policy in International Business* 283.

Horrigan, Bryan, 'Fault lines in the intersection between corporate governance and social responsibility (2002) 25(2) *University of New South Wales Law Journal* 515.

Huang, Jin and Andrew Xuefeng Qian, ' "One country, two systems", three law families and four legal regions: the emerging inter-regional conflicts of law in China' (1995) 5 *Duke Journal of Comparative & International Law* 289.

Huertas, Thomas F., 'A market paradigm' (August 1993) *International Financial Law Review: Special Supplement* 3–5.

Hui, Taylor and Vivien Teu, 'China QFII rules revised – significant developments for foreign fund managers' (November 2006) 20(9) *China Law & Practice* 16–18.

Hunt, Alan, 'The ideology of law: advances and problems in recent applications of the concept of ideology to the analysis of law' (1985) 19 *Law & Society Review* 11.

Igarashi, Magasaki, 'Chinese bonds in the introduction of foreign capital' 82 *China Newsletter* 9–15.

Jensen, Michael and Richard Ruback, 'The market for corporate control: the scientific evidence' (1983) 11 *Journal of Financial Economics* 5.

Kahn-Freund, Otto, 'On uses and misuses of Comparative Law' (1974) 37 *Modern Law Review* 1.

Lam, J., 'The Closure of GITIC' (1999) 4 *Journal of International Business Law* 127.

Lau, Kun Luen Alex, 'People's Republic of China: the new Shanghai Stock Exchange listing rules: an egg hatched or an egg within an egg' (1999) 20(7) *Company Lawyer* 243–250.

Lau, K.L. Alex, 'Proposals for Chinese company law reform' (2006) 27(12) *Company Lawyer* 376–380.

Laurenceson, James and J.C.H. Chai, 'The economic performance of China's state-owned industrial enterprises' (2000) 9(23) *Journal of Contemporary China* 21.

Lee, Tahirih V., 'Risky business: courts, culture and the market place' (1993) 47 *University of Miami Law Review* 1335.

Legrand, Pierre, 'Comparative legal studies and commitment to theory' (1995) 58 *Modern Law Review* 263.

Legrand, Pierre, 'The impossibility of legal transplants' (1997) *4 Maastricht Journal of European Comparative Law* 111.

Levine, Tyrrell and Kim Woodard, 'The new face of Chinese M&A' (April 2006) 169(3) *Far Eastern Economic Review* 18–22.

Li, Ji Kevin Lam and Jane W. Moy, 'Ownership reform amongst state firms in China and its implications' (2005) 43(4) *Management Decision* 568.

Li, Qiang, 'The new M&A Code and the new takeover rules: impact on future M&A transactions', *China Law Update: Capital Markets* (CCH Hong Kong Limited 2007).

Linning, Alan, 'Disciplinary focus of the SFC' (July–August 2003) 4(4) *Hong Kong Securities* 26.

Lim, Helen, 'New share offerings in the PRC' (May 2001) 15(4) *China Law & Practice* 20–23.

Lin, Z. Jun, 'Internationalization of public accounting: Chinese experience' (1998) 13(2) *Managerial Auditing Journal* 84.

Liu, Hongchuan and Zili Ren, 'Halfway to effective shareholder protection' (March 1993) 17(2) *China Law & Practice* 29.

Liu, Kin Cheung, 'State control and performance evaluation: the case of a state-owned enterprise in China' (1995) 8(6) *International Journal of Public Sector Management* 39.

Liu, Jinrong and Chengwei Liu, 'China re-opens its doors to the IPO market' (July/August 2006) 20(6) *China Law & Practice* 22.

Lo, Jackie, 'New PRC Securities Law fails to fully unify regulation of securities issues in China' (February 1999) 13(1) *China Law and Practice* 21.

Low, Chee Keong, 'Regulating the regulators', **12**(12) *Company Secretary* (December 2002) 42.

Neumann Peter A. and Tony Zhang, 'China's new foreign-funded M&A provisions: greater legal protection or legalized protectionism' (October 2006) 20(8) *China Law & Practice* 21.

Niu, Tiehang, 'Stock Market integration in Hong Kong and China' (November 1997) 6(16) *Journal of Contemporary China* 487–512.

Nolan, P., 'Large firms and industrial reform in former planned economies: the case of China' (1996) 20(1) *Cambridge Journal of Economics* 1–29.

Nottle, R., 'The development of securities markets in China in the 1990s' (1993) 11 *Company and Securities Law Journal* 503.

Peerenboom, Randall, 'Globalization, path dependency and the limits of law: administrative law reform and the rule of law in the People's Republic' (2001) 19 *Berkeley Journal of International Law* 161.

Potter, Pitman B., 'The legal framework for securities markets in China: the challenge of maintaining state control and inducing investing confidence' (1992) 7 *China Law Reporter* 61.

Qi, Ben, 'China's new M&A rules: a revisionist's view' (January 2007) 3(1) *Asialaw M & A Review* 23.

Randall, Christopher, 'Hong Kong gets tough on market misconduct' (June 2003) 1(2) *Asialaw* 24–26.

Roe, Mark J., 'Chaos and evolution in law and economics' (1996) 109(3) *Harvard Law Review* 641.

Roe, Mark, 'Political preconditions to separating ownership from corporate control' (2000) 53 *Stanford Law Review* 539.

Ruskola, Teema, 'Conceptualizing corporations and kinship: Comparative Law and development theory in a Chinese perspective' (1999–2000) 52 *Stanford Law Review* 1599.

Schroeder, P., 'Rebuilding China's securities markets' (May–June 1991) *The China Business Review* 20–21.

Shan, Weijian, 'The mystery of China's sinking stocks' (December 2005) 168(11) *Far Eastern Economic Review* 5.

Shepherd, Craig, and Tim Mak, 'Double-barrelled assault on market misconduct' (June 2003) 11(1) *Asia Pacific Forum News* 19–21.

Shi, Steven and Drake Weisert, 'Corporate governance with Chinese characteristics' (February 2003) 13(2) *Company Secretary* 10.

Silbey, Susan, 'Making a place for a cultural analysis of law' (1992) 17 *Law and Social Inquiry* 41.

Smyth, Russell and Zhai Qingguo, 'Reforming China's large-scale state-owned enterprises: the petrochemical sector' (2001) 5:2 *Asia Pacific Journal of Economics and Business* 82–104.

Spisto, Michael, 'Stakeholder interests in corporate governance: is a new model of governance a change for the better for South Africa? Part 1' (2005) 18 *Australian Journal of Corporate Law* 129.

Stout, Lynne, 'On the nature of corporations' (2004) 9(2) *Deakin Law Review* 775.

Tan, Lay Hong, 'The legal and regulatory framework of securities markets in the PRC' (1998) 7(1) *Asia Pacific Law Review* 69.

Teubner, Gunther, 'Legal irritants: good faith in British law or how unifying law ends up in new divergences' (1998) 61 *Modern Law Review* 30.

Tian, Gang, 'China's post-1979 uneven regional policy: Shanghai and Guangdong' (March 1997) 6(14) *Journal of Contemporary China* 61–78.

Tomasic, Roman, 'Company Law and the limits of the rule of law in China' (January 1995) 4(4) *Australian Journal of Corporate Law* 470–487.

Tomasic, Roman, 'Insolvency law principles and the Draft Bankruptcy Law of the People's Republic of China' (Special Issue on PRC Securities and Insolvency Law) (December 1998) 9(3) *Australian Journal of Corporate Law* 211–233.

Tomasic, Roman, 'An overview and assessment of the Draft Securities Law of the People's Republic of China' (Special Issue on PRC Securities and Insolvency Law) (December 1998) 9(3) *Australian Journal of Corporate Law* 284–299.

Tomasic, Roman, and Neil Andrews, 'Special Issue on corporate governance in post-WTO China' (2004) 17(1) *Australian Journal of Corporate Law* 1–5.

Tomasic, Roman, and Margaret Wang, 'Reforming China's corporate bankruptcy laws' (2005) 18(3) *Australian Journal of Corporate Law* 220–232.

Tomasic, Roman, and Jian Fu, 'Legal regulation and corporate governance in China's top 100 listed companies' (2006) 27(9) *The Company Lawyer* 278–287.

Wei, Jun and Stephen Curley, 'Listing rights extended for foreign investment enterprises' (July/August 2001) 15(6) *China Law & Practice* 52.

Wilhelm, Kathy, 'Casinos by another name' (8 March 2001) **164**(9), *Far Eastern Economic Review* 46, at 47.

Wilson, Therese, 'The pursuit of profit at all costs: corporate law as a barrier to corporate social responsibility' (2005) 30:6 *Alternative Law Journal* 278.

Wright, Chris, 'China takes note of governance', *HSBC China Supplement* (December 2002) *Asiamoney* 19–20.

Wu, Chi Kuen Simon, 'Single securities market in China' (2006) 14(1) *Asia Pacific Law Review* 19.

Xiao, Yu, 'Ending the split share structure: government interferes to correct a long-standing plague' *Beijing Review* (28 May 2005), accessed at http://www.bjreview.com.cn/En-2005/05–28-e/bus-2.htm in January 2006.

Xu, Guojian, Lu Guoming & Pek-Siang Tee, 'Stock market access paves the way for new utilization of insurance funds' (December 2004/January 2005) 18(10) *China Law & Practice* 54–56.

Xu, Guojian, Lu Guoming and Pek-Siang Tee, 'A big step forward for China's insurance industry: building broader and safer avenues for the utilization of insurance funds' (November 2005) 19(9) *China Law & Practice*.

Yang, TieCheng, Alan Xu and Allen Zhong, 'Steady as she goes – China's new Securities Law' (December 2005–January 2006) 19(10) *China Law & Practice* 16.

Yang, TieCheng, Zhang Nan & Alan Xu, 'A rule pushed by the market: China's new measures for offering and underwriting securities' (December 2006–January 2007) 20(10) *China Law & Practice* 25–27.

Yee, Lawrence S. and Jason Yu, 'Time to go: new CSRC de-listing regulations' (April 2001) 15(3), *China Law & Practice* 58.

Yin, Sherry, Edward Fung and Ying Zhu, 'CSRC's new circular puts spin-off listings in the spotlight' (September 2004) 18(7) *China Law & Practice* 41–43.

Young, Angus, Grace Li and Alex Lau, 'Corporate governance in China: The role of the state and ideology in shaping reforms' (2007) 28(7) *Company Lawyer* 204–211.

Yu, David, 'Foreign funds rush into strategic investment in PRC-listed companies' (January 2007) 3(1) *Asialaw M & A Review* 22.

Yu, David & Wayne Cehn, 'Controls on foreign acquisitions of Chinese enterprises' (January 2007) 3(1) *Asialaw M & A Review* 11–13.

Zaloom, E. Anthony and Hongchuan Liu, 'New rules for A-share issues' (September 1999) 13(8) *China Law & Practice* 42.

Zhang, Chi, Thomas C. Heller and Michael M. May, 'Carbon intensity of electricity generation and CDM baseline: case studies of three Chinese provinces' (2005) 33 *Energy Policy* 451.

Zhang, Jean and May Liang, 'Employee stock options in China', *China Law Update: Capital Markets* (CCH Hong Kong 2007).

'Fair Shares' (November 2005) *Company Secretary* 18.

'QFII updates', (July–August 2003) 4(4) *Hong Kong Securities* 28.

'State Commission outlines shareholding system', special report by the State Commission for Restructuring the Economic System, *JPRS-CAR-92-059*, 3 August 1992, pp. 34–9; 'Article on joint stock companies, stock markets', *JPRS-CAR-92-079*, 21 October 1992 pp. 20–27; and 'Shanghai re-establishes securities market', *JPRS-CAR-90-011*, 12 February 1990 pp. 31–4

'On China's stock market development', *JPRS-CAR-93-018*, 19 March 1993. pp. 16–19. *Asiamoney*, October 2002, p. 36 (available at www.asiamoney.com).

Website resources

China Securities Regulatory Commission, *China's Securities and Futures Markets* (April 2004), available at the CSRC website http://www.csrc.gov.cn/CSRCSite/eng/esmintr.htm (56 pages).

'Listing requirements', available at the Shanghai stock exchange website: http://www.sse.com.cn accessed December 2005.

World Federation of Exchanges, 'Equity 1.1: domestic market capitalization' (6 May 2005) http://www.fibv.com/publications/EQUITY104.pdf accessed 18 March 2006.

Hong Kong Trade Development Council's 'Market Profile on Chinese Mainland' (updated to 6 October 2006) available via the Trade Development Council's website at http://www.tdc.com.hk/.

List of all H-share companies available at the Hong Kong Exchanges and Clearing Ltd China Stock Markets Web at http://www.hkex.com.hk/csm/.

Webb, David, 'Listing rules review part 2: board games', Webb-site.com newsletter at http://www.webb-site.com/articles/boardgames.htm, 21 February 2002.

Webb, David Webb-site.com newsletter, '2005 Christmas Pick – regulatory note', 15 December 2005, at http://www.webb-site.com/.

Webb.site, at http://webb-site.com/articles/gatesway.htm, 'Gates' Way to China', Newsletter dated 9 August 2004.

Website of Beiren Group Corporation accessed at http://www.eprint.cn/forum/beirenen/index.htm also available at http://www.beiren.com/EN/About.asp accessed on 18 January 2007.

News Release issued 16 June 2006, Mitsubishi Printing Presses, 'MHI to manufacture printing machinery in China in joint venture with Beiren Printing Machinery Holdings', accessed at http://www.mhi-mpp.com/e/releas/e_060616.html.

US Securities and Exchange Commission: http://www.sec.gov/rules/final/33-8128.htm

Asia times online, 'China's equity markets: buyer beware', 9 May 2003, available at http://www.atimes.com/.

Asia times online, 'China's stock market binge', 30 August 2003, available at http://www.atimes.com/.

Asia times online, 'The stock market a casino for communists', 9 October 2004, available at http://www.atimes.com/.

Asia times online, 'China moves to cage its rampaging bears', 20 January 2005, available at http://www.atimes.com/.

BGC website: about Beiren at http://www.eprint.cn/forum/beirenen/index.htm accessed on 18 January 2007.

China's economic times (Zhongguo jingji shibao) 2001-07-05 accessible at http://images.chinainfobank.com/report/wto/file/che07.htm (in Chinese).

China Business Information Network, 'China: court hearing begins on bankruptcy of GITIC in Shenzhen' (22 April 1999), available at <1999 WL 5618970>.

Cosh, Andy and Paul Guest, 'The long run performance of hostile takeovers: UK evidence' (Working Paper No. 215, ESRC Centre for Business Research, University of Cambridge, 2001) 4–5, 30–1 http://www.cbr.cam.ac.uk/pdf/WP215.pdf.

Deloitte China, *Comparison of IFRSs and New Chinese Accounting Standards* (August 2006) available at http://www.iasplus.com/country.china.htm.

FDI, 'Foreign investors allowed to invest in trust and securities', available through the China Economic Information Network at http://www.ce.cei.gov.cn/.

The Hong Kong Institute of Company Secretaries, 'Independent directors crucial to corporate governance', News Release, Thursday 18 September 2003, accessed at http://www.hkics.org.hk/whatsnew/ on 22 November 2003.

The Hong Kong Institute of Company Secretaries, 'Good Governance Guides No. 1.1'; 'Good Governance Guides No. 1.2', accessed at http://www.hkics.org.hk/governance/goodgovernance/ on 22 November 2003.

Lehman, Lee & Xu, vol. 1, no. 10, *China Law Digest Newsletter*, 13 December 2002 http://chinalawdigest@lehmanlaw.com, received via email on 13 December 2002.

Lehman Lee & Xu, 'Mergers and Acquisitions in China', *China Law Digest Newsletter*, 19 May 2006 <http://www.chinalawdigest@lehmanlaw.com, received via email on 19 May 2006.

Loh, Christine, 'Mandate under challenge: Christine Loh's Newsletter', received by email on 4 May 2003 from cloh@civic-exchange.org.

Reuters, 'China takes aim at corporate abuses with jail', 26 December 2005, Reuters website accessed at http://in.today.reuters.com on 27 December 2005.

'Shares of Shenyang Machine Tool Group draws hot response', published at http://www.liaoning-gateway.com, dated 21 November 2006 and downloaded 24 January 2007.

Newspaper articles

From the *South China Morning Post* (Hong Kong) (SCMP):

Carrie Lee, 'Hurdles cleared by Guangzhou Shipyard', SCMP 18 June 1993.

Kent Chen, 'Poor bond sales will not affect float plan', SCMP 18 June 1993.

Christine Chan, 'Beiren Printing to float six subsidiaries', SCMP 18 June 1993.

Ivan Tong and Carrie Lee, 'Petrochemical may hold back giant flotation', SCMP 24 June 1993.
SCMP Staff Reporters, 'State Council orders bigger Tsingtao float', SCMP 27 June 1993.
Gareth Hewett, 'Speaking out will help bring more Tsingtao's', SCMP 16 July 1993.
Carrie Lee, 'Shipyard offer to kick off next week', SCMP 16 July 1993.
Kerry Wong, 'Lower prices on offer for next mainland listings', SCMP 18 July 1993.
Ray Heath, 'Shipyard's major unit faces 20pc dip in profit', SCMP 21 July 1993.
'A closer look at US book building', SCMP 22 July 1993.
Ray Heath, 'SFC rejects any stabilization scheme for Shanghai Petro', SCMP 22 July 1993.
Ivan Tong, 'Beiren's parent sends it ready for outside world', SCMP 23 July 1993.
Ivan Tong, 'Local market viewed as test for China listings', SCMP 27 July 1993.
Gareth Hewett, 'Merrill chief warns mainland listings could be lost', SCMP 28 July 1993.
Kerry Wong, 'Brokers back new offerings', SCMP 30 July 1993.
Simon Davies, 'Beiren pricing sets it apart from the crowd', SCMP 30 July 1993.
Kerry Wong, 'Brokers back new offerings', SCMP 30 July 1993.
Mark Evans, 'Utilities lead index surge to top off winning week', SCMP 31 July 1993.
'Stabilisation should be written into law', SCMP 2 August 1993.
Kerry Wong, 'Call to improve underwriting practices of HK', SCMP 8 August 1993.
'Fortune found at the back door', SCMP 14 September 1993.
'Guangzhou Shipyard in demand', SCMP 1 October 1993.
Hu Cui-Ping, 'Steel giant plans $3.9 stock offer', SCMP 20 October 1993.
Wong Joon San, 'Shipyard set to list in Shanghai', SCMP 25 October 1993.
Kent Chen, 'Further overseas listings planned for US or Europe', SCMP 29 October 1993.
Christine Chan, 'Paper profit of 28pc in shipyard float', SCMP 29 October 1993.
Kerry Wong, 'Listing loophole causes anxiety', SCMP 14 November 1993.
Duncan Mount, 'Low issue price ensures sharp rise for Kunming', SCMP 12 December 1993.
Foo Choy Peng, 'Electric Trio seek power of the world giants', SCMP 3 March 1994.

Renee Lai, 'Dongfang to step up output of turbines', SCMP 11 March 1994.
See also Renee Lai, 'Analysts see price worry for Dongfang', SCMP 15 March 1994.
Geoffrey Crothall, 'Government bonds draw good support', SCMP 4 April 1994.
'Guangzhou Shipyard beats forecast', SCMP 6 April 1994.
'Stock price forced up by traders', SCMP 13 April 1994.
'Guangzhou Shipyard pays $17.7m for site', SCMP 20 April 1994.
Renee Lai, 'China companies' acid test', SCMP 26 April 1994.
Kerry Wong and Ivan Tong, 'China in plea to bail out Bohai', SCMP 15 May 1994.
Renee Lai, 'Dongfang to price shares at lower end', SCMP 17 May 1994.
Renee Lai, 'Dongfang listing likely to do well', SCMP 19 May 1994.
Gareth Hewett, 'H-shares offer more disclosure', SCMP 31 May 1994.
Renee Lai, 'Rock-bottom price for Qingling designed to lure', SCMP 21 July 1994.
Gareth Hewett, 'Guangzhou Shipyard lifts profit', SCMP 6 August 1994.
Renee Lai, 'Shipbuilder in venture with US steelmaker', SCMP 9 August 1994.
Renee Lai, 'Mainland taxes force shipbuilder to change focus', SCMP 12 August 1994.
Renee Lai, 'Listing code clears up uncertainties', SCMP 20 August 1994.
Renee Lai, 'Exchange rate gain will not reflect in profit', SCMP 24 August 1994.
Renee Lai, 'Accountants' society queries Guangzhou Shipyard's 1993 report', SCMP 25 August 1994.
Randall Collis, 'Ageing of global merchant fleet tipped to push mainland up among the giants', SCMP 3 November 1994.
Sean Kennedy, 'Morgan pushes Asian ADRs', SCMP 10 November 1994.
Renee Lai, 'Warburg exercises option to buy Harbin Power shares on market', SCMP 21 December 1994.
Gareth Hewett, 'Patience needed for huge gains', SCMP 19 January 1995.
'Chinese Press Digest', SCMP 20 January 1995.
Renee Lai, 'Beiren spree on non-core items worries analyst', SCMP 11 April 1995.
Renee Lai, 'Beiren controversy finally cleared up', SCMP 12 April 1995.
Ray Heath, 'Warburg sells $1b shares in Yizheng', SCMP 26 April 1995.
K.K. Chadha, 'Pacific Basin launches ship', SCMP 12 May 1995.
Foo Choy Peng, 'Investors bring down network in rush for shares', SCMP 17 June 1995.
Foo Choy Peng, 'Tianjin Bohai Chemical Industry (Group) public issue is about 28 times over-subscribed', SCMP 19 June 1995.

Foo Choy Peng, 'Dongfang gets record response', SCMP 6 July 1995.
Gareth Hewett, 'Caution needed in buying H shares', SCMP 12 July 1995.
Nicholas Ionides, 'Nomura escapes censure', SCMP 21 July 1995.
Foo Choy Peng, 'China revamps listings', SCMP 25 July 1995.
Gareth Hewett, 'H-share profits face VAT wipeout', SCMP 7 August 1995.
'Different approaches taken by companies', SCMP 10 August 1995.
'Share hand-out prevents listing', SCMP 30 August 1995.
Foo Choy Peng, 'Costs squeeze Shanghai profits', SCMP 25 September 1995.
Foo Choy Peng, 'Dongfang's A-share in star display', SCMP 11 October 1995.
Renee Lai, 'Analysts play down fear on interest costs for H shares', SCMP 8 November 1995.
Christine Chan, 'Tax worries panic H-share investors', SCMP 17 November 1995.
'Group nets $9m contract', SCMP 23 December 1995.
'Wit and wisdom of 1995 put to the test', SCMP 31 December 1995.
'Shipyard sales increase', SCMP 17 January 1996.
'Chinese press digest', SCMP 18 January 1996.
Nicholas Reynolds, 'Venture delay hits shipyard profits', SCMP 11 February 1996.
Renee Lai, 'Shipyard dives 44pc on turnover', SCMP 16 April 1996.
Renee Lai, 'Tsingtao sees earnings dip as costs squeeze profit margin', SCMP 17 April 1996.
Christine Chan, 'H-share to lobby for 17pc rebate', SCMP 18 April 1996.
Renee Lai and Christine Chan, 'Firms crushed in transition to free-market rules', SCMP 9 May 1996.
'Market summary "Tsingtao Brewery" ', SCMP 12 May 1996.
Kent Chen, 'GSI share performance fails to reflect strength', SCMP 19 May 1996.
'Record for Guangzhou', SCMP 3 June 1996.
'Shake-up likely at Tsingtao', SCMP 4 June 1996.
'Loans for state firms', SCMP 22 June 1996.
'Entrepreneur to join Tsingtao management', SCMP 25 June 1996.
Renee Lai, 'Tsingtao in move for loans of $93m', SCMP 11 July 1996.
'Tax changes hit Guangzhou yard', SCMP 2 August 1996.
Lana Wong, 'Guangzhou Shipyard dives 33 pc', SCMP 30 August 1996.
Josephine Ma, 'Export rebate cuts may cost Guangzhou Shipyard', SCMP 31 August 1996.
Christine Chan, 'H-share tax rate remains', SCMP 26 March 1997.
Wang Xiang Wei and Agencies, 'Beijing drafts list of firms for state support', SCMP 29 March 1997.

'GSI gains plummet as tax changes hurt, building prices fall', SCMP 12 April 1997.
Lana Wong, 'Tax rebate cut hits shipbuilder', SCMP 15 April 1997.
Renee Lai, 'H shares feel pressure', SCMP 26 April 1997.
Renee Lai, 'Luoyang Glass pulls funds from broker', SCMP 20 June 1997.
Lana Wong, 'Tsingtao plans to put funds to expansive use', SCMP 7 July 1997.
Lana Wong, 'Tsingtao Brewery launches holding company to steer acquisition drive', SCMP 9 July 1997.
Renee Lai, 'Tsingtao subsidiary in debts reshuffle', SCMP 4 August 1997.
'H shares intrigue investors', SCMP 8 August 1997.
'China–Iran ship deal', SCMP 18 August 1997.
Lana Wong, 'Tsingtao in bid to benefit listed arm' SCMP 28 August 1997.
Renee Lai, 'Mainland firms line up for Hong Kong share listing', SCMP 11 September 1997.
Renee Lai, 'Joint venture perfect tonic for ailing brewery', SCMP 11 September 1997.
'Bloated giants may weigh down progress', SCMP 11 September 1997.
Cheung Lai-kuen, 'Shandong eyes allies for state enterprises', SCMP 18 September 1997.
Renee Lai, 'Tsingtao poised to swallow two breweries in Shandong', SCMP 5 November 1997.
'Tsingtao Brewery Co: Recommendation: Sell', under section heading 'Amoy set for property killing', SCMP 9 November 1997.
Renee Lai, 'Tsingtao in brewery-takeover talks as part of Shandong Acquisition drive', SCMP 16 January 1998.
Renee Lai, 'Guangzhou Shipyard confident of surviving regional turmoil', SCMP 21 January 1998.
Renee Lai, 'Tsingtao goes stale', SCMP 21 April 1998.
Denise Tsang, 'Shipyard secures crane contract', SCMP 28 April 1998.
Eric Ng, 'The week that was', SCMP 30 August 1998.
Stewart Oldfield, 'Tsingtao under pressure', SCMP 20 September 1998.
'Shipyard gains export credits', SCMP 22 September 1998.
'Shipyard receives $1.1b loans', SCMP 23 September 1998.
Lana Wong, 'Beijing edict boosts domestic builders', SCMP 26 December 1998.
'Gzitic hotel offered, says firm', SCMP 1 January 1999.
Christine Chan, 'Tsingtao shopping for growth', SCMP 23 April 1999.
Christine Chan, 'Dongfang Electrical recoups most of funds locked in bank', SCMP 24 April 1999.
Joseph Lo, 'Shipyard sues Itics for $483m loans due', SCMP 26 April 1999.

Christine Chan, 'Tsingtao steps up size of purchases', SCMP 25 August 1999.
'Mass consumption', SCMP 24 October 1999.
Lana Wong, 'Tsingtao receives buy-back approval', SCMP 29 October 1999.
Christine Chan, 'Tsingtao buy-back tour', SCMP 2 November 1999.
'Tsingtao to blaze trail for healthy firms', SCMP 4 November 1999.
Christine Chan, 'Tianjin Bohai sets out on new track', SCMP 29 December 1999.
Enoch Yiu, 'Shares bill eases curbs on IPOs', SCMP 23 October 2000.
Simon Pritchard, 'A case for rules and disclosure', SCMP 10 November 2000.
Mathew Miller, 'Hainan construction company wins landmark case against CSRC', SCMP 20 December 2000.
Bei Hu, 'Regulator fights ruling', SCMP 6 January 2001.
Bei Hu, 'Narcissus shareholders sue CSRC, Shanghai exchange over delisting', SCMP 27 April 2001.
'Smarter scrutiny', SCMP 30 May 2001.
Staff Reporter in Shanghai, 'Court raps watchdog for breaking regulations', SCMP 7 July 2001.
'CSRC loses Kaili appeal', SCMP 8 July 2001.
Enoch Yiu, 'SFC proposes price support for IPOs', SCMP 9 February 2002.
Cai ShuMo and Deng YingXia, 'Corporate governance: obstacles and new developments', SCMP 12 April 2002.
Bei Hu, 'Listed firms face sweeping review of corporate governance', SCMP 11 May 2002.
Enoch Yiu, 'SFC agrees to allow price-stabilising actions for 30 days on $100m offers', SCMP 10 July 2002.
Hui Yuk-Min, 'Watchdog finds governance faults at Tianjin Capital', SCMP 23 August 2002.
Geoffrey Baker, 'New Avenue for M & A transactions', SCMP 28 October 2002.
Reuters, 'Beijing urges brokerages to bolster markets', SCMP 29 October 2002.
Peggy Sito, 'New SOE rules considered short of foreign needs', SCMP 5 November 2002.
Bei Hu, 'Door opens to foreign investors', SCMP 8 November 2002.
Bei Hu, 'Company trio get suspended jail terms for fraud', SCMP 15 November 2002.
Thomas E. Jones, 'Trailblazing developments in state sector and capital markets', SCMP 9 December 2002.
Bei Hu, 'Citigroup seeks QFII licence', SCMP 21 March 2003.

Enoch Yiu, 'Market reforms show progress', SCMP 25 March 2003.
Eric Ng, 'Jilin Chemical stock frozen', SCMP 26 April 2003.
Mark O'Neil and Hui Yuk-Min, 'Lianhua Supermarket delays HK listing', SCMP 20 May 2003.
Peggy Sito, 'Supermarket chain cleared for listing', SCMP 31 May 2003.
Enoch Yiu, 'HKEx to shame shoddy sponsors', SCMP 31 May 2003.
Bloomberg, 'Motorcycle firm avoids expulsion', SCMP 1 September 2003.
Eric Ng, 'Sinopec parent ponders injection of assets', SCMP 25 September 2003.
Eric Ng, 'Sinopec units sign supply contract', SCMP 13 November 2003.
Toh Han Shih, 'Mainland salaries for executives to top HK', SCMP 24 November 2003.
Bei Hu, 'Mainland reforms listing panel', SCMP 12 December 2003.
Enoch Yiu, 'Exchange wants SFC to be sole regulator of listing sponsors', SCMP 24 December 2003.
Bloomberg, 'China moves closer to a unified regulatory regime', SCMP 29 December 2003.
Mark O'Neil, 'Mainland tries to rein in blatant asset stripping', SCMP 29 December 2003.
Bei Hu and Jane Moir, 'More bang to H shares' explosive run', SCMP 30 December 2003.
Eric Ng, 'Sinopec lifts refining target on demand surge', SCMP 20 January 2004.
Bei Hu, 'Independents shunned by China firms', SCMP 7 February 2004.
Bei Hu, 'Shenzhen expands state share sales', SCMP 10 February 2004.
Eric Ng, 'Scarce materials may idle 25pc of new steel output', SCMP 8 March 2004.
Anette Jonsson and Ben Kwok, 'SMIC debut takes the gloss off China IPOs', SCMP 19 March 2004.
Eric Ng, 'Maanshan defies clampdown', SCMP 14 April 2004.
Anette Jonsson, 'New listings losing their appeal', SCMP 16 July 2004.
Eric Ng, 'Mainland refiners count down to 2007', SCMP 6 September 2004.
Elaine Chan, 'State firms urged to slow pace of overseas listing', SCMP 8 September 2004.
Eric Ng, 'Refining growth goes into overdrive', SCMP 18 September 2004.
China Economic Quarterly, 'Hazy forecast for capital reform', SCMP 22 November 2004.
Elaine Chan, 'CSRC urges fund managers to toe line', SCMP 10 December 2004.
Bloomberg in Beijing, 'Big Four's bad-debt sales reach 605b yuan', SCMP 30 December 2004.

Elaine Chan, 'Mainland investors decide to stay away from equities', SCMP 11 January 2005.
Jamil Anderlini, 'Banks bail out three bankrupt mainland brokers', SCMP 10 August 2005.
Jane Moir and Toh Han Shih, 'Regulators look into suspicious trade in Kelon shares', SCMP 10 August 2005.
Bei Hu, 'China Securities to be folded in bailout', SCMP 12 August 2005.
Andy Cheng, 'Bond offer shelved on fears over share policy', SCMP 12 August 2005.
Bei Hu, 'Let the share buyers beware', SCMP 10 October 2005.
Mark O'Neill, 'State fund chases investments', SCMP 14 October 2005.
Jamil Anderlini, 'Tight US listing rules expected to ease', SCMP 25 October 2005.
Shi Jiangtao and Josephine Ma, '"Serious pollution" of river after blast finally admitted', SCMP 24 November 2005.
Eric Ng, 'Oil majors choose risk over insurance', SCMP 28 November 2005.
Mark O'Neill, 'PetroChina braces for legal and financial fallout from spill', SCMP 7 December 2005.
Shi Jiangtao, 'Vice-mayor of spill city kills himself', SCMP 8 December 2005.
Chan Siu-Sin, 'State enterprises suffer record losses', SCMP 26 March 2006.
Guo Aibing, 'Officials talk up mainland market: stocks reverse losses after message on positive long-term outlook despite correction', SCMP 7 June 2007.
Tom Miller and Amy Gu, 'Foreign funds cash out of A shares: QFII assets fall 13pc even as record bank withdrawals show strong domestic appetite', SCMP 12 June 2007.
Cameron Dueck, 'Mainland hot zone for M&A deals: interest in Chinese companies sparks busiest first half ever, with transactions up 58.3pc', SCMP 15 June 2007.

From other electronic newspapers

'Stricter IPO standards set out: securities watchdog', *China Daily*, 23 September 2003, accessed at http://www.china.org.cn/english/BAT/75731.htm on 5 January 2006.
'Securities watchdog opens up listing process', *Shanghai Daily* 12 December 2003, accessed at http://www.china.org.cn/english/BAT/82214.htm on 5 January 2006.
XinhuaNet, 'New law justifies banking watchdog', China Daily website, 28 December 2003, available at http://www.chinadaily.com.cn/.
Jiang Jing Jing, 'H-share index to continue rising', *China Business Weekly* 13 January 2004, accessed at http://www.chinadaily.com.cn/en/doc/2004-01/13/content_299406.htm on 20 December 2006.

C.H. Kwan, Senior Fellow, Research Institute of Economy, Trade and Industry, IAI. Article written for *The Straits Times*, downloaded 23 November 2004 at http://www.rieti.go.jp/en/.

Bernard Wasow, 'Should we trust China?', *The Globalist* 30 March 2004, available at http://www.theglobalist.com/.

XinhuaNet, 'Watchdog outlines overseas listing criteria', *Xinhuanet* 12 August 2004, accessed at http://www1.cei.gov.cn/ce/doc/cep2/200408122313.htm on 31 December 2004.

'New measure to protect small investors', *China Daily* 28 September 2004, accessed at http://www.china.org.cn/english/BAT/108231.htm.

'Banks to get green light for fund biz', *XinhuaNet* 11 November 2004; accessed at http://www.cei.gov.cn/ce/.

'China lifts barrier on local bank fund units', *XinhuaNet* 12 November 2004 accessed at http://www.cei.gov.cn/ce/.

Xin Bei, 'Securities watchdog should be watched', *China Daily* 18 November 2004, accessed at http://www.china.org.cn/english/BAT/112499.htm on 5 January 2006.

'Resumption of new IPOs unlikely in short term', *China Daily* 22 November 2004, accessed at *People's Daily Online* website: http://english.people.com.cn/ on 11 January 2006.

'Lawsuit mechanism mulled for capital market investors', Xinhua News Agency, 5 December 2004, accessed at http://www.china.org.cn/english/2004/Dec/114026.htm on 5 January 2006.

'China decides to resume issuance of IPOs', *People's Daily Online*, 14 January 2005; accessed at http://english.people.com.cn/ on 10 January 2005.

'Reshuffle of securities firms gathers pace', *China Daily* 24 January 2005, accessed at http://www.china.org.cn/english/BAT/118613.htm on 5 January 2006.

Beijing Portal, 'China amends Securities Law to boost slumping stock market', 27 April 2005, accessed at http://www.beijingportal.com.cn/7838/2005/04/27/1820@2613061.htm on 27 December 2005.

'Anheuser lifts Tsingtao stake to 27%', *China Daily*/ HK edition, 12 May 2005; available at http://www.chinadaily.com.cn/english/.

Xinhua, 'China issues proposals promoting experiments on split share structure', *People's Daily Online* 31 May 2005, accessed at http://www.people.com.cn/200505/31/.

'Share or cash compensation most welcome in split share reform', Xinhua, *People's Daily Online*, 9 July 2005, accessed at http://english.people.com.cn/200507/09/ on 11 January 2006.

'Foreign security firms allowed into China market', *China Daily* 7 December 2005, accessed at http://www.china.org.cn/english/2005/Dec/151182.htm on 5 January 2006.

Reuters, 'China takes aim at corporate abuses with jail' 26 December 2005 Reuters, accessed at http://in.today/reuters.com/ on 27 December 2005.

JCN Newswire, 'MHI's Printing Machinery JV in China celebrates first production press; Full-scale Launch of High-quality, High-speed Multicolor Sheet-fed Presses', *JCN Newswire*, 15 December 2006, accessed at http://www.japancorp.net/ on 18 January 2006.

Xinhua Finance, 'Xinhua FTSE Index launches H-Share Index for QDIIs and other Chinese Institutional Investors' 12 July 2006, accessed at http://www.xinhuafinance.com/en/media-center/news-and-events/press-releases on 20 December 2006.

Xinhua Finance, 'Bank of Communication makes fast track entry to Xinhua FTSE Indices', 15 May 2007, at http://www.xinhuafinance.com/.

News Release, 'Xinhua FTSE launches sector indices for A200 benchmark', 16 May 2007 at http://www.xinhuaftse.com/.

Xinhua Finance, 'Xinhua Finance/ MNI China Business Survey: indexes slump', 29 May 2007 at http://www.xinhuafinance.com/.

Helen Yuan and Xiaowei Li, 'China's steel exports forecast slump by 23 percent (Update3)', Bloomberg 19 December 2006, accessed at http://www.bloomberg.com/apps/news on 20 December 2006.

XinhuaNet, '77% stock investors lose money: survey', XinhuaEnglish 26 December 2006, accessed at http://content.sina.com/news/ on 11 January 2006.

Tom Young, 'Threshold rule dampens Hong Kong listings', *International Financial Law Review Bulletin*, News analysis 18 April 2007.

Simon Crompton, 'Second-ever dual listing closes in China', *International Financial Law Review Bulletin*, News analysis 27 April 2007.

Other secondary resources

S.G. Warburg Research, *Company Update Hong Kong*, Circular dated 6th October 1993 'Tsingtao Brewery' (168.HK).

'China's brewing industry gears for expansion', 7 October 2004, Breaking News on Food and Beverage in Asia Pacific, available at http://www.ap-foodtechnology.com/news/.

Phil Ruthven, 'Continued economic growth will make this the Chinese Century', *On Line Opinion* 17 November 2003, available at http://www.onlineopinion.com.au/.

'Features: regulations for the overseas listing of the subsidiary of a domestic listed company' (November 2004) CNPUPDATE Greater China Supplement, accessed at http://www.cnplaw.com/en/cnpupdate/2005 on 13 July 2007.

'Tsingtao and Anheuser-Busch strengthen strategic alliance: Anheuser-Busch increases economic interest in Tsingtao to 27 percent', 11 April

2005, at http://anheuserbusch.com/press_room/2005/Tsingtao_041105.html.

'Study: corporate boards in China', ChinaCSR.com posted on 19 October 2006, available at http://www.chinacsr.com/2006/10/19/study-corporate-boards-in-china/; accessed on 24 October 2006.

Darren Boey, 'Chinese stocks, lifted by Yuan, head for records (Update 2)', Bloomberg, 11 December 2006, accessed at http://www.Bloomberg.com/apps/news on 20 December 2006.

'Hong Kong exchange: in the ascendancy: why Hong Kong is the venue of choice for Chinese IPOs' (September 2006) *International Financial Law Review*, accessed at http://www.iflr.com/includes/magazine on 3 October 2006.

Hang Seng Index website with information on the following indexes available at http://www.xinhuaftse.com: Hang Seng Mainland 25, Hang Seng China Enterprises Index, Hang Seng China-Affiliated Corporations Index.

See also 'Xinhua/FTSE China 25 selected by Hang Seng as basis of new ETF', Press Release dated 9 June 2005, accessed at http://www.xfn.com/en.media/press_05_59.html on 12 January 2006.

Information also available at the Hong Kong Stock Exchange website at http://www.hkex.com.hk.

Graeme Dobell, ABC Radio National, 'CHINA: Millions rush for share in stockmarket', Asia Pacific radio interview with Professor Harry Gelber, broadcast 18 May 2007.

Index